2005 SUPPLEMENT TO CONSTITUTIONAL LAW THE AMERICAN CONSTITUTION CONSTITUTIONAL RIGHTS AND LIBERTIES CASES–COMMENTS–QUESTIONS

Ninth Editions

By

Jesse H. Choper
Earl Warren Professor of Public Law,
University of California, Berkeley

Richard H. Fallon, Jr.
Professor of Law
Harvard University

Yale Kamisar
Professor of Law, University of San Diego
Clarence Darrow Distinguished University Professor Emeritus of Law,
University of Michigan

Steven H. Shiffrin
Professor of Law,
Cornell University

AMERICAN CASEBOOK SERIES®

THOMSON
WEST™

Mat #40383180

610 Opperman Drive
P.O. Box 64526
St. Paul, MN 55164–0526
1–800–328–9352

ISBN 0–314–16206–2

TEXT IS PRINTED ON 10% POST CONSUMER RECYCLED PAPER

Preface

This Supplement contains significant developments that have occurred since February 20, 2001—the "cut-off" date of the principal books.

The editorial style of this Supplement follows that of the principal books. In designating the places in the principal books at which the supplementary material is to be inserted, the following abbreviations have been used:

Constitutional Law: Cases, Comments & Questions—CON LAW

The American Constitution: Cases & Materials—AMER CON

Constitutional Rights & Liberties: Cases & Materials—RTS & LIB

Chapter and section titles from the principal books have been reproduced in this Supplement to facilitate identification of the material to be inserted.

JESSE H. CHOPER
RICHARD H. FALLON, JR.
YALE KAMISAR
STEVEN H. SHIFFRIN

July, 2005

*

Table of Contents

*

Table of Cases

The principal cases are in bold type. Cases cited or discussed in the text are roman type. References are to pages. Cases cited in principal cases and within other quoted materials are included.

2005 SUPPLEMENT TO

CONSTITUTIONAL LAW

THE AMERICAN CONSTITUTION

CONSTITUTIONAL RIGHTS AND LIBERTIES

CASES–COMMENTS–QUESTIONS

Ninth Editions

*

NATURE AND SCOPE OF JUDICIAL REVIEW

POLITICAL QUESTIONS

CON LAW: P. 34, at end of note 3

AMER CON: P. 30, at end of note 3

RTS & LIB: P. 30, at end of note 3

In VIETH v. JUBELIRER, 541 U.S. 267, 124 S.Ct. 1769, 158 L.Ed.2d 546 (2004), SCALIA, J., concluded for a four-Justice plurality that no judicially manageable standards exist to determine when partisan political gerrymanders of voting districts violate the Constitution. The plurality opinion appeared to accept that partisan gerrymanders would violate the Constitution if they went "too far" in deliberately advantaging the candidates of one party and disadvantaging those of another. It insisted, however, that legislatures were not categorically forbidden to take partisan advantage into account in designing voting districts, and it maintained that the courts lack sufficiently clear standards, rooted in the Constitution, for determining when partisan scheming exceeded constitutional bounds.

KENNEDY, J., concurred in the judgment dismissing the plaintiffs' complaint. He agreed with the plurality that no constitutionally adequate and judicially manageable standard for identifying forbidden partisan gerrymanders "has emerged in this case," but he declined to pronounce partisan gerrymandering claims categorically non-justiciable, based on the possibility that an administrable standard might emerge in the future.

Writing for the plurality, SCALIA, J., retorted: "The first thing to be said about Justice Kennedy's disposition is that it is not legally available. The District Court in this case considered the plaintiffs' claims *justiciable* but dismissed them because the standard for unconstitutionality had not been met. It is logically impossible to affirm that dismissal without either (1) finding that the unconstitutional-districting standard applied by the District Court, or some other standard that it *should* have applied, has not been met, or (2) finding (as we have) that the claim is nonjusticiable. Justice Kennedy seeks to affirm 'because, in the case before us, we have no standard.' But it is *our* job, not the plaintiffs', to explicate the standard that makes the facts alleged by the plaintiffs adequate or inadequate to state a claim.

"[What] are the lower courts to make of [Kennedy, J.'s] pronouncement? We suggest that they must treat it as a reluctant fifth vote against justiciability at district and statewide levels—a vote that may change in some future case but that holds, for the time being, that this matter is nonjusticiable." Do you agree?

In separate dissenting opinions, Stevens, J., Souter, J. (joined by Ginsburg, J.), and Breyer, J., all disagreed about the absence of judicially manageable standards and indeed identified the (diverse) standards that they would apply.

As is perhaps necessarily true in cases turning on the presence or absence of judicially manageable standards, the political question analysis in *Vieth* was intricately bound up with the Justices' assessments of the merits of the claim before them. Judicially manageable standards could almost surely have been devised if judicial manageability were all that mattered. The principal division within the Court was over whether standards existed that were both judicially manageable and otherwise constitutionally appropriate. As Scalia, J., put it: "This Court may not willy-nilly apply standards—even manageable standards—having no relation to constitutional harms."

Vieth appears as a principal case involving voting rights under the Equal Protection Clause at p. 218 of this Supplement.

CON LAW: P. 40, at end of note 6

AMER CON: P. 34, at end of note 6

RTS & LIB: P. 34, at end of note 6

7. *Cases with political implications.* In two decisions arising from the 2000 presidential election in the state of Florida, *Bush v. Palm Beach County Canvassing Board*, 531 U.S. 70, 121 S.Ct. 471, 148 L.Ed.2d 366 (2000) (per curiam), and *Bush v. Gore*, 531 U.S. 98, 121 S.Ct. 525, 148 L.Ed.2d 388 (2000) (per curiam), there were colorable arguments, raised in amicus curiae briefs, that at least some of the issues involved political questions in the technical sense. In particular, amici argued that the Twelfth Amendment commits to Congress the question whether a state's electors have been chosen in accord with Art. II's requirements. Yet the Court did not refer to the political question doctrine in either decision, nor did Rehnquist, C.J.'s concurring opinion in *Bush v. Gore*, joined by Scalia and Thomas, JJ., even though it rested on Art. II grounds. Should the Court, possibly for prudential reasons, have taken the political question argument more seriously? Does the Justices' failure to grapple with political question arguments signal their growing sense of the Court's irreducibly central role in the constitutional scheme? *But cf. Vieth v. Jubelirer, supra.*

CONGRESSIONAL REGULATION OF JUDICIAL POWER

CON LAW: P. 47, at end of note 7

INS v. ST. CYR, 533 U.S. 289, 121 S.Ct. 2271, 150 L.Ed.2d 347 (2001), the Court cited the "substantial" constitutional questions that would otherwise be presented as a principal ground for holding that federal statutes barring judicial "review" of certain deportation orders issued by the INS did not deprive the federal courts of habeas corpus jurisdiction to determine whether the agency's decisions rest on an accurate interpretation of the substantive law. The Court, per STEVENS, J., rooted its constitutional concerns in Art. I, § 9, cl. 2, which restricts Congress' capacity to suspend the writ of habeas corpus: "[A]t the absolute minimum, the Suspension Clause protects the writ 'as it existed in 1789.' [At] its historical core, the writ of habeas corpus has served as a means of reviewing the legality of executive detention [and, in cases involving executive detention, has provided a basis for review of] errors of law, including the erroneous application or interpretation of statutes." SCALIA, J. (joined by Rehnquist, C.J., Thomas, J., and in part by O'Connor, J.) dissented both on statutory and constitutional grounds. He thought it plain as a matter of statutory construction that Congress had stripped the courts of habeas as well as other forms of jurisdiction, and he saw no constitutional violation, contending that the Suspension Clause guards against temporary suspensions of the "privilege" of habeas corpus as defined by statute at any particular time, but does not "guarantee[] any particular habeas right that enjoys immunity from suspension."

NATIONAL LEGISLATIVE POWER

THE NATIONAL COMMERCE POWER

NEW LIMITATIONS AT THE END OF THE 20TH CENTURY

CON LAW: P. 104, at end of note 1

AMER CON: P. 79, at end of note 1

(a) GONZALES v. RAICH, ___ U.S. ___, 125 S.Ct. 2195, ___ L.Ed.2d ___ (2005), per STEVENS, J., upheld Congress' power to apply the Controlled Substances Act—which was part of "a comprehensive regime to combat the international and interstate traffic in illicit drugs"—to "prohibit the local cultivation and use of marijuana" even when in compliance with state law authorizing its use for medical purposes:

"The similarities between this case and *Wickard* are striking. [*Wickard*] establishes that Congress can regulate purely intrastate activity that is not itself 'commercial,' in that it is not produced for sale, if it concludes that failure to regulate that class of activity would undercut the regulation of the interstate market in that commodity. [In] *Wickard,* we had no difficulty concluding that Congress had a rational basis for believing that, when viewed in the aggregate, leaving home-consumed wheat outside the regulatory scheme would have a substantial influence on price and market conditions. Here too, Congress had a rational basis for concluding that leaving home-consumed marijuana outside federal control would similarly affect price and market conditions [given] the likelihood that the high demand in the interstate market will draw such marijuana into that market. [In] both cases, the regulation is squarely within Congress' commerce power because production of the commodity meant for home consumption, be it wheat or marijuana, has a substantial effect on supply and demand in the national market for that commodity.

"[Respondents] nonetheless insist that the CSA cannot be constitutionally applied to their activities because Congress did not make a specific finding that the intrastate cultivation and possession of marijuana for medical purposes based on the recommendation of a physician would substantially affect the larger interstate marijuana market. Be that as it may, we have never required ['that legislation must contain detailed findings proving that each activity regulated within a comprehensive statute is essential to the statutory scheme'], absent a special concern such as the protection of free speech. [Given] the enforcement difficulties that attend distinguishing between marijuana cultivated locally and marijuana grown elsewhere, and concerns about diversion into illicit channels, we have no difficulty concluding that Congress had a rational basis for believing that failure to regulate the intrastate manufacture and possession of marijuana would leave a gaping hole in the CSA.

"[I]n both *Lopez* and *Morrison,* the parties asserted that a particular statute or provision fell outside Congress' commerce power in its entirety. This distinction is pivotal for we have often reiterated that '[w]here the class of activities is regulated and that class is within the reach of federal power', the courts have no power 'to excise, as trivial, individual instances' of the class."*Perez.* [Unlike] *Lopez* and *Morrison,* the activities regulated by the CSA are quintessentially economic [—] production, distribution, and consumption of commodities for which there is an established, and lucrative, interstate market.

"[I]f, as the principal dissent contends, the personal cultivation, possession, and use of marijuana for medicinal purposes is beyond the 'outer limits' of Congress' Commerce Clause authority,' (O'Connor, J., dissenting), it must also be true that such personal use of marijuana (or any other homegrown drug) for recreational purposes is also beyond those 'outer limits,' whether or not a State elects to authorize or even regulate such use. Justice Thomas' separate dissent suffers from the same sweeping implications. [One] need not have a degree in economics to understand why a nationwide exemption for the vast quantity of marijuana (or other drugs) locally cultivated for personal use (which presumably would include use by friends, neighbors, and family members) may have a substantial impact on the interstate market for this extraordinarily popular substance. The congressional judgment that an exemption for such a significant segment of the total market would undermine the orderly enforcement of the entire regulatory scheme is entitled to a strong presumption of validity. Indeed, that judgment is not only rational, but 'visible to the naked eye,' *Lopez,* under any commonsense appraisal of the probable consequences of such an open-ended exemption.

"[L]imiting the activity to marijuana possession and cultivation 'in accordance with state law' cannot serve to place respondents' activities beyond congressional reach. The Supremacy Clause unambiguously provides that if there is any conflict between federal and state law, federal law shall prevail. * * *[38] [The] notion that California law has surgically excised a discrete activity that is hermetically sealed off from the larger interstate marijuana market is a dubious proposition,[a] and, more importantly, one that Congress could have rationally rejected."

SCALIA, J., concurred in the judgment to describe a "more nuanced doctrinal foundation" and to respond to O'Connor, J.'s dissent: Although *Lopez* and *Morrison* "rejected the argument that Congress may regulate *noneconomic* activity based solely on the effect that it may have on interstate commerce through a

38. California's decision (made 34 years after the CSA was enacted) to impose "stric[t] controls" on the "cultivation and possession of marijuana for medical purposes," (Thomas, J., dissenting), cannot retroactively divest Congress of its authority under the Commerce Clause.

[Thomas, J.'s dissent responded: "The majority apparently believes that even if States prevented any medical marijuana from entering the illicit drug market, and thus even if there were no need for the CSA to govern medical marijuana users, we should uphold the CSA under the *Commerce* Clause and the *Necessary* and Proper Clause. [T]o invoke the Supremacy Clause, as the majority does, is to beg the question. The CSA displaces California's Compassionate Use Act if the CSA is constitutional as applied to respondents' conduct, but that is the very question at issue."

a. The Court refers here to O'Connor, J's argument "that California's Compassionate Use Act and similar state legislation may well isolate activities relating to medicinal marijuana from the illicit market," through controls such as the requirement of a "recommendation by a physician" and "an identification card system for qualified patients."

remote chain of inferences," under the Necessary and Proper Clause, Congress has "regulatory authority over intrastate activities that are not themselves part of interstate commerce [even when they] do not themselves substantially affect interstate commerce [if they are] 'an essential part of a larger regulation of economic activity, in which the regulatory scheme could be undercut unless the intrastate activity were regulated.' [*Lopez*.] Unlike the power to regulate activities that have a substantial effect on interstate commerce, the power to enact laws enabling effective regulation of interstate commerce can only be exercised in conjunction with congressional regulation of an interstate market. [Therefore, that] simple possession [of drugs] is a noneconomic activity is immaterial to whether it can be prohibited as a necessary part of a larger regulation. Rather, Congress's authority to enact all of these prohibitions of intrastate controlled-substance activities depends only upon whether they are appropriate means of achieving the legitimate end of eradicating [illegal] substances from interstate commerce. [T]hat the CSA regulates an area typically left to state regulation [is] not enough to render federal regulation an inappropriate means."

O'CONNOR, J., joined by Rehnquist, C.J., and Thomas, J., dissented: "This case exemplifies the role of States as laboratories. The States' core police powers have always included authority to define criminal law and to protect the health, safety, and welfare of their citizens. [Today's] decision suggests that the federal regulation of local activity is immune to Commerce Clause challenge because Congress chose to act with an ambitious, all-encompassing statute, rather than piecemeal. [If so], then *Lopez* stands for nothing more than a drafting guide: Congress should have described the relevant crime as "transfer or possession of a firearm anywhere in the nation"—thus including commercial and noncommercial activity, and clearly encompassing some activity with assuredly substantial effect on interstate commerce. [This is] a signal to Congress to enact legislation that is more extensive and more intrusive into the domain of state power. If the Court always defers to Congress as it does today, little may be left to the notion of enumerated powers. * * *

"A number of objective markers are available to confine the scope of constitutional review here. Both federal and state legislation [recognize] that medical and nonmedical (i.e., recreational) uses of drugs are realistically distinct and can be segregated, and regulate them differently. [Moreover] it is relevant that this case involves the interplay of federal and state regulation in areas of criminal law and social policy, where 'States lay claim by right of history and expertise.' *Lopez* (Kennedy, J., concurring); see also *Morrison*. [To] ascertain whether Congress' encroachment is constitutionally justified in this case, then, I would focus here on the personal cultivation, possession, and use of marijuana for medicinal purposes.

"[It] will not do to say that Congress may regulate noncommercial activity simply because it may have an effect on the demand for commercial goods, or because the noncommercial endeavor can, in some sense, substitute for commercial activity. Most commercial goods or services have some sort of privately producible analogue. Home care substitutes for daycare. Charades games substitute for movie tickets. Backyard or windowsill gardening substitutes for going to the supermarket. To draw the line wherever private activity affects the demand for market goods is to draw no line at all, and to declare everything economic.

"[As for *Wickard*, in] contrast to the CSA's limitless assertion of power, Congress provided an exemption within the AAA for small producers. [Thus] *Wickard* did not hold or imply that small-scale production of commodities is always economic, and automatically within Congress' reach.

"[C]haracterizing this as a case about the Necessary and Proper Clause does not change the analysis significantly. [S]omething more than mere assertion is required when Congress purports to have power over local activity whose connection to an interstate market is not self-evident. Otherwise, the Necessary and Proper Clause will always be a back door for unconstitutional federal regulation. [And] here, in part because common sense suggests that medical marijuana users may be limited in number, [the] effect of those activities on interstate drug traffic is not self-evidently substantial.

"In this regard, again, this case is readily distinguishable from *Wickard* [because] the parties had 'stipulated a summary of the economics of the wheat industry' [which showed] that consumption of homegrown wheat was the most variable factor in the size of the national wheat crop, and that on-site consumption could have the effect of varying the amount of wheat sent to market by as much as 20 percent. [The] Court recognizes that 'the record in the *Wickard* case itself established the causal connection between the production for local use and the national market' and argues that 'we have before us findings by Congress *to the same effect.*' The Court refers to a series of declarations in the introduction to the CSA saying that (1) local distribution and possession of controlled substances causes 'swelling' in interstate traffic; (2) local production and distribution cannot be distinguished from interstate production and distribution; (3) federal control over intrastate incidents 'is essential to effective control' over interstate drug trafficking. These bare declarations cannot be compared to the record before the Court in *Wickard.* [If] as the Court claims, today's decision does not break with precedent, how can it be that voluminous findings, documenting extensive hearings about the specific topic of violence against women, did not pass constitutional muster in *Morrison,* while the CSA's abstract, unsubstantiated, generalized findings about controlled substances do?"

THOMAS, J., dissented: "The Government contends that banning ['a distinct and separable subclass (local growers and users of state-authorized, medical marijuana)'] is 'necessary and proper for carrying into Execution' its regulation of interstate drug trafficking. However, in order to be 'necessary,' the intrastate ban must be more than 'a reasonable means [of] effectuat[ing] the regulation of interstate commerce.' [See] (majority opinion) (employing rational-basis review). It must be 'plainly adapted' to regulating interstate marijuana trafficking—in other words, there must be an 'obvious, simple, and direct relation' between the intrastate ban and the regulation of interstate commerce. *Sabri v. United States,* [p. 8 of this Supplement] (Thomas, J., concurring in judgment).

"[E]ven assuming Congress has 'obvious' and 'plain' reasons why regulating intrastate cultivation and possession is necessary to regulating the interstate drug trade, none of those reasons applies to medical marijuana. [E]ven assuming that States' controls[b] allow some seepage of medical marijuana into the illicit drug market, [i]t is difficult to see how this vast market could be affected by diverted medical cannabis, let alone in a way that makes regulating intrastate medical marijuana obviously essential to controlling the interstate drug market. [I]t is implausible that this Court could set aside entire portions of the United States Code as outside Congress' power in *Lopez* and *Morrison,* but it cannot engage in the more restrained practice of invalidating particular applications of the CSA that are beyond Congress' power. This Court has regularly entertained as-applied challenges under constitutional provisions, including the Commerce Clause, see *Katzenbach v. McClung*; *Heart of Atlanta Motel*; *Wickard.* There is no reason why,

b. See fn. a to the Court's opinion.

when Congress exceeds the scope of its commerce power, courts may not invalidate Congress' overreaching on a case-by-case basis. The CSA undoubtedly regulates a great deal of interstate commerce, but that is no license to regulate conduct that is neither interstate nor commercial, however minor or incidental. * * *

"In *Lopez,* I argued that allowing Congress to regulate intrastate, noncommercial activity under the Commerce Clause would confer on Congress a general 'police power' over the Nation. This is no less the case if Congress ties its power to the Necessary and Proper Clause rather than the Commerce Clause. [The] means selected by Congress to regulate interstate commerce cannot be 'prohibited' by, or inconsistent with the 'letter and spirit' of, the Constitution. *McCulloch.* * * *

"The majority's rewriting of the Commerce Clause seems to be rooted in the belief that, unless the Commerce Clause covers the entire web of human activity, Congress will be left powerless to regulate the national economy effectively. The interconnectedness of economic activity is not a modern phenomenon unfamiliar to the Framers. *Lopez* (Thomas, J., concurring). Moreover, the Framers understood what the majority does not appear to fully appreciate: There is a danger to concentrating too much, as well as too little, power in the Federal Government. This Court has carefully avoided stripping Congress of its ability to regulate *inter* state commerce, but it has casually allowed the Federal Government to strip States of their ability to regulate *intra* state commerce—not to mention a host of local activities, like mere drug possession, that are not commercial."

CON LAW: P. 106, at end of note 2(d)

AMER CON: P. 80, at end of note 2(d)

PIERCE COUNTY v. GUILLEN, 537 U.S. 129, 123 S.Ct. 720, 154 L.Ed.2d 610 (2003), per THOMAS, J., upheld Congress' power to grant a privilege from pretrial discovery in state and federal courts, for information (e.g., data regarding "potential accident sites, hazardous roadway conditions"), "compiled or collected" in connection with a federal program funding highway improvement: the law was "aimed at improving safety in the channels of commerce and increasing protection for the instrumentalities of interstate commerce."

THE NATIONAL TAXING AND SPENDING POWERS
REGULATION THROUGH SPENDING

CON LAW: P. 121, at end of Section

AMER CON: P. 92, at end of Section

SABRI v. UNITED STATES, 541 U.S. 600, 124 S.Ct. 1941, 158 L.Ed.2d 891 (2004), per SOUTER, J., held that Congress had power to make it a crime to bribe state or local officials whose government agency received federal funds in excess of $10,000 in any year: "Congress has authority under the Spending Clause to appropriate federal monies to promote the general welfare, and it has corresponding authority under the Necessary and Proper Clause to see to it that taxpayer dollars appropriated under that power are in fact spent for the general welfare, and not frittered away in graft or on projects undermined when funds are siphoned off or corrupt public officers are derelict about demanding value for dollars. See generally *McCulloch* (establishing review for means-ends rationality under the Necessary and Proper Clause). [Unlike *Dole*, the statute] is authority to bring federal power to bear directly on individuals who convert public spending into unearned private gain, not a means for bringing federal economic might to bear on a State's own choices of public policy."

Sabri argued that, even though his alleged actions related to the federal funds, the statute itself must specifically require proof that the bribe will be "traceably skimmed from specific federal payment." The Court responded: "Money is fungible, bribed officials are untrustworthy stewards of federal funds, and corrupt contractors do not deliver dollar-for-dollar value. [M]oney can be drained off here because a federal grant is pouring in there. And officials are not any the less threatening to the objects behind federal spending just because they may accept general retainers. [See] *Westfall v. United States,* 274 U.S. 256, 259, 47 S.Ct. 629, 71 L.Ed. 1036 (1927) (majority opinion by Holmes, J.) (upholding federal law criminalizing fraud on a state bank member of federal system, even where federal funds not directly implicated). [Sabri's claim has] to be seen as an overbreadth challenge; the most he could seriously say was that the statute could not be enforced against him, because it could not be enforced against someone else whose behavior would be outside the scope of Congress's Article I authority to legislate. [We] have recognized the validity of facial attacks alleging overbreadth (though not necessarily using that term) in relatively few settings, and, [outside these], and absent a good reason, we do not extend an invitation to bring overbreadth claims."

Although concurring in the judgment on the basis of pre-*Lopez* and *Morrison* precedents, THOMAS, J. observed that "the Court appears to hold that the Necessary and Proper Clause authorizes the exercise of any power that is no more than a 'rational means' to effectuate one of Congress' enumerated powers. This conclusion derives from the Court's characterization of the seminal case *M'Culloch*, as having established a 'means-ends rationality' test, a characterization that I am not certain is correct. [The Court] does not explain how there could be any federal interest in 'prosecut [ing] a bribe paid to a city's meat inspector in connection with a substantial transaction just because the city's parks department had received a federal grant of $10,000,' *United States v. Santopietro,* 166 F.3d 88, 93 (C.A.2 1999). It would be difficult to describe the chain of inferences and assumptions in which the Court would have to indulge to connect such a bribe to a federal interest in any federal funds or programs as being 'plainly adapted' to their protection."

APPLYING NATIONAL POWERS TO STATE GOVERNMENTS: INTERGOVERNMENTAL IMMUNITIES

STATE IMMUNITY FROM FEDERAL REGULATION

CON LAW: P. 144, add before note 4

AMER CON: P. 112, add before note 3

(c) JINKS v. RICHLAND COUNTY, 538 U.S. 456, 123 S.Ct. 1667, 155 L.Ed.2d 631 (2003), per SCALIA, J., unanimously upheld a federal statute—enacted pursuant to Congress' Art I, § 8, cl. 9 power to "constitute" lower federal courts—providing that the state statute of limitations will be tolled on state law claims, that are joined to federal causes of action filed in federal court, if the federal court declines to exercise jurisdiction over those claims which then must be refiled in state court: Although "we need not (and do not) hold that Congress has unlimited power to regulate practice and procedure in state courts," state statutes of limitations do not "fall into the category of 'procedure' immune from congressional regulation."

DISTRIBUTION OF FEDERAL POWERS: SEPARATION OF POWERS

CONGRESSIONAL ACTION AFFECTING "PRESIDENTIAL" POWERS

DELEGATION OF RULEMAKING POWER

CON LAW: P. 158, add before note (b)

WHITMAN v. AMERICAN TRUCKING ASSN'S, INC., 531 U.S. 457, 121 S.Ct. 903, 149 L.Ed.2d 1 (2001), per SCALIA, J. held that Clean Air Act's delegation to the EPA to set air quality standards—"the attainment and maintenance of which [are] requisite to protect the public health" with "an adequate margin of safety"—stated an "intelligible principle." THOMAS, J., agreed, but was "not convinced that the intelligible principle doctrine serves to prevent all cessions of legislative power. [On] a future [day], I would be willing to address the question whether our delegation jurisprudence has strayed too far from our Founders' understanding of separation of powers."

INDIVIDUAL RIGHTS AND THE WAR ON TERRORISM [NEW SECTION]

CON LAW: P. 193, before Section 4

AMER CON: P. 145, before Section 4

RTS & LIB: P. 283, before Chapter 5

HAMDI v. RUMSFELD

542 U.S. 507, 124 S.Ct. 2633, 159 L.Ed.2d 578 (2004).

JUSTICE O'CONNOR announced the judgment of the Court and delivered an opinion, in which THE CHIEF JUSTICE, JUSTICE KENNEDY, and JUSTICE BREYER join.

[Petitioner Yaser Hamdi is an American citizen, born in Louisiana, who by 2001 resided in Afghanistan. In the immediate aftermath of the al Qaeda terrorist attacks of September 11, 2001, Congress passed a resolution authorizing the President to "use all necessary and appropriate force" against "nations, organizations, or persons" that he determines "planned, authorized, committed, or aided" in the September 11 attacks. Authorization for Use of Military Force (AUMF). A short time later, the President ordered the Armed Forces to Afghanistan to subdue al Qaeda and oust the ruling Taliban regime. At a time when American forces were engaged in active combat, Hamdi was seized late in 2001 by the Northern Alliance, a military group opposed to the Taliban government, and turned over to the U.S. military as a Taliban fighter who had been captured on the battlefield. He was initially taken to the American naval base at Guantanamo Bay, Cuba, but when it was learned that he was an American citizen, he was transferred to a naval brig in the United States. In detaining Hamdi, the government took the position that he was an "enemy combatant," who had fought against the United States and its allies, and that his enemy combatant status justifies the U.S. in holding him indefinitely without bringing any formal criminal charges against him.]

[Hamdi's father filed this habeas petition, alleging, inter alia, that the Government was holding his son in violation of the fifth and fourteenth amendments. Hamdi's father contended that less than two months before the September 11 attacks his son went to Afghanistan to do "relief work" and could not have received any military training. The Government responded with a declaration from a Defense Department official (the Mobbs declaration) asserting in conclusory terms that Hamdi was affiliated with a Taliban army unit during a time when the Taliban was fighting U.S. allies. The Government maintained that Hamdi's habeas corpus petition should be dismissed on the basis of the Mobbs declaration.]

[The] threshold question before us is whether the Executive has the authority to detain citizens who qualify as "enemy combatants." There is some debate as to the proper scope of this term, and the Government has [made clear] that, for purposes of this case, the "enemy combatant" that it is seeking to detain is an individual who, it alleges, was "part of or supporting forces hostile to the United States or coalition partners" in Afghanistan and who "engaged in an armed conflict against the United States" there. We therefore answer only the narrow question before us: whether the detention of citizens falling within that definition is authorized.

* * * We do not reach the question whether Article II provides [the requisite] authority [even though] 18 U.S.C. § 4002(a) states that "[n]o citizen shall be imprisoned or otherwise detained by the United States except pursuant to an Act of Congress." [We conclude, however, that] AUMF is explicit congressional authorization for the detention of individuals in the narrow category we describe (assuming, without deciding, that such authorization is required). [The] AUMF authorizes the President to use "all necessary and appropriate force" against "nations, organizations, or persons" associated with the September 11, 2001, terrorist attacks. There can be no doubt that individuals who fought against the United States in Afghanistan as part of the Taliban, [are] individuals Congress sought to target in passing the AUMF. We conclude that detention of individuals falling into the limited category we are considering, for the duration of the particular conflict in which they were captured, is so fundamental and accepted an incident to war as to be an exercise of the "necessary and appropriate force" Congress has authorized the President to use.

[Hamdi] contends that the AUMF does not authorize indefinite or perpetual detention. Certainly, we agree that indefinite detention for the purpose of interrogation is not authorized. Further, we understand Congress' grant of authority for the use of "necessary and appropriate force" to include the authority to detain for the duration of the relevant conflict, and our understanding is based on longstanding law-of-war principles. If the practical circumstances of a given conflict are entirely unlike those of the conflicts that informed the development of the law of war, that understanding may unravel. But that is not the situation we face as of this date. Active combat operations against Taliban fighters apparently are ongoing in Afghanistan.

[O'Connor, J. then turned to precedents concerning the constitutionality of military detention during wartime and concluded that cases from the Civil War and World War II, especially *Ex Parte Quirin*, 317 U.S. 1, 63 S. Ct. 1, 87 L.Ed. 3 (1942), recognized the lawfulness of applying the "laws of war," including their provisions permitting the detention of enemy combatants without subjecting them to criminal trials, to citizens as well as non-citizens. Quirin, a citizen, was found to be subject to trial and punishment in a military tribunal (rather than an Article III court) because he had violated the laws of war by spying on his own country during wartime, and "his citizenship did not change this result."]

[Even] in cases in which the detention of enemy combatants is legally authorized, [however,] there remains the question of what process is constitutionally due to a citizen who disputes his enemy-combatant status.[A]ll agree that, absent suspension, the writ of habeas corpus remains available to every individual detained within the United States. U.S. Const., Art. I, § 9, cl. 2. [All] agree suspension of the writ has not occurred here. Thus, it is undisputed that Hamdi was properly before an Article III court to challenge his detention under 28 U.S.C. § 2241, [which provides that the courts of the

United States may "within their respective jurisdictions" issue the write to order the release of prisoners held "in custody in violation of the Constitution, laws, or treaties of the United States"]

[The] simple outline of § 2241 makes clear both that Congress envisioned that habeas petitioners would have some opportunity to present and rebut facts and that courts in cases like this retain some ability to vary the ways in which they do so as mandated by due process. The Government recognizes the basic procedural protections required by the habeas statute, but asks us to hold that, given both the flexibility of the habeas mechanism and the circumstances presented in this case, the presentation of the Mobbs Declaration to the habeas court completed the required factual development. It suggests two separate reasons for its position that no further process is due.

First, the Government urges [that] because it is "undisputed" that Hamdi's seizure took place in a combat zone, the habeas determination can be made purely as a matter of law, with no further hearing or factfinding necessary. This argument is easily rejected. [The] circumstances surrounding Hamdi's seizure cannot in any way be characterized as "undisputed."

[The] Government's second argument [is] that further factual exploration is unwarranted and inappropriate in light of the extraordinary constitutional interests at stake. Under the Government's most extreme rendition of this argument, "[r]espect for separation of powers and the limited institutional capabilities of courts in matters of military decision-making in connection with an ongoing conflict" ought to eliminate entirely any individual process, restricting the courts to investigating only whether legal authorization exists for the broader detention scheme. At most, the Government argues, courts should review its determination that a citizen is an enemy combatant under a very deferential "some evidence" standard. [Under] this review, a court would assume the accuracy of the Government's articulated basis for Hamdi's detention, as set forth in the Mobbs Declaration, and assess only whether that articulated basis was a legitimate one

[The] ordinary mechanism that we use for balancing such serious competing interests, and for determining the procedures that are necessary to ensure that a citizen is not "deprived of life, liberty, or property, without due process of law," is the test that we articulated in *Mathews v. Eldridge* [CON LAW p. 557, RTS & LIB p. 484]. *Mathews* dictates that the process due in any given instance is determined by weighing "the private interest that will be affected by the official action" against the Government's asserted interest, "including the function involved" and the burdens the Government would face in providing greater process. * * *

It is beyond question that substantial interests lie on both sides of the scale in this case. Hamdi's "private interest [affected] by the official action," is the most elemental of liberty interests—the interest in being free from physical detention by one's own government. * * * "We have always been careful not to 'minimize the importance and fundamental nature' of the individual's right to liberty," and we will not do so today.

Nor is the weight on this side of the *Mathews* scale offset by the circumstances of war or the accusation of treasonous behavior, for "[i]t is clear that commitment for *any* purpose constitutes a significant deprivation of liberty that requires due process protection," and at this stage in the *Mathews* calculus, we consider the interest of the *erroneously* detained individual. [A]s critical as the Government's interest may be in detaining those who actually pose an immediate threat to the national security of the United States during ongoing international conflict, history and common sense teach us that an unchecked system of detention carries the potential to become a means for oppression and abuse of others who do not present that sort of threat. [We] reaffirm today the fundamental nature of a citizen's right to be free from involuntary confinement by his own government without due process of law, and we weigh the opposing governmental interests against the curtailment of liberty that such confinement entails.

On the other side of the scale are the weighty and sensitive governmental interests in ensuring that those who have in fact fought with the enemy during a war do not return to battle against the United States. [Without] doubt, our Constitution recognizes that core strategic matters of warmaking belong in the hands of those who are best positioned and most politically accountable for making them.

[The] Government also argues at some length that its interests in reducing the process available to alleged enemy combatants are heightened by the practical difficulties that would accompany a system of trial-like process. In its view, military officers who are engaged in the serious work of waging battle would be unnecessarily and dangerously distracted by litigation half a world away, and discovery into military operations would both intrude on the sensitive secrets of national defense and result in a futile search for evidence buried under the rubble of war. To the extent that these burdens are triggered by heightened procedures, they are properly taken into account in our due process analysis.

Striking the proper constitutional balance here is of great importance to the Nation during this period of ongoing combat. But it is equally vital that our calculus not give short shrift to the values that this country holds dear or to the privilege that is American citizenship. It is during our most challenging and uncertain moments that our Nation's commitment to due process is most severely tested; and it is in those times that we must preserve our commitment at home to the principles for which we fight abroad.

[We hold] that a citizen-detainee seeking to challenge his classification as an enemy combatant must receive notice of the factual basis for his classification, and a fair opportunity to rebut the Government's factual assertions before a neutral decisionmaker. [These] essential constitutional promises may not be eroded.

At the same time, the exigencies of the circumstances may demand that, aside from these core elements, enemy combatant proceedings may be tailored to alleviate their uncommon potential to burden the Executive at a time of ongoing military conflict. Hearsay, for example, may need to be accepted as the most reliable available evidence from the Government in such a proceeding. Likewise, the Constitution would not be offended by a presumption in favor of the Government's evidence, so long as that presumption remained a rebuttable one and fair opportunity for rebuttal were provided. [A] burden-shifting scheme of this sort would meet the goal of ensuring that the errant tourist, embedded journalist, or local aid worker has a chance to prove military error while giving due regard to the Executive once it has put forth meaningful support for its conclusion that the detainee is in fact an enemy combatant. In the words of *Mathews,* process of this sort would sufficiently address the "risk of erroneous deprivation" of a detainee's liberty interest while eliminating certain procedures that have questionable additional value in light of the burden on the Government.

We think it unlikely that this basic process will have the dire impact on the central functions of warmaking that the Government forecasts. The parties agree that initial captures on the battlefield need not receive the process we have discussed here; that process is due only when the determination is made to *continue* to hold those who have been seized. The Government has made clear in its briefing that documentation regarding battlefield detainees already is kept in the ordinary course of military affairs. Any factfinding imposition created by requiring a knowledgeable affiant to summarize these records to an independent tribunal is a minimal one. [It] does not infringe on the core role of the military for the courts to exercise their own time-honored and constitutionally mandated roles of reviewing and resolving claims like those presented here.

[In holding as we do] we necessarily reject the Government's assertion that separation of powers principles mandate a heavily circumscribed role for the courts in such circumstances. Indeed, the position that the courts must forgo any examination of the individual case and focus exclusively on the legality of the broader detention scheme cannot be mandated by any reasonable view of separation of powers, as this approach serves only to *condense* power into a single branch of government. We have long since made clear that a state of war is not a blank check for the President when it comes to the rights of the Nation's citizens. *Youngstown.* Whatever power the United States Constitution envisions for the Executive in its exchanges with other nations or with enemy organizations in times of conflict, it most assuredly envisions a role for all three branches when individual liberties are at stake. [Likewise], unless Congress acts to suspend it, the Great Writ of habeas corpus allows the Judicial Branch to play a necessary role in maintaining this delicate balance of governance, serving as an important judicial check on the Executive's discretion in the realm of detentions. [Absent] suspension of the writ by Congress, a citizen detained as an enemy combatant is entitled to [due] process.

[There] remains the possibility that the standards we have articulated could be met by an appropriately authorized and properly constituted military tribunal. [In] the absence of such process, however, a court that receives a petition for a writ of habeas corpus from an alleged enemy combatant must itself ensure that the minimum requirements of due process are achieved.

[Hamdi] asks us to hold that the [lower court] also erred by denying him immediate access to counsel upon his detention and by disposing of the case without permitting him to meet with an attorney. Since our grant of certiorari in this case, Hamdi has been appointed counsel, with whom he has met for consultation purposes on several occasions, and with whom he is now being granted unmonitored meetings. He unquestionably has the right to access to counsel in connection with the proceedings on remand. No further consideration of this issue is necessary at this stage of the case. * * *

JUSTICE SOUTER, with whom JUSTICE GINSBURG joins, concurring in part, dissenting in part, and concurring in the judgment.

[It] is undisputed that the Government has not charged [Hamdi] with espionage, treason, or any other crime under domestic law. It is likewise undisputed that for one year and nine months, on the basis of an Executive designation of Hamdi as an "enemy combatant," the Government denied him the right to send or receive any communication beyond the prison where he was held and, in particular, denied him access to counsel to represent him.[1] The Government asserts a right to hold Hamdi under these conditions indefinitely, that is, until the Government determines that the United States is no longer threatened by the terrorism exemplified in the attacks of September 11, 2001. * * *

The plurality rejects [the Government's arguments trying to limit] the exercise of habeas jurisdiction and so far I agree with its opinion. The plurality does, however, accept the Government's position that if Hamdi's designation as an enemy combatant is correct, his detention (at least as to some period) is authorized by [the] AUMF. Here I disagree and respectfully dissent. * * *

The threshold issue is how broadly or narrowly to read the Non–Detention Act, the tone of which is severe: "No citizen shall be imprisoned or otherwise detained by the United States except pursuant to an Act of Congress." [For] a number of reasons, the prohibition within § 4001(a) has to be read broadly to accord the statute a long reach and to impose a burden of justification on the Government.

First, the circumstances in which the Act was adopted point the way to this interpretation. The provision superseded a cold-war statute, the Emergency Detention Act of 1950, which had authorized the Attorney General, in time of emergency, to detain anyone reasonably thought likely to engage in espionage or sabotage. That statute was repealed in 1971 out of fear that it could authorize a repetition of the World War II internment of citizens of Japanese ancestry; Congress meant to preclude another episode like the one described in *Korematsu v. United States*.

[Even] if history had spared us the cautionary example of the internments in World War II, [there] would be a compelling reason to read § 4001(a) to demand manifest authority to detain before detention is authorized. [For] reasons of inescapable human nature, the branch of the Government asked to counter a serious threat is not the branch on which to rest the Nation's entire reliance in striking the balance between the will to win and the cost in liberty on the way to victory. [A] reasonable balance is more likely to be reached on the judgment of a different branch. [Hence] the need for an assessment by Congress before citizens are subject to lockup, and likewise the need for a clearly expressed congressional resolution of the competing claims.

Under this principle of reading § 4001(a) robustly to require a clear statement of authorization to detain, none of the Government's arguments suffices to justify Hamdi's detention. [The] Government's [principal] claim, accepted by the Court, [is] that the terms of the Force Resolution are

1. The Government has since February 2004 permitted Hamdi to consult with counsel as a matter of policy, but does not concede that it has an obligation to allow this.

adequate to authorize detention of an enemy combatant under the circumstances described. [But the statute] never so much as uses the word detention, and there is no reason to think Congress might have perceived any need to augment Executive power to deal with dangerous citizens within the United States, given the well-stocked statutory arsenal of defined criminal offenses covering the gamut of actions that a citizen sympathetic to terrorists might commit.

[There] is one argument for treating the Force Resolution as sufficiently clear to authorize detention of a citizen consistently with § 4001(a). Assuming the argument to be sound, however, the Government is in no position to claim its advantage.

Because the Force Resolution authorizes the use of military force in acts of war by the United States, the argument goes, it is reasonably clear that the military and its Commander in Chief are authorized to deal with enemy belligerents according to the treaties and customs known collectively as the laws of war. [There] is no need [to] address the merits of such an argument in all possible circumstances. For now it is enough to recognize that the Government's stated legal position in its campaign against the Taliban (among whom Hamdi was allegedly captured) is apparently at odds with its claim here to be acting in accordance with customary law of war and hence to be within the terms of the Force Resolution in its detention of Hamdi. [Hamdi would] seem to qualify for treatment as a prisoner of war under the Third Geneva Convention, to which the United States is a party. [By] holding him incommunicado, however, the Government obviously has not been treating him as a prisoner of war, and in fact the Government claims that no Taliban detainee is entitled to prisoner of war status. This treatment appears to be a violation of the Geneva Convention provision that even in cases of doubt, captives are entitled to be treated as prisoners of war "until such time as their status has been determined by a competent tribunal."

[Since] the Government has given no reason either to deflect the application of § 4001(a) or to hold it to be satisfied, I need to go no further; the Government hints of a constitutional challenge to the statute, but it presents none here. I will, however, stray across the line between statutory and constitutional territory just far enough to note the weakness of the Government's mixed claim of inherent, extrastatutory authority under a combination of Article II of the Constitution and the usages of war. It [is] instructive to recall Justice Jackson's observation that the President is not Commander in Chief of the country, only of the military. *Youngstown.*

There may be room for one qualification to Justice Jackson's statement, however: in a moment of genuine emergency, when the Government must act with no time for deliberation, the Executive may be able to detain a citizen if there is reason to fear he is an imminent threat to the safety of the Nation and its people (though I doubt there is any want of statutory authority). This case, however, does not present that question, because an emergency power of necessity must at least be limited by the emergency; Hamdi has been locked up for over two years.

[Because] I find Hamdi's detention forbidden by § 4001(a) and unauthorized by the Force Resolution, I would not reach any questions of what process he may be due in litigating disputed issues in a proceeding under the habeas statute or prior to the habeas enquiry itself. [Since] this disposition does not command a majority of the Court, however, the need to give practical effect to the conclusions of eight members of the Court rejecting the Government's position calls for me to join with the plurality in ordering remand on terms closest to those I would impose. Although I think litigation of Hamdi's status as an enemy combatant is unnecessary, the terms of the plurality's remand will allow Hamdi to offer evidence that he is not an enemy combatant, and he should at the least have the benefit of that opportunity. * * *

JUSTICE SCALIA, with whom JUSTICE STEVENS joins, dissenting.

[Where] the Government accuses a citizen of waging war against it, our constitutional tradition has been to prosecute him in federal court for treason or some other crime. Where the exigencies of war prevent that, the Constitution's Suspension Clause, Art. I, § 9, cl. 2, allows Congress to relax the usual protections temporarily. Absent suspension, however, the Executive's assertion of military exigency has not been thought sufficient to permit detention without charge.

[The] writ of habeas corpus was preserved in the Constitution [as] a means to protect against "the practice of arbitrary imprisonments [in] all ages, [one of] the favourite and most formidable instruments of tyranny." Indeed, availability of the writ under the new Constitution (along with the requirement of trial by jury in criminal cases) was his basis for arguing that additional, explicit procedural protections were unnecessary.

[The] allegations here, of course, are no ordinary accusations of criminal activity. [Hamdi] has been imprisoned because the Government believes he participated in the waging of war against the United States. The relevant question, then, is whether there is a different, special procedure for imprisonment of a citizen accused of wrongdoing *by aiding the enemy in wartime.*

Justice O'Connor, writing for a plurality of this Court, asserts that captured enemy combatants (other than those suspected of war crimes) have traditionally been detained until the cessation of hostilities and then released. That is probably an accurate description of wartime practice with respect to enemy *aliens.* The tradition with respect to American citizens, however, has been quite different. Citizens aiding the enemy have been treated as traitors subject to the criminal process.

[T]here are times when military exigency renders resort to the traditional criminal process impracticable. English law accommodated such exigencies by allowing legislative suspension of the writ of habeas corpus for brief periods [and the Constitution does likewise]. [Of] course the extensive historical evidence of criminal convictions and habeas suspensions does not *necessarily* refute the Government's position in this case. [Even] if suspension of the writ on the one hand, and committal for criminal charges on the other hand, have been the only *traditional* means of dealing with citizens who levied war against their own country, it is theoretically possible that the Constitution does not *require* a choice between these alternatives.

I believe, however, that substantial evidence does refute that possibility. First, the text of the 1679 Habeas Corpus Act makes clear that indefinite imprisonment on reasonable suspicion is not an available option of treatment for those accused of aiding the enemy, absent a suspension of the writ. In the

United States, this Act was read as "enforc[ing] the common law" and shaped the early understanding of the scope of the writ.

[Cases from the Civil War and World War II are not to the contrary. In] *Ex parte Milligan*, [71 U.S. (4 Wall.) 2 (1866)], the Court issued the writ to an American citizen who had been tried by military commission [rather than an Article III court] for offenses that included conspiring to overthrow the Government. [The] Court rejected in no uncertain terms the Government's assertion that military jurisdiction was proper "under the laws and usages of war" [because, the Court said, those laws and usages, whatever they are,] "can never be applied to citizens in states which have upheld the authority of the government, and where the courts are open and their process unobstructed."

[In denying the controlling authority of *Milligan*, the] Government places primary reliance upon *Quirin*, a World War II case upholding the trial by military commission of eight German saboteurs, one of whom, Hans Haupt, was a U.S. citizen. The case was not this Court's finest hour. The Court upheld the commission and denied relief in a brief per curiam issued the day after oral argument concluded; a week later the Government carried out the commission's death sentence upon six saboteurs, including Haupt. The Court eventually explained its reasoning in a written opinion issued several months later [in which it] purported to interpret the language of *Milligan* quoted above [in] the following manner: "Elsewhere in its opinion [the] Court was at pains to point out that Milligan, a citizen twenty years resident in Indiana, who had never been a resident of any of the states in rebellion, was not an enemy belligerent either entitled to the status of a prisoner of war or subject to the penalties imposed upon unlawful belligerents. We construe the Court's statement as to the inapplicability of the law of war to Milligan's case as having particular reference to the facts before it." * * *

In my view this seeks to revise *Milligan* rather than describe it. [But] *Quirin* would still not justify denial of the writ here. In *Quirin* it was uncontested that the petitioners were members of enemy forces. [W]here those jurisdictional facts are not conceded—where the petitioner insists that he is not a belligerent—*Quirin* left the pre-existing law in place: Absent suspension of the writ, a citizen held where the courts are open is entitled either to a criminal trial or to a judicial decree requiring his release.

The plurality finds justification for Hamdi's imprisonment in the [AUMF]. [This] is not remotely a congressional suspension of the writ, and no one claims that it is. [If] the Suspension Clause does not guarantee the citizen that he will either be tried or released, unless the conditions for suspending the writ exist and the grave action of suspending the writ has been taken; if it merely guarantees the citizen that he will not be detained unless Congress by ordinary legislation says he can be detained; it guarantees him very little indeed.

It should not be thought, however, that the plurality's evisceration of the Suspension Clause augments, principally, the power of Congress. As usual, the major effect of its constitutional improvisation is to increase the power of the Court. Having found a congressional authorization for detention of citizens where none clearly exists; and having discarded the categorical procedural protection of the Suspension Clause; the plurality then proceeds, under the guise of the Due Process Clause, to prescribe what procedural protections *it* thinks appropriate.

[There] is a certain harmony of approach in the plurality's making up for Congress's failure to invoke the Suspension Clause and its making up for the Executive's failure to apply what it says are needed procedures—an approach that reflects what might be called a Mr. Fix-it Mentality. The plurality seems to view it as its mission to Make Everything Come Out Right, rather than merely to decree the consequences, as far as individual rights are concerned, of the other two branches' actions and omissions. Has the Legislature failed to suspend the writ in the current dire emergency? Well, we will remedy that failure by prescribing the reasonable conditions that a suspension should have included. And has the Executive failed to live up to those reasonable conditions? Well, we will ourselves make that failure good, so that this dangerous fellow (if he is dangerous) need not be set free. The problem with this approach is not only that it steps out of the courts' modest and limited role in a democratic society; but that by repeatedly doing what it thinks the political branches ought to do it encourages their lassitude and saps the vitality of government by the people.

Several limitations give my views in this matter a relatively narrow compass. They apply only to citizens, accused of being enemy combatants, who are detained within the territorial jurisdiction of a federal court. This is not likely to be a numerous group; currently we know of only two, Hamdi and Jose Padilla. [Moreover], the accused citizen-enemy combatant may lawfully be detained once prosecution is in progress or in contemplation. [The] Government has been notably successful in securing conviction, and hence long-term custody or execution, of those who have waged war against the state.

I frankly do not know whether these tools are sufficient to meet the Government's security needs, including the need to obtain intelligence through interrogation. It is far beyond my competence, or the Court's competence, to determine that. But it is not beyond Congress's. If the situation demands it, the Executive can ask Congress to authorize suspension of the writ—which can be made subject to whatever conditions Congress deems appropriate, including even the procedural novelties invented by the plurality today. To be sure, suspension is limited by the Constitution to cases of rebellion or invasion. But whether the attacks of September 11, 2001, constitute an "invasion," and whether those attacks still justify suspension several years later, are questions for Congress rather than this Court. If civil rights are to be curtailed during wartime, it must be done openly and democratically, as the Constitution requires, rather than by silent erosion through an opinion of this Court. * * *

JUSTICE THOMAS, dissenting.

The Executive Branch, acting pursuant to the powers vested in the President by the Constitution and with explicit congressional approval, has determined that Yaser Hamdi is an enemy combatant and should be detained. This detention falls squarely within the Federal Government's war powers, and we lack the expertise and capacity to second-guess that decision. As such, petitioners' habeas challenge should fail, and there is no reason to remand the case. The plurality reaches a contrary conclusion by failing adequately to consider basic principles of the constitutional structure as it relates to national security and foreign affairs and by using the balancing scheme of *Mathews v. Eldridge*. I do not think that the Federal Government's war powers can be balanced away by this Court. Arguably, Congress could provide for additional procedural protections, but until it does, we have no right to insist upon them. But even if I were to agree with the general approach the plurality takes, I could not accept the particulars. The plurality utterly fails to account for the Government's compelling interests and for our own institutional inability to weigh competing concerns correctly. * * *

"It is 'obvious and unarguable' that no governmental interest is more compelling than the security of the Nation." The national security, after all, is the primary responsibility and purpose of the Federal Government. [The] Founders intended that the President have primary responsibility—along with the necessary power—to protect the national security and to conduct the Nation's foreign relations. They did so principally because the structural advantages of a unitary Executive are essential in these domains. [These] structural advantages are most important in the national-security and foreign-affairs contexts. "Of all the cares or concerns of government, the direction of war most peculiarly demands those qualities which distinguish the exercise of power by a single hand." The Federalist No. 74, (A.Hamilton). [This] Court has long recognized these features and has accordingly held that the President has *constitutional* authority to protect the national security and that this authority carries with it broad discretion. * * *

Congress, to be sure, has a substantial and essential role in both foreign affairs and national security. But it is crucial to recognize that *judicial* interference in these domains destroys the purpose of vesting primary responsibility in a unitary Executive. * * *

I acknowledge that the question whether Hamdi's executive detention is lawful is a question properly resolved by the Judicial Branch, though the question comes to the Court with the strongest presumptions in favor of the Government. The plurality agrees that Hamdi's detention is lawful if he is an enemy combatant. But the question whether Hamdi is actually an enemy combatant is "of a kind for which the Judiciary has neither aptitude, facilities nor responsibility and which has long been held to belong in the domain of political power not subject to judicial intrusion or inquiry." That is, although it is appropriate for the Court to determine the judicial question whether the President has the asserted authority, we lack the information and expertise to question whether Hamdi is actually an enemy combatant, a question the resolution of which is committed to other branches.

[The] Government's asserted authority to detain an individual that the President has determined to be an enemy combatant, at least while hostilities continue, comports with the Due Process Clause. [The] Executive's decision that a detention is necessary to protect the public need not and should not be subjected to judicial second-guessing. Indeed, at least in the context of enemy-combatant determinations, this would defeat the unity, secrecy, and dispatch that the Founders believed to be so important to the warmaking function. I therefore cannot agree with Justice Scalia's conclusion that the Government must choose between using standard criminal processes and suspending the writ.

[Scalia, J.'s] position raises an additional concern. [He] apparently does not disagree that the Federal Government has all power necessary to protect the Nation. If criminal processes do not suffice, however, Justice Scalia would require Congress to suspend the writ. But the fact that the writ may not be suspended "unless when in Cases of Rebellion or Invasion the public Safety may require it," poses two related problems. First, this condition might not obtain here or during many other emergencies during which this detention authority might be necessary. Congress would then have to choose between acting unconstitutionally[4] and depriving the President of the tools he needs to protect the Nation. Second, I do not see how suspension would make constitutional otherwise unconstitutional detentions ordered by the President. It simply removes a remedy. Justice Scalia's position might therefore require one or both of the political branches to act unconstitutionally in order to protect the Nation. But the power to protect the Nation must be the power to do so lawfully.

Accordingly, I conclude that the Government's detention of Hamdi as an enemy combatant does not violate the Constitution. By detaining Hamdi, the President, in the prosecution of a war and authorized by Congress, has acted well within his authority. * * *

Ultimately, the plurality's dismissive treatment of the Government's asserted interests arises from its apparent belief that enemy-combatant determinations are not part of "the actual prosecution of a war" or one of the "central functions of warmaking." This seems wrong: Taking *and holding* enemy combatants is a quintessential aspect of the prosecution of war. * * *

I acknowledge that under the plurality's approach, it might, at times, be appropriate to give detainees access to counsel and notice of the factual basis for the Government's determination. But properly accounting for the Government's interests also requires concluding that access to counsel and to the factual basis would not always be warranted. Though common sense suffices, the Government thoroughly explains that counsel would often destroy the intelligence gathering function. Equally obvious is the Government's interest in not fighting the war in its own courts, and protecting classified information. * * *

Two other war-on-terrorism cases decided the same day as *Hamdi* settled important questions involving the jurisdiction of the federal courts to review the detentions of suspected terrorists, but they did not resolve any substantive constitutional issues. RASUL v. BUSH, 540 U.S. 1175, 124 S.Ct. 1494, 158 L.Ed.2d 75 (2004), per STEVENS, J., rejecting the government's reliance on a World War II precedent, ruled that U.S. courts have jurisdiction under the same habeas corpus statute involved in *Hamdi* to consider challenges to the legality of the detentions of foreign nationals captured abroad and imprisoned at a U.S. naval base at Guantanamo Bay, Cuba. Significantly, however, the Court left open the question of what substantive rights the detainees might

4. I agree with Justice Scalia that this Court could not review Congress' decision to suspend the writ.

assert. Cf. *United States v. Verdugo–Urquidez*, 494 U.S. 259, 110 S.Ct. 1056, 108 L.Ed.2d 222 (1990) (fourth amendment does not apply to property owned by a nonresident alien and located in another country). Neither did the Court make it wholly clear whether its opinion would apply to prisoners detained by the U.S. in foreign locations other than Guantanamo, on which the U.S. has a permanent lease. Scalia, J., joined by Rehnquist, C.J., and Thomas, J., dissented, arguing that the federal courts lacked statutory jurisdiction to review the Guantanamo detentions at all.

RUMSFELD v. PADILLA, 542 U.S. 426, 124 S.Ct. 2711, 159 L.Ed.2d 513 (2004), held only that an American citizen seized in the U.S. and held as an enemy combatant had brought his legal challenge in the wrong federal district court. It thus left open the question whether the "enemy combatant" label could be applied to an American citizen who, unlike Hamdi, was apprehended in the U.S. and not on a foreign battlefield.

EXECUTIVE PRIVILEGE AND IMMUNITY

CON LAW: P. 201, before note 7

AMER CON: P. 149, after note 6

CHENEY v. U.S. DIST. CT., 542 U.S. 367, 124 S.Ct. 2576, 159 L.Ed.2d 459 (2004): Public interest groups filed suit under the Federal Advisory Committee Act (FACA) seeking information from the Vice President and other senior Executive Branch officials about the members and activities of a task force (NEPDG) established to develop a national energy policy for the President. To show FACA's applicability, plaintiffs obtained an extensive discovery order regarding NEPDG's activities which requested even more information than they would be entitled to if they succeeded in proving that FACA applied. The D.C. Circuit, relying on *Nixon*, denied the government's petition for mandamus to vacate the district court's discovery order and to dismiss the Vice President as a defendant because of principles of separation of powers. The Court, per KENNEDY, J., remanded to the D.C. Circuit to reconsider:

"Accepted mandamus standards are broad enough to allow a court to prevent a lower court from interfering with a coequal branch's ability to discharge its constitutional responsibilities. [The] need for information for use in civil cases, while far from negligible, does not share the urgency or significance of the criminal subpoena requests in *Nixon*. * * * Withholding materials from a tribunal in an ongoing criminal case when the information is necessary to the court in carrying out its tasks 'conflict[s] with the function of the courts under Art. III.' [Withholding] the information in this case, however, does not hamper another branch's ability to perform its 'essential functions' in quite the same way. [Even if] FACA's statutory objectives would be to some extent frustrated, [it] cannot, in fairness, be compared to *Nixon*, where a court's ability to fulfill its constitutional responsibility to resolve cases and controversies within its jurisdiction hinges on the availability of certain indispensable information.

"[This] Court has held, on more than one occasion, that '[t]he high respect that is owed to the office of the Chief Executive ... is a matter that should inform the conduct of the entire proceeding, including the timing and scope of discovery,' *Clinton*, and that the Executive's 'constitutional responsibilities and status [are] factors counseling judicial deference and restraint' in the conduct of litigation against it, *Nixon v. Fitzgerald*. [Given] the breadth of the discovery requests in this case compared to the narrow subpoena orders in *Nixon*, our precedent provides no support for the proposition [adopted by the district court] that the Executive Branch 'shall bear the burden' of invoking executive privilege with sufficient specificity and of making particularized objections. [Our] precedents suggest just the opposite. See, e.g., *Clinton* (holding that the Judiciary may direct 'appropriate process' to the Executive).

"In recognition of these concerns, there is sound precedent in the District of Columbia itself for district courts to explore other avenues, short of forcing the Executive to invoke privilege, when they are asked to enforce against the Executive Branch unnecessarily broad subpeonas. [But the D.C. Circuit] labored under the mistaken assumption that the assertion of executive privilege is a necessary precondition to the Government's separation-of-powers objections."[a]

a. Stevens, J., who joined the Court's opinion, also concurred separately. Thomas, J., joined by Scalia, concurred and dissented in part, and Ginsburg, J., joined by Souter, J., dissented, all four Justices addressing procedural mandamus issues.

STATE POWER TO REGULATE

STATE REGULATION WHEN CONGRESS' POWER IS "DORMANT": HISTORY AND FUNDAMENTAL ISSUES

CONGRESSIONAL AUTHORIZATION OF STATE REGULATION

CON LAW: P. 214, after note 1

AMER CON: P. 161, after note 1

See also *Hillside Dairy, Inc. v. Lyons*, 539 U.S. 59, 123 S.Ct. 2142, 156 L.Ed.2d 54 (2003) (demanding a clear indication of congressional intent to authorize state regulations that burden or discriminate against interstate commerce).

CASES AND DOCTRINE

REGULATIONS THAT BURDEN OUT-OF-STATE SUPPLIERS SEEKING IN-STATE MARKETS: BASIC THEMES AND DISTINCTIONS

CON LAW: P. 226, at end of note 2

AMER CON: P. 172, at end of note 2

GRANHOLM v. HEALD, ___ U.S. ___, 125 S.Ct. 1885, 161 L.Ed.2d 796 (2005), held that state regulatory schemes allowing "in-state wineries to sell wine to consumers in that state but [prohibiting] out-of state wineries from doing so," or otherwise burdening direct deliveries from out-of-state vintners, violated the dormant commerce clause. After emphasizing that facially discriminatory statutes are virtually per se illegal, the Court, per Kennedy, J., devoted most of its opinion to refuting arguments that the state discrimination was authorized either by the 21st Amendment or by a federal statute, the Webb–Kenyon Act. Absent an authorization from one of these sources, Kennedy, J., found inadequate evidence that the state's legitimate interests, including an interest in keeping alcohol out of the hands of minors, could not be served adequately by non-discriminatory alternatives. Thomas, J., joined by Rehnquist, C.J., and Stevens and O'Connor, JJ., dissented, arguing that discriminatory state regulation of liquor imported from other states was authorized both by the 21st Amendment and the Webb–Kenyon Act and thus was exempt from the dormant commerce clause.

INTERSTATE PRIVILEGES AND IMMUNITIES CLAUSE

CON LAW: P. 264, after note 4

AMER CON: P. 202, after note 3

Discriminatory effects. A statute that does not facially discriminate against out-of-staters, but nonetheless has discriminatory effects, can violate the Privileges and Immunities Clause under at least some circumstances, the Court held unanimously in HILLSIDE DAIRY, INC. v. LYONS, 539 U.S. 59, 123 S.Ct. 2142, 156 L.Ed.2d 54 (2003). A complex California scheme of milk price supports required in-state processors both to pay minimum prices to farmers and to make payments into an "equalization fund," distributions from which went to processors based on the nature of their ultimate products (including, for example, cheese, cottage cheese, and butter) and the prices that those products commanded. Prior to 1997, California did not require payments to the equalization fund for out-of-state milk purchases. When the state amended its plan to require payments into the equalization fund based on purchases of milk from out-of-state (as well as California) producers, out-of-state farmers filed suit alleging violations of the dormant commerce clause and the Privileges and Immunities Clause. The lower court dismissed the Privileges and Immunities challenge on the ground that the California scheme did not facially discriminate against out-of-state producers. The Court, per Stevens, J., reversed, relying principally on *Chalker v. Birmingham & Northwestern Ry. Co.*, 249 U.S. 522, 39 S.Ct. 366, 63 L.Ed.748 (1919), which had invalidated a tax that did not facially discriminate on the basis of citizenship, but imposed a higher rate on persons with their principal offices out of state: "Whether *Chalker* should be interpreted as merely applying the [Privileges and Immunities] Clause to classifications that are but proxies for differential treatment against out-of-state residents, or as prohibiting any classification with the practical effect of discriminating against such residents, is a matter we need not decide at this stage of the case. Under either interpretation, [the] absence of an express statement in the California laws identifying out-of-state citizenship as a basis for disparate treatment is not a sufficient basis for rejecting this claim."

CON LAW: P. 269, after note 1

STATE POWER TO TAX

In AMERICAN TRUCKING ASS'NS, INC. v. MICHIGAN PUBLIC SERV. COMM'N, ___ U.S. ___, 125 S.Ct. 2419, ___ L.Ed.2d (2005), the Court per Breyer, J., held unanimously that a Michigan provision charging a flat fee of $100 on all trucks engaging in in-state commercial hauling did not violate the dormant commerce clause. The Court emphasized that states commonly tax intra-state service providers. It then distinguished *American Trucking Ass'ns v. Scheiner*, 483 U.S. 266, 107 S.Ct. 2829, 97 L.Ed.2d 226 (1987), which invalidated a flat tax of $25 that Pennsylvania levied on all trucks that used its roads (even if for purely interstate traffic): "The present fee [taxes] purely local activity; it does not tax an interstate truck's entry into the state. [Consequently], we lack any reason to infer that Michigan's lump-sum levy erects [an] impermissible discriminatory roadblock" despite unsupported assertions that the fee would discourage interstate trucks from also engaging in intra-state hauling and thus protect in-state service providers.

SUBSTANTIVE PROTECTION OF ECONOMIC INTERESTS

OTHER LIMITS ON ECONOMIC LEGISLATION: THE PROHIBITION AGAINST "TAKING" "PRIVATE PROPERTY" WITHOUT JUST COMPENSATION

PURPOSE OF "TAKING"

CON LAW: P. 306, at end

AMER CON: P. 234, at end of note

RTS & LIB: P. 70, at end

KELO v. NEW LONDON

___ U.S. ___, 125 S.Ct. 2655, ___ L.Ed.2d ___ (2005).

JUSTICE STEVENS delivered the opinion of the Court.

[Decades of economic decline prompted state and local officials to target New London, Conn. (hereinafter City), and especially its Fort Trumbell area, for economic revitalization. The New London Development Corp. (NLDC), a private entity designed to help the City in planning economic development, was revitalized. Shortly thereafter, the pharmaceutical company Pfizer announced that it would build a $300 million facility on a site immediately adjacent to Fort Trumbell. Local planners hoped that the new facility would serve as a catalyst to the area's rejuvenation.

[The city council approved the NLDC plan and authorized the entity to purchase property or to acquire it by exercising eminent domain in the City's name. When petitioners in the case, nine persons who owned 15 properties in Fort Trumbell, refused to sell, the City initiated condemnation proceedings. There is no allegation that any of their properties was blighted or otherwise in poor condition. Rather, they were condemned only because they happened to be in the development area.

[Petitioner brought this action in state court, maintaining that the City's taking of their properties would violate the "public use" restriction in the taking clause. The state supreme court disagreed.]

Two polar propositions are perfectly clear. On the one hand, it has long been accepted that the sovereign may not take the property of *A* for the sole purpose of transferring it to another private party *B*, even though *A* is paid just compensation. On the other hand, it is equally clear that a State may transfer property from one private party to another if future "use by the public" is the purpose of the taking; the condemnation of land for a railroad with common-carrier duties is a familiar example. Neither of these propositions, however, determines the disposition of this case.

As for the first proposition, the City would no doubt be forbidden from taking petitioners' land for the purpose of conferring a private benefit on a particular private party. [Nor] would the City be allowed to take property under the mere pretext of a public purpose, when its actual purpose was to bestow a private benefit. The takings before us, however, would be executed pursuant to a "carefully considered" development plan. The trial judge and all the members of the Supreme Court of Connecticut agreed that there was no evidence of an illegitimate purpose in this case. Therefore, as was true of the statute challenged in *Midkiff*, the City's development plan was not adopted "to benefit a particular class of identifiable individuals."

On the other hand, this is not a case in which the City is planning to open the condemned land—at least not in its entirety—to use by the general public. Nor will the private lessees of the land in any sense be required to operate like common carriers, making their services available to all comers. But although such a projected use would be sufficient to satisfy the public use requirement, this "Court long ago rejected any literal requirement that condemned property be put into use for the general public." *Midkiff*.

[The] disposition of this [case] turns on the question whether the City's development plan serves a "public purpose." Without exception, our cases have defined that concept broadly, reflecting our longstanding policy of deference to legislative judgments in this field. [The Court then discusses *Berman* and *Midkiff* at considerable length.]

[For] more than a century, our public use jurisprudence has wisely eschewed rigid formulas and intrusive scrutiny in favor of affording legislatures broad latitude in determining what public needs justify the use of the takings power.

Those who govern the City were not confronted with the need to remove blight in the Fort Trumbull area, but their determination that the area was sufficiently distressed to justify a program of economic rejuvenation is entitled to our deference. The City has carefully formulated an economic development plan that it believes will provide appreciable benefits to the community, including—but by no means limited to—new jobs and increased tax revenue. As with other exercises in urban planning and development, the City is endeavoring to coordinate a variety of commercial, residential, and recreational uses of land, with the hope that they will form a whole greater than the sum of its parts. [Given] the comprehensive character of the plan, the thorough deliberation that preceded its adoption, and the limited scope of our review, it is appropriate for us, as it was in *Berman*, to resolve the challenges of the individual owners, not on a piecemeal basis, but rather in light of the entire plan. Because that plan unquestionably serves a public purpose, the takings challenged here satisfy the public use requirement of the Fifth Amendment.

To avoid this result, petitioners urge us to adopt a new bright-line rule that economic development does not qualify as a public use. Putting aside the unpersuasive suggestion that the City's plan will provide only purely economic benefits, neither precedent nor logic supports petitioners' proposal. Promoting economic development is a traditional and long accepted function of government. There is, moreover, no principled way of distinguishing economic development from the other public purposes that we have recognized. In our cases upholding takings that facilitated agriculture and mining, for example, we emphasized the importance of those industries to the welfare of the States in question; in *Berman,* we endorsed the purpose of transforming a blighted area into a "well-balanced" community through redevelopment; in *Midkiff,* we upheld the interest in breaking up a land oligopoly that "created artificial deterrents to the normal functioning of the State's residential land market;" and in *Ruckelshaus v. Monsanto Co.*, 467 U.S. 986, 104 S.Ct. 2862, 81 L.Ed.2d 815 (1984), we accepted Congress' purpose of eliminating a "significant barrier to entry in the pesticide market," It would be incongruous to hold that the City's interest in the economic benefits to be derived from the development of the Fort Trumbull area has less of a public character than any of those other interests. Clearly, there is no basis for exempting economic development from our traditionally broad understanding of public purpose.

Petitioners contend that using eminent domain for economic development impermissibly blurs the boundary between public and private takings. Again, our cases foreclose this objection. Quite simply, the government's pursuit of a public purpose will often benefit individual private parties. For example, in *Midkiff,* the forced transfer of property conferred a direct and significant benefit on those lessees who were previously unable to purchase their homes. [The] owner of the department store in *Berman* objected to "taking from one businessman for the benefit of another businessman," referring to the fact that under the redevelopment plan land would be leased or sold to private developers for redevelopment. Our rejection of that contention has particular relevance to the instant case: "The public end may be as well or better served through an agency of private enterprise than through a department of government—or so the Congress might conclude. We cannot say that public ownership is the sole method of promoting the public purposes of community redevelopment projects."

It is further argued that without a bright-line rule nothing would stop a city from transferring citizen *A*'s property to citizen *B* for the sole reason that citizen *B* will put the property to a more productive use and thus pay more taxes. Such a one-to-one transfer of property, executed outside the confines of an integrated development plan, is not presented in this case. While such an unusual exercise of government power would certainly raise a suspicion that a private purpose was afoot, the hypothetical cases posited by petitioners can be confronted if and when they arise. They do not warrant the crafting of an artificial restriction on the concept of public use.

Alternatively, petitioners maintain that for takings of this kind we should require a "reasonable certainty" that the expected public benefits will actually accrue. Such a rule, however, would represent an even greater departure from our precedent. "When the legislature's purpose is legitimate and its means are not irrational, our cases make clear that empirical debates over the wisdom of takings—no less than debates over the wisdom of other kinds of socioeconomic legislation—are not to be carried out in the federal courts." *Midkiff.*

[Just] as we decline to second-guess the City's considered judgments about the efficacy of its development plan, we also decline to second-guess the City's determinations as to what lands it needs to acquire in order to effectuate the project.

In affirming the City's authority to take petitioners' properties, we do not minimize the hardship that condemnations may entail, notwithstanding the payment of just compensation. We emphasize that nothing in our opinion precludes any State from placing further restrictions on its exercise of the takings power. Indeed, many States already impose "public use" requirements that are stricter than the federal baseline. Some of these requirements have been established as a matter of state constitutional law, while others are expressed in state eminent domain statutes that carefully limit the grounds upon which takings may be exercised. [The] necessity and wisdom of using eminent domain to promote economic development are certainly matters of legitimate public debate. This Court's authority, however, extends only to determining whether the City's proposed condemnations are for a "public use" within the meaning of the Fifth Amendment to the Federal Constitution. Because over a century of our case law interpreting that provision dictates an affirmative answer to that question, we may not grant petitioners the relief that they seek. * * *

JUSTICE KENNEDY, concurring.

I join the opinion for the Court and add these further observations.

This Court has declared that a taking should be upheld as consistent with the Public Use Clause, as long as it is "rationally related to a conceivable public purpose." *Midkiff* [A] court applying rational-basis review under the Public Use Clause should strike down a taking that, by a clear showing, is intended to favor a particular private party, with only incidental or pretextual public benefits, just as a court applying rational-basis review under the Equal Protection Clause must strike down a government classification that is clearly intended to injure a particular class of private parties, with only incidental or pretextual public justifications.

[A] court confronted with a plausible accusation of impermissible favoritism to private parties should treat the objection as a serious one and review the record to see if it has merit, though with the presumption that the government's actions were reasonable and intended to serve a public purpose. Here, the trial court [did so] and concluded [that] benefitting Pfizer was not "the primary motivation or effect of this development plan." [This] case, then, survives the meaningful rational basis review that in my view is required under the Public Use Clause. [While] there may be categories of cases in which the transfers are so suspicious, or the procedures employed so prone to abuse, or the purported benefits are so trivial or implausible, that courts should presume an impermissible private purpose, no such circumstances are present in this case. * * *

JUSTICE O'CONNOR, with whom THE CHIEF JUSTICE, JUSTICE SCALIA, and JUSTICE THOMAS join, dissenting.

[Under] the banner of economic development, all private property is now vulnerable to being taken and transferred to another private owner, so long as it might be upgraded—i.e., given to an owner who will use it in a way that the legislature deems more beneficial to the public—in the process. To reason, as the Court does, that the incidental public benefits resulting from the subsequent ordinary use of private property render economic development takings "for public use" is to wash out any distinction between private and public use of property—and thereby effectively to delete the words "for public use" from the Takings Clause of the Fifth Amendment.

[We] have read the Fifth Amendment's language to impose two distinct conditions on the exercise of eminent domain: "the taking must be for a 'public use' and 'just compensation' must be paid to the owner." [While] the Takings Clause presupposes that government can take private property without the owner's consent, the just compensation requirement spreads the cost of condemnations and thus "prevents the public from loading upon one individual more than his just share of the burdens of government." The public use requirement, in turn, imposes a more basic limitation, circumscribing the very scope of the eminent domain power: Government may compel an individual to forfeit her property for the *public's* use, but not for the benefit of another private person. This requirement promotes fairness as well as security.

Where is the line between "public" and "private" property use? We give considerable deference to legislatures' determinations about what governmental activities will advantage the public. But were the political branches the sole arbiters of the public-private distinction, the Public Use Clause would amount to little more than hortatory fluff. An external, judicial check on how the public use requirement is interpreted, however limited, is necessary if this constraint on government power is to retain any meaning.

[This] case returns us for the first time in over 20 years to the hard question of when a purportedly "public purpose" taking meets the public use requirement. It presents an issue of first impression: Are economic development takings constitutional? I would hold that they are not.

[In *Berman* and *Midkiff*], we emphasized the importance of deferring to legislative judgments about public purpose. Because courts are ill-equipped to evaluate the efficacy of proposed legislative initiatives, we rejected as unworkable the idea of courts' " 'deciding on what is and is not a governmental function [and] invalidating legislation on the basis of their view on that question at the moment of decision, a practice which has proved impracticable in other fields.' "

[Yet] for all the emphasis on deference, *Berman* and *Midkiff* hewed to a bedrock principle without which our public use jurisprudence would collapse: "A purely private taking could not withstand the scrutiny of the public use requirement; it would serve no legitimate purpose of government and would thus be void." *Midkiff.*

[The] Court's holdings in *Berman* and *Midkiff* were true to the principle underlying the Public Use Clause. In both those cases, the extraordinary, precondemnation use of the targeted property inflicted affirmative harm on society—in *Berman* through blight resulting from extreme poverty and in *Midkiff* through oligopoly resulting from extreme wealth. And in both cases, the relevant legislative body had found that eliminating the existing property use was necessary to remedy the harm. Thus a public purpose was realized when the harmful use was eliminated. Because each taking *directly* achieved a public benefit, it did not matter that the property was turned over to private use. Here, in contrast, New London does not claim that [petitioners'] well-maintained homes are the source of any social harm. Indeed, it could not so claim without adopting the absurd argument that any single-family home that might be razed to make way for an apartment building, or any church that might be replaced with a retail store, or any small business that might be more lucrative if it were instead part of a national franchise, is inherently harmful to society and thus within the government's power to condemn.

In moving away from our decisions sanctioning the condemnation of harmful property use, the Court today significantly expands the meaning of public use. It holds that the sovereign may take private property currently put to ordinary private use, and give it over for new, ordinary private use, so long as the new use is predicted to generate some secondary benefit for the public—such as increased tax revenue, more jobs, maybe even aesthetic pleasure. But nearly any lawful use of real private property can be said to generate some incidental benefit to the public. Thus, if predicted (or even guaranteed) positive side-effects are enough to render transfer from one private party to another constitutional, then the words "for public use" do not realistically exclude *any* takings, and thus do not exert any constraint on the eminent domain power.

[The Court] protests that it does not sanction the bare transfer from A to B for B's benefit. It suggests two limitations on what can be taken after today's decision. First, it maintains a role for courts in ferreting out takings whose sole purpose is to bestow a benefit on the private transferee—without detailing how courts are to conduct that complicated inquiry. For his part, Justice Kennedy suggests that courts may divine illicit purpose by a careful review of the record and the process by which a legislature arrived at the decision to take—without specifying what courts should look for in a case with different facts, how they will know if they have found it, and what to do if they do not. Whatever the details of Justice Kennedy's as-yet-undisclosed test, it is difficult to envision anyone but the "stupid staff[er]" failing it. The trouble with economic development takings is that private benefit and incidental public benefit are, by definition, merged and mutually reinforcing. In this case, for example, any boon for Pfizer or the plan's developer is difficult to disaggregate from the promised public gains in taxes and jobs.

Even if there were a practical way to isolate the motives behind a given taking, the gesture toward a purpose test is theoretically flawed. If it is true that incidental public benefits from new private use are enough to ensure the "public purpose" in a taking, why should it matter, as far as the Fifth Amendment is concerned, what inspired the taking in the first place? How much the government does or does not desire to benefit a favored private party has no bearing on whether an economic development taking will or will not generate secondary benefit for the public. And whatever the reason for a given condemnation, the effect is the same from the constitutional perspective—private property is forcibly relinquished to new private ownership.

A second proposed limitation is implicit in the Court's opinion. The logic of today's decision is that eminent domain may only be used to upgrade—not downgrade—property. At best this makes the Public Use Clause redundant with the Due Process Clause, which already prohibits irrational government action. [In] any event, this constraint has no realistic import. For who among us can say she already makes the most productive or attractive possible use of her property? The specter of condemnation hangs over all property. Nothing is to prevent the State from replacing any Motel 6 with a Ritz-Carlton, any home with a shopping mall, or any farm with a factory.

The Court also puts special emphasis on facts peculiar to this case: The NLDC's plan is the product of a relatively careful deliberative process; it proposes to use eminent domain for a multipart, integrated plan rather than for isolated property transfer; it promises an array of incidental benefits (even aesthetic ones), not just increased tax revenue; it comes on the heels of a legislative determination that New London is a depressed municipality. Justice Kennedy, too, takes great comfort in these facts. But none has legal significance to blunt the force of today's holding. If legislative prognostications about the secondary public benefits of a new use can legitimate a taking, there is nothing in the Court's rule or in Justice Kennedy's gloss on that rule to prohibit property transfers generated with less care, that are less comprehensive, that happen to result from less elaborate process, whose only projected advantage is the incidence of higher taxes, or that hope to transform an already prosperous city into an even more prosperous one.

[The] Court suggests that property owners should turn to the States, who may or may not choose to impose appropriate limits on economic development takings. This is an abdication of our responsibility. States play many important functions in our system of dual sovereignty, but compensating for our refusal to enforce properly the Federal Constitution (and a provision meant to curtail state action, no less) is not among them. * * *

Any property may now be taken for the benefit of another private party, but the fallout from this decision will not be random. The beneficiaries are likely to be those citizens with disproportionate influence and power in the political process, including large corporations and development firms. As for the victims, the government now has license to transfer property from those with fewer resources to those with more. The Founders cannot have intended this perverse result. * * *

JUSTICE THOMAS, dissenting.

[The] Framers [allowed] the government to take property not for "public necessity," but instead for "public use." Amdt. 5. Defying this understanding, the Court replaces the Public Use Clause with a " '[P]ublic [P]urpose' " Clause (or perhaps the "Diverse and Always Evolving Needs of Society" Clause), a restriction that is satisfied, the Court instructs, so long as the purpose is "legitimate" and the means "not irrational." This deferential shift in phraseology enables the Court to hold, against all common sense, that a costly urban-renewal project whose stated purpose is a vague promise of new jobs and increased tax revenue, but which is also suspiciously agreeable to the Pfizer Corporation, is for a "public use."

[Today's] decision is simply the latest in a string of our cases construing the Public Use Clause to be a virtual nullity, without the slightest nod to its original meaning. In my view, the Public Use Clause, originally understood, is a meaningful limit on the government's eminent domain power. Our cases have strayed from the Clause's original meaning, and I would reconsider them. * * *

The most natural reading of the [Public Use] Clause is that it allows the government to take property only if the government owns, or the public has a legal right to use, the property, as opposed to taking it for any public purpose or necessity whatsoever. * * * Tellingly, the phrase "public use" contrasts with the very different phrase "general Welfare" used elsewhere in the Constitution. The Framers would have used some such broader term if they had meant the Public Use Clause to have a similarly sweeping scope. Other founding-era documents made the contrast between these two usages still more explicit. * * *

Our current Public Use Clause jurisprudence [has] rejected [the] natural reading of the Clause. The Court adopted its modern reading blindly, with little discussion of the Clause's history and original meaning, in two distinct lines of cases: first, in cases adopting the "public purpose" interpretation of the Clause, and second, in cases deferring to legislatures' judgments regarding what constitutes a valid public purpose. Those questionable cases converged in the boundlessly broad and deferential conception of "public use" adopted by this Court in *Berman* and *Midkiff*, cases that take center stage in the Court's opinion. The weakness of those two lines of cases, and consequently *Berman* and *Midkiff*, fatally undermines the doctrinal foundations of the Court's decision. Today's questionable application of these cases is further proof that the "public purpose" standard is not susceptible of principled application. This Court's reliance by rote on this standard is ill advised and should be reconsidered.

[There] is no justification [for] affording almost insurmountable deference to legislative conclusions that a use serves a "public use." To begin with, a court owes no deference to a legislature's judgment concerning the quintessentially legal question of whether the government owns, or the public has a legal right to use, the taken property. Even under the "public purpose" interpretation, moreover, it is most implausible that the Framers intended to defer to legislatures as to what satisfies the Public Use Clause, uniquely among all the express provisions of the Bill of Rights. We would not defer to a legislature's determination of the various circumstances that establish, for example, when a search of a home would be reasonable, or when a convicted double-murderer may be shackled during a sentencing proceeding without on-the-record findings, or when state law creates a property interest protected by the Due Process Clause.

Still worse, it is backwards to adopt a searching standard of constitutional review for nontraditional property interests, such as welfare benefits, while deferring to the legislature's determination as to what constitutes a public use when it exercises the power of eminent domain, and thereby invades individuals' traditional rights in real property. The Court has elsewhere recognized "the overriding respect for the sanctity of the home" when the issue is only whether the government may search a home. Yet today the Court tells us that we are not to "second-guess the City's considered judgments" when the issue is, instead, whether the government may take the infinitely more intrusive step of tearing down petitioners' homes. Something has gone seriously awry with this Court's interpretation of the Constitution. Though citizens are safe from the government in their homes, the homes themselves are not. Once one accepts, as the Court at least nominally does, that the Public Use Clause is a limit on the eminent domain power of the Federal Government and the States, there is no justification for the almost complete deference it grants to legislatures as to what satisfies it.

* * * I would revisit our Public Use Clause cases and consider returning to the original meaning of the Public Use Clause: that the government may take property only if it actually uses or gives the public a legal right to use the property.

The consequences of today's decision are not difficult to predict, and promise to be harmful. So-called "urban renewal" programs provide some compensation for the properties they take, but no compensation is possible for the subjective value of these lands to the individuals displaced and the indignity inflicted by uprooting them from their homes. Allowing the government to take property solely for public purposes is bad enough, but extending the concept of public purpose to encompass any economically beneficial goal guarantees that these losses will fall disproportionately on poor communities. Those communities are not only systematically less likely to put their lands to the highest and best social use, but are also the least politically powerful. If ever there were justification for intrusive judicial review of constitutional provisions that protect "discrete and insular minorities," surely that principle would apply with great force to the powerless groups and individuals the Public Use Clause protects. The deferential standard this Court has adopted for the Public Use Clause is therefore deeply perverse.

[The] Court relies almost exclusively on this Court's prior cases to derive today's far-reaching, and dangerous, result. But the principles this Court should employ to dispose of this case are found in the Public Use Clause itself. [When] faced with a clash of constitutional principle and a line of unreasoned cases wholly divorced from the text, history, and structure of our founding document, we should not hesitate to resolve the tension in favor of the Constitution's original meaning. * * *

WHEN IS "REGULATION" OF PROPERTY TANTAMOUNT TO A "TAKING"?

CON LAW: P. 324, end of subsection

AMER CON: P. 233, end of note

RTS & LIB: P.88, end of subsection

PALAZZOLO v. RHODE ISLAND, 533 U.S. 606, 121 S.Ct. 2448, 150 L.Ed.2d 592 (2001): Petitioner and others formed a corporation in 1959 that purchased 18 acres of coastal wetlands. Then, as now, most of the property was salt marsh, subject to tidal flooding. Petitioner subsequently became the sole stockholder. In 1971, the State created the Rhode Island Coastal Resources Management Council (Council) and charged it with protecting the state's coastal properties. The Council's regulations designated salt marshes like those owned by petitioner's corporation as potential "coastal wetlands" on which development was greatly limited. Seven years later, the corporate charter was revoked and title to the property passed to petitioner as the sole owner. After his applications to develop his property had been rejected by the Council, petitioner filed an inverse condemnation action, maintaining that the state's wetland regulations, as applied by the Council to his land, had taken his property without compensation. The state supreme court held, inter alia, that (1) petitioner's takings claim was not ripe; (2) he could not challenge regulations predating 1978, when he succeeded to legal ownership of the property; and (3) because the challenged regulations predated his acquisition of title, he could not have had any reasonable investment-backed expectations that he could develop his property; thus he could not recover under *Penn Central*. A 5–4 majority, per KENNEDY, J., disagreed:

"[The] state court held the postregulation acquisition of title was fatal to the claim for deprivation of all economic use [and] to the *Penn Central* claim. [While] the first holding was couched in terms of background principles of state property law [and] the second in terms of petitioner's reasonable investment-backed expectations, [the] two holdings together amount to a single, sweeping, rule: A purchaser of a successive title holder like petitioner is deemed to have notice of an earlier-enacted restriction and is barred from claiming that it effects a taking.

"[The] State may not put so potent a Hobbesian stick into the Lockean bundle. [Were] we to accept the State's rule, the post-enactment transfer of title would absolve the State of its obligation to defend any action restricting land use, no matter how extreme or unreasonable. A State would be allowed, in effect, to put an expiration date on the Takings Clause. This ought not to be the rule. Future generations, too, have a right to challenge unreasonable limitations on the use and value of land.

"Nor does the justification of notice take into account the effect on owners at the time of enactment, who are prejudiced as well. Should an owner attempt to challenge a new regulation, but not survive the process of ripening his or her claim (which, as this case demonstrates, will often take years), under the proposed rule the right to compensation may not be asserted by an heir or successor, and so may not be asserted at all. The State's rule would work a critical alteration to the nature of property, as the newly regulated landowner is stripped of the ability to transfer the interest which was possessed prior to the regulation. The State may not by this means secure a windfall for itself.

"[The state supreme court] held that all economically beneficial use was not deprived because the uplands portion of the property can still be improved. On this point, we agree with the court's decision. Petitioner accepts [the] state trial court's finding that his parcel retains $200,000 in development value under the State's wetlands regulations. He asserts, nonetheless, that he has suffered a total taking and contends the Council cannot sidestep the holding in *Lucas* 'by the simple expedient of leaving a landowner a few crumbs of value.' * * *

"Assuming a taking is otherwise established, a State may not evade the duty to compensate on the premise that the landowner is left with a token interest. This is not the situation of the landowner in this case, however. A regulation permitting a landowner to build a substantial residence on an 18-acre parcel does not leave the property 'economically idle.' *Lucas.*

"[The] State Supreme Court erred in finding petitioner's claims were unripe and in ruling that acquisition of title after the effective date of the regulations barred the takings claims. The court did not err in finding that petitioner failed to establish a deprivation of all economic value, for it is undisputed that the parcel retains significant worth for construction of a residence. The claims under the *Penn Central* analysis were not examined, and for this purpose the case should be remanded."

O'Connor and Scalia, JJ., both joined the Court's opinion, but each wrote a separate concurring opinion expressing disagreement over "what role the temporal relationship between regulatory enactment and title acquisition plays in a proper *Penn Central* analysis."

As O'Connor, J., viewed the matter: "[I]nterference with investment-backed expectations is one of a number of factors that a court must examine. Further, the regulatory regime in place at the time the claimant acquires the property at issue helps to shape the reasonableness of those expectations. [The] temptation to adopt what amount to per se rules in either direction must be resisted. The Takings Clause requires careful examination and weighing of all the relevant circumstances in this context. The court below therefore must consider on remand the array of relevant factors under *Penn Central* before deciding whether any compensation is due."

Scalia, J., contended: "[T]hat a restriction existed at the time the purchaser took title (other than a restriction forming part of the 'background principles of the State's law of property and nuisance,' *Lucas*) should have no bearing upon the determination of whether the restriction is so substantial as to constitute a taking. The 'investment-backed expectations' that the law will take into account do not include the assumed validity of a restriction that in fact deprives property of so much of its value as to be unconstitutional. Which is to say that a *Penn Central taking*, no less than a total taking, is not absolved by the transfer of title."

TAHOE–SIERRA PRESERVATION COUNCIL, INC. v. TAHOE REGIONAL PLANNING AGENCY

535 U.S. 302, 122 S.Ct.1465, 152 L.Ed.2d 517 (2002).

Justice Stevens delivered the opinion of the Court.

[Respondent Tahoe Regional Planning Agency (TRPA), the creation of a regional planning compact adopted by California and Nevada and approved by Congress, imposed two moratoria, totaling 32 months, in the Lake Tahoe Basin while formulating a comprehensive land-use plan for the area. Prior to the adoption of the final plan, the Compact itself prohibited the development of new subdivisions, condominiums and apartment buildings. Shortly after the final plan was adopted in 1984, petitioners, real estate owners affected by the moratoria and an association representing such owners, filed suit, claiming that TRPA's actions constituted a taking of their property without just compensation.

[The Ninth Circuit held that because the regulations had only a temporary impact on petitioners' fee interest, and thus no categorical taking had occurred, *Lucas* did not apply. It also concluded that *Penn Central*'s ad hoc balancing approach was the appropriate framework for analyzing whether a taking had occurred, but that petitioners had not challenged the District Court's conclusion that they had failed to make out a claim under *Penn Central.*]

The question presented is whether a moratorium on development imposed during the process of devising a comprehensive land-use plan constitutes a per se taking of property requiring compensation under the Takings Clause of the United States Constitution. This case actually involves two moratoria ordered by respondent Tahoe Regional Planning Agency (TRPA) to maintain the status quo while studying the impact of development on Lake Tahoe and designing a strategy for environmentally sound growth. [As] a result of these two directives, virtually all development on a substantial portion of the property subject to TRPA's jurisdiction was prohibited for a period of 32 months.

[The] relevant facts are undisputed. The Court of Appeals, while reversing the District Court on a question of law, accepted all of its findings of fact, and no party challenges those findings. [All agree that Lake Tahoe is "uniquely beautiful" and that it has deservedly been called a "national treasure that must be protected and preserved."] [The] upsurge of development in the area has caused "increased nutrient loading of the lake largely because of the increase in impervious coverage of land in the Basin resulting from that development." [Given] this trend, the District Court predicted that "unless the process is stopped, the lake will lose its clarity and its trademark blue color, becoming green and opaque for eternity." * * *

For petitioners, it is enough that a regulation imposes a temporary deprivation—no matter how brief—of all economically viable use to trigger a per se rule that a taking has occurred. Petitioners assert that our opinions in *First English* and *Lucas* have already endorsed their view, and that it is a logical application of the principle that the Takings Clause was "designed to bar Government from forcing some people alone to bear burdens which, in all fairness and justice, should be borne by the public as a whole." *Armstrong* v. *United States,* 364 U.S. 40, 80 S.Ct. 1563, 4 L.Ed. 2d 1554 (1960).

[In] our view the answer to the abstract question whether a temporary moratorium effects a taking is neither "yes, always" nor "no, never"; the answer depends upon the particular circumstances of the case. Resisting "[t]he temptation to adopt what amount to per se rules in either direction," *Palazzolo* (O'Connor, J., concurring), we conclude that the circumstances in this case are best analyzed within the *Penn Central* framework.

[When] the government physically takes possession of an interest in property for some public purpose, it has a categorical duty to compensate the former owner, regardless of whether the interest that is taken constitutes an entire parcel or merely a part thereof. Thus, compensation is mandated when a leasehold is taken and the government occupies the property for its own purposes, even though that use is temporary. Similarly, when the government appropriates part of a rooftop in order to provide cable TV access for apartment tenants, or when its planes use private airspace to approach a government airport, it is required to pay for that share no matter how small. But a government regulation that merely prohibits landlords from evicting tenants unwilling to pay a higher rent, that bans certain private uses of a portion of an owner's property, or that forbids the private use of certain airspace, does not constitute a categorical taking.

[This] longstanding distinction between acquisitions of property for public use, on the one hand, and regulations prohibiting private uses, on the other, makes it inappropriate to treat cases involving physical takings as controlling precedents for the evaluation of a claim that there has been a "regulatory taking," and vice versa. * * * Treating [all land-use regulations] as per se takings would transform government regulation into a luxury few governments could afford. By contrast, physical appropriations are relatively rare, easily identified, and usually represent a greater affront to individual property rights.[19] * * *

Perhaps recognizing this fundamental distinction, petitioners wisely do not place all their emphasis on analogies to physical takings cases. Instead, they rely principally on our decision in *Lucas*—a regulatory takings case that, nevertheless, applied a categorical rule—to argue that the *Penn Central* framework is inapplicable here. * * *

Justice Brennan's opinion for the Court in *Penn Central* [made] it clear that even though multiple factors are relevant in the analysis of regulatory takings claims, in such cases we must focus on "the parcel as a whole." [This] requirement that "the aggregate must be viewed in its entirety" explains why, for example, a regulation that prohibited commercial transactions in eagle feathers, but did not bar other uses or impose any physical invasion or restraint upon them, was not a taking. *Andrus* v. *Allard*. It also clarifies why restrictions on the use of only limited portions of the parcel, such as set-back ordinances, or a requirement that coal pillars be left in place to prevent mine subsidence, were not considered regulatory takings. In each of these cases, we affirmed that "where an owner possesses a full 'bundle' of property rights, the destruction of one 'strand' of the bundle is not a taking."

While the foregoing cases considered whether particular regulations had "gone too far" and were therefore invalid, none of them addressed the separate remedial question of how compensation is measured once a regulatory taking is established. [In] *First English*, the Court unambiguously and repeatedly characterized the issue to be decided as a "compensation question" or a "remedial

19. According to The Chief Justice's dissent, even a temporary, use-prohibiting regulation should be governed by our physical takings cases because, under *Lucas*, "from the landowner's point of view," the moratorium is the functional equivalent of a forced leasehold. Of course, from both the landowner's and the government's standpoint there are critical differences between a leasehold and a moratorium. Condemnation of a leasehold gives the government possession of the property, the right to admit and exclude others, and the right to use it for a public purpose. A regulatory taking, by contrast, does not give the government any right to use the property, nor does it dispossess the owner or affect her right to exclude others.

The Chief Justice stretches *Lucas*' "equivalence" language too far. For even a regulation that constitutes only a minor infringement on property may, from the landowner's perspective, be the functional equivalent of an appropriation. *Lucas* carved out a narrow exception to the rules governing regulatory takings for the "extraordinary circumstance" of a permanent deprivation of all beneficial use. The exception was only partially justified based on the "equivalence" theory cited by his dissent. It was also justified on the theory that, in the "relatively rare situations where the government has deprived a landowner of all economically beneficial uses," it is less realistic to assume that the regulation will secure an "average reciprocity of advantage," or that government could not go on if required to pay for every such restriction. But as we explain, these assumptions hold true in the context of a moratorium.

question." [And] the Court's statement of its holding was equally unambiguous: "We merely hold that where the government's activities *have already worked a taking* of all use of property, no subsequent action by the government can relieve it of the duty to provide compensation for the period during which the taking was effective." (emphasis added). In fact, *First English* expressly disavowed any ruling on the merits of the takings issue* * *.

The categorical rule that we applied in *Lucas* states that compensation is required when a regulation deprives an owner of "*all* economically beneficial uses" of his land. Under that rule, a statute that "wholly eliminated the value" of Lucas' fee simple title clearly qualified as a taking. But our holding was limited to "the extraordinary circumstance when *no* productive or economically beneficial use of land is permitted." The emphasis on the word "no" in the text of the opinion was, in effect, reiterated in a footnote explaining that the categorical rule would not apply if the diminution in value were 95% instead of 100%. Anything less than a "complete elimination of value," or a "total loss," the Court acknowledged, would require the kind of analysis applied in *Penn Central*.

Certainly, our holding that the permanent "obliteration of the value" of a fee simple estate constitutes a categorical taking does not answer the question whether a regulation prohibiting any economic use of land for a 32–month period has the same legal effect. Petitioners seek to bring this case under the rule announced in *Lucas* by arguing that we can effectively sever a 32–month segment from the remainder of each landowner's fee simple estate, and then ask whether that segment has been taken in its entirety by the moratoria. Of course, defining the property interest taken in terms of the very regulation being challenged is circular. With property so divided, every delay would become a total ban; the moratorium and the normal permit process alike would constitute categorical takings. Petitioners' "conceptual severance" argument is unavailing because it ignores *Penn Central*'s admonition that in regulatory takings cases we must focus on "the parcel as a whole." [Thus,] the District Court erred when it disaggregated petitioners' property into temporal segments corresponding to the regulations at issue and then analyzed whether petitioners were deprived of all economically viable use during each period. The starting point for the court's analysis should have been to ask whether there was a total taking of the entire parcel; if not, then *Penn Central* was the proper framework.[26]

[Neither] *Lucas,* nor *First English,* nor any of our other regulatory takings cases compels us to accept petitioners' categorical submission. In fact, these cases make clear that the categorical rule in *Lucas* was carved out for the "extraordinary case" in which a regulation permanently deprives property of all value; the default rule remains that, in the regulatory taking context, we require a more fact specific inquiry. Nevertheless, we will consider whether the interest in protecting individual property owners from bearing public burdens "which, in all fairness and justice, should be borne by the public as a whole," *Armstrong,* justifies creating a new rule for these circumstances.

[The] ultimate constitutional question is whether the concepts of "fairness and justice" that underlie the Takings Clause will be better served by [a categorical rule] or by a *Penn Central* inquiry into all of the relevant circumstances in particular cases. From that perspective, the extreme categorical rule that any deprivation of all economic use, no matter how brief, constitutes a compensable

26. The Chief Justice's dissent makes the same mistake by carving out a 6–year interest in the property, rather than considering the parcel as a whole, and treating the regulations covering that segment as analogous to a total taking under *Lucas*.

taking surely cannot be sustained. Petitioners' broad submission would apply to numerous "normal delays in obtaining building permits, changes in zoning ordinances, variances, and the like," as well as to orders temporarily prohibiting access to crime scenes, businesses that violate health codes, fire-damaged buildings, or other areas that we cannot now foresee. [A] rule that required compensation for every delay in the use of property would render routine government processes prohibitively expensive or encourage hasty decision-making. Such an important change in the law should be the product of legislative rulemaking rather than adjudication.

More importantly, for reasons set out [by] Justice O'Connor in her concurring opinion in *Palazzolo*, we are persuaded that the better approach to claims that a regulation has effected a temporary taking "requires careful examination and weighing of all the relevant circumstances." [In] rejecting petitioners' per se rule, we do not hold that the temporary nature of a land-use restriction precludes finding that it effects a taking; we simply recognize that it should not be given exclusive significance one way or the other.

A narrower rule that excluded the normal delays associated with processing permits, or that covered only delays of more than a year, would certainly have a less severe impact on prevailing practices, but it would still impose serious financial constraints on the planning process. Unlike the "extraordinary circumstance" in which the government deprives a property owner of all economic use, moratoria like [those at issue here] are used widely among land-use planners to preserve the status quo while formulating a more permanent development strategy. In fact, the consensus in the planning community appears to be that moratoria, or "interim development controls" as they are often called, are an essential tool of successful development. Yet even the weak version of petitioners' categorical rule would treat these interim measures as takings regardless of the good faith of the planners, the reasonable expectations of the landowners, or the actual impact of the moratorium on property values.

[It] may well be true that any moratorium that lasts for more than one year should be viewed with special skepticism. But given the fact that the District Court found that the 32 months required by TRPA to formulate the 1984 Regional Plan was not unreasonable, we could not possibly conclude that every delay of over one year is constitutionally unacceptable. Formulating a general rule of this kind is a suitable task for state legislatures. In our view, the duration of the restriction is one of the important factors that a court must consider in the appraisal of a regulatory takings claim, but with respect to that factor as with respect to other factors, the "temptation to adopt what amount to per se rules in either direction must be resisted." *Palazzolo,* (O'Connor, J., concurring). [The] interest in "fairness and justice" will be best served by relying on the familiar *Penn Central* approach when deciding cases like this, rather than by attempting to craft a new categorical rule. * * *

Chief Justice Rehnquist, with whom Justice Scalia and Justice Thomas join, dissenting.

For over half a decade petitioners were prohibited from building homes, or any other structures, on their land. Because the Takings Clause requires the government to pay compensation when it deprives owners of all economically viable use of their land, see *Lucas*, and because a ban on all development lasting almost six years does not resemble any traditional land-use planning device, I dissent.

[The] Court ignores much of the impact of respondent's conduct on petitioners. Instead, it relies on the flawed determination of the Court of Appeals that the relevant time period lasted only from August 1981 until April 1984. During that period, [regulations] prohibited development pending the adoption of a new regional land-use plan. The adoption of the 1984 Regional Plan (hereinafter Plan or 1984 Plan) did not, however, change anything from the petitioners' standpoint. After the adoption of the 1984 Plan, petitioners still could make no use of their land.

[The] District Court enjoined the 1984 Plan because the Plan did not comply with the environmental requirements of respondent's regulations and of the Compact itself. Respondent is surely responsible for its own regulations, and it is also responsible for the Compact as it is the governmental agency charged with administering the Compact. It follows that respondent was the "moving force" behind petitioners' inability to develop its land from April 1984 through the enactment of the 1987 plan. * * * Because respondent caused petitioners' inability to use their land from 1981 through 1987, that is the appropriate period of time from which to consider their takings claim.

[The] Court refuses to apply *Lucas* on the ground that the deprivation was "temporary." Neither the Takings Clause nor our case law supports such a distinction. For one thing, a distinction between "temporary" and "permanent" prohibitions is tenuous. The "temporary" prohibition in this case that the Court finds is not a taking lasted almost six years. The "permanent" prohibition that the Court held to be a taking in *Lucas* lasted less than two years. The "permanent" prohibition in *Lucas* lasted less than two years because the law, as it often does, changed.

[Under] the Court's decision today, the takings question turns entirely on the initial label given a regulation, a label that is often without much meaning. There is every incentive for government to simply label any prohibition on development "temporary," or to fix a set number of years. As in this case, this initial designation does not preclude the government from repeatedly extending the "temporary" prohibition into a long-term ban on all development. The Court now holds that such a designation by the government is conclusive even though in fact the moratorium greatly exceeds the time initially specified. Apparently, the Court would not view even a 10–year moratorium as a taking under *Lucas* because the moratorium is not "permanent."

[The] Court also reads *Lucas* as being fundamentally concerned with value, rather than with the denial of "all economically beneficial or productive use of land." But *Lucas* repeatedly discusses its holding as applying where "*no* productive or economically beneficial use of land is permitted." * * * *Lucas* is implicated when the government deprives a landowner of "all economically beneficial or productive use of land." The District Court found, and the Court agrees, that the moratorium "temporarily" deprived petitioners of " 'all economically viable use of their land.' " Because the rationale for the *Lucas* rule applies just as strongly in this case, the "temporary" denial of all viable use of land for six years is a taking.

[When] a regulation merely delays a final land use decision, we have recognized that there are other background principles of state property law that prevent the delay from being deemed a taking. We thus noted in *First English* that our discussion of temporary takings did not apply "in the case of normal delays in obtaining building permits, changes in zoning ordinances, variances, and the like." We reiterated this last Term: "The right to improve property, of course, is subject to the reasonable exercise of state authority, including the enforcement of valid zoning and land-use restrictions." *Palazzolo*. Zoning regulations existed as far back as colonial Boston. [Thus,] the short-term delays attendant to zoning and permit regimes are a longstanding feature of state property law and part of a landowner's reasonable investment-backed expectations.

But a moratorium prohibiting all economic use for a period of six years is not one of the longstanding, implied limitations of state property law. Typical moratoria * * * prohibit only certain categories of development, such as fast-food restaurants, or adult businesses, or all commercial development. Such moratoria do not implicate *Lucas* because they do not deprive landowners of all economically beneficial use of their land. As for moratoria that prohibit all development, these do not have the lineage of permit and zoning requirements and thus it is less certain that property is acquired under the "implied limitation" of a moratorium prohibiting all development.

[But] this case does not require us to decide as a categorical matter whether moratoria prohibiting all economic use are an implied limitation of state property law, because the duration of this "moratorium" far exceeds that of ordinary moratoria. [Because] the prohibition on development of nearly six years in this case cannot be said to resemble any "implied limitation" of state property law, it is a taking that requires compensation.

Lake Tahoe is a national treasure and I do not doubt that respondent's efforts at preventing further degradation of the lake were made in good faith in furtherance of the public interest. But, as is the case with most governmental action that furthers the public interest, the Constitution requires that the costs and burdens be borne by the public at large, not by a few targeted citizens. * * *

JUSTICE THOMAS, with whom JUSTICE SCALIA joins, dissenting.

I join the Chief Justice's dissent. I write separately to address the majority's conclusion that the temporary moratorium at issue here was not a taking because it was not a "taking of 'the parcel as a whole.'" While this questionable rule has been applied to various alleged regulatory takings, it was, in my view, rejected in the context of *temporal* deprivations of property by *First English*, which held that temporary and permanent takings "are not different in kind" when a landowner is deprived of all beneficial use of his land. I had thought that *First English* put to rest the notion that the "relevant denominator" is land's infinite life. Consequently, a regulation effecting a total deprivation of the use of a so-called "temporal slice" of property is compensable under the Takings Clause unless background principles of state property law prevent it from being deemed a taking; "total deprivation of use is, from the landowner's point of view, the equivalent of a physical appropriation." *Lucas*.

A taking is exactly what occurred in this case. No one seriously doubts that the land use regulations at issue rendered petitioners' land unsusceptible of *any* economically beneficial use. This was true at the inception of the moratorium, and it remains true today. These individuals and families were deprived of the opportunity to build single-family homes as permanent, retirement, or vacation residences on land upon which such construction was authorized when purchased. * * *

I would hold that regulations prohibiting all productive uses of property are subject to *Lucas*' per se rule, regardless of whether the property so burdened retains theoretical useful life and value if, and when, the "temporary" moratorium is lifted. To my mind, such potential future value bears on the amount of compensation due and has nothing to do with the question whether there was a taking in the first place. * * *

WHAT CONSTITUTES "PROPERTY" FOR PURPOSES OF THE TAKINGS CLAUSE?

CON LAW: P. 330, end of subsection

RTS & LIB: P. 94, end of subsection

Compare *Phillips* with BROWN v. LEGAL FOUNDATION OF WASHINGTON, 538 U.S. 216, 123 S.Ct. 1406, 155 L.Ed.2d 376 (2003): Under the IOLTA program established by the Washington Supreme Court, (a) all client fund that can generate net earnings for the client must be deposited in non-IOLTA accounts; (b) funds that cannot earn net interest for the client are deposited in IOLTA accounts; (c) banks are directed to pay the net interest on the IOLTA accounts to the Legal Foundation of Washington, and (d) the Foundation uses all such funds for tax-exempt, law-related charitable and educational purposes. Petitioners claimed that the "taking" of the interest earned on their funds in the IOLTA accounts violated the Just Compensation Clause. A 5–4 majority, per STEVENS, J., disagreed:

" 'The Fifth Amendment does not proscribe the taking of property; it proscribes taking without just compensation.' * * * Applying the teaching of [our] cases to the question before us, it is clear that [neither petitioner] is entitled to any compensation for the nonpecuniary consequences of the taking of the interest on his deposited funds, and that any pecuniary compensation must be measured by his net losses rather than the value of the public's gain. For that reason, both the majority and the dissenters on the Court of Appeals [for the Ninth Circuit] agreed that if petitioner's net loss was zero, the compensation that is due is also zero.

"[The Washington State plan] unambiguously requires lawyers and Limited Practice Officers (LPOs) to deposit funds in non–IOLTA accounts whenever these funds could generate net earnings for the client. Thus, if the LPOs who deposited petitioner's money in IOLTA accounts could have generated net income, the LPOs violated the court's Rules. Any conceivable net loss to petitioners was the consequence of the LPOs' incorrect private decisions rather than any state action. Such mistakes may well give petitioners a valid claim against the LPOs, but they would provide no support for a claim for compensation from the State * * *.

"A state law that requires client funds that could not otherwise generate net earnings for the client to be deposited in an IOLTA account is not a 'regulatory taking.' A law that requires that the interest on these funds be transferred to a different owner for a legitimate public use, however, could be a per se taking requiring the payment of 'just compensation' to the client. Because that compensation is measured by the owner's pecuniary loss—which is zero whenever the Washington law is obeyed—there has been no violation of the Just Compensation Clause [in] this case."

SCALIA, J., joined by Rehnquist, C.J., and Kennedy and Thomas, JJ., dissented: "As the Court correctly notes, Washington's IOLTA program comprises two steps. First, the State mandates that certain client trust funds by placed in an IOLTA account, where those funds generate interest. Second, the State seizes the interest earned on those accounts to fund [the Foundation]. With regard to step one, we held in *Phillips* that any interest earned on client funds held in IOLTA accounts belongs to the owner of the principal, not the State or the State's designated recipient of the interest. As to step two, the Court assumes, arguendo, that the appropriation of petitioners' interest constitutes a 'taking,' but holds that just compensation is zero because without the mandatory pooling arrangements (step one) of IOLTA, petitioners' funds could not have generated any interest in the first place. This holding contravenes our decision in *Phillips*—effectively refusing to treat the interest as the property of petitioners we held it to be—and brushes aside 80 years of precedent on determining just compensation.

"When a State has taken private property for a public use, the Fifth Amendment requires compensation in the amount of the market value of the property on the date it is appropriated. [Our] cases have recognized only two situations in which this standard is not to be used: when market value is too difficult to ascertain, and when payment of market value would result in 'manifest injustice' to the owner or the public.

"In holding that any just compensation that might be owned is zero, the Court neither pretends to ascertain the market value of the confiscated property nor asserts that the case falls within one of the two exceptions where market value need not be determined. Instead, the Court proclaims that just compensation is to be determined by the former property owner's 'net loss,' and endorses simultaneously two competing and irreconcilable theories of how that loss should be measured. The Court proclaims its agreement with the Ninth Circuit majority that just compensation is the interest petitioners *would have earned* had their funds been deposited in *non-IOLTA* accounts. [At] the same time, the Court approves the view of the Ninth Circuit *dissenters* that just compensation is the amount of interest *actually earned* in petitioners' IOLTA accounts, minus the amount that would have been lost in transaction costs had petitioners sought to keep the money for themselves. The Court cannot have it both ways—as the Ninth Circuit itself realized—but even if it could, neither of the two options from which lower courts may now choose is consistent with *Phillips* or our precedents that equate just compensation with the fair market value of the property taken."[a]

a. Kennedy, J., added a dissent, noting that "[by] mandating that the interest from these accounts serve causes the justices of the Washington Supreme Court prefer, [the State] grants to itself a monopoly which might then be used for the forced support of certain viewpoints. [The] First Amendment consequences of the State's action have not been addressed in this case, but the potential for a serious violation is there. Today's holding, then, is doubly unfortunate. One constitutional violation (the taking of property) likely will lead to another (compelled speech)."

PROTECTION OF INDIVIDUAL RIGHTS; DUE PROCESS, THE BILL OF RIGHTS, AND NONTEXTUAL CONSTITUTIONAL RIGHTS

NATURE AND SCOPE OF FOURTEENTH AMENDMENT DUE PROCESS; APPLICABILITY OF THE BILL OF RIGHTS TO THE STATES

THE ORDERED LIBERTY—"FUNDAMENTAL FAIRNESS," "TOTAL INCORPORATION" AND "SELECTIVE INCORPORATION" THEORIES

CON LAW: P. 345, after extract from *Duncan*:

AMER CON: P. 242, after extract from *Duncan*:

RTS & LIB: P. 107, after extract from *Duncan*:

Compare the comments of White, J. in *Duncan* with those of Kennedy, J. for a 5–4 majority in *Roper v. Simmons*, set forth at p. 62 of this Supplement.

THE RETROACTIVE EFFECT OF A HOLDING OF UNCONSTITUTIONALITY

CON LAW: P. 389, after note 3

AMER CON: P. 256, after note 3

RTS & LIB: P. 399, after note 3

4. *Retroactivity in the context of the death sentence.* SCHRIRO v. SUMMERLIN, 542 U.S. 348, 124 S.Ct. 2519, 159 L.Ed.2d 442 (2004): Respondent was convicted of murder and sentenced to death under Arizona's capital sentencing scheme then in effect, which authorized the trial judge, rather than the jury, to determine the presence of aggravating circumstances making the defendant eligible for the death sentence. (The aggravating circumstances included whether the offense was committed in an "especially heinous," "cruel," or "depraved" manner.) The state supreme court affirmed. While respondent was seeking federal habeas review, the Supreme Court decided *Apprendi v. New Jersey*, 530 U.S. 466, 120 S.Ct. 2348, 147 L.Ed.2d 435 (2000) and *Ring v. Arizona*, 536 U.S. 584, 536 S.Ct. 2428, 153 L.Ed.2d 556 (2002). *Apprendi* required that facts increasing the penalty for a crime beyond the prescribed statutory maximum be submitted to a

jury and proved beyond a reasonable doubt. Applying the *Apprendi* principle to the Arizona death sentencing scheme, *Ring* held that because Arizona law authorized the death penalty only if an aggravating factor was present, the existence of such a factor had to be proved to a jury rather than to a judge. The Ninth Circuit invalidated respondent's death sentence on alternative grounds: (1) The new rule announced in *Ring* was substantive rather than procedural; and (2) the rule was a "watershed" procedural rule entitled to retroactive effect. A 5–4 majority per SCALIA, J., reversed, finding both grounds inadequate:

"New *substantive* rules generally apply retroactively. This includes decisions that narrow the scope of a criminal statute by interpreting it terms [as] well as constitutional determinations that place particular conduct on persons covered by the statute beyond the State's power to punish. [Such] rules apply retroactively because they 'necessarily carry a significant risk that a defendant stands convicted of "an act that the law does not make criminal" or faces a punishment that the law cannot impose upon him.

"New rules of procedure on the other hand, generally do not apply retroactively. [They] merely raise the possibility that someone convicted with use of the invalidated procedure might have been acquitted otherwise. Because of this more speculative connection to innocence, we give retroactive effect to only a small set of ' "watershed rules of criminal procedure" implicating the fundamental fairness and accuracy of the criminal proceeding.' [*Teague*] That a new procedural rule is 'fundamental' in some abstract sense is not enough; the rule must be one 'without which the likelihood of an accurate conviction is *seriously* diminished.' [*Teague*, emphasis added].

"A rule is substantive rather than procedural if it alters the range of conduct or the class of persons that the law punishes. [In] contrast, rules that regulate only the *manner of determining* the defendant's culpability are procedural.

"Judged by this standard, *Ring*'s holding is properly classified as procedural. [*Ring*] altered the range of permissible methods for determining whether a defendant's conduct is punishable by death, requiring that a jury rather than a judge find the essential facts bearing on punishment. Rules that allocate decision making authority in this fashion are prototypical procedural rules * * *.

"[As for the argument] that *Ring* falls under the retroactivity exception for 'watershed rules of criminal procedure' implicating the fundamental fairness and accuracy of the criminal proceeding' [quoting *Teague*], [the] question here is not [whether] the Framers believed that juries are more accurate factfinders than judges [or] whether juries actually *are* more accurate factfinders than judges * * *. Rather, the questions is whether judicial factfinding so 'seriously diminishe[s]' accuracy that there is an 'impermissibly large risk' of punishing conduct the law does not reach. [*Teague*]. The evidence is simply too equivocal to support that conclusion.

"First, for every argument why juries are more accurate factfinders, there is another why they are less accurate. [The] mixed reception that the right to jury trial has been given in other countries, [though] irrelevant to the meaning and continued existence of that right under our Constitution, surely makes it implausible that judicial factfinding so '*seriously* diminishe[s]' accuracy as to produce an 'impermissibly large risk' of injustice. When so many presumably reasonable minds continue to disagree over whether juries are better factfinders *at all*, we cannot confidently say that judicial factfinding *seriously* diminishes accuracy.

"Our decision in *DeStefano v. Woods*, 392 U.S. 631, 88 S.Ct. 2093, 20 L.Ed.2d 1308 (1968), is on point. There we refused to give retroactive effect to *Duncan v. Louisiana*, which applied the Sixth Amendment's jury-trial guarantee to the States. While *DeStefano* was decided under our pre-*Teague* retroactivity framework, its reasoning is germane. We noted that '[we] would not assert [that] every criminal trial—or any particular trial—held before a judge alone is unfair or that a defendant may never be as fairly treated by a judge as he would be by a jury,' [If] under *DeStefano* a trial held entirely without a jury was not impermissibly inaccurate, it is hard to see how a trial in which a judge finds only aggravating factors could be.

"[The] dissent contends that juries are more accurate because they better reflect community standards in deciding whether, for example, a murder is heinous, cruel, or depraved *as determined by community standards*. It is easy to find enhanced accuracy in jury determination when one redefines the statute's substantive scope in such manner as to ensure that result * * *.

"The right to jury trial is fundamental to our system of criminal procedure, and States are bound to enforce the Sixth Amendment's guarantees as we interpret them. But it does not follow that, when a criminal defendant has had a full trial and one round of appeals in which the State faithfully applied the Constitution as we understood it at the time, he may nevertheless continue to litigate his claims indefinitely in hopes that we will one day have a change of heart. *Ring* announce a new procedural rule that does not apply retroactively to cases already final on direct review."

Breyer, J., joined by Stevens, Souter and Ginsburg, JJ., dissented: "[*Ring*] held that a jury, not a judge, must make the findings necessary to qualify a person for punishment by death. In my view, that holding amounts to a 'watershed' procedural ruling that a federal habeas court must apply when considering a constitutional challenge to a 'final' death sentence—i.e., a sentence that was already final on direct review when *Ring* was decided.

"*Teague* sets forth the relevant retroactivity criteria. A new procedural rule applies retroactively in habeas proceedings if the new procedure is (1) 'implicit in the concept of ordered liberty,' implicating 'fundamental fairness,' and (2) 'central to an accurate determination of innocence or guilt,' such that its absence 'creates an impermissibly large risk that the innocent will be convicted.' In the context of a death sentence, where the matter is not one of 'innocence or guilt,' the second criterion asks whether the new procedure is '*central to an accurate determination' that death is a legally appropriate punishment.*

"[The] majority says that *Ring*'s [rule] cannot satisfy *Teague*'s accuracy-enhancing requirement, for two reasons. First, it [states that] one cannot say 'confidently' that 'judicial factfinding *seriously* diminishes accuracy.' Second, it relies on *DeStefano v. Woods*, the case in which this Court considered whether *Duncan v. Louisiana*, which extended the Sixth Amendment jury trial guarantee to the States, should apply retroactively. The Court decided that *Duncan* should *not* have retroactive effect. 'If,' the majority concludes, 'a trial held entirely without a jury was not impermissibly inaccurate, it is hard to see how a trial in which a judge finds only aggravating factors could be.'

"The majority, however, overlooks three additional considerations that lead me to the opposite conclusion.

"First, the factfinder's role in determining the applicability of aggravating factors in a death case is a special role that can involve, not simply the finding of brute facts, but also the making of death-related, community-based value judgments. * * * Words like 'especially heinous,' 'cruel,' or 'depraved'—particularly when asked in the context of a death sentence proceeding—require reference to community-based standards, standards that incorporate values.

"[Second,] *Teague's* basic purpose strongly favors retroactive application of *Ring*'s rule. *Teague*'s retroactivity principles reflect the Court's effort to balance competing considerations. On the one hand, interests related to certain of the Great Writ's basic objectives—protecting the innocent against erroneous conviction or punishment and assuring fundamentally fair procedures—favor applying a new procedural rule retroactively. So too does the legal system's commitment to 'equal justice'—i.e., to 'assur[ing] a uniformity of ultimate treatment among prisoners.'

"Where death-sentence-related factfinding is at issue, these considerations have unusually strong force. This Court has made clear that in a capital case 'the Eighth Amendment requires a greater degree of accuracy [than] would be true in a noncapital case.' Hence, the risk of error that the law can tolerate is correspondingly diminished.

"[Consider,] too, the law's commitment to uniformity. Is treatment 'uniform' when two offenders each have been sentenced to death through the use of procedures that we now know violate the Constitution—but one is allowed to go to his death while the other receives a new, constitutionally proper sentencing proceeding? Outside the capital sentencing context, one might understand the nature of the difference that the word 'finality' implies: One prisoner is already serving a final sentence, the other's has not yet begun. But a death sentence is different in that it seems to be, and it is, an entirely future event—an event not yet undergone by either prisoner. And in respect to that event, both prisoners are, in every important respect, in the same position. I understand there is a 'finality-based' difference. But given the dramatically different nature of death, that difference diminishes in importance.

"[*Teague*] recognizes that important interests argue against, and indeed generally forbid, retroactive application of new procedural rules. These interests include the 'interest in insuring that there will at some point be the certainty that comes with an end to litigation'; the desirability of assuring that 'attention will ultimately be focused not on whether a conviction was free from error but rather on whether the prisoner can be restored to a useful place in the community'; and the fact that society does not have endless resources to spend upon retrials, which (where witnesses have become unavailable and other evidence stale) may well produce unreliable results.

"Certain of these interests are unusually weak where capital sentencing proceedings are at issue. Retroactivity here, for example, would not require inordinate expenditure of state resources. A decision making *Ring* retroactive would affect approximately 110 individuals on death row. This number, however large in absolute terms, is small compared with the approximately 1.2 million individuals presently confined in state prisons. Consequently, the impact on resources is likely to be much less than if a rule affecting the ordinary criminal process were made retroactive.

"[Finally,] I believe we should discount ordinary finality interests in a death case, for those interests are comparative in nature and death-related collateral proceedings, in any event, may stretch on for many years regardless.

"Third, DeStefano fails to give the majority the support for which it hopes. *DeStefano* did decide that *Duncan's* holding—that the Sixth Amendment jury trial right applies to the States—should *not* have retroactive effect. But the Court decided *DeStefano* before *Teague*. And it explicitly took into account '(a) the purpose to be served by the new standards, (b) the extent of the reliance by law enforcement authorities on the old standards, and (c) the effect on the administration of justice of a retroactive application of the new standards.'

"The latter two factors, 'reliance' and 'effect on the administration of justice,' argued strongly against retroactivity. Retroactivity there, unlike here, would have thrown the prison doors open wide—at least in Louisiana and possibly in other States as well. The Court believed that the first factor—'the purpose to be served by the new standards'—also favored prospective application only. But the Court described that purpose broadly, as 'prevent[ing] arbitrariness and repression'; it recognized that some judge-only trials might have been fair; and it concluded that the values served by the jury trial guarantee 'would not measurably be served by requiring retrial of *all* persons convicted in the past' without a jury.

"By contrast, this case involves only a small subclass of defendants deprived of jury trial rights, the relevant harm within that subclass is more widespread, the administration of justice problem is far less serious, and the reliance interest less weighty. For these reasons, I believe the *DeStefano* Court would have come out differently had it been considering *Ring*'s rule.

"[The] majority does not deny that *Ring*'s rule makes *some* contribution to greater accuracy. It simply is unable to say 'confidently' that the absence of *Ring*'s rule creates an 'impermissibly large risk' that the death penalty was improperly imposed. For the reasons stated, I believe that the risk is one that the law need not and should not tolerate. Judged in light of *Teague's* basic purpose, *Ring*'s requirement that a jury, and not a judge, must apply the death sentence aggravators announces a watershed rule of criminal procedure that should be applied retroactively in habeas proceedings."[a]

THE RIGHT OF "PRIVACY" (OR "AUTONOMY" OR "PERSONHOOD")

FAMILY LIVING ARRANGEMENTS, PARENTAL RIGHTS, AND THE "RIGHT TO MARRY"

CON LAW: P. 455, after note 3

AMER CON: P. 519, after note 3

RTS & LIB: P.380, after note 3

Until recently, observes David D. Meyer, *Lochner Redeemed: Family Privacy After Troxel and Carhart*, 48 UCLA L.Rev. 1125 (2001), the Court has differentiated its review of abortion laws from its review of other intrusions on family privacy. However, the decisions in *Carhart* and *Troxel* "suggest that the Court is moving toward a roughly similar approach in both sorts of family-privacy cases. More significantly, the cases signal that the polestar of the Court's emerging approach is 'reasonableness,' the very standard that the Court is supposed to have safely entombed along with *Lochner* itself." Although the Court seems to fear that its interventionism in the family-privacy field "will be viewed as indistinguishable

a. See also *Beard v. Banks*, 124 U.S. 2504, 124 S.Ct. 2504, 159 L.Ed.2d 494 (2004).

from its activism in the age of *Lochner*," Professor Meyer concludes that "the Court must soon reconcile itself to the realization that, in this one limited area of state regulation, the flexible, value-laden test of reasonableness is precisely the right one."

CRITICISM OF *BOWERS v. HARDWICK*

CON LAW: P. 474, after note 3

AMER CON: P. 533, after note 3

RTS & LIB: P. 399, after note 3

LAWRENCE v. TEXAS

539 U.S. 558, 123 S.Ct. 2472, 156 L.Ed.2d 508 (2003).

JUSTICE KENNEDY delivered the opinion of the Court.

[Responding to a reported weapons disturbance, Houston police entered petitioner's apartment and observed petitioner and another adult man, petitioner Garner, engaging in a consensual sexual act. The two men were arrested and charged with "deviate sexual intercourse, namely anal sex, with a member of the same sex (a man)." The applicable state law prohibited two persons of the same sex from engaging in "deviate sexual intercourse" and defined the crime as follows:

> "(A) any contact between any part of the genitals of one person and the mouth or anus of another person; or
>
> "(B) the penetration of the genitals or the anus of another person with an object."

[Petitioners were convicted. The Texas Court of Appeals rejected their constitutional arguments, considering *Bowers* controlling.]

Liberty protects the person from unwarranted government intrusions into a dwelling or other private places. In our tradition the State is not omnipresent in the home. And there are other spheres of our lives and existence, outside the home, where the State should not be a dominant presence. Freedom extends beyond spatial bounds. Liberty presumes an autonomy of self that includes freedom of thought, belief, expressions, and certain intimate conduct. The instant case involves liberty of the person both in its spatial and more transcendent dimensions.

[Although we granted certiorari to consider whether petitioners' convictions violated the Equal Protection or Due Process Clauses or whether *Bowers* should be overruled,] [w]e conclude the case should be resolved by determining whether the petitioners were free as adults to engage in the private conduct in the exercise of their liberty under [Due Process.] For this inquiry we deem it necessary to reconsider the Court's holding in *Bowers*. [The Court then discusses *Griswold, Eisenstadt, Roe v. Wade* and *Carey*.]

The facts in *Bowers* had some similarities to the instant case. [One] difference between the two cases is that the Georgia statute prohibited the conduct whether or not the participants were of the same sex, while the Texas statute, as we have seen, applies only to participants of the same sex.

[The] Court began its substantive discussion in *Bowers* as follows: "The issue presented is whether the Federal Constitution confers a fundamental right upon homosexuals to engage in sodomy and hence invalidates the laws of the many States that still make such conduct illegal and have done so for a very long time." That statement, we now conclude, discloses the Court's own failure to appreciate the extent of the liberty at stake. To say that the issue in *Bowers* was simply the right to engage in certain sexual conduct demeans the claim the individual put forward, just as it would demean a married couple were it to be said marriage is simply about the right to have sexual intercourse. The laws involved in *Bowers* and here are, to be sure, statutes that purport to do no more than prohibit a particular sexual act. Their penalties and purposes, though, have more far-reaching consequences, touching upon the most private human conduct, sexual behavior, and in the most private of places, the home. The statutes do seek to control a personal relationship that, whether or not entitled to formal recognition in the law, is within the liberty of persons to choose without being punished as criminals.

This, as a general rule, should counsel against attempts by the State, or a court, to define the meaning of the relationship or to set its boundaries absent injury to a person or abuse of an institution the law protects. It suffices for us to acknowledge that adults may choose to enter upon this relationship in the confines of their homes and their own private lives and still retain their dignity as free persons. When sexuality finds overt expression in intimate conduct with another person, the conduct can be but one element in a personal bond that is more enduring. The liberty protected by the Constitution allows homosexual persons the right to make this choice.

Having misapprehended the claim of liberty there presented to it, and thus stating the claim to be whether there is a fundamental right to engage in consensual sodomy, the *Bowers* Court said: "Proscriptions against that conduct have ancient roots." In academic writings, and in many of the scholarly amici briefs filed to assist the Court in this case, there are fundamental criticisms of the historical premises relied upon by the majority and concurring opinions in *Bowers*. We need not enter this debate in the attempt to reach a definitive historical judgment, but the following considerations counsel against adopting the definitive conclusions upon which *Bowers* placed such reliance.

At the outset it should be noted that there is no longstanding history in this country of laws directed at homosexual conduct as a distinct matter. [The] absence of legal prohibitions focusing on homosexual conduct may be explained in part by noting that according to some scholars the concept of the homosexual as a distinct category of person did not emerge until the late 19th century. [Thus] early American sodomy laws were not directed at homosexuals as such but instead sought to prohibit nonprocreative sexual activity more generally. This does not suggest approval of homosexual conduct. It does tend to show that this particular form of conduct was not thought of as a separate category from like conduct between heterosexual persons.

Laws prohibiting sodomy do not seem to have been enforced against consenting adults acting in private. [Instead] of targeting relations between consenting adults in private, 19th-century sodomy prosecutions typically involved relations between men and minor girls or minor boys, relations between adults involving force, relations between adults implicating disparity in status, or relations between men and animals.

[The infrequency of prosecutions in consensual cases] makes it difficult to say that society approved of a rigorous and systematic punishment of the consensual acts committed in private and by adults. The longstanding criminal prohibition of homosexual sodomy upon which the *Bowers* decision placed such reliance is as consistent with a general condemnation of nonprocreative sex as it is with an established tradition of prosecuting acts because of their homosexual character.

[Far] from possessing "ancient roots," *Bowers,* American laws targeting same-sex couples did not develop until the last third of the 20th century. The reported decisions concerning the prosecution of consensual, homosexual sodomy between adults for the years 1880–1995 are not always clear in the details, but a significant number involved conduct in a public place.

It was not until the 1970's that any State singled out same-sex relations for criminal prosecution, and only nine States have done so. [Over] the course of the last decades, States with same-sex prohibitions have moved toward abolishing them.

[In] summary, the historical grounds relied upon in *Bowers* are more complex than the majority opinion and the concurring opinion by Chief Justice Burger indicate. Their historical premises are not without doubt and, at the very least, are overstated.

It must be acknowledged, of course, that the Court in *Bowers* was making the broader point that for centuries there have been powerful voices to condemn homosexual conduct as immoral. [This does not] answer the question before us, however. The issue is whether the majority may use the power of the State to enforce these views on the whole society through operation of the criminal law. "Our obligation is to define the liberty of all, not to mandate our own moral code." *Casey.*

[In the past half century there has been] an emerging awareness that liberty gives substantial protection to adult persons in deciding how to conduct their private lives in matters pertaining to sex. "[H]istory and tradition are the starting point but not in all cases the ending point of the substantive due process inquiry." *Sacramento v. Lewis* (Kennedy J., concurring).

This emerging recognition should have been apparent when *Bowers* was decided. In 1955 the American Law Institute promulgated the Model Penal Code and made clear that it did not recommend or provide for "criminal penalties for consensual sexual relations conducted in private." [In] 1961 Illinois changed its laws to conform to the Model Penal Code. Other States soon followed.

In *Bowers* the Court referred to the fact that before 1961 all 50 States had outlawed sodomy, and that at the time of the Court's decision 24 States and the District of Columbia had sodomy laws. Justice Powell pointed out that these prohibitions often were being ignored, however. Georgia, for instance, had not sought to enforce its law for decades.

[The] sweeping references by Chief Justice Burger to the history of Western civilization and to Judeo–Christian moral and ethical standards did not take account of other authorities pointing in an opposite direction. A committee advising the British Parliament recommended in 1957 repeal of laws punishing homosexual conduct. Parliament enacted the substance of those recommendations 10 years later. [Of] even more importance, almost five years before *Bowers* was decided the European Court of Human Rights considered a case with parallels to *Bowers* and to today's case. [The] court held that the laws proscribing [consensual homosexual conduct] were invalid under the European Convention on Human Rights. *Dudgeon v. United Kingdom.*

[In] our own constitutional system the deficiencies in *Bowers* became even more apparent in the years following its announcement. The 25 States with laws prohibiting the relevant conduct referenced in the *Bowers* decision are reduced now to 13, of which 4 enforce their laws only against homosexual conduct. In those States where sodomy is still proscribed, whether for same-sex or heterosexual conduct, there is a pattern of nonenforcement with respect to consenting adults acting in private. The State of Texas admitted in 1994 that as of that date it had not prosecuted anyone under those circumstances.

Two principal cases decided after *Bowers* cast its holding into even more doubt. [The court then discusses *Casey* and *Romer v. Evans,* infra.]

[As] an alternative argument in this case, counsel for the petitioners and some amici contend that *Romer* provides the basis for declaring the Texas statute invalid under the Equal Protection Clause. That is a tenable argument, but we conclude the instant case requires us to address whether *Bowers* itself has continuing validity. Were we to hold the statute invalid under the Equal Protection Clause some might question whether a prohibition would be valid if drawn differently, say, to prohibit the conduct both between same-sex and different-sex participants.

Equality of treatment and the due process right to demand respect for conduct protected by the substantive guarantee of liberty are linked in important respects, and a decision on the latter point advances both interests. If protected conduct is made criminal and the law which does so remains unexamined for its substantive validity, its stigma might remain even if it were not enforceable as drawn for equal protection reasons. When homosexual conduct is made criminal by the law of the State, that declaration in and of itself is an invitation to subject homosexual persons to discrimination both in the public and in the private spheres. The central holding of *Bowers* has been brought in question by this case, and it should be addressed. Its continuance as precedent demeans the lives of homosexual persons.

The stigma this criminal statute imposes, moreover, is not trivial. The offense, to be sure, is but [a] minor offense in the Texas legal system. Still, it remains a criminal offense with all that imports for the dignity of the persons charged. The petitioners will bear on their record the history of their criminal convictions. Just this Term we rejected various challenges to state laws requiring the registration of sex offenders. We are advised that if Texas convicted an adult for private, consensual homosexual conduct under the statute here in question the convicted person would come within the registration laws of a least four States were he or she to be subject to their jurisdiction. This underscores the consequential nature of the punishment and the state-sponsored condemnation attendant to the criminal prohibition. Furthermore, the Texas criminal conviction carries with it the other collateral consequences always following a conviction, such as notations on job application forms, to mention but one example.

The foundations of *Bowers* have sustained serious erosion from our recent decisions in *Casey* and *Romer*. When our precedent has been thus weakened, criticism from other sources is of greater significance. In the United States criticism of *Bowers* has been substantial and continuing, disapproving of its reasoning in all respects, not just as to its historical assumptions. See, e.g., Charles Fried, *Order and Law: Arguing the Reagan Revolution—A Firsthand Account* 81–84 (1991); Richard Posner, *Sex and Reason* 341–350 (1992). The courts of five different States have declined to follow it in interpreting provisions in their own state constitutions parallel to the Due Process Clause of the Fourteenth Amendment.

To the extent *Bowers* relied on values we share with a wider civilization, it should be noted that the reasoning and holding in *Bowers* have been rejected elsewhere. The European Court of Human Rights has followed not *Bowers* but its own decision in *Dudgeon v. United Kingdom*. Other nations, too, have taken action consistent with an affirmation of the protected right of homosexual adults to engage in intimate, consensual conduct. The right the petitioners seek in this case has been accepted as an integral part of human freedom in many other countries. There has been no showing that in this country the governmental interest in circumscribing personal choice is somehow more legitimate or urgent.

[In] *Casey* we noted that when a Court is asked to overrule a precedent recognizing a constitutional liberty interest, individual or societal reliance on the existence of that liberty cautions with particular strength against reversing course. [The] holding in *Bowers,* however, has not induced detrimental reliance comparable to some instances where recognized individual rights are involved. Indeed, there has been no individual or societal reliance on *Bowers* of the sort that could counsel against overturning its holding once there are compelling reasons to do so. *Bowers* itself causes uncertainty, for the precedents before and after its issuance contradict its central holding.

The rationale of *Bowers* does not withstand careful analysis. In his dissenting opinion in Bowers Justice Stevens came to these conclusions: "Our prior cases make two propositions abundantly clear. First, the fact that the governing majority in a State has traditionally viewed a particular practice as immoral is not a sufficient reason for upholding a law prohibiting the practice; neither history nor tradition could save a law prohibiting miscegenation from constitutional attack. Second, individual decisions by married persons, concerning the intimacies of their physical relationship, even when not intended to produce offspring, are a form of 'liberty' protected by the Due Process Clause of the Fourteenth Amendment. Moreover, this protection extends to intimate choices by unmarried as well as married persons."

Justice Stevens' analysis, in our view, should have been controlling in *Bowers* and should control here.

Bowers was not correct when it was decided, and it is not correct today. It ought not to remain binding precedent. *Bowers* should be and now is overruled.

The present case [involves] two adults who, with full and mutual consent from each other, engaged in sexual practices common to a homosexual lifestyle. The petitioners are entitled to respect for their private lives. The State cannot demean their existence or control their destiny by making their private sexual conduct a crime. Their right to liberty under the Due Process Clause gives them the full right to engage in their conduct without intervention of the government. "It is a promise of the Constitution that there is a realm of personal liberty which the government may not enter." *Casey*. The Texas statute furthers no legitimate state interest which can justify its intrusion into the personal and private life of the individual.

Had those who drew and ratified the Due Process Clauses of the Fifth Amendment or the Fourteenth Amendment known the components of liberty in its manifold possibilities, they might have been more specific. They did not presume to have this insight. They knew times can blind us to certain truths and later generations can see that laws once thought necessary and proper in fact serve only to oppress. As the Constitution endures, persons in every generation can invoke its principles in their own search for greater freedom. * * *

JUSTICE O'CONNOR, concurring in the judgment.

[O'Connor, J., did not join the Court in overruling *Bowers*, but agreed that Texas' statute banning "same-sex sodomy" was unconstitutional, relying on the Equal Protection Clause. See p. 216 of this Supplement.]

JUSTICE SCALIA, with whom THE CHIEF JUSTICE and JUSTICE THOMAS join, dissenting.

[N]owhere does the Court's opinion declare that homosexual sodomy is a "fundamental right" under the Due Process Clause; nor does it subject the Texas law to the standard of review that would be appropriate (strict scrutiny) if homosexual sodomy *were* a "fundamental right." Thus, while overruling the *outcome* of *Bowers,* the Court leaves strangely untouched its central legal conclusion: "[R]espondent would have us announce [a] fundamental right to engage in homosexual sodomy. This we are quite unwilling to do." Instead the Court simply describes petitioners' conduct as "an exercise of their liberty"—which it undoubtedly is—and proceeds to apply an unheard-of form of rational-basis review that will have far-reaching implications beyond this case.

I begin with the Court's surprising readiness to reconsider a decision rendered a mere 17 years ago in *Bowers*. I do not myself believe in rigid adherence to stare decisis in constitutional cases; but I do believe that we should be consistent rather than manipulative in invoking the doctrine. Today's opinions in support of reversal do not bother to distinguish—or indeed, even bother to mention—the paean to stare decisis coauthored by three Members of today's majority in *Casey*. There, when stare decisis meant preservation of judicially invented abortion rights, the widespread criticism of *Roe* was strong reason to *reaffirm* it: "Where, in the performance of its judicial duties, the Court decides a case in such a way as to resolve the sort of intensely divisive controversy reflected in *Roe*[,] [its] decision has a dimension that the resolution of the normal case does not carry. [T]o overrule under fire in the absence of the most compelling reason [would] subvert the Court's legitimacy beyond any serious question." Today, however, the widespread opposition to *Bowers,* a decision resolving an issue as "intensely divisive" as the issue in *Roe,* is offered as a reason in favor of *overruling* it. Gone, too, is any "enquiry" (of the sort conducted in *Casey*) into whether the decision sought to be overruled has "proven 'unworkable.' "

Today's approach to stare decisis invites us to overrule an erroneously decided precedent (including an "intensely divisive" decision) *if:* (1) its foundations have been "eroded" by subsequent decisions; (2) it has been subject to "substantial and continuing" criticism; and (3) it has not induced "individual or societal reliance" that counsels against overturning. The problem is that *Roe* itself—which today's majority surely has no disposition to overrule—satisfies these conditions to at least the same degree as *Bowers.*

(1) A preliminary digressive observation with regard to the first factor: The Court's claim that *Casey* "casts some doubt" upon the holding in *Bowers* (or any other case, for that matter) does not withstand analysis. As far as its holding is concerned, *Casey* provided a *less* expansive right to abortion than did *Roe, which was already on the books when Bowers was decided.* And if the Court is referring not to the holding of *Casey,* but to the dictum of its famed sweet-mystery-of-life passage (" 'At the heart of liberty is the right to define one's own concept of existence, of meaning, of the universe, and of the mystery of human life' "): That "casts some doubt" upon either the totality of our jurisprudence or else (presumably the right answer) nothing at all. I have never heard of a law that attempted to restrict one's "right to define" certain concepts; and if the passage calls into question the government's power to regulate *actions based on* one's self-defined "concept of existence, etc.," it is the passage that ate the rule of law.

I do not quarrel with the Court's claim that *Romer* "eroded" the "foundations" of *Bowers'* rational-basis holding. But *Roe* and *Casey* have been equally "eroded" by *Washington v. Glucksberg,* [infra,] which held that *only* fundamental rights which are " 'deeply rooted in this Nation's history and tradition' " qualify for anything other than rational basis scrutiny under the doctrine of "substantive due process." *Roe* and *Casey,* of course, subjected the restriction of abortion to heightened scrutiny without even attempting to establish that the freedom to abort *was* rooted in this Nation's tradition.

(2) *Bowers,* the Court says, has been subject to "substantial and continuing [criticism], disapproving of its reasoning in all respects, not just as to its historical assumptions." Exactly what those nonhistorical criticisms are, and whether the Court even agrees with them, are left unsaid, although the Court does cite two [books.][b] Of course, *Roe* too (and by extension *Casey*) had been (and still is) subject to unrelenting criticism, including criticism from the two commentators cited by the Court today.

(3) That leaves, to distinguish the rock-solid, unamendable disposition of *Roe* from the readily overrulable *Bowers,* only the third factor. "[T]here has been," the Court says, "no individual or societal reliance on *Bowers* of the sort that could counsel against overturning its [holding]." It seems to me that the "societal reliance" on the principles confirmed in *Bowers* and discarded today has been overwhelming. Countless judicial decisions and legislative

b. [One of the *Bowers* critics cited by the majority] actually writes: "[*Bowers*] is correct nevertheless that the right to engage in homosexual acts is not deeply rooted in America's history and tradition." Posner, *Sex and Reason,* at 343.

enactments have relied on the ancient proposition that a governing majority's belief that certain sexual behavior is "immoral and unacceptable" constitutes a rational basis for regulation. [Justice Scalia then discusses numerous lower court cases.] We ourselves relied extensively on *Bowers* when we concluded, in *Barnes v. Glen Theatre, Inc.*, that Indiana's public indecency statute furthered "a substantial government interest in protecting order and morality," (plurality opinion). State laws against bigamy, same-sex marriage, adult incest, prostitution, masturbation, adultery, fornication, bestiality, and obscenity are likewise sustainable only in light of *Bowers* 'validation of laws based on moral choices. Every single one of these laws is called into question by today's decision; the Court makes no effort to cabin the scope of its decision to exclude them from its holding. [The] impossibility of distinguishing homosexuality from other traditional "morals" offenses is precisely why *Bowers* rejected the rational-basis challenge. "The law," it said, "is constantly based on notions of morality, and if all laws representing essentially moral choices are to be invalidated under the Due Process Clause, the courts will be very busy indeed."[c]

What a massive disruption of the current social order, therefore, the overruling of *Bowers* entails. Not so the overruling of *Roe,* which would simply have restored the regime that existed for centuries before 1973, in which the permissibility of and restrictions upon abortion were determined legislatively State-by-State. *Casey,* however, chose to base its *stare decisis* determination on a different "sort" of reliance. "[P]eople," it said, "have organized intimate relationships and made choices that define their views of themselves and their places in society, in reliance on the availability of abortion in the event that contraception should fail." This falsely assumes that the consequence of overruling *Roe* would have been to make abortion unlawful. It would not; it would merely have *permitted* the States to do so. Many States would unquestionably have declined to prohibit abortion, and others would not have prohibited it within six months (after which the most significant reliance interests would have expired). Even for persons in States other than these, the choice would not have been between abortion and childbirth, but between abortion nearby and abortion in a neighboring State.

To tell the truth, it does not surprise me, and should surprise no one, that the Court has chosen today to revise the standards of stare decisis set forth in *Casey.* It has thereby exposed *Casey*'s extraordinary deference to precedent for the result-oriented expedient that it is.

Having decided that it need not adhere to stare decisis, the Court still must establish that *Bowers* was wrongly decided and that the Texas statute, as applied to petitioners, is unconstitutional.

[The Texas law at issue] undoubtedly imposes constraints on liberty. So do laws prohibiting prostitution, recreational use of heroin, and, for that matter, working more than 60 hours per week in a bakery. But there is no right to "liberty" under the Due Process Clause, though today's opinion repeatedly makes that claim. [The] Fourteenth Amendment *expressly allows*

c. While the Court does not overrule *Bowers* "holding that homosexual sodomy is not a 'fundamental right,' it is worth noting that the 'societal reliance' upon that aspect of the decision has been substantial as well. See 10 U.S.C. § 654(b)(1) ('A member of the armed forces shall be separated from the armed forces [if] the member has engaged in [a] homosexual act or acts'). [Scalia, J., then discusses many lower court cases.]"

States to deprive their citizens of "liberty," *so long as "due process of law" is provided* * * *.

Our opinions applying the doctrine known as "substantive due process" hold that the Due Process Clause prohibits States from infringing *fundamental* liberty interests, unless the infringement is narrowly tailored to serve a compelling state interest. *Washington v. Glucksberg*. We have held repeatedly, in cases the Court today does not overrule, that *only* fundamental rights qualify for this so-called "heightened scrutiny" protection—that is, rights which are " 'deeply rooted in this Nation's history and tradition,' " [Scalia, J., then discusses *Reno v. Flores, Michael H. v. Gerald D., Meyer v. Nebraska* and other cases.][d] All other liberty interests may be abridged or abrogated pursuant to a validly enacted state law if that law is rationally related to a legitimate state interest.

Bowers held, first, that criminal prohibitions of homosexual sodomy are not subject to heightened scrutiny because they do not implicate a "fundamental right" under the Due Process Clause. Noting that "[p]roscriptions against that conduct have ancient roots," that "[s]odomy was a criminal offense at common law and was forbidden by the laws of the original 13 States when they ratified the Bill of Rights," and that many States had retained their bans on sodomy, *Bowers* concluded that a right to engage in homosexual sodomy was not "deeply rooted in this Nation's history and tradition."

The Court today does not overrule this holding. Not once does it describe homosexual sodomy as a "fundamental right" or a "fundamental liberty interest," nor does it subject the Texas statute to strict scrutiny. Instead, [the] Court concludes that the application of Texas's statute to petitioners' conduct fails the rational-basis test, and overrules *Bowers* 'holding to the contrary[:] "The Texas statute furthers no legitimate state interest which can justify its intrusion into the personal and private life of the individual." ' "

I shall address that rational-basis holding presently. First, however, I address some aspersions that the Court casts upon *Bowers'* conclusion that homosexual sodomy is not a "fundamental right"—even though, as I have said, the Court does not have the boldness to reverse that conclusion.

The Court's description of "the state of the law" at the time of *Bowers* only confirms that *Bowers* was right. [The *Griswold*] case *expressly disclaimed* any reliance on the doctrine of "substantive due process," and grounded the so-called "right to privacy" in penumbras of constitutional provisions *other than* the Due Process Clause. *Eisenstadt*, likewise had nothing to do with "substantive due process"; it invalidated a Massachusetts law prohibiting the distribution of contraceptives to unmarried persons solely on the basis of the Equal Protection Clause. * * *

d. The Court is quite right that "history and tradition are the starting point but not in all cases the ending point of the substantive due process inquiry." An asserted "fundamental liberty interest" must not only be "deeply rooted in this Nation's history and tradition," *Washington v. Glucksberg*, but it must *also* be "implicit in the concept of ordered liberty," so that "neither liberty nor justice would exist if [it] were sacrificed." Moreover, liberty interests unsupported by history and tradition, though not deserving of "heightened scrutiny," are *still* protected from state laws that are not rationally related to any legitimate state interest. As I proceed to discuss, it is this latter principle that the Court applies in the present case.

Roe v. Wade recognized that the right to abort an unborn child was a "fundamental right" protected by the Due Process Clause. The *Roe* Court, however, made no attempt to establish that this right was " 'deeply rooted in this Nation's history and tradition' "; instead, it based its conclusion that "the Fourteenth Amendment's concept of personal liberty [is] broad enough to encompass a woman's decision whether or not to terminate her pregnancy" on its own normative judgment that anti-abortion laws were undesirable. We have since rejected *Roe*'s holding that regulations of abortion must be narrowly tailored to serve a compelling state interest, see *Casey*, (joint opinion of O'Connor, Kennedy, and Souter, JJ.); (Rehnquist, C.J., concurring in judgment in part and dissenting in part)—and thus, by logical implication, *Roe*'s holding that the right to abort an unborn child is a "fundamental right."

[After] discussing the history of antisodomy laws, the Court proclaims that, "it should be noted that there is no longstanding history in this country of laws directed at homosexual conduct as a distinct matter." This observation in no way casts into doubt the "definitive [historical] conclusion" on which *Bowers* relied: that our Nation has a longstanding history of laws prohibiting *sodomy in general*—regardless of whether it was performed by same-sex or opposite-sex couples * * *.

It is (as *Bowers* recognized) entirely irrelevant whether the laws in our long national tradition criminalizing homosexual sodomy were "directed at homosexual conduct as a distinct matter." Whether homosexual sodomy was prohibited by a law targeted at same-sex sexual relations or by a more general law prohibiting both homosexual and heterosexual sodomy, the only relevant point is that it *was* criminalized—which suffices to establish that homosexual sodomy is not a right "deeply rooted in our Nation's history and tradition." The Court today agrees that homosexual sodomy was criminalized and thus does not dispute the facts on which Bowers *actually* relied.

Next the Court makes the claim, again unsupported by any citations, that "[l]aws prohibiting sodomy do not seem to have been enforced against consenting adults acting in private." The key qualifier here is "acting in private"—since the Court admits that sodomy laws *were* enforced against consenting adults (although the Court contends that prosecutions were "infrequent."). I do not know what "acting in private" means; surely consensual sodomy, like heterosexual intercourse, is rarely performed on stage. If all the Court means by "acting in private" is "on private premises, with the doors closed and windows covered," it is entirely unsurprising that evidence of enforcement would be hard to come by. * * * Surely that lack of evidence would not sustain the proposition that consensual sodomy on private premises with the doors closed and windows covered was regarded as a "fundamental right," even though all other consensual sodomy was criminalized. [*Bowers*'] conclusion that homosexual sodomy is not a fundamental right "deeply rooted in this Nation's history and tradition" is utterly unassailable.

Realizing that fact, the Court instead says: "[W]e think that our laws and traditions in the past half century are of most relevance here. These references show *an emerging awareness* that liberty gives substantial protection to adult persons in deciding how to conduct their private lives *in matters pertaining to sex.*" (Emphasis added). Apart from the fact that such an "emerging awareness" does not establish a "fundamental right," the statement is factually false. States continue to prosecute all sorts of crimes by adults "in matters pertaining to sex": prostitution, adult incest, adultery, obscenity, and child pornography. Sodomy laws, too, have been enforced "in the past half century," in which there have been 134 reported cases involving prosecutions for consensual, adult, homosexual sodomy.

[In] any event, an "emerging awareness" is by definition not "deeply rooted in this Nation's history and tradition[s]," as we have said "fundamental right" status requires. Constitutional entitlements do not spring into existence because some States choose to lessen or eliminate criminal sanctions on certain behavior. Much less do they spring into existence, as the Court seems to believe, because *foreign nations* decriminalize conduct. The *Bowers* majority opinion *never* relied on "values we share with a wider civilization," but rather rejected the claimed right to sodomy on the ground that such a right was not " 'deeply rooted in *this Nation's* history and tradition' " (emphasis added).

I turn now to the ground on which the Court squarely rests its holding: the contention that there is no rational basis for the law here under attack. This proposition is so out of accord with our jurisprudence—indeed, with the jurisprudence of *any* society we know—that it requires little discussion.

The Texas statute undeniably seeks to further the belief of its citizens that certain forms of sexual behavior are "immoral and unacceptable," *Bowers*—the same interest furthered by criminal laws against fornication, bigamy, adultery, adult incest, bestiality, and obscenity. *Bowers* held that this *was* a legitimate state interest. The Court today reaches the opposite conclusion. The Texas statute, it says, "furthers *no legitimate state interest* which can justify its intrusion into the personal and private life of the individual," (emphasis added). The Court embraces instead Justice Stevens' declaration in his *Bowers* dissent, that "the fact that the governing majority in a State has traditionally viewed a particular practice as immoral is not a sufficient reason for upholding a law prohibiting the practice." This effectively decrees the end of all morals legislation. If, as the Court asserts, the promotion of majoritarian sexual morality is not even a *legitimate* state interest, none of the above-mentioned laws can survive rational-basis review. * * *

Today's opinion is the product of a Court, which is the product of a law-profession culture, that has largely signed on to the so-called homosexual agenda, by which I mean the agenda promoted by some homosexual activists directed at eliminating the moral opprobrium that has traditionally attached to homosexual conduct. I noted in an earlier opinion the fact that the American Association of Law Schools (to which any reputable law school *must* seek to belong) excludes from membership any school that refuses to ban from its job-interview facilities a law firm (no matter how small) that does not wish to hire as a prospective partner a person who openly engages in homosexual conduct.

One of the most revealing statements in today's opinion is the Court's grim warning that the criminalization of homosexual conduct is "an invitation to subject homosexual persons to discrimination both in the public and in the private spheres." It is clear from this that the Court has taken sides in the culture war, departing from its role of assuring, as neutral observer, that the democratic rules of engagement are observed. Many Americans do not want persons who openly engage in homosexual conduct as partners in their business, as scoutmasters for their children, as teachers in their children's schools, or as boarders in their home. They view this as protecting themselves and their families from a lifestyle that they believe to be immoral and destructive. The Court views it as "discrimination" which it is the function of our judgments to deter. So imbued is the Court with the law profession's anti-anti-homosexual culture, that it is seemingly unaware that the attitudes of that culture are not obviously "mainstream"; that in most States what the Court calls "discrimination" against those who engage in homosexual acts is perfectly legal; that proposals to ban such "discrimination" under Title VII have repeatedly been rejected by Congress; that in some cases such "discrimination" is *mandated* by federal statute, see 10 U.S.C. § 654(b)(1) (mandating discharge from the armed forces of any service member who engages in or intends to engage in homosexual acts); and that in some cases such "discrimination" is a constitutional right, see *Boy Scouts of America v. Dale*.

Let me be clear that I have nothing against homosexuals, or any other group, promoting their agenda through normal democratic means. Social perceptions of sexual and other morality change over time, and every group has the right to persuade its fellow citizens that its view of such matters is the best. [But] persuading one's fellow citizens is one thing, and imposing one's views in absence of democratic majority will is something else. I would no more *require* a State to criminalize homosexual acts—or, for that matter, display *any* moral disapprobation of them—than I would *forbid* it to do so. What Texas has chosen to do is well within the range of traditional democratic action, and its hand should not be stayed through the invention of a brand-new "constitutional right" by a Court that is impatient of democratic change. It is indeed true that "later generations can see that laws once thought necessary and proper in fact serve only to oppress," and when that happens, later generations can repeal those laws. But it is the premise of our system that those judgments are to be made by the people, and not imposed by a governing caste that knows best.

One of the benefits of leaving regulation of this matter to the people rather than to the courts is that the people, unlike judges, need not carry things to their logical conclusion. The people may feel that their disapprobation of homosexual conduct is strong enough to disallow homosexual marriage, but not strong enough to criminalize private homosexual acts—and may legislate accordingly. The Court today pretends that it possesses a similar freedom of action, so that that we need not fear judicial imposition of homosexual marriage, as has recently occurred in Canada (in a decision that the Canadian Government has chosen not to appeal). At the end of its opinion—after having laid waste the foundations of our rational-basis jurisprudence—the Court says that the present case "does not involve whether the government must give formal recognition to any relationship that homosexual persons seek to enter." Do not believe it. More illuminating than this bald, unreasoned disclaimer is the progression of thought displayed by an earlier passage in the Court's opinion, which notes the constitutional protections afforded to "personal decisions relating to *marriage,* procreation, contraception, family relationships, child rearing, and education," and then declares that "[p]ersons in a homosexual relationship may seek autonomy for these purposes, just as heterosexual persons do" (emphasis added). Today's opinion dismantles the structure of constitutional law that has permitted a distinction to be made between heterosexual and homosexual unions, insofar as formal recognition in marriage is concerned. If moral disapprobation of homosexual conduct is "no legitimate state interest" for purposes of proscribing that conduct; and if, as the Court coos (casting aside all pretense of neutrality), "[w]hen sexuality finds overt expression in intimate conduct with another person, the conduct can be but one element in a personal bond that is more enduring"; what justification could there possibly be for denying the benefits of marriage to homosexual couples exercising "[t]he liberty protected by the Constitution"? Surely not the encouragement of procreation, since the sterile and the elderly are allowed to marry. This case "does not involve" the issue of homosexual marriage only if one entertains the belief that principle and logic have nothing to do with the decisions of this Court. Many will hope that, as the Court comfortingly assures us, this is so.

The matters appropriate for this Court's resolution are only three: Texas's prohibition of sodomy neither infringes a "fundamental right" (which the Court does not dispute), nor is unsupported by a rational relation to what the Constitution considers a legitimate state interest, nor denies the equal protection of the laws. I dissent.[a]

JUSTICE THOMAS, dissenting.

I join Justice Scalia's dissenting opinion. I write separately to note that the law before the Court today "is . . . uncommonly silly." *Griswold* (Stewart, J., dissenting). If I were a member of the Texas Legislature, I would vote to repeal it. Punishing someone for expressing his sexual preference through noncommercial consensual conduct with another adult does not appear to be a worthy way to expend valuable law enforcement resources.

Notwithstanding this, I recognize that as a member of this Court I am not empowered to help petitioners and others similarly situated. My duty, rather, is to "decide cases 'agreeably to the Constitution and laws of the United States.'" And, just like Justice Stewart, I "can find [neither in the Bill of Rights nor any other part of the Constitution a] general right of privacy" or as the Court terms it today, the "liberty of the person both in its spatial and more transcendent dimensions."

THE DEATH PENALTY AND RELATED PROBLEMS: CRUEL AND UNUSUAL PUNISHMENT

CON LAW: P. 537, end of section

AMER CON: P. 445, end of section

RTS & LIB: P. 463, end of section

NEW RESTRICTIONS ON IMPOSITION OF THE DEATH PENALTY [NEW PART]

ROPER v. SIMMONS

___ U.S. ___, 125 S.Ct. 1183, 161 L.Ed.2d 1 (2005).

JUSTICE KENNEDY delivered the opinion of the Court.

[At age 17, Simmons committed murder. After he turned 18, he was tried, convicted and sentenced to death. After Simmons's appeal and subsequent

a. For portions of Scalia, J.'s dissenting opinion responding to O'Connor, J.'s concurring argument that the Texas statute violates equal protection, see p. ___ of this Supplement.

petitions for state and federal post-conviction relief were rejected, the Court handed down *Atkins v. Virginia*, 536 U.S. 304, 122 S.Ct. 2242, 153 L.Ed.2d 335 (2002), holding that the cruel and unusual punishments clause prohibits the execution of a mentally retarded person. Although *Stanford v. Kentucky*, 492 U.S. 361, 109 S.Ct. 2969, 106 L.Ed.2d 306 (1989), which had upheld the death penalty for juvenile offenders younger than 18 (but not younger than 16) was still on the books, Simmons filed a new petition for state post-conviction relief, maintaining that *Atkins*' reasoning applied to juvenile offenders as well. The Missouri Supreme Court agreed, holding that in the decade and a half since *Stanford* had been decided a national consensus had developed against the execution of offenders under 18.]

[*Atkins*] held that standards of decency have evolved since *Penry v. Lynaugh*, 492 U.S. 302, 109 S.Ct. 2934, 106 L.Ed.2d 256 (1989) [holding that the Constitution does not categorically prohibit the execution of mentally retarded people convicted of capital offenses] and now demonstrate that the execution of the mentally retarded is cruel and unusual punishment. The Court noted objective indicia of society's standards, as expressed in legislative enactments and state practice with respect to execution of the mentally retarded.

[*Atkins*] neither repeated nor relied upon the statement in *Stanford* that the Court's independent judgment has no bearing on the acceptability of a particular punishment under the Eighth Amendment. Instead we returned to the rule, established in decisions predating *Stanford*, that " 'the Constitution contemplates that in the end our own judgment will be brought to bear on the question of the acceptability of the death penalty under the Eighth Amendment.' " * * *

Just as the *Atkins* Court reconsidered the issue decided in *Penry*, we now reconsider the issue decided in *Stanford*. The beginning point is a review of objective indicia of consensus, as expressed in particular by the enactments of legislatures that have addressed the question. This data gives us essential instruction. We then must determine, in the exercise of our own independent judgment, whether the death penalty is a disproportionate punishment for juveniles.

The evidence of national consensus against the death penalty for juveniles is similar, and in some respects parallel, to the evidence *Atkins* held sufficient to demonstrate a national consensus against the death penalty for the mentally retarded. When *Atkins* was decided, 30 States prohibited the death penalty for the mentally retarded [including 12 that had abandoned the death penalty altogether]. By a similar calculation in this case, 30 States prohibit the juvenile death penalty [again including 12 that had abandoned the death penalty altogether].

[Though] less dramatic than the change from *Penry* to *Atkins*, we still consider the change from *Stanford* to this case to be significant. As noted in *Atkins*, with respect to the States that had abandoned the death penalty for the mentally retarded since *Penry,* "[i]t is not so much the number of these States that is significant, but the consistency of the direction of change."

[As] in *Atkins,* the objective indicia of consensus in this case—the rejection of the juvenile death penalty in the majority of States; the infrequency of its use even where it remains on the books; and the consistency in the trend toward abolition of the practice—provide sufficient evidence that today our society views juveniles, in the words *Atkins* used respecting the mentally retarded, as "categorically less culpable than the average criminal."

[Because] the death penalty is the most severe punishment, the Eighth Amendment applies to it with special force. Capital punishment must be limited to those offenders who commit "a narrow category of the most serious crimes" and whose extreme culpability makes them "the most deserving of execution." *Atkins*. This principle is implemented throughout the capital sentencing process. States must give narrow and precise definition to the aggravating factors that can result in a capital sentence. In any capital case a defendant has wide latitude to raise as a mitigating factor "any aspect of [his or her] character or record and any of the circumstances of the offense that the defendant proffers as a basis for a sentence less than death." * * *

Three general differences between juveniles under 18 and adults demonstrate that juvenile offenders cannot with reliability be classified among the worst offenders. First, as any parent knows and [as] scientific and sociological studies [tend] to confirm, "[a] lack of maturity and an underdeveloped sense of responsibility are found in youth more often than in adults and are more understandable among the young. These qualities often result in impetuous and ill-considered actions and decisions." [In] recognition of the comparative immaturity and irresponsibility of juveniles, almost every State prohibits those under 18 years of age from voting, serving on juries, or marrying without parental consent.

[The] second area of difference is that juveniles are more vulnerable or susceptible to negative influences and outside pressures, including peer pressure. [The] third broad difference is that the character of a juvenile is not as well formed as that of an adult.

[These] differences render suspect any conclusion that a juvenile falls among the worst offenders. [From] a moral standpoint it would be misguided to equate the failings of a minor with those of an adult, for a greater possibility exists that a minor's character deficiencies will be reformed. * * *

In concluding that neither retribution nor deterrence provides adequate justification for imposing the death penalty on juvenile offenders, we cannot deny or overlook the brutal crimes too many juvenile offenders have committed. Certainly it can be argued, although we by no means concede the point, that a rare case might arise in which a juvenile offender has sufficient psychological maturity, and at the same time demonstrates sufficient depravity, to merit a sentence of death. Indeed, this possibility is the linchpin of one contention pressed by petitioner and his amici. They assert that even assuming the truth of the observations we have made about juveniles' diminished culpability in general, jurors nonetheless should be allowed to consider mitigating arguments related to youth on a case-by-case basis, and in some cases to impose the death penalty if justified.

We disagree. The differences between juvenile and adult offenders are too marked and well understood to risk allowing a youthful person to receive the death penalty despite insufficient culpability. An unacceptable likelihood exists that the brutality or cold-blooded nature of any particular crime would overpower mitigating arguments based on youth as a matter of course, even where the juvenile offender's objective immaturity, vulnerability, and lack of true depravity should require a sentence less severe than death. In some cases a defendant's youth may even be counted against him.

[To] the extent *Stanford* was based on review of the objective indicia of consensus that obtained in 1989, it suffices to note that those indicia have changed. It should be observed, furthermore, that the *Stanford* Court should have considered those States that had abandoned the death penalty altogether as part of the consensus against the juvenile death penalty; a State's decision to bar the death penalty altogether of necessity demonstrates a judgment that the death penalty is inappropriate for all offenders, including juveniles. Last, to the extent *Stanford* was based on a rejection of the idea that this Court is required to bring its independent judgment to bear on the proportionality of the death penalty for a particular class of crimes or offenders, it suffices to note that this rejection was inconsistent with prior Eighth Amendment decisions. It is also inconsistent with the premises of our recent decision in *Atkins*. * * *

Our determination that the death penalty is disproportionate punishment for offenders under 18 finds confirmation in the stark reality that the United States is the only country in the world that continues to give official sanction to the juvenile death penalty. This reality does not become controlling, for the task of interpreting the Eighth Amendment remains our responsibility. Yet at least from the time of the Court's decision in *Trop v. Dulles*, 356 U.S. 86, 78 S.Ct. 590, 2 L.Ed.2d 630 (1958), the Court has referred to the laws of other countries and to international authorities as instructive for its interpretation of the Eighth Amendment's prohibition of "cruel and unusual punishments."

[Article] 37 of the United Nations Convention on the Rights of the Child, which every country in the world has ratified save for the United States and Somalia, contains an express prohibition on capital punishment for crimes committed by juveniles under 18. [No] ratifying country has entered a reservation to the provision prohibiting the execution of juvenile offenders. Parallel prohibitions are contained in other significant international covenants.

[Petitioner] does not contest that only seven countries other than the United States have executed juvenile offenders since 1990: Iran, Pakistan, Saudi Arabia, Yemen, Nigeria, the Democratic Republic of Congo, and China. Since then each of these countries has either abolished capital punishment for juveniles or made public disavowal of the practice. In sum, it is fair to say that the United States now stands alone in a world that has turned its face against the juvenile death penalty.

[It] is proper that we acknowledge the overwhelming weight of international opinion against the juvenile death penalty, resting in large part on the understanding that the instability and emotional imbalance of young people may often be a factor in the crime. The opinion of the world community, while not controlling our outcome, does provide respected and significant confirmation for our own conclusions.

[It] does not lessen our fidelity to the Constitution or our pride in its origins to acknowledge that the express affirmation of certain fundamental rights by other nations and peoples simply underscores the centrality of those same rights within our own heritage of freedom. * * * [a]

JUSTICE SCALIA, with whom THE CHIEF JUSTICE and JUSTICE THOMAS join, dissenting.

[The Court] finds, on the flimsiest of grounds, that a national consensus which could not be perceived in our people's laws barely 15 years ago now solidly exists. Worse still, the Court says in so many words that what our people's laws say about the issue does not, in the last analysis, matter. [The] Court thus proclaims itself sole arbiter of our Nation's moral standards—and in the course of discharging that awesome responsibility purports to take guidance from the views of foreign courts and legislatures. Because I do not believe that the meaning of our Eighth Amendment, any more than the meaning of other provisions of our Constitution, should be determined by the subjective views of five Members of this Court and like-minded foreigners, I dissent. * * *

Words have no meaning if the views of less than 50% of death penalty States can constitute a national consensus. Our previous cases have required overwhelming opposition to a challenged practice, generally over a long period of time. [In] an attempt to keep afloat its implausible assertion of national consensus, the Court throws overboard a proposition well established in our Eighth Amendment jurisprudence. "It should be observed," the Court says, "that the *Stanford* Court should have considered those States that had abandoned the death penalty altogether as part of the consensus against the juvenile death penalty. [The] insinuation that the Court's new method of counting contradicts only "the *Stanford* Court" is misleading. *None* of our cases dealing with an alleged constitutional limitation upon the death penalty has counted, as States supporting a consensus in favor of that limitation, States that have eliminated the death penalty entirely. [That] 12 States favor *no* executions says something about consensus against the death penalty, but nothing—absolutely nothing—about consensus that offenders under 18 deserve special immunity from such a penalty.

[If] the Eighth Amendment set forth an ordinary rule of law, it would indeed be the role of this Court to say what the law is. But the Court having pronounced that the Eighth Amendment is an ever-changing reflection of "the evolving standards of decency" of our society, it makes no sense for the Justices then to *prescribe* those standards rather than discern them from the practices of our people. On the evolving-standards hypothesis, the only legitimate function of this Court is to identify a moral consensus of the American people. By what conceivable warrant can nine lawyers presume to be the authoritative conscience of the Nation? * * *

a. In a brief concurring opinion, Stevens, J., joined by Ginsburg, J., observed that "[if] the meaning of [the Eighth] Amendment has been frozen when it was originally drafted, it would impose no impediment to the execution of 7-year-old children. [That] our understanding of the Constitution does change from time to time has been settled since John Marshall breathed life into the text."

Today's opinion provides a perfect example of why judges are ill equipped to make the type of legislative judgments the Court insists on making here. To support its opinion that States should be prohibited from imposing the death penalty on anyone who committed murder before age 18, the Court looks to scientific and sociological studies, picking and choosing those that support its position. It never explains why those particular studies are methodologically sound; none was ever entered into evidence or tested in an adversarial proceeding. * * *

We need not look far to find studies contradicting the Court's conclusions. [The] American Psychological Association (APA), which claims in this case that scientific evidence shows persons under 18 lack the ability to take moral responsibility for their decisions, has previously taken precisely the opposite position before this very Court. * * *

Even putting aside questions of methodology, the studies cited by the Court offer scant support for a categorical prohibition of the death penalty for murderers under 18. At most, these studies conclude that, *on average,* or *in most cases,* persons under 18 are unable to take moral responsibility for their actions. Not one of the cited studies opines that all individuals under 18 are unable to appreciate the nature of their crimes.

The Court concludes [that] juries cannot be trusted with the delicate task of weighing a defendant's youth along with the other mitigating and aggravating factors of his crime. This startling conclusion undermines the very foundations of our capital sentencing system, which entrusts juries with "mak[ing] the difficult and uniquely human judgments that defy codification and that 'buil[d] discretion, equity, and flexibility into a legal system.' " The Court says that juries will be unable to appreciate the significance of a defendant's youth when faced with details of a brutal crime. This assertion is based on no evidence; to the contrary, the Court itself acknowledges that the execution of under–18 offenders is "infrequent" even in the States "without a formal prohibition on executing juveniles," suggesting that juries take seriously their responsibility to weigh youth as a mitigating factor.

Nor does the Court suggest a stopping point for its reasoning. If juries cannot make appropriate determinations in cases involving murderers under 18, in what other kinds of cases will the Court find jurors deficient? We have already held that no jury may consider whether a mentally deficient defendant can receive the death penalty, irrespective of his crime. See *Atkins*. Why not take other mitigating factors, such as considerations of childhood abuse or poverty, away from juries as well? Surely jurors "overpower[ed]" by "the brutality or cold-blooded nature" of a crime, could not adequately weigh these mitigating factors either.

[Though] the views of our own citizens are essentially irrelevant to the Court's decision today, the views of other countries and the so-called international community take center stage. * * *

[The] basic premise of the Court's argument—that American law should conform to the laws of the rest of the world—ought to be rejected out of hand. In fact the Court itself does not believe it. In many significant respects the laws of most other countries differ from our law—including not only such explicit provisions of our Constitution as the right to jury trial and grand jury indictment, but even many interpretations of the Constitution prescribed by this Court itself. The Court-pronounced exclusionary rule, for example, is distinctively American. [Since] then a categorical exclusionary rule has been "universally rejected" by other countries, including those with rules prohibiting illegal searches and police misconduct, despite the fact that none of these countries "appears to have any alternative form of discipline for police that is effective in preventing search violations."

[The] Court has been oblivious to the views of other countries when deciding how to interpret our Constitution's requirement that "Congress shall make no law respecting an establishment of religion." [And] let us not forget the Court's abortion jurisprudence, which makes us one of only six countries that allow abortion on demand until the point of viability.

[The Court's statement that] "the express affirmation of certain fundamental rights by other nations and peoples simply underscores the centrality of those same rights within our own heritage of freedom" * * * flatly misdescribes what is going on here. Foreign sources are cited today, *not* to underscore our "fidelity" to the Constitution, our "pride in its origins," and "our own [American] heritage." To the contrary, they are cited *to set aside* the centuries-old American practice—a practice still engaged in by a large majority of the relevant States—of letting a jury of 12 citizens decide whether, in the particular case, youth should be the basis for withholding the death penalty. What these foreign sources "affirm," rather than repudiate, is the Justices' own notion of how the world ought to be, and their diktat that it shall be so henceforth in America. The Court's parting attempt to downplay the significance of its extensive discussion of foreign law is unconvincing. "Acknowledgment" of foreign approval has no place in the legal opinion of this Court *unless it is part of the basis for the Court's judgment*—which is surely what it parades as today. * * *[b]

RING v. ARIZONA, 536 U.S. 584, 122 S.Ct. 2428, 153 L.Ed.2d 556 (2002): Under Arizona law a defendant convicted of a capital offense cannot be sentenced to death unless the judge, conducting a sentencing hearing, finds at least one aggravating circumstance and no mitigating circumstances sufficiently substantial to call for leniency. After Ring was convicted of felony-murder, the trial judge conducted a sentencing hearing and sentenced him to death. On appeal, Ring argued that Arizona's capital sentencing scheme violated the Sixth Amendment right to jury trial by entrusting to a judge the finding of fact warranting the death penalty. Overruling *Walton v. Arizona*, 497 U.S. 639, 110 S.Ct. 3047, 111 L.Ed.2d. 511 (1990), a 7–2 majority per Ginsburg, J., agreed:

b. Because she did not believe that a "genuine *national* consensus against the juvenile death penalty has yet developed" or that "the Court's moral proportionality argument justifies a categorical, age-based constitutional rule," O'Connor, J., wrote a separate dissent. Although the evidence of an international consensus did not "alter [her] determination that the Eighth Amendment does not, at this time, forbid capital punishment of 17-year-old murderers in all cases," she "disagree[d] with Justice Scalia's contention that foreign and international law have no place in our Eighth Amendment jurisprudence. Over the course of nearly half a century, the Court has consistently referred to foreign and international law as relevant to its assessment of evolving standards of decency. [This] inquiry reflects the special character of the Eighth Amendment, which, as the Court has long held, draws its meaning directly from the maturing values of civilized society. Obviously, American law is distinctive in many respects, not least where the specific provisions of our Constitution and the history of its exposition so dictate. [But] this Nation's evolving understanding of human dignity certainly is neither wholly isolated from, nor inherently at odds with, the values prevailing in other countries."

"In *Walton* this Court held that Arizona's sentencing scheme was compatible with the Sixth Amendment because the additional facts found by the judge qualified as sentencing considerations, not as elements of the offense of capital murder. Ten years later, however, we decided *Apprendi* v. *New Jersey*, 530 U.S. 466, 120 S.Ct. 2348, 147 L.Ed. 2d 435 (2000), which held that the Sixth Amendment does not permit a defendant to be 'exposed [to] a penalty *exceeding* the maximum he would receive if punished according to the facts reflected in the jury verdict alone.[a] This prescription governs, *Apprendi* determined, even if the State characterizes the additional findings made by the judge as 'sentencing factor[s]'.

"*Apprendi*'s reasoning is irreconcilable with *Walton*'s holding in this regard, and today we overrule *Walton* in relevant part. Capital defendants, no less than noncapital defendants, we conclude, are entitled to a jury determination of any fact on which the legislature conditions an increase in their maximum punishment.

"[The] right to trial by jury guaranteed by the Sixth Amendment would be senselessly diminished if it encompassed the factfinding necessary to increase a defendant's sentence by two years, but not the factfinding necessary to put him to death. We hold that the Sixth Amendment applies to both."

Although unable to accept *Apprendi*, Breyer J., concurred in the judgment on the ground that "the Eighth Amendment requires that a jury, not a judge, make the decision to sentence a defendant to death":

"I am convinced by the reasons that Justice Stevens [gave in *Spaziano v. Florida*, 468 U.S. 447, 104 S.Ct. 3154, 82 L.Ed. 2d 340 (1984) (Stevens, J., joined by Brennan and Marshall, JJ., concurring in part and dissenting in part).] [Justice Steven's reasons] include (1) his belief that retribution provides the main justification for capital punishment, and (2) his assessment of the jury's comparative advantage in determining, in a particular case, whether capital punishment will serve that end.

"[In] respect to retribution, jurors possess an important comparative advantage over judges. In principle, they are more attuned to ('the community's moral sensibility,' *Spaziano* (Stevens, J.), concurring in part and dissenting in part), because they 'reflect more accurately the composition and experiences of the community as a whole.' Hence they are more likely to 'express the conscience of the community on the ultimate question of life or death,' and better able to determine in the particular case the need for retribution, namely, 'an expression of the community's belief that certain crimes are themselves so grievous an affront to humanity that the only adequate response may be the penalty of death.' *Gregg* (joint opinion of Stewart, Powell, and Stevens, JJ.).

"[The] importance of trying to translate a community's sense of capital punishment's appropriateness in a particular case is underscored by the continued division of opinion as to whether capital punishment is in all circumstances, as currently administered, 'cruel and unusual.' Those who make this claim point, among other things, [to] the potentially arbitrary application of the death penalty, adding that the race of the victim and socio-economic factors seem to matter.

a. In *Apprendi*, defendant was convicted of possession of a firearm, an offense carrying a maximum penalty of ten years under state law. The sentencing judge found by a preponderance of the evidence that Apprendi's crime had been motivated by racial animus. That finding triggered application of the state's "hate crime enhancement," which doubled Apprendi's maximum authorized sentence. He was sentenced to 12 years in prison, 2 years over the maximum that would have applied but for the enhancement. The Court held that Apprendi's sentence violated the right to "a jury determination that [he] is guilty of every element of the crime [charged] beyond a reasonable doubt."

[They] argue that the delays that increasingly accompany sentences of death make those sentences unconstitutional because of 'the suffering inherent in a prolonged wait for execution.' [They] point to the inadequacy of representation in capital cases, a fact that aggravates the other failings. [And] they note that other nations have increasingly abandoned capital punishment. * * *

"Many communities may have accepted some or all of these claims, for they do not impose capital sentences.* * * Leaving questions of arbitrariness aside, this diversity argues strongly for procedures that will help assure that, in a particular case, the community indeed believes application of the death penalty is appropriate, not 'cruel,' 'unusual,' or otherwise unwarranted.

"For these reasons, the danger of unwarranted imposition of the penalty cannot be avoided unless 'the decision to impose the death penalty is made by a jury rather than by a single governmental official.' *Spaziano* (Stevens, J.). And I conclude that the Eighth Amendment requires individual jurors to make, and to take responsibility for, a decision to sentence a person to death."[b]

O'Connor, J., joined by Rehnquist, C.J., dissented: "I understand why the Court holds that the reasoning of *Apprendi* is irreconcilable with *Walton*. Yet in choosing which to overrule, I would choose *Apprendi*, not *Walton*.

"Not only was the decision in *Apprendi* unjustified in my view, but it has also had a severely destabilizing effect on our criminal justice system. I predicted in my dissent that the decision would 'unleash a flood of petitions by convicted defendants seeking to invalidate their sentences in whole or in part on the authority of [*Apprendi*].' As of May 31, 2002, less than two years after *Apprendi* was announced, the United States Courts of Appeals had decided approximately 1,802 criminal appeals in which defendants challenged their sentences, and in some cases even their convictions, under *Apprendi*. These federal appeals are likely only the tip of the iceberg, as federal criminal prosecutions represent a tiny fraction of the total number of criminal prosecutions nationwide.

"[The] decision today is only going to add to these already serious effects. The Court effectively declares five States' capital sentencing schemes unconstitutional. There are 168 prisoners on death row in these States, each of whom is now likely to challenge his or her death sentence. [Whether or not many of these challenges will ultimately be successful], the need to evaluate these claims will greatly burden the courts in these five States. In addition, I fear that the prisoners on death row in [five other states], which the Court identifies as having hybrid sentencing schemes in which the jury renders an advisory verdict but the judge makes the ultimate sentencing determination, may also seize on today's decision to challenge their sentences. There are 529 prisoners on death row in these States."

According to death penalty experts, there is general agreement that the likelihood of receiving a death sentence is greater from a judge than a jury. Ronald J. Tabak, co-chair of an ABA committee on the death penalty, pointed out that "far, far more often when the judge overrides the jury, it is in order to impose the death penalty when the jury has recommended life"—and this is especially so "when the judge is up for election." N.Y. Times, June 25, 2002, p. A19. One expert who has gathered statistics from Alabama, Stephen B. Bright of the

b. A concurring opinion by Scalia, J., joined by Thomas, J., is omitted.

Southern Center for Human Rights, reported that "you have 83 overrides from life to death and only 7 from death to life." James S. Liebman of Columbia Law School added that "about a quarter of the [187 people on] death row in Alabama is made up of people whom juries sentenced to life in prison but judges sentenced to death." Id. In Delaware, the only state with both an advisory system and *appointed* judges, judges have overridden seven jury recommendations, all from death to life. See id.

PROCEDURAL DUE PROCESS IN NON-CRIMINAL CASES

DEPRIVATION OF "LIBERTY" AND "PROPERTY" INTERESTS

CON LAW: P. 556, end of subsection

RTS & LIB: P. 483, end of subsection

CASTLE ROCK v. GONZALES, ___ U.S. ___, 125 S.Ct. 2796, ___ L.Ed.2d (2005): Respondent obtained a restraining order from a Colorado state trial court commanding her estranged husband not to molest or disturb her or any of her three daughters (ages 10, 9 and 7) and to remain away from the family home. However, upon reasonable notice respondent's husband could have a mid-week dinner visit with the children arranged by the parties.

What the Court called "the critical language" of the restraining order came from the preprinted notice that appeared on the back. This language, which essentially restated the relevant state statutory provisions, warned that "a knowing violation of a restraining order is a crime" and "will also constitute contempt of court"; a person violating the order "may be arrested without notice" if "probable cause" exists that the person "knowingly violated this order"; and that law enforcement personnel "shall use every reasonable means to enforce this restraining order [or], if an arrest would be impractical under the circumstances, seek a warrant for the arrest of the restrained person" when "probable cause" exists that "the restrained person has violated or attempted to violate any provision of this order * * *."

One afternoon, although no advance arrangements had been made, respondent's husband took the three children while they were playing outside the family home. When respondent noticed the children were missing, she suspected her husband had taken them and contacted the Castle Rock police. She showed them a copy of the restraining order and requested that it be enforced, but the police told her there was nothing they could do about the order and suggested that she call the police again if the children did not return home later in the evening. An hour later, respondent's husband called and told her that he had taken the children to a certain amusement park. She called the police again to inform them of this new development and asked them to check out her husband or his vehicle at the amusement park. Once again, the police declined to do anything, except to tell her to wait until later in the evening and see if her husband returned the girls. Respondent contacted the police three more times that evening, but all they did was tell her to wait some more. Several hours after respondent's last contact with the police, her husband entered the police station, opened fire with a semi-automatic weapon, and was killed by the return fire. Inside his vehicle, parked outside the stationhouse, the police found the bodies of all three daughters, whom he had murdered.

Respondent brought a § 1983 action against the town of Castle Rock, alleging that it had violated her fourteenth amendment due process rights because its police department had "an official policy or custom of failing to respond properly to complaints of restraining order violations" and "tolerate[d] the non-enforcement of restraining orders by its police officers." On rehearing en banc, a majority of the Tenth Circuit held that respondent had "a protected property interest in the enforcement of the terms of her restraining order" and that the town had deprived her of due process because "the police never 'heard' nor seriously entertained her request to enforce and protect her interests in the restraining order." A 7–2 majority, per SCALIA, J., disagreed: "Our cases recognize that a benefit is not a protected entitlement if government officials may grant or deny it in their discretion. [The Tenth Circuit concluded that the Colorado statute dealing with restraining orders] established the Colorado Legislature's clear intent 'to alter the fact that the police were not enforcing domestic abuse restraining orders,' and thus its intent 'that the recipient of a domestic abuse restraining order have an entitlement to its enforcement.' * * *"

"We do not believe these provisions of Colorado law truly made enforcement of the restraining orders *mandatory*. A well established tradition of police discretion has long coexisted with apparently mandatory arrest statutes. [Against] that backdrop, a true mandate of police action would require some stronger indication from the Colorado Legislature than 'shall use every reasonable means to enforce a restraining order' (or even 'shall arrest [or] seek a warrant'). [It] is hard to imagine that a Colorado peace officer would not have some discretion to determine that–despite probable cause to believe a restraining order has been violated–the circumstances of the violation or the competing duties of that officer or his agency counsel decisively against enforcement in a particular instance. The practical necessity for discretion is particularly apparent in a case such as this one, where the suspected violator is not actually present and his whereabouts are unknown.

"Respondent does not specify the precise means of enforcement that the Colorado restraining-order statute assertedly mandated–whether her interest lay in having police arrest her husband, having them seek a warrant for his arrest, or having them 'use every reasonable means, up to and including arrest, to enforce the order's terms.' Such indeterminancy is not the hallmark of a duty that is mandatory. Nor can someone be safely deemed 'entitled' to something when the identity of the alleged entitlement is vague. [The] dissent, after suggesting various formulations of the entitlement in question, ultimately contends that the obligations under the statute were quite precise: either make an arrest or (if that is impractical) seek an arrest warrant. The problem with this is that the seeking of an arrest warrant would be an entitlement to nothing but procedure–which we have held inadequate even to support standing, see *Lujan v. Defenders of Wildlife*, [CON LAW p. 1539; RTS & LIB p. 1444]; much less can it be the basis for a property interest. After the warrant is sought, it remains within the discretion of a judge whether to grant it, and after it is granted, it remains within the discretion of the police whether and when to execute it. Respondent would have been assured nothing but the seeking of a warrant. This is not the sort of 'entitlement' out of which a property interest is created.

"Even if the statute could be said to have made enforcement of restraining orders 'mandatory' because of the domestic-violence context of the underlying statute, that would not necessarily mean that state law gave *respondent* an entitlement to *enforcement* of the mandate. Making the actions of government employees obligatory can serve various legitimate ends other than the conferral of a benefit on a specific class of people. [This] principle underlies, for example, a Colorado district attorney's discretion to prosecute a domestic assault, even though the victim withdraws her charge.

"Respondent's alleged interest stems only from a State's *statutory* scheme—from a restraining order that was authorized by and tracked precisely the statute on which the Court of Appeals relied. She does not assert that she has any common-law or contractual entitlement to enforcement. If she was given a statutory entitlement, we would expect to see some indication of that in the statute [itself.] Perhaps most importantly, the statute spoke directly to the protected person's power to 'initiate contempt proceedings against the restrained person if the order [was] issued in a civil action or request the prosecuting attorney to initiate contempt proceedings if the order [was] issued in a criminal action.' The protected person's express power to 'initiate' civil contempt proceedings contrasts tellingly with the mere ability to 'request' initiation of criminal contempt proceedings—and even more dramatically with the complete silence about any power to 'request' (much less demand) that an arrest be made.

"The creation of a personal entitlement to something as vague and novel as enforcement of restraining orders cannot 'simply g[o] without saying' (Stevens, J., dissenting). We conclude that Colorado has not created such an entitlement.

"Even if we were to think otherwise concerning the creation of an entitlement by Colorado, it is by no means clear that an individual entitlement to enforcement of a restraining order could constitute a 'property' interest for purposes of the Due Process Clause. Such a right would not, of course, resemble any traditional conception of property. Although that alone does not disqualify it from due process protection, as. *Roth* and its progeny show, the right to have a restraining order enforced does not 'have some ascertainable monetary value,' as even our '*Roth*-type property-as-entitlement' cases have implicitly required. Merrill, *The Landscape of Constitutional Property*, 86 Va.L.Rev., 885 964 (2000). Perhaps most radically, the alleged property interest here arises *incidentally*, not out of some new species of government benefit or service, but out of a function that government actors have always performed—to wit, arresting people who they have probable cause to believe have committed a criminal offense. The indirect nature of a benefit was fatal to the due process claim of the nursing-home residents in *O'Bannon v. Town Court Nursing Center* [CON LAW p. 557; RTS & LIB p. 484].

"[In] light of today's decision and that in *DeShaney*, the benefit that a third party may receive from having someone else arrested for a crime generally does not trigger protections under the Due Process Clause, neither in its procedural nor in its 'substantive' manifestations. This result reflects our continuing reluctance to treat the Fourteenth Amendment as 'a font of tort law,' *Parratt v. Taylor*, but it does not mean States are powerless to provide victims with personally enforceable remedies. Although the framers of the Fourteenth Amendment and the Civil Rights Act of 1871 (the original source of § 1983), did not create a system by which police departments are generally held financially accountable for crimes that better policing might have prevented, the people of Colorado are free to craft such a system under state law."

Souter, J., joined by Breyer, J., joined the Court's opinion, but also wrote a concurring opinion: "[The] Court emphasizes the traditional public focus of law enforcement as reason to doubt that these particular legal requirements to provide police services, however unconditional their form, presuppose enforceable individual rights to a certain level of police protection. The Court also notes that the terms of the Colorado statute involved here recognize and preserve the traditional discretion afforded law enforcement officers. Gonzales's claim of a property right thus runs up against police discretion in the face of an individual demand to enforce, and discretion to ignore an individual instruction not to enforce (because, say, of a domestic reconciliation); no one would argue that the beneficiary of a Colorado order like the one here would be authorized to control a court's contempt power or order the police to refrain from arresting. These considerations argue against inferring any guarantee of a level of protection or safety that could be understood as the object of a 'legitimate claim of entitlement,' *Roth*, in the nature of property arising under Colorado law. Consequently, the classic predicate for federal due process protection of interests under state law is missing.

"[There appears to be another reason] for rejecting [respondent's] call to apply *Roth*, a reason that would apply even if the statutory mandates to the police were absolute, leaving the police with no discretion when the beneficiary of a protective order insists upon its enforcement. The Due Process Clause extends procedural protection to guard against unfair deprivation by state officials of substantive state-law property rights or entitlements; the federal process protects the property created by state law. But Gonzales claims a property interest in a state-mandated process in and of itself. This argument is at odds with the rule that '[p]rocess is not an end in itself. Its constitutional purpose is to protect a substantive interest to which the individual has a legitimate claim of entitlement.' In putting to rest the notion that the scope of an otherwise discernible property interest could be limited by related state-law procedures, this Court observed that '[t]he categories of substance and procedure are distinct * * *. "Property" cannot be defined by the procedures provided for its deprivation.' *Loudermill*. Just as a State cannot diminish a property right, once conferred, by attaching less than generous procedure to its deprivation, neither does a State create a property right merely by ordaining beneficial procedure unconnected to some articulable substantive guarantee. This is not to say that state rules of executive procedure may not provide significant reasons to infer an articulable property right meant to be protected; but it is to say that we have not identified property with procedure as such. State rules of executive procedure, however important, may be nothing more than rules of executive procedure.

"Thus, in every instance of property recognized by this Court as calling for federal procedural protection, the property has been distinguishable from the procedural obligations imposed on state officials to protect it. Whether welfare benefits, attendance at public schools, utility services, public employment, professional licenses, and so on, the property interest recognized in our cases has always existed apart from state procedural protection before the Court has recognized a constitutional claim to protection by federal process. To accede to Gonzales's argument would therefore work a sea change in the scope of federal due process, for she seeks federal process as a substitute simply for state process. (And she seeks damages [under] § 1983, for denial of process to which she claimed a federal right.) There is no articulable distinction between the object of Gonzales's asserted entitlement and the process she desires in order to protect her entitlement; both amount to certain steps to be taken to by the police to protect her family and herself. Gonazles's claim would thus take us beyond *Roth* or any recognized theory of Fourteenth Amendment due process, by collapsing the distinction between property protected and the process that protects it, and would federalize every mandatory state-law direction to executive officers whose performance on the job can be vitally significant to individuals affected."

Stevens, J., joined by Ginsburg, J., dissented: "The central question in this case is [whether,] as a matter of Colorado law, respondent had a right to police assistance comparable to the right she would have possessed to any other service the government or a private firm might have undertaken to provide. * * * Unfortunately, [the majority] has chosen to ignore our settled practice by providing its *own* answer to that question. [Even] if the Court had good reason to doubt the Court of Appeals' determination of a state law, it would, in my judgment, be a far wiser course to certify the question to the Colorado Supreme Court. * * *

"Three flaws in the Court's rather superficial analysis of the merits highlight the unwisdom of its decision to answer the state-law question de novo. First, the Court places undue weight on the various statutes throughout the country that seemingly mandate police enforcement but are generally understood to provide police discretion. As a result, the Court gives short shrift to the unique case of 'mandatory arrest' statutes in the domestic violence context; States passed a wave of these statutes in the 1980's and 1990's with the unmistakable goal of eliminating police discretion in this area. Second, the Court's formalistic analysis fails to take seriously the fact that the Colorado statute at issue in this case was enacted for the benefit of the narrow class of persons who are beneficiaries of domestic restraining orders, and that the order at issue in this case was specifically intended to provide protection to respondent and her children. Finally, the Court is simply wrong to assert that a citizen's interest in the government's commitment to provide police enforcement in certain defined circumstances does not resemble any 'traditional conception of property'; in fact, a citizen's property interest in such a commitment is just as concrete and worthy of protection as her interest in any other important service the government or a private firm has undertaken to provide.

"[When] Colorado passed its statute in 1994, it joined the ranks of 15 States that mandated arrest for domestic violence offenses and 19 States that mandated arrest for domestic restraining order violations. [It] is clear that the elimination of police discretion was integral to Colorado and its fellow States' solution to the problem of underenforcement in domestic violence cases. Since the text of Colorado's statute perfectly captures this legislative purpose, it is hard to imagine what the Court has in mind when it insists on 'some stronger indication from the Colorado Legislature.' "

"While Colorado case law does not speak to the question, it is instructive that other state courts interpreting their analogous statutes have not only held that they eliminate the police's traditional discretion to refuse enforcement, but have also recognized that they create rights enforceable against the police under state law. [To] what extent the Colorado Supreme Court would agree with the views of these courts is, of course, an open question, but it does seem rather brazen for the majority to assume that the Colorado Supreme Court would repudiate this consistent line of persuasive authority from other States.

"Indeed, the Court fails to come to terms with the wave of domestic violence statutes that provides the crucial context for understanding Colorado's law. [The] innovation of the domestic violence statutes was to make police enforcement, not 'more mandatory,' but simply *mandatory*. If, as the Court says, the existence of a protected 'entitlement' turns on whether 'government officials may grant or deny it in their discretion,' the new mandatory statutes undeniably create an entitlement to police enforcement of restraining orders.

"[The] statute directs that, upon probable cause of a violation, 'a peace officer shall arrest, of, if an arrest would be impractical under the circumstances, seek a warrant for the arrest of a restrained person.' Regardless of whether the enforcement called for in this case was arrest or the seeking of an arrest warrant (the answer to that question probably changed over the course of the night as the respondent gave the police more information about the husband's whereabouts), the crucial point is that, under the statute, the police were *required* to provide enforcement; *they lacked the discretion to do nothing*. The Court suggests that the fact that 'enforcement' may encompass different acts infects any entitlement to enforcement with 'indeterminacy.' But this objection is also unfounded. Our cases have never required the object of an entitlement to be some mechanistic, unitary thing. Suppose a State entitled every citizen whose income was under a certain level to receive health care at a state clinic. The provision of health care is not a unitary thing–doctors and administrators must decide what tests are called for and what procedures are required, and these decisions often involve difficult applications of judgment. But it could not credibly be said that a citizen lacks an entitlement to health care simply because the content of that entitlement is not the same in every given situation. Similarly, the enforcement of a restraining order is not some amorphous, indeterminate thing. Under the statute, if the police have probable cause that a violation has occurred, enforcement consists of either making an immediate arrest or seeking a warrant and then executing an arrest–traditional, well-defined tasks that law enforcement officers perform every day. * * *

"Because the statute's guarantee of police enforcement is triggered by, and operates only in reference to, a judge's granting of a restraining order in favor or an identified 'protected person,' there is simply no room to suggest that such a person has received merely an 'incidental' or 'indirect' benefit. As one state court put it, domestic restraining order statutes 'identify with precision when, to whom, and under what circumstances police protection must be afforded. The legislative purpose in requiring the police to enforce individual restraining orders clearly is to protect the named persons for whose protection the order is issued, not to protect the community at large by general law enforcement activity.' * * *

"Given that Colorado law has quite clearly eliminated the police's discretion to deny enforcement, respondent is correct that she had [a] 'legitimate claim of entitlement' to enforcement. Recognizing respondent's property interest in the enforcement of her restraining order is fully consistent with our precedent. This Court has 'made clear that the property interests protected by procedural due process extend well beyond actual ownership of real estate, chattels, or money.' The 'types of interests protected as "property" are varied and, as often as not, intangible, "relating to the whole domain of social and economic fact." ' *Logan v. Zimmerman Brush Co.*

"Police enforcement of a restraining order is a government service that is no less concrete and no less valuable than other government services, such as education. The relative novelty of recognizing this type of property interest is explained by the relative novelty of the domestic violence statutes creating a mandatory arrest duty; before this innovation, the unfettered discretion that characterized police enforcement defeated any citizen's 'legitimate claim of entitlement' to this service. Novel or not, respondent's claim finds strong support in the principles that underlie our due process jurisprudence. In this case, Colorado law *guaranteed* the provision of a certain service, in certain defined circumstances, to a certain class of beneficiaries, and respondent reasonably relied on that guarantee. [Surely,] if respondent had contracted with a private security firm to provide her and her daughters with protection from her husband, it would be apparent that she possessed a property interest in such a contract. Here, Colorado undertook a comparable obligation, and respondent—with restraining order in hand—justifiably relied on that undertaking. Respondent's claim of entitlement to this promised service is no less legitimate than the other claims our cases have upheld, and no less concrete than a hypothetical agreement with a private firm. The fact that it is based on a statutory enactment and a judicial order extended for her special protection, rather than on a formal contract, does not provide a principled basis for refusing to consider it 'property' worthy of constitutional protection. * * *

"Because respondent had a property interest in the enforcement of the restraining order, state officials could not deprive her of that interest without observing fair procedures. Her description of the police behavior in this case and the department's callous policy of failing to respond properly to reports of restraining order violations clearly alleges a due process violation. At the very least, due process requires that the relevant state decisionmaker *listen* to the claimant and then *apply the relevant criteria* in reaching this decision."

CONSTITUTIONAL—CRIMINAL PROCEDURE

ARREST, SEARCH AND SEIZURE

PROTECTED AREAS AND INTERESTS

AMER CON: P. 403, at end of section

RTS & LIB: P. 160, at end of section

KYLLO v. UNITED STATES

533 U.S. 27, 121 S.Ct. 2038, 150 L.Ed.2d 94 (2001).

JUSTICE SCALIA delivered the opinion of the Court.

[Suspicious that marijuana was being grown in Kyllo's home in a triplex, federal agents used a thermal imaging device to scan the triplex to determine if the heat emanating from it was consistent with the high-intensity lamps typically used for indoor marijuana growth. Based in part on the thermal imaging (which disclosed that Kyllo's garage roof and a side wall were relatively hot compared to the rest of his home), the agents obtained a warrant to search Kyllo's home. The search revealed marijuana growing.]

This case presents the question whether the use of a thermal-imaging device aimed at a private home from a public street to detect relative amounts of heat within the home constitutes a "search" within the meaning of the Fourth Amendment. * * *

It would be foolish to contend that the degree of privacy secured to citizens by the Fourth Amendment has been entirely unaffected by the advance of technology. For example, [the] technology enabling human flight has exposed to public view (and hence, we have said, to official observation) uncovered portions of the house and its curtilage that once were private. The question we confront today is what limits there are upon this power of technology to shrink the realm of guaranteed privacy.

The *Katz* test—whether the individual has an expectation of privacy that society is prepared to recognize as reasonable—has often been criticized as circular, and hence subjective and unpredictable. While it may be difficult to refine *Katz* when the search of areas such as telephone booths, automobiles, or even the curtilage and uncovered portions of residences are at issue, in the case of the search of the interior of homes—the prototypical and hence most commonly litigated area of protected privacy—there is a ready criterion, with roots deep in the common law, of the minimal expectation of privacy that *exists,* and that is acknowledged to be *reasonable.* To withdraw protection of this minimum expectation would be to permit police technology to erode the privacy guaranteed by the Fourth Amendment. We think that obtaining by sense-enhancing technology any information regarding the interior of the home that could not otherwise have been obtained without physical "intrusion into a constitutionally protected area" constitutes a search—at least where (as here) the technology in question is not in general public use. This assures preservation of that degree of privacy against government that existed when the Fourth Amendment was adopted. On the basis of this criterion, the information obtained by the thermal imager in this case was the product of a search.[2]

The Government maintains, however, that the thermal imaging must be upheld because it detected "only heat radiating from the external surface of the house." The dissent makes this its leading point, contending that there is a fundamental difference between what it calls "off-the-wall" observations and "through-the-wall surveillance." But just as a thermal imager captures only heat emanating from a house, so also a powerful directional microphone picks up only sound emanating from a house—and a satellite capable of scanning from many miles away would pick up only visible light emanating from a house. We rejected such a mechanical interpretation of the Fourth Amendment in *Katz,* where the eavesdropping device picked up only sound waves that reached the exterior of the phone booth. Reversing that approach would leave the homeowner at the mercy of advancing technology—including imaging technology that could discern all human activity in the home. While the technology used in the present case was relatively crude, the rule we adopt must take account of more sophisticated systems that are already in use or in development.[3]

[The] Government also contends that the thermal imaging was constitutional because it did not "detect private activities occurring in private areas." [The] Fourth Amendment's protection of the home has never been tied to measurement of the quality or quantity of information obtained. [Thus,] in *Karo,* the only thing detected was a can of ether in the home; and in *Arizona v. Hicks,* 480 U.S. 321, 107 S.Ct. 1149, 94 L.Ed.2d 347 (1987), the only thing detected by a physical search that went beyond what officers lawfully present could observe in "plain view" was

2. The dissent's repeated assertion that the thermal imaging did not obtain information regarding the interior of the home, is simply inaccurate. A thermal imager reveals the relative heat of various rooms in the home. The dissent may not find that information particularly private or important, but there is no basis for saying it is not information regarding the interior of the home. The dissent's comparison of the thermal imaging to various circumstances in which outside observers might be able to perceive, without technology, the heat of the home—for example, by observing snowmelt on the roof—is quite irrelevant. The fact that equivalent information could sometimes be obtained by other means does not make lawful the use of means that violate the Fourth Amendment. The police might, for example, learn how many people are in a particular house by setting up year-round surveillance; but that does not make breaking and entering to find out the same information lawful. In any event, on the night of January 16, 1992, no outside observer could have discerned the relative heat of Kyllo's home without thermal imaging.

3. The ability to "see" through walls and other opaque barriers is a clear, and scientifically feasible, goal of law enforcement research and development. The National Law Enforcement and Corrections Technology Center, a program within the United States Department of Justice, features on its Internet Website projects that include a "Radar-Based Through-the-Wall Surveillance System," "Handheld Ultrasound Through the Wall Surveillance," and a "Radar Flashlight" that "will enable law officers to detect individuals through interior building walls." www.nlectc.org/techproj/ (visited May 3, 2001). Some devices may emit low levels of radiation that travel "through-the-wall," but others, such as more sophisticated thermal imaging devices, are entirely passive, or "off-the-wall" as the dissent puts it.

the registration number of a phonograph turntable. These were intimate details because they were details of the home, just as was the detail of how warm—or even how relatively warm—Kyllo was heating his residence.

Limiting the prohibition of thermal imaging to "intimate details" would not only be wrong in principle; it would be impractical in application, failing to provide "a workable accommodation between the needs of law enforcement and the interests protected by the Fourth Amendment." To begin with, there is no necessary connection between the sophistication of the surveillance equipment and the "intimacy" of the details that it observes—which means that one cannot say (and the police cannot be assured) that use of the relatively crude equipment at issue here will always be lawful. [We] would have to develop a jurisprudence specifying which home activities are "intimate" and which are not. And even when (if ever) that jurisprudence were fully developed, no police officer would be able to know *in advance* whether his through-the-wall surveillance picks up "intimate" details—and thus would be unable to know in advance whether it is constitutional.

The dissent's proposed standard—whether the technology offers the "functional equivalent of actual presence in the area being searched"—would seem quite similar to our own at first blush. The dissent concludes that *Katz* was such a case, but then inexplicably asserts that if the same listening device only revealed the volume of the conversation, the surveillance would be permissible. Yet if, without technology, the police could not discern volume without being actually present in the phone booth, Justice Stevens should conclude a search has occurred. [The] same should hold for the interior heat of the home if only a person present in the home could discern the heat. Thus the driving force of the dissent, despite its recitation of the above standard, appears to be a distinction among different types of information—whether the "homeowner would even care if anybody noticed." The dissent offers no practical guidance for the application of this standard, and for reasons already discussed, we believe there can be none. The people in their houses, as well as the police, deserve more precision.

We have said that the Fourth Amendment draws "a firm line at the entrance to the house." That line, we think, must be not only firm but also bright—which requires clear specification of those methods of surveillance that require a warrant. While it is certainly possible to conclude from the videotape of the thermal imaging that occurred in this case that no "significant" compromise of the homeowner's privacy has occurred, we must take the long view, from the original meaning of the Fourth Amendment forward.

[Where,] as here, the Government uses a device that is not in general public use, to explore details of the home that would previously have been unknowable without physical intrusion, the surveillance is a "search" and is presumptively unreasonable without a warrant.

Since we hold the Thermovision imaging to have been an unlawful search, it will remain for the District Court to determine whether, without the evidence it provided, the search warrant issued in this case was supported by probable cause—and if not, whether there is any other basis for supporting admission of the evidence that the search pursuant to the warrant produced.

JUSTICE STEVENS, with whom the CHIEF JUSTICE, JUSTICE O'CONNOR, and JUSTICE KENNEDY join, dissenting. * * *

While the Court "take[s] the long view" and decides this case based largely on the potential of yet-to-be-developed technology that might allow "through-the-wall surveillance," this case involves nothing more than off-the-wall surveillance by law enforcement officers to gather information exposed to the general public from the outside of petitioner's home. All that the infrared camera did in this case was passively measure heat emitted from the exterior surfaces of petitioner's home; all that those measurements showed were relative differences in emission levels, vaguely indicating that some areas of the roof and outside walls were warmer than others. As still images from the infrared scans show, no details regarding the interior of petitioner's home were revealed. Unlike an x-ray scan, or other possible "through-the-wall" techniques, the detection of infrared radiation emanating from the home did not accomplish "an unauthorized physical penetration into the premises," nor did it "obtain information that it could not have obtained by observation from outside the curtilage of the house." *Karo.*

Indeed, the ordinary use of the senses might enable a neighbor or passerby to notice the heat emanating from a building, particularly if it is vented, as was the case here. Additionally, any member of the public might notice that one part of a house is warmer than another part or a nearby building if, for example, rainwater evaporates or snow melts at different rates across its surfaces. Such use of the senses would not convert into an unreasonable search if, instead, an adjoining neighbor allowed an officer onto her property to verify her perceptions with a sensitive thermometer. Nor, in my view, does such observation become an unreasonable search if made from a distance with the aid of a device that merely discloses that the exterior of one house, or one area of the house, is much warmer than another. Nothing more occurred in this case. * * *

Notwithstanding the implications of today's decision, there is a strong public interest in avoiding constitutional litigation over the monitoring of emissions from homes, and over the inferences drawn from such monitoring. Just as "the police cannot reasonably be expected to avert their eyes from evidence of criminal activity that could have been observed by any member of the public," *Greenwood,* so too public officials should not have to avert their senses or their equipment from detecting emissions in the public domain such as excessive heat, traces of smoke, suspicious odors, odorless gases, airborne particulates, or radioactive emissions, any of which could identify hazards to the community. In my judgment, monitoring such emissions with "sense-enhancing technology," and drawing useful conclusions from such monitoring, is an entirely reasonable public service.

On the other hand, the countervailing privacy interest is at best trivial. After all, homes generally are insulated to keep heat in, rather than to prevent the detection of heat going out, and it does not seem to me that society will suffer from a rule requiring the rare homeowner who both intends to engage in uncommon activities that produce extraordinary amounts of heat, and wishes to conceal that production from outsiders, to make sure that the surrounding area is well insulated. * * *

Despite the Court's attempt to draw a line that is "not only firm but also bright," the contours of its new rule are uncertain because its protection apparently dissipates as soon as the relevant technology is "in general public use." Yet how much use is general public use is not even hinted at by the Court's opinion, which makes the somewhat doubtful assumption that the thermal imager used in this case does not satisfy that criterion.[5] In any event, putting aside its lack of

5. The record describes a device that numbers close to a thousand manufactured units; that has a predecessor numbering in the neighborhood of 4,000 to 5,000 units; that competes with a similar product numbering from 5,000 to 6,000 units; and that is "readily available to the public" for commercial, personal, or law enforcement purposes, and is just an 800-num-

clarity, this criterion is somewhat perverse because it seems likely that the threat to privacy will grow, rather than recede, as the use of intrusive equipment becomes more readily available.

It is clear, however, that the category of "sense-enhancing technology" covered by the new rule, is far too broad. It would, for example, embrace potential mechanical substitutes for dogs trained to react when they sniff narcotics. But in *United States v. Place,* 462 U.S. 696, 707, 103 S.Ct. 2637, 77 L.Ed.2d 110 (1983), we held that a dog sniff that "discloses only the presence or absence of narcotics" does "not constitute a 'search' within the meaning of the Fourth Amendment," and it must follow that sense-enhancing equipment that identifies nothing but illegal activity is not a search either. Nevertheless, the use of such a device would be unconstitutional under the Court's rule, as would the use of other new devices that might detect the odor of deadly bacteria or chemicals for making a new type of high explosive. * * *

Because the new rule applies to information regarding the "interior" of the home, it is too narrow as well as too broad. Clearly, a rule that is designed to protect individuals from the overly intrusive use of sense-enhancing equipment should not be limited to a home. If such equipment did provide its user with the functional equivalent of access to a private place—such as, for example, the telephone booth involved in *Katz,* or an office building—then the rule should apply to such an area as well as to a home.

[The] two reasons advanced by the Court as justifications for the adoption of its new rule are both unpersuasive. First, the Court suggests that its rule is compelled by our holding in *Katz,* because in that case, as in this, the surveillance consisted of nothing more than the monitoring of waves emanating from a private area into the public domain. Yet there are critical differences between the cases. In *Katz,* the electronic listening device attached to the outside of the phone booth allowed the officers to pick up the content of the conversation inside the booth, making them the functional equivalent of intruders because they gathered information that was otherwise available only to someone inside the private area; it would be as if, in this case, the thermal imager presented a view of the heat-generating activity inside petitioner's home. By contrast, the thermal imager here disclosed only the relative amounts of heat radiating from the house; it would be as if, in *Katz,* the listening device disclosed only the relative volume of sound leaving the booth, which presumably was discernible in the public domain. * * *

Second, the Court argues that the permissibility of "through-the-wall surveillance" cannot depend on a distinction between observing "intimate details" such as "the lady of the house [taking] her daily sauna and bath," and noticing only "the nonintimate rug on the vestibule floor" or "objects no smaller than 36 by 36 inches." This entire argument assumes, of course, that the thermal imager in this case could or did perform "through-the-wall surveillance" that could identify any detail "that would previously have been unknowable without physical intrusion." In fact, the device could not, and did not enable its user to identify either the lady of the house, the rug on the vestibule floor, or anything else inside the house, whether smaller or larger than 36 by 36 inches.

[Although] the Court is properly and commendably concerned about the threats to privacy that may flow from advances in the technology available to the

ber away from being rented from "half a dozen national companies" by anyone who wants one. Since, by virtue of the Court's new rule, the issue is one of first impression, perhaps it should order an evidentiary hearing to determine whether these facts suffice to establish "general public use."

law enforcement profession, it has unfortunately failed to heed the tried and true counsel of judicial restraint. Instead of concentrating on the rather mundane issue that is actually presented by the case before it, the Court has endeavored to craft an all-encompassing rule for the future. It would be far wiser to give legislators an unimpeded opportunity to grapple with these emerging issues rather than to shackle them with prematurely devised constitutional constraints. * * *

POLICE INTERROGATION AND CONFESSIONS

Can Congress "Repeal" *Miranda?*

AMER CON: P. 387, after note 2

RTS & LIB: P. 251, after note 2

Congress vs. the Court. How significant is it that in *Dickerson* the Court confronted a federal statute that purported to overrule one of the Court's most famous cases? Consider Craig Bradley, *Behind the Dickerson Decision*, Trial, Oct. 2000, at 80: "In *Dickerson*, the majority sent a strong message to Congress: Stay off our turf."

Was § 3501 a good faith response to the Court's invitation to Congress to produce alternative safeguards to the *Miranda* rules? No, answers Susan R. Klein, *Identifying and (Re)Formulating Prophylactic Rules, Safe Harbors, and Incidental Rights in Constitutional Criminal Procedure*, 99 Mich. L. Rev. 1030, 1057 (2001), § 3501 was "an angry, disrespectful, and disingenuous attempt" to "overrule a decision [Congress] loathed." Consider, too, Michael C. Dorf & Barry Friedman, *Shared Constitutional Interpretation,* 2000 Sup. Ct. 61 (forthcoming): "[Section § 3501] was a slap at the Court and if any Court was likely to slap back, it was this one. For the Court that in recent years has given [us] *Boerne v. Flores* and other decisions favoring its own power at the expense of Congress, Section 3501 was a gnat that ran into the windshield of whatever it was that *Miranda* held."

INDIVIDUAL RIGHTS AND THE WAR ON TERRORISM
[New Section]

RTS & LIB: P. 283, before Chapter 5

HAMDI v. RUMSFELD

542 U.S. 507, 124 S.Ct. 2633, 159 L.Ed.2d 578 (2004).

[P. ___ of this Supplement].

FREEDOM OF EXPRESSION AND ASSOCIATION

WHAT SPEECH IS NOT PROTECTED?

OWNERSHIP OF SPEECH [NEW PART]

CON LAW: P. 645, after note 4

AMER CON: P. 632, after note 4

RTS & LIB: P. 572, after note 4

Former President Ford had contracted with Harper & Row and Readers Digest to publish his memoirs and granted them the right to license prepublication excerpts concentrating on his pardon of former President Nixon. Some weeks before a licensed article in Time was to appear, an unknown person presented the editor of The Nation with an unauthorized copy of the 200,000 word Ford manuscript from which the editor wrote a 2,250 word article entitled, "The Ford Memoirs—Behind the Nixon Pardon." The article included 26 verbatim quotations totaling 300 words of Ford's copyrighted expression and was timed to scoop Time. Accordingly, Time cancelled its article and refused to pay the publishers the remaining half of its $25,000 contract price.

In defense against the publishers' copyright claim, The Nation maintained that its publication was protected by the fair use provision of the Copyright Revision Act of 1976, 17 U.S.C. § 107 and by the first amendment. HARPER & ROW v. NATION ENTERPRISES, 471 U.S. 539, 105 S.Ct. 2218, 85 L.Ed.2d 588 (1985), per O'CONNOR, J., concluded that neither defense was viable and that the fair use provision properly accommodated the relevant first amendment interests: "Article I, § 8, of the Constitution provides that: 'The Congress shall have Power * * * to Promote the Progress of Science and useful Arts, by securing for limited Times to Authors and Inventors the exclusive Right to their respective Writings and Discoveries.' '[This] limited grant is a means by which an important public purpose may be achieved. It is intended to motivate the creative activity of authors and inventors by the provision of a special reward, and to allow the public access to the products of their genius after the limited period of exclusive control has expired.' The monopoly created by copyright thus rewards the individual author in order to benefit the public. This principle applies equally to works of fiction and nonfiction. The book at issue here, for example, was two years in the making, and began with a contract giving the author's copyright to the publishers in exchange for their services in producing and marketing the work. In preparing the book, Mr. Ford drafted essays and word portraits of public figures and participated in hundreds of taped interviews that were later distilled to chronicle his personal viewpoint. It is evident that the monopoly granted by copyright actively served its intended purpose of inducing the creation of new material of potential historical value.

"Section 106 of the Copyright Act confers a bundle of exclusive rights to the owner of the copyright. [T]hese rights—to publish, copy, and distribute the author's work—vest in the author of an original work from the time of its creation. In practice, the author commonly sells his rights to publishers who offer royalties in exchange for their services in producing and marketing the author's work. The copyright owner's rights, however, are subject to certain statutory exceptions. Among these is § 107 which codifies the traditional privilege of other authors to make 'fair use' of an earlier writer's work.[1] In addition, no author may copyright facts or ideas. § 102. The copyright is limited to those aspects of the work—termed 'expression'—that display the stamp of the author's originality.

"[T]here is no dispute that the unpublished manuscript of 'A Time to Heal,' as a whole, was protected by § 106 from unauthorized reproduction. Nor do respondents dispute that verbatim copying of excerpts of the manuscript's original form of expression would constitute infringement unless excused as fair use. Yet copyright does not prevent subsequent users from copying from a prior author's work those constituent elements that are not original—for example, quotations borrowed under the rubric of fair use from other copyrighted works, facts, or materials in the public domain—as long as such use does not unfairly appropriate the author's original contributions. Perhaps the controversy between the lower courts in this case over copyrightability is more aptly styled a dispute over whether The Nation's appropriation of unoriginal and uncopyrightable elements encroached on the originality embodied in the work as a whole. Especially in the realm of factual narrative, the law is currently unsettled regarding the ways in which uncopyrightable elements combine with the author's original contributions to form protected expression.

"We need not reach these issues, however, as The Nation has admitted to lifting verbatim quotes of the author's original language [constituting] some 13% of The Nation article. [To thereby] lend authenticity to its account of the forthcoming memoirs, The Nation effectively arrogated to itself the right of first publication, an important marketable subsidiary right. For the reasons set forth below, we find that this use of the copyrighted manuscript, even stripped to the verbatim quotes conceded by The Nation to be copyrightable expression, was not a fair use within the meaning of the Copyright Act.

"[The] nature of the interest at stake is highly relevant to whether a given use is fair. [The] right of first publication implicates a threshold decision by the author whether and in what form to release his work. First publication is inherently different from other § 106 rights in that only one person can be the first publisher; as the contract with Time illustrates, the commercial value of the right lies primarily in exclusivity. [Under] ordinary circumstances, the author's

1. Section 107 states: "Notwithstanding the provisions of section 106, the fair use of a copyrighted work [for] purposes such as criticism, comment, news reporting, teaching (including multiple copies for classroom use), scholarship, or research, is not an infringement of copyright. In determining whether the use made of a work in any particular case is a fair use the factors to be considered shall include—

"(1) the purpose and character of the use, including whether such use is of a commercial nature or is for nonprofit educational purposes;

"(2) the nature of the copyrighted work;

"(3) the amount and substantiality of the portion used in relation to the copyrighted work as a whole; and

"(4) the effect of the use upon the potential market for or value of the copyrighted work."

right to control the first public appearance of his undisseminated expression will outweigh a claim of fair use.

"Respondents, however, contend that First Amendment values require a different rule under the circumstances of this case. [Respondents] advance the substantial public import of the subject matter of the Ford memoirs as grounds for excusing a use that would ordinarily not pass muster as a fair use—the piracy of verbatim quotations for the purpose of 'scooping' the authorized first serialization. Respondents explain their copying of Mr. Ford's expression as essential to reporting the news story it claims the book itself represents. In respondents' view, not only the facts contained in Mr. Ford's memoirs, but 'the precise manner in which [he] expressed himself was as newsworthy as what he had to say.' Respondents argue that the public's interest in learning this news as fast as possible outweighs the right of the author to control its first publication.

"The Second Circuit noted, correctly, that copyright's idea/expression dichotomy 'strike[s] a definitional balance between the First Amendment and the Copyright Act by permitting free communication of facts while still protecting an author's expression.' No author may copyright his ideas or the facts he narrates.

"Respondents' theory, however, would expand fair use to effectively destroy any expectation of copyright protection in the work of a public figure. Absent such protection, there would be little incentive to create or profit in financing such memoirs and the public would be denied an important source of significant historical information. The promise of copyright would be an empty one if it could be avoided merely by dubbing the infringement a fair use 'news report' of the book. * * *

"In our haste to disseminate news, it should not be forgotten that the Framers intended copyright itself to be the engine of free expression. By establishing a marketable right to the use of one's expression, copyright supplies the economic incentive to create and disseminate ideas. * * *

"Moreover, freedom of thought and expression 'includes both the right to speak freely and the right to refrain from speaking at all.' We do not suggest this right not to speak would sanction abuse of the copyright owner's monopoly as an instrument to suppress facts. [But] 'the essential thrust of the First Amendment is to prohibit improper restraints on the *voluntary* public expression of ideas; it shields the man who wants to speak or publish when others wish him to be quiet. There is necessarily, and within suitably defined areas, a concomitant freedom *not* to speak publicly, one which serves the same ultimate end as freedom of speech in its affirmative aspect.' *Estate of Hemingway v. Random House, Inc.,* 23 N.Y.2d 341, 348, 296 N.Y.S.2d 771, 776, 244 N.E.2d 250, 255 (1968). * * *

"In view of the First Amendment protections already embodied in the Copyright Act's distinction between copyrightable expression and uncopyrightable facts and ideas, and the latitude for scholarship and comment traditionally afforded by fair use, we see no warrant for expanding the doctrine of fair use to create what amounts to a public figure exception to copyright. Whether verbatim copying from a public figure's manuscript in a given case is or is not fair must be judged according to the traditional equities of fair use."

In assessing the equities, the Court found the purpose of the article to count against fair use, noting that the publication "went beyond simply reporting uncopyrightable information" and made "a 'news event' out of its unauthorized first publication," that the publication was "commercial as opposed to non-profit," that The Nation intended to supplant the "right of first publication," and that it acted in bad faith, for it "knowingly exploited a purloined manuscript." In considering the nature of the copyrighted work, the Court found it significant not only that Ford's work was yet unpublished, but also that The Nation had focused "on the most expressive elements of the work" in a way that exceeded "that necessary to disseminate the facts" and in a "clandestine" fashion that afforded no "opportunity for creative or quality control" by the copyright holder. In evaluating the amount and substantiality of the portion used, the Court cited the district court finding that "The Nation took what was essentially the heart of the book" and pointed to the "expressive value of the excerpts and their key role in the infringing work." Finally, the Court observed that the effect of the use on the market for the copyrighted work was the most important element. It found the Time contract cancellation to be "clear cut evidence of actual damage."

BRENNAN, J., joined by White and Marshall, JJ., dissented: "When The Nation was not quoting Mr. Ford, [its] efforts to convey the historical information in the Ford manuscript did not so closely and substantially track Mr. Ford's language and structure as to constitute an appropriation of literary form.

"[The] Nation is thus liable in copyright only if the quotation of 300 words infringed any of Harper & Row's exclusive rights under § 106 of the Act. [Limiting] the inquiry to the propriety of a subsequent author's use of the copyright owner's literary form is not easy in the case of a work of history. Protection against only substantial appropriation of literary form does not ensure historians a return commensurate with the full value of their labors. The literary form contained in works like 'A Time to Heal' reflects only a part of the labor that goes into the book. It is the labor of collecting, sifting, organizing and reflecting that predominates in the creation of works of history such as this one. The value this labor produces lies primarily in the information and ideas revealed, and not in the particular collocation of words through which the information and ideas are expressed. Copyright thus does not protect that which is often of most value in a work of history and courts must resist the tendency to reject the fair use defense on the basis of their feeling that an author of history has been deprived of the full value of his or her labor. A subsequent author's taking of information and ideas is in no sense piratical because copyright law simply does not create any property interest in information and ideas.

"The urge to compensate for subsequent use of information and ideas is perhaps understandable. An inequity seems to lurk in the idea that much of the fruit of the historian's labor may be used without compensation. This, however, is not some unforeseen by-product of a statutory scheme intended primarily to ensure a return for works of the imagination. Congress made the affirmative choice that the copyright laws should apply in this way: 'Copyright does not preclude others from using the ideas or information revealed by the author's work. It pertains to the literary [form] in which the author expressed intellectual concepts.' This distinction is at the essence of copyright. The copyright laws serve as the 'engine of free expression,' only when the statutory monopoly does not choke off multifarious indirect uses and consequent broad dissemination of information and ideas. To ensure the progress of arts and sciences and the integrity of First Amendment values, ideas and information must not be freighted with claims of proprietary right.[13]

13. This congressional limitation on the scope of copyright does not threaten the production of history. That this limitation results in significant diminution of economic incentives is far from apparent. In any event noneconomic incentives motivate much historical research and writing. For example, former public officials often have great incentive to

"In my judgment, the Court's fair use analysis has fallen to the temptation to find copyright violation based on a minimal use of literary form in order to provide compensation for the appropriation of information from a work of history."

Since news reporting is ordinarily conducted for profit and marked by attempts to "scoop" the opposition and by attempts to create "news events," Brennan, J., found the drawing of any negative implications from these factors to be inconsistent with congressional recognition in § 107 that news reporting is a prime example of fair use. He found reliance on bad faith to be equally unwarranted: "No court has found that The Nation possessed the Ford manuscript illegally or in violation of any common law interest of Harper & Row; all common law causes of action have been abandoned or dismissed in this case. Even if the manuscript had been 'purloined' by someone, nothing in this record imputes culpability to The Nation. On the basis of the record in this case, the most that can be said is that The Nation made use of the contents of the manuscript knowing the copyright owner would not sanction the use.

"[T]he Court purports to rely on [the] factual findings that The Nation had taken 'the heart of the book.' This reliance is misplaced, and would appear to be another result of the Court's failure to distinguish between information and literary form. When the District Court made this finding, it was evaluating not the quoted words at issue here but the 'totality' of the information and reflective commentary in the Ford work. The vast majority of what the District Court considered the heart of the Ford work, therefore, consisted of ideas and information The Nation was free to use. It may well be that, as a qualitative matter, most of the value of the manuscript did lie in the information and ideas the Nation used. But appropriation of the 'heart' of the manuscript in this sense is irrelevant to copyright analysis because copyright does not preclude a second author's use of information and ideas.

"At least with respect to the six particular quotes of Mr. Ford's observations and reflections about President Nixon, I agree with the Court's conclusion that The Nation appropriated some literary form of substantial quality. I do not agree, however, that the substantiality of the expression taken was clearly excessive or inappropriate to The Nation's news reporting purpose.

"Had these quotations been used in the context of a critical book review of the Ford work, there is little question that such a use would be fair use within the meaning of § 107 of the Act. The amount and substantiality of the use—in both quantitative and qualitative terms—would have certainly been appropriate to the purpose of such a use. It is difficult to see how the use of these quoted words in a news report is less appropriate.

"The Nation's publication indisputably precipitated Time's eventual cancellation. But that does not mean that The Nation's use of the 300 quoted words caused this injury to Harper & Row. Wholly apart from these quoted words, The Nation published significant information and ideas from the Ford manuscript. [If] The Nation competed with Time, the competition was not for a share of the market in excerpts of literary form but for a share of the market in the new information in the Ford work. * * *

"Because The Nation was the first to convey the information in this case, it did perhaps take from Harper & Row some of the value that publisher sought to

"tell their side of the story." And much history is the product of academic scholarship. Perhaps most importantly, the urge to preserve the past is as old as human kind.

garner for itself through the contractual arrangement with Ford and the license to Time. Harper & Row had every right to seek to monopolize revenue from that potential market through contractual arrangements but it has no right to set up copyright [as] a shield from competition in that market because copyright does not protect information. The Nation had every right to seek to be the first to publish that information. * * *

"The Court's exceedingly narrow approach to fair use permits Harper & Row to monopolize information. This holding 'effect[s] an important extension of property rights and a corresponding curtailment in the free use of knowledge and of ideas.' The Court has perhaps advanced the ability of the historian—or at least the public official who has recently left office—to capture the full economic value of information in his or her possession. But the Court does so only by risking the robust debate of public issues that is the 'essence of self-government.' *Garrison*. The Nation was providing the grist for that robust debate. The Court imposes liability upon The Nation for no other reason than that The Nation succeeded in being the first to provide certain information to the public."

Notes and Questions

1. Assume The Nation acquires a "purloined" manuscript of Chief Justice Burger's memoirs. Assume Time is soon to publish exclusive excerpts from his forthcoming book. The editors of The Nation want to run a news story about the book before the Time article appears. They want to know whether they can write a story, whether they can quote from the book, what they should do to reduce the risk in writing the story, and whether their right to quote from the book would be enhanced if they made their story a book review. Advise.

2. Will *Harper & Row* chill freedom of the press? Does it matter? To what extent was the Court influenced by the belief that there was no immediate need for the public to know about the Ford memoirs? Suppose California outlaws broadcast presentations in California of presidential election results (and exit polls or the like) until after the California polls have closed. Constitutional?[a]

3. *Gertz* was reluctant to make ad hoc judgments as to whether statements are or are not of general or public interest. Should the Court be similarly reluctant to make ad hoc judgments as to the bona fide news purpose of an article,[b] as to whether expression goes to the "heart of the book," or whether quoted words are "necessary" to communicate the "facts"? Is there an alternative to the making of such judgments?[c]

a. For commentary, see Fischer, *Network "Early Calls" of Elections,* 14 Sw.U.L.Rev. 428 (1984); Note, *Exit Polls and the First Amendment,* 98 Harv.L.Rev. 1927 (1985); Comment, *Restricting the Broadcast of Election Day Projections: A Justifiable Protection of the Right to Vote,* 9 U.Dayton L.Rev. 297 (1984).

b. Compare *Regan v. Time, Inc.,* 468 U.S. 641, 104 S.Ct. 3262, 82 L.Ed.2d 487 (1984): 18 U.S.C. § 474 makes it a crime to photograph United States currency, but exceptions for articles and books for newsworthy purposes are permitted so long as certain size and color requirements are satisfied. 18 U.S.C. § 504. The Court, per White, J., invalidated the purpose requirement: "A determination concerning the newsworthiness [of] a photograph cannot help but be based on the content of the photograph and the message it delivers. [Regulations] which permit the Government to discriminate on the basis of the content of the message cannot be tolerated under the First Amendment. The purpose requirement of § 504 is therefore constitutionally infirm." Stevens, J., dissenting on this point, observed that if the Court's language were applied literally, the constitutionality of the fair use provision of the Copyright Act would be "highly suspect."

c. For a variety of approaches to the fair use issue, see Dratler, *Distilling the Witches' Brew of Fair Use in Copyright Law,* 43 U.Miami L.Rev. 233 (1988); Elkin–Koren, *Cyberlaw* and Social Change, 14 Cardoza Arts & Ent.

4. Melville Nimmer had argued that in most cases the idea/expression dichotomy is central to resolving the clash between copyright and the first amendment. *Does Copyright Abridge the First Amendment Guarantees of Free Speech and Press?* 17 U.C.L.A.L.Rev. 1180 (1970). Is the distinction satisfactory?[d] Consider *Cohen v. California,* protecting Cohen's use of the phrase "Fuck the Draft": "[W]e cannot indulge the facile assumption that one can forbid particular words without running a substantial risk of suppressing ideas in the process." Cohen's counsel was—Professor Nimmer. Does *Nimmer On Copyright* collide with *Nimmer on Freedom of Speech?* For Nimmer's answer, see id. § 2.05(c), at 72–77; § 3.04, at 28 n. 11.

5. The 1976 Copyright Act generally provided copyright protection until 50 years after an author's death. The Copyright Term Extension Act of 1998 ("CTEA") extended the term to 70 years for new and existing copyrights. ELDRED v. ASHCROFT, 537 U.S. 186, 123 S.Ct. 769, 154 L.Ed.2d 683 (2003), per GINSBURG, J., upheld the Act against a claim that the extended copyright protection to already existing intellectual property was unconstitutional: "Petitioners [argue] that the CTEA is a content-neutral regulation of speech that fails heightened judicial review under the First Amendment. We reject petitioners' plea for imposition of uncommonly strict scrutiny on a copyright scheme that incorporates its own speech-protective purposes and safeguards. The Copyright Clause and First Amendment were adopted close in time. This proximity indicates that, in the Framers' view, copyright's limited monopolies are compatible with free speech principles. Indeed, copyright's purpose is to *promote* the creation and publication of free expression. * * *

"In addition to spurring the creation and publication of new expression, copyright law contains built-in First Amendment accommodations. First, it distinguishes between ideas and expression and makes only the latter eligible for copyright protection. [Due] to this distinction, every idea, theory, and fact in a copyrighted work becomes instantly available for public exploitation at the moment of publication. * * *

"Second, the 'fair use' defense allows the public to use not only facts and ideas contained in a copyrighted work, but also expression itself in certain circumstances. [The] fair use defense affords considerable 'latitude for scholarship and comment,' and even for parody. The CTEA itself supplements these traditional First Amendment safeguards. First, it allows libraries, archives, and similar institutions to 'reproduce' and 'distribute, display, or perform in facsimile or digital form' copies of certain published works 'during the last 20 years of any term of copyright [for] purposes of preservation, scholarship, or research' if the work is not already being exploited commercially and further copies are unavailable at a reasonable price. Second, Title II of the CTEA, known as the Fairness in

L.Rev. 215 (1996); Fewer, *Constitutionalizing Copyright: Freedom of Expression and the Limits of Copyright in Canada,* U.Toronto Fac. L.Rev. 175 (1997); Fisher, *Reconstructing the Fair Use Doctrine,* 101 Harv.L.Rev. 1659 (1988); Gordon, *Fair Use as Market Failure: A Structural and Economic Analysis of the Betamax Case and Its Predecessors,* 82 Colum.L.Rev. 1600 (1982); Leval, *Toward a Fair Use Standard,* 103 Harv.L.Rev. 1105 (1990); Nanantel, *Copyright and a Democratic Civil Society,* 106 Yale L.J. 283 (1996); Weinreb, *Fair's Fair: A Comment on the Fair Use Doctrine,* 103 Harv.L.Rev. 1137 (1990).

d. For commentary, see Benkler, *Free as the Air to Common Use, First Amendment Constraints on Enclosure of the First Amendment Domain,* 74 N.Y.U.L. Rev. 354 (1999); Lemley & Volokh, *Freedom of Speech and Injunctions in Intellectual Property Cases,* 48 Duke L.J. 147 (1998); Goldstein, *Copyright and the First Amendment,* 70 Colum.L.Rev. 983 (1970); Patterson & Birch, *Copyright and Free Speech Rights,* 4 J. Intell. Prop.L. 1 (1997); Zimmerman, *Information as Speech, Information as Goods,* 33 Wm. & Mary L.Rev 665 (1992).

Music Licensing Act of 1998, exempts small businesses, restaurants, and like entities from having to pay performance royalties on music played from licensed radio, television, and similar facilities. * * *

"The First Amendment securely protects the freedom to make—or decline to make—one's own speech; it bears less heavily when speakers assert the right to make other people's speeches. To the extent such assertions raise First Amendment concerns, copyright's built-in free speech safeguards are generally adequate to address them. [W]hen, as in this case, Congress has not altered the traditional contours of copyright protection, further First Amendment scrutiny is unnecessary."

Breyer, J., dissented: "The Copyright Clause and the First Amendment seek related objectives—the creation and dissemination of information. When working in tandem, these provisions mutually reinforce each other, the first serving as an 'engine of free expression,' the second assuring that government throws up no obstacle to its dissemination. At the same time, a particular statute that exceeds proper Copyright Clause bounds may set Clause and Amendment at cross-purposes, thereby depriving the public of the speech-related benefits that the Founders, through both, have promised. [The] majority [invokes] the 'fair use' exception, and it notes that copyright law itself is restricted to protection of a work's expression, not its substantive content. Neither the exception nor the restriction, however, would necessarily help those who wish to obtain from electronic databases material that is not there—say, teachers wishing their students to see albums of Depression Era photographs, to read the recorded words of those who actually lived under slavery, or to contrast, say, Gary Cooper's heroic portrayal of Sergeant York with filmed reality from the battlefield of Verdun. Such harm, and more, will occur despite the 1998 Act's exemptions and despite the other 'First Amendment safeguards' in which the majority places its trust. The statute falls outside the scope of legislative power that the Copyright Clause, read in light of the First Amendment, grants to Congress."[e]

SHOULD NEW CATEGORIES BE CREATED?

HARM TO CHILDREN AND THE OVERBREADTH DOCTRINE

CON LAW: P. 688, after note 5

AMER CON: P. 669, after note 5

RTS & LIB: P. 615, after note 5

6. *Digital child pornography.* The Child Pornography Act of 1996 (the "CPPA") in addition to outlawing child pornography involving minors, extends its

e. Although the majority argued that the act created incentives for the copyright holders to further invest in and disseminate their property, Breyer, J., rejoined: "This claim cannot justify this statute, however, because the rationale is inconsistent with the basic purpose of the Copyright Clause—as understood by the Framers and by this Court. The Clause assumes an initial grant of monopoly, designed primarily to encourage creation, followed by termination of the monopoly grant in order to promote dissemination of already-created works. It assumes that it is the *disappearance* of the monopoly grant, not its *perpetuation,* that will, on balance, promote the dissemination of works already in existence. This view of the Clause does not deny the empirical possibility that grant of a copyright monopoly to the heirs or successors of a long-dead author could *on occasion* help publishers resurrect the work, say, of a long-lost Shakespeare. But it does deny Congress the Copyright Clause power to base its actions primarily upon that empirical possibility—lest copyright grants become perpetual, lest on balance they restrict dissemination, lest too often they seek to bestow benefits that are solely retroactive." Stevens, J., also dissented.

coverage to prohibit images that "appear to be, of a minor engaging in sexually explicit conduct" or marketed in a way that "conveys the impression" that it depicts a "minor engaging in sexually explicit conduct." ASHCROFT v. FREE SPEECH COALITION, per KENNEDY, J., declared these provisions to be unconstitutional: "The CPPA [extends] to images that appear to depict a minor engaging in sexually explicit activity without regard to the *Miller* requirements. The materials need not appeal to the prurient interest. Any depiction of sexually explicit activity, no matter how it is presented, is proscribed. The CPPA applies to a picture in a psychology manual, as well as a movie depicting the horrors of sexual abuse. It is not necessary, moreover, that the image be patently offensive. Pictures of what appear to be 17-year-olds engaging in sexually explicit activity do not in every case contravene community standards.

"The CPPA prohibits speech despite its serious literary, artistic, political, or scientific value. The statute proscribes the visual depiction of [the idea] of teenagers engaging in sexual activity that is a fact of modern society and has been a theme in art and literature throughout the ages." Kennedy, J., argued that the Act could potentially apply to versions of Romeo and Juliet and films like Traffic and American Beauty.

"[The government] argues that the CPPA is necessary because pedophiles may use virtual child pornography to seduce children. There are many things innocent in themselves, however, such as cartoons, video games, and candy, that might be used for immoral purposes, yet we would not expect those to be prohibited because they can be misused. The Government, of course, may punish adults who provide unsuitable materials to children, and it may enforce criminal penalties for unlawful solicitation. The precedents establish, however, that speech within the rights of adults to hear may not be silenced completely in an attempt to shield children from it. [The Government] submits further that virtual child pornography whets the appetites of pedophiles and encourages them to engage in illegal conduct. This rationale cannot sustain the provision in question. The mere tendency of speech to encourage unlawful acts is not a sufficient reason for banning it. * * *

"Finally, the Government says that the possibility of producing images by using computer imaging makes it very difficult for it to prosecute those who produce pornography by using real children. Experts, we are told, may have difficulty in saying whether the pictures were made by using real children or by using computer imaging. The necessary solution, the argument runs, is to prohibit both kinds of images. The argument, in essence, is that protected speech may be banned as a means to ban unprotected speech. This analysis turns the First Amendment upside down. The Government may not suppress lawful speech as the means to suppress unlawful speech."[a]

THOMAS, J., concurred: "In my view, the Government's most persuasive asserted interest [is] the prosecution rationale that persons who possess and disseminate pornographic images of real children may escape conviction by claiming that the images are computer-generated, thereby raising a reasonable doubt as to their guilt. At this time, however, the Government asserts only that defendants raise such defenses, not that they have done so successfully. In fact, the Government points to no case in which a defendant has been acquitted based on a

a. In overthrowing the "conveys the impression provision," Kennedy, J., argued that it applied to a substantial amount of material that could not be reached by anti-pandering obscenity law and wrongfully proscribed possession of material that was distributed in a manner conveying a false impression even when the possessor knew the impression was false."

computer-generated images defense. While this speculative interest cannot support the broad reach of the CPPA, technology may evolve to the point where it becomes impossible to enforce actual child pornography laws because the Government cannot prove that certain pornographic images are of real children. * * *

"The Court suggests that the Governments interest in enforcing prohibitions against real child pornography cannot justify prohibitions on virtual child pornography, because 'this analysis turns the First Amendment upside down.' [But] if technological advances thwart prosecution of unlawful speech, the Government may well have a compelling interest in barring or otherwise regulating some narrow category of lawful speech in order to enforce effectively laws against pornography made through the abuse of real children."

O'Connor, J., concurring in part and dissenting in part, agreed that the act's attempt to ban sexually explicit images of adults that appear to be children was overbroad, but, in a portion of her opinion joined by Rehnquist, C.J., and Scalia, J., she argued that the prohibitions of computer generated sexually explicit images appearing to be children or conveying that impression were constitutional: "[D]efendants indicted for the production, distribution, or possession of actual-child pornography may evade liability by claiming that the images attributed to them are in fact computer-generated. Respondents may be correct that no defendant has successfully employed this tactic. But, given the rapid pace of advances in computer-graphics technology, the Governments concern is reasonable. Computer-generated images lodged with the Court bear a remarkable likeness to actual human beings. [T]his Court's cases do not require Congress to wait for harm to occur before it can legislate against it.

"The Court concludes that the CPPAs ban on virtual-child pornography is overbroad. The basis for this holding is unclear. [Respondents] provide no examples of films or other materials that are wholly computer-generated and contain images that 'appea[r] to be' of minors engaging in indecent conduct, but that have serious value or do not facilitate child abuse."

Rehnquist, C.J., joined in part by Scalia, J.,[b] dissenting, would have construed the statute to apply to "visual depictions of youthful looking adult actors engaged in actual sexual activity; mere suggestions of sexual activity, such as youthful looking adult actors squirming under a blanket, are more akin to written descriptions than visual depictions, and thus fall outside the purview of the statute. The reference to simulated has been part of the definition of sexually explicit conduct since the statute was first passed. But the inclusion of simulated conduct, alongside actual conduct, does not change the hard core nature of the image banned. The reference to simulated conduct simply brings within the statute's reach depictions of hard core pornography that are made to look genuine including the main target of the CPPA, computer generated images virtually indistinguishable from real children engaged in sexually explicit conduct. Neither actual conduct nor simulated conduct, however, is properly construed to reach depictions such as those in a film portrayal of Romeo and Juliet which are far removed from the hard core pornographic depictions that Congress intended to reach.

"To the extent the CPPA prohibits possession or distribution of materials that convey the impression of a child engaged in sexually explicit conduct, that prohibition can and should be limited to reach the sordid business of pandering which lies outside the bounds of First Amendment protection. [The] First Amend-

b. Scalia, J., did not join a portion of Rehnquist, C.J.'s opinion discussing the statute's legislative history.

ment may protect the video shopowner or film distributor who promotes material as 'entertaining' or 'acclaimed' regardless of whether the material contains depictions of youthful looking adult actors engaged in nonobscene but sexually suggestive conduct. The First Amendment does not, however, protect the panderer. Thus, materials promoted as conveying the impression that they depict actual minors engaged in sexually explicit conduct do not escape regulation merely because they might warrant First Amendment protection if promoted in a different manner. * * *

"In sum, while potentially impermissible applications of the CPPA may exist, I doubt that they would be substantial in relation to the statute's plainly legitimate sweep. The aim of ensuring the enforceability of our Nation's child pornography laws is a compelling one. The CPPA is targeted to this aim by extending the definition of child pornography to reach computer-generated images that are virtually indistinguishable from real children engaged in sexually explicit conduct. The statute need not be read to do any more than precisely this, which is not offensive to the First Amendment."

JUDICIAL ELECTIONS [NEW PART]

CON LAW: P. 710, after note 10

AMER CON: P. 691, after note 10

RTS & LIB: P. 637, after note 10

REPUBLICAN PARTY OF MINNESOTA v. WHITE, 536 U.S. 765, 122 S.Ct. 2528, 153 L.Ed.2d 694 (2002), per SCALIA, J., invalidated a Minnesota Supreme Court canon of judicial conduct that prohibited candidates for judicial election in that State from announcing their views on disputed legal and political issues ("the announce clause"): "[T]he announce clause both prohibits speech on the basis of its content and burdens a category of speech that is 'at the core of our First Amendment freedoms'—speech about the qualifications of candidates for public office. The Court of Appeals concluded that the proper test to be applied to determine the constitutionality of such a restriction is what our cases have called strict scrutiny; the parties do not dispute that this is correct. Under the strict-scrutiny test, respondents have the burden to prove that the announce clause is (1) narrowly tailored, to serve (2) a compelling state interest.

"The Court of Appeals concluded that respondents had established two interests as sufficiently compelling to justify the announce clause: preserving the impartiality of the state judiciary and preserving the appearance of the impartiality of the state judiciary. Respondents reassert these two interests before us, arguing that the first is compelling because it protects the due process rights of litigants, and that the second is compelling because it preserves public confidence in the judiciary. Respondents are rather vague, however, about what they mean by 'impartiality.' [Clarity] on this point is essential before we can decide whether impartiality is indeed a compelling state interest, and, if so, whether the announce clause is narrowly tailored to achieve it.

"One meaning of 'impartiality' in the judicial context—and of course its root meaning—is the lack of bias for or against either *party* to the proceeding. Impartiality in this sense assures equal application of the law. That is, it guarantees a party that the judge who hears his case will apply the law to him in the same way he applies it to any other party. This is the traditional sense in which the term is used. * * *

"We think it plain that the announce clause is not narrowly tailored to serve impartiality (or the appearance of impartiality) in this sense. Indeed, the clause is barely tailored to serve that interest *at all*, inasmuch as it does not restrict speech for or against particular *parties*, but rather speech for or against particular *issues*. To be sure, when a case arises that turns on a legal issue on which the judge (as a candidate) had taken a particular stand, the party taking the opposite stand is likely to lose. But not because of any bias against that party, or favoritism toward the other party. *Any* party taking that position is just as likely to lose. * * *

"It is perhaps possible to use the term 'impartiality' in the judicial context (though this is certainly not a common usage) to mean lack of preconception in favor of or against a particular *legal* view. This sort of impartiality would be concerned, not with guaranteeing litigants equal application of the law, but rather with guaranteeing them an equal chance to persuade the court on the legal points in their case. Impartiality in this sense may well be an interest served by the announce clause, but it is not a *compelling* state interest, as strict scrutiny requires. A judge's lack of predisposition regarding the relevant legal issues in a case has never been thought a necessary component of equal justice, and with good reason. For one thing, it is virtually impossible to find a judge who does not have preconceptions about the law. [The] Minnesota Constitution positively forbids the selection to courts of general jurisdiction of judges who are impartial in the sense of having no views on the law. Minn. Const., Art. VI, § 5 ('Judges of the supreme court, the court of appeals and the district court shall be learned in the law'). And since avoiding judicial preconceptions on legal issues is neither possible nor desirable, pretending otherwise by attempting to preserve the 'appearance' of that type of impartiality can hardly be a compelling state interest either.

"A third possible meaning of "impartiality" (again not a common one) might be described as openmindedness. This quality in a judge demands, not that he have no preconceptions on legal issues, but that he be willing to consider views that oppose his preconceptions, and remain open to persuasion, when the issues arise in a pending case. This sort of impartiality seeks to guarantee each litigant, not an *equal* chance to win the legal points in the case, but at least *some* chance of doing so. It may well be that impartiality in this sense, and the appearance of it, are desirable in the judiciary, but we need not pursue that inquiry, since we do not believe the Minnesota Supreme Court adopted the announce clause for that purpose.

"[S]tatements in election campaigns are such an infinitesimal portion of the public commitments to legal positions that judges (or judges-to-be) undertake, that this object of the prohibition is implausible. Before they arrive on the bench (whether by election or otherwise) judges have often committed themselves on legal issues that they must later rule upon. More common still is a judge's confronting a legal issue on which he has expressed an opinion while on the bench. Most frequently, of course, that prior expression will have occurred in ruling on an earlier case. But judges often state their views on disputed legal issues outside the context of adjudication—in classes that they conduct, and in books and speeches. Like the ABA Codes of Judicial Conduct, the Minnesota Code not only permits but encourages this. See Minn. Code of Judicial Conduct, Canon 4(B) (2002) ('A judge may write, lecture, teach, speak and participate in other extra-judicial activities concerning the law * * * '); Minn. Code of Judicial Conduct, Canon 4(B), Comment. (2002) ('To the extent that time permits, a judge is encouraged to do so * * * '). That is quite incompatible with the notion that the need for openmindedness (or for the appearance of openmindedness) lies behind the prohibition at issue here. * * *

"Justice Stevens asserts that statements made in an election campaign pose a special threat to openmindedness because the candidate, when elected judge, will have a particular reluctance to contradict them. That might be plausible, perhaps, with regard to campaign *promises*. [But] the Minnesota Supreme Court has adopted a separate prohibition on campaign 'pledges or promises,' which is not challenged here. The proposition that judges feel significantly greater compulsion, or appear to feel significantly greater compulsion, to maintain consistency with *nonpromissory* statements made during a judicial campaign than with such statements made before or after the campaign is not self-evidently true. It seems to us quite likely, in fact, that in many cases the opposite is true. We doubt, for example, that a mere statement of position enunciated during the pendency of an election will be regarded by a judge as more binding—or as more likely to subject him to popular disfavor if reconsidered—than a carefully considered holding that the judge set forth in an earlier opinion denying some individual's claim to justice. In any event, it suffices to say that respondents have not carried the burden imposed by our strict-scrutiny test to establish this proposition (that campaign statements are uniquely destructive of openmindedness) on which the validity of the announce clause rests.

"Moreover, the notion that the special context of electioneering justifies an *abridgment* of the right to speak out on disputed issues sets our First Amendment jurisprudence on its head. '[D]ebate on the qualifications of candidates' is 'at the core of our electoral process and of the First Amendment freedoms,' not at the edges. [We] have never allowed the government to prohibit candidates from communicating relevant information to voters during an election.

"Justice Ginsburg would do so—and much of her dissent confirms rather than refutes our conclusion that the purpose behind the announce clause is not openmindedness in the judiciary, but the undermining of judicial elections. She contends that the announce clause must be constitutional because due process would be denied if an elected judge sat in a case involving an issue on which he had previously announced his view. She reaches this conclusion because, she says, such a judge would have a 'direct, personal, substantial, and pecuniary interest' in ruling consistently with his previously announced view, in order to reduce the risk that he will be 'voted off the bench and thereby lose [his] salary and emoluments,' But elected judges—regardless of whether they have announced any views beforehand—*always* face the pressure of an electorate who might disagree with their rulings and therefore vote them off the bench. [So] if, as Justice Ginsburg claims, it violates due process for a judge to sit in a case in which ruling one way rather than another increases his prospects for reelection, then—quite simply—the practice of electing judges is itself a violation of due process. * * *

"Justice Ginsburg devotes the rest of her dissent to attacking arguments we do not make. For example, [we] neither assert nor imply that the First Amendment requires campaigns for judicial office to sound the same as those for legislative office. [But] in any case, Justice Ginsburg greatly exaggerates the difference between judicial and legislative elections. She asserts that 'the rationale underlying unconstrained speech in elections for political office—that representative government depends on the public's ability to choose agents who will act at its behest—does not carry over to campaigns for the bench.' This complete separation of the judiciary from the enterprise of 'representative government' might have some truth in those countries where judges neither make law themselves nor set aside the laws enacted by the legislature. It is not a true picture of the American system. Not only do state-court judges possess the power to 'make' common law, but they have the immense power to shape the States' constitutions as well. * * *

"There is an obvious tension between the article of Minnesota's popularly approved Constitution which provides that judges shall be elected, and the Minnesota Supreme Court's announce clause which places most subjects of interest to the voters off limits. [The] disparity is perhaps unsurprising, since the ABA, which originated the announce clause, has long been an opponent of judicial elections. [That] opposition may be well taken (it certainly had the support of the Founders of the Federal Government), but the First Amendment does not permit it to achieve its goal by leaving the principle of elections in place while preventing candidates from discussing what the elections are about."

O'CONNOR, J., concurred: "I join the opinion of the Court but write separately to express my concerns about judicial elections generally. * * * I am concerned that, even aside from what judicial candidates may say while campaigning, the very practice of electing judges undermines this interest. [I]f judges are subject to regular elections they are likely to feel that they have at least some personal stake in the outcome of every publicized case. Elected judges cannot help being aware that if the public is not satisfied with the outcome of a particular case, it could hurt their reelection prospects. * * *

"Moreover, contested elections generally entail campaigning. And campaigning for a judicial post today can require substantial funds. Unless the pool of judicial candidates is limited to those wealthy enough to independently fund their campaigns, a limitation unrelated to judicial skill, the cost of campaigning requires judicial candidates to engage in fundraising. Yet relying on campaign donations may leave judges feeling indebted to certain parties or interest groups. Even if judges were able to refrain from favoring donors, the mere possibility that judges' decisions may be motivated by the desire to repay campaign contributors is likely to undermine the public's confidence in the judiciary.

"Despite these significant problems, 39 States currently employ some form of judicial elections for their appellate courts, general jurisdiction trial courts, or both. [M]innesota has chosen to select its judges through contested popular elections instead of through an appointment system or a combined appointment and retention election system * * * . In doing so the State has voluntarily taken on the risks to judicial bias described above. As a result, the State's claim that it needs to significantly restrict judges' speech in order to protect judicial impartiality is particularly troubling. If the State has a problem with judicial impartiality, it is largely one the State brought upon itself by continuing the practice of popularly electing judges."

KENNEDY, J., concurred: "[C]ontent-based speech restrictions that do not fall within any traditional exception should be invalidated without inquiry into narrow tailoring or compelling government interests. The speech at issue here does not come within any of the exceptions to the First Amendment recognized by the Court. [The] political speech of candidates is at the heart of the First Amendment, and direct restrictions on the content of candidate speech are simply beyond the power of government to impose. * * *

"This case does not present the question whether a State may restrict the speech of judges because they are judges—for example, as part of a code of judicial conduct; the law at issue here regulates judges only when and because they are candidates. [Petitioner] Gregory Wersal was not a sitting judge but a challenger; he had not voluntarily entered into an employment relationship with the State or surrendered any First Amendment rights. His speech may not be controlled or abridged in this manner. Even the undoubted interest of the State in the excellence of its judiciary does not allow it to restrain candidate speech by reason of its content. Minnesota's attempt to regulate campaign speech is impermissible."

STEVENS, J., joined by Souter, Ginsburg and Breyer JJ., dissented: "By recognizing a conflict between the demands of electoral politics and the distinct characteristics of the judiciary, we do not have to put States to an all or nothing choice of abandoning judicial elections or having elections in which anything goes. As a practical matter, we cannot know for sure whether an elected judge's decisions are based on his interpretation of the law or political expediency. In the absence of reliable evidence one way or the other, a State may reasonably presume that elected judges are motivated by the highest aspirations of their office. But we do know that a judicial candidate, who announces his views in the context of a campaign, is effectively telling the electorate: 'Vote for me because I believe X, and I will judge cases accordingly.' Once elected, he may feel free to disregard his campaign statements, but that does not change the fact that the judge announced his position on an issue likely to come before him *as a reason to vote for him*. Minnesota has a compelling interest in sanctioning such statements.

"A candidate for judicial office who goes beyond the expression of 'general observation about the law [in] order to obtain favorable consideration' of his candidacy demonstrates either a lack of impartiality or a lack of understanding of the importance of maintaining public confidence in the impartiality of the judiciary. * * *

"Even when 'impartiality' is defined in its narrowest sense to embrace only 'the lack of bias for or against either party to the proceeding,' the announce clause serves that interest. Expressions that stress a candidate's unbroken record of affirming convictions for rape, for example, imply a bias in favor of a particular litigant (the prosecutor) and against a class of litigants (defendants in rape cases). * * *

"The Court boldly asserts that respondents have failed to carry their burden of demonstrating 'that campaign statements are uniquely destructive of openmindedness,' But the very purpose of most statements prohibited by the announce clause is to convey the message that the candidate's mind is not open on a particular issue. [T]he judicial reputation for impartiality and openmindedness is compromised by electioneering that emphasizes the candidate's personal predilections rather than his qualifications."[4]

GINSBURG, J., joined by Stevens, Souter and Breyer, JJ., dissented: "I would differentiate elections for political offices, in which the First Amendment holds full sway, from elections designed to select those whose office it is to administer justice without respect to persons. Minnesota's choice to elect its judges, I am persuaded, does not preclude the State from installing an election process geared to the judicial office.

"Legislative and executive officials serve in representative capacities. They are agents of the people; their primary function is to advance the interests of their constituencies. Candidates for political offices, in keeping with their representative role, must be left free to inform the electorate of their positions on specific

4. Justice Kennedy would go even further and hold that no content-based restriction of a judicial candidate's speech is permitted under the First Amendment. While he does not say so explicitly, this extreme position would preclude even Minnesota's prohibition against 'pledges or promises' by a candidate for judicial office. Minn. Code of Judicial Conduct, Canon 5(A)(3)(d)(i) (2002). A candidate could say 'vote for me because I promise to never reverse a rape conviction,' and the Board could do nothing to formally sanction that candidate. The unwisdom of this proposal illustrates why the same standards should not apply to speech in campaigns for judicial and legislative office.

issues. Armed with such information, the individual voter will be equipped to cast her ballot intelligently, to vote for the candidate committed to positions the voter approves. * * *

"Judges, however, are not political actors. They do not sit as representatives of particular persons, communities, or parties; they serve no faction or constituency. [Even] when they develop common law or give concrete meaning to constitutional text, judges act only in the context of individual cases, the outcome of which cannot depend on the will of the public. * * *

"Thus, the rationale underlying unconstrained speech in elections for political office—that representative government depends on the public's ability to choose agents who will act at its behest—does not carry over to campaigns for the bench. [In] view of the magisterial role judges must fill in a system of justice, a role that removes them from the partisan fray, States may limit judicial campaign speech by measures impermissible in elections for political office.

"The Court sees in this conclusion, and in the Announce Clause that embraces it, 'an obvious tension': The Minnesota electorate is permitted to select its judges by popular vote, but is not provided information on 'subjects of interest to the voters'—in particular, the voters are not told how the candidate would decide controversial cases or issues if elected. This supposed tension, however, rests on the false premise that by departing from the federal model with respect to who chooses judges, Minnesota necessarily departed from the federal position on the *criteria* relevant to the exercise of that choice. * * *

"Although the Court is correct that th[e] 'pledges or promises' provision is not directly at issue in this case, the Court errs in overlooking the interdependence of that prohibition and the one before us. In my view, the constitutionality of the Announce Clause cannot be resolved without an examination of that interaction in light of the interests the pledges or promises provision serves. [Pledges] or promises of conduct in office, however commonplace in races for the political branches, are inconsistent 'with the judge's obligation to decide cases in accordance with his or her role.' This judicial obligation to avoid prejudgment corresponds to the litigant's right, protected by the Due Process Clause of the Fourteenth Amendment, to 'an impartial and disinterested tribunal in both civil and criminal cases,' The proscription against pledges or promises thus represents an accommodation of 'constitutionally protected interests [that] lie on both sides of the legal equation.' Balanced against the candidate's interest in free expression is the litigant's 'powerful and independent constitutional interest in fair adjudicative procedure.' * * *

"When a judicial candidate promises to rule a certain way on an issue that may later reach the courts, the potential for due process violations is grave and manifest. If successful in her bid for office, the judicial candidate will become a judge, and in that capacity she will be under pressure to resist the pleas of litigants who advance positions contrary to her pledges on the campaign trail. If the judge fails to honor her campaign promises, she will not only face abandonment by supporters of her professed views, she will also 'ris[k] being assailed as a dissembler,' willing to say one thing to win an election and to do the opposite once in office.

"A judge in this position therefore may be thought to have a 'direct, personal, substantial, [and] pecuniary interest' in ruling against certain litigants, for she may be voted off the bench and thereby lose her salary and emoluments unless she honors the pledge that secured her election. Given this grave danger to litigants from judicial campaign promises, States are justified in barring expression of such commitments, for they typify the 'situatio[n] * * * in which experience teaches that the probability of actual bias on the part of the judge [is] too high to be constitutionally tolerable.' By removing this source of 'possible temptation' for a judge to rule on the basis of self-interest, the pledges or promises prohibition furthers the State's 'compellin[g] interest in maintaining a judiciary fully capable of performing' its appointed task * * * .

"Prohibiting a judicial candidate from pledging or promising certain results if elected directly promotes the State's interest in preserving public faith in the bench. When a candidate makes such a promise during a campaign, the public will no doubt perceive that she is doing so in the hope of garnering votes. And the public will in turn likely conclude that when the candidate decides an issue in accord with that promise, she does so at least in part to discharge her undertaking to the voters in the previous election and to prevent voter abandonment in the next. The perception of that unseemly quid pro quo—a judicial candidate's promises on issues in return for the electorate's votes at the polls—inevitably diminishes the public's faith in the ability of judges to administer the law without regard to personal or political self-interest.[4] * * *

"Uncoupled from the Announce Clause, the ban on pledges or promises is easily circumvented. By prefacing a campaign commitment with the caveat, 'although I cannot promise anything,' or by simply avoiding the language of promises or pledges altogether, a candidate could declare with impunity how she would decide specific issues. Semantic sanitizing of the candidate's commitment would not, however, diminish its pernicious effects on actual and perceived judicial impartiality. * * *

"By targeting statements that do not technically constitute pledges or promises but nevertheless 'publicly mak[e] known how [the candidate] would decide' legal issues, the Announce Clause prevents this end run around the letter and spirit of its companion provision. No less than the pledges or promises clause itself, the Announce Clause is an indispensable part of Minnesota's effort to maintain the health of its judiciary, and is therefore constitutional for the same reasons."

DISTINGUISHING BETWEEN CONTENT REGULATION AND MANNER REGULATION: UNCONVENTIONAL FORMS OF COMMUNICATION

CON LAW: P. 737, after note 3

AMER CON: P. 718, after note 3

RTS & LIB: P. 664, after note 3

4. *Arcara extended?* The Richmond Redevelopment and Housing Authority barred Hicks from trespassing on property where public low income housing existed in the absence of permission from the manager of the housing project. VIRGINIA v. HICKS, 539 U.S. 113, 123 S.Ct. 2191, 156 L.Ed.2d 148 (2003), per Scalia, J., held that the bar was not substantially overbroad since it prevented a

4. The author of the Court's opinion declined on precisely these grounds to tell the Senate whether he would overrule a particular case: "Let us assume that I have people arguing before me to do it or not to do it. I think it is quite a thing to be arguing to somebody who you know has made a representation in the course of his confirmation hearings, and that is, by way of condition to his being confirmed, that he will do this or do that. I think I would be in a very bad position to adjudicate the case without being accused of having a less than impartial view of the matter."

wide range of conduct, and that even if Hicks wanted to enter the property to speak or leaflet, the bar would properly be applied: "Neither the basis for the barment sanction (the prior trespass) nor its purpose (preventing prior trespasses) has anything to do with the First Amendment."[e]

IS SOME PROTECTED SPEECH LESS EQUAL THAN OTHER PROTECTED SPEECH?

NEAR OBSCENE SPEECH

CON LAW: P. 748, after note 3

AMER CON: P. 723, after note 3

RTS & LIB: P. 675, after note 3

4. Yet another adult business zoning case, LOS ANGELES v. ALAMEDA BOOKS, 535 U.S. 425, 122 S.Ct. 1728, 152 L.Ed.2d 670 (2002) per O'CONNOR, J., found a sufficient showing of secondary effects to permit Los Angeles not only to disperse adult businesses, but also to prohibit more than one adult entertainment business within the same building, i.e., a company could not have an adult bookstore and an adult video arcade in the same building.

SCALIA, J., concurring, would have gone further: "[I]n a case such as this our First Amendment traditions make secondary effects analysis quite unnecessary. The Constitution does not prevent those communities that wish to do so from regulating, or indeed entirely suppressing, the business of pandering sex."

KENNEDY, J., concurring, interpreted *Renton* to require a city to "advance some basis to show that its regulation has the purpose and effect of suppressing secondary effects, while leaving the quantity and accessibility of speech substantially intact. The ordinance may identify the speech based on content, but only as a shorthand for identifying the secondary effects outside. A city may not assert that it will reduce secondary effects by reducing speech in the same proportion. [The] rationale of the ordinance must be that it will suppress secondary effects and not by suppressing speech." Kennedy, J., found that Los Angeles ordinance met this burden.

SOUTER, J., joined by Stevens and Ginsburg, JJ., and in part by Breyer, J., dissented: "[W]hile it may be true that an adult business is burdened only because of its secondary effects, it is clearly burdened only if its expressive products have adult content. Thus, the Court has recognized that this kind of regulation, though called content neutral, occupies a kind of limbo between full-blown, content-based restrictions and regulations that apply without any reference to the substance of what is said.

"It would in fact make sense to give this kind of zoning regulation a First Amendment label of its own, and if we called it content correlated, we would not only describe it for what it is, but keep alert to a risk of content-based regulation that it poses. The risk lies in the fact that when a law applies selectively only to speech of particular content, the more precisely the content is identified, the greater is the opportunity for government censorship. Adult speech refers not merely to sexually explicit content, but to speech reflecting a favorable view of being explicit about sex and a favorable view of the practices it depicts; a

e. Souter, J., joined by Breyer, J., concurred.

restriction on adult content is thus also a restriction turning on a particular viewpoint, of which the government may disapprove.

"This risk of viewpoint discrimination is subject to a relatively simple safeguard, however. If combating secondary effects of property devaluation and crime is truly the reason for the regulation, it is possible to show by empirical evidence that the effects exist, that they are caused by the expressive activity subject to the zoning, and that the zoning can be expected either to ameliorate them or to enhance the capacity of the government to combat them (say, by concentrating them in one area), without suppressing the expressive activity itself. This capacity of zoning regulation to address the practical problems without eliminating the speech is, after all, the only possible excuse for speaking of secondary-effects zoning as akin to time, place, or manner regulations." Souter, J., argued that Los Angeles had not met this burden.[a]

COMMERCIAL SPEECH

CON LAW: P. 778, after note 2

AMER CON: P. 739, after note 2

RTS & LIB: p. 705, after note 2

3. THOMPSON v. WESTERN STATES MEDICAL CENTER, 535 U.S. 357, 122 S.Ct. 1497, 152 L.Ed.2d 563 (2002), per O'CONNOR, J., invalidated advertising restrictions on compounded drugs not subject to FDA standard drug approval requirements in part by concluding that the government did not meet its burden to show that less restrictive alternatives were unavailable.

BREYER, J., joined by Rehnquist, C.J., and Stevens and Ginsburg, JJ., dissenting, argued that the Court's approach to such issues should be flexible. He contended that the Court rightly applied the less demanding *Central Hudson* test because "it has concluded that, from a constitutional perspective, commercial speech does not warrant application of the Court's strictest speech-protective tests. And it has reached this conclusion in part because restrictions on commercial speech do not often repress individual self-expression; they rarely interfere with the functioning of democratic political processes; and they often reflect a democratically determined governmental decision to regulate a commercial venture in order to protect, for example, the consumer, the public health, individual safety, or the environment. [The] Court, in my view, gives insufficient weight to the Government's regulatory rationale, and too readily assumes the existence of practical alternatives. It thereby applies the commercial speech doctrine too strictly. [A]n overly rigid commercial speech doctrine will transform what ought to be a legislative or regulatory decision about the best way to protect the health and safety of the American public into a constitutional decision prohibiting the legislature from enacting necessary protections. As history in respect to the Due Process Clause shows, any such transformation would involve a tragic constitutional misunderstanding."

4. *Defining commercial speech.* In 1996 Nike, Inc. was confronted with allegations that it mistreated and underpaid workers at foreign facilities. Nike attempted to answer these charges with press releases, letters to editors, university presidents and athletic directors, and with a commissioned report by Andrew Young about working conditions in its factories. Kasky, a California resident, sued as a private attorney general under a California statute prohibiting unfair and

a. Breyer, J., joined this section of the opinion, but not the portion quoted supra.

deceptive practices. Kasky alleged that in order to boost sales, Nike made a number of false statements and/or material omissions of fact. Assume that some of Nike's communications went to customers and that some did not. Are any of the communications "commercial speech"? All of them? Compare *Kasky v. Nike, Inc.*, 27 Cal.4th 939, 119 Cal. Rptr.2d 296, 45 P.3d 243 (2002) with *Nike, Inc. v. Kasky*, 539 U.S. 654, 123 S.Ct. 2554, 156 L.Ed.2d 580 (2003)(Breyer, J., joined by O'Connor, J., dissenting from dismissal of the writ as improvidently granted).

LORILLARD TOBACCO CO. v. REILLY

533 U.S. 525, 121 S.Ct. 2404, 150 L.Ed.2d 532 (2001).

JUSTICE O'CONNOR delivered the opinion of the Court.

In January 1999, the Attorney General of Massachusetts promulgated comprehensive regulations governing the advertising and sale of cigarettes, smokeless tobacco, and cigars. Petitioners, a group of cigarette, smokeless tobacco, and cigar manufacturers and retailers, filed suit in Federal District Court claiming that the regulations violate federal law and the United States Constitution.

I. [The purpose] of the cigarette and smokeless tobacco regulations is "to eliminate deception and unfairness in the way cigarettes and smokeless tobacco products are marketed, sold and distributed in Massachusetts in order to address the incidence of cigarette smoking and smokeless tobacco use by children under legal age [and] in order to prevent access to such products by underage consumers." The similar purpose of the cigar regulations is "to eliminate deception and unfairness in the way cigars and little cigars are packaged, marketed, sold and distributed in Massachusetts [so that] consumers may be adequately informed about the health risks associated with cigar smoking, its addictive properties, and the false perception that cigars are a safe alternative to cigarettes [and so that] the incidence of cigar use by children under legal age is addressed [in] order to prevent access to such products by underage consumers." The regulations have a broader scope than [a settlement agreement with the tobacco industry in 1999], reaching advertising, sales practices, and members of the tobacco industry not covered by the agreement. The regulations place a variety of restrictions on outdoor advertising, point-of-sale advertising, retail sales transactions, transactions by mail, promotions, sampling of products, and labels for cigars.

The cigarette and smokeless tobacco regulations being challenged before this Court provide: "(2) Retail Outlet Sales Practices. Except as otherwise provided in [§ 21.04(4)], it shall be an unfair or deceptive act or practice for any person who sells or distributes cigarettes or smokeless tobacco products through a retail outlet located within Massachusetts to engage in any of the following retail outlet sales practices: * * * (c) Using self-service displays of cigarettes or smokeless tobacco products; (d) Failing to place cigarettes and smokeless tobacco products out of the reach of all consumers, and in a location accessible only to outlet personnel." §§ 21.04(2)(c)–(d).

"(5) Advertising Restrictions. Except as provided in [§ 21.04(6)], it shall be an unfair or deceptive act or practice for any manufacturer, distributor or retailer to engage in any of the following practices: (a) Outdoor advertising, including advertising in enclosed stadiums and advertising from within a retail establishment that is directed toward or visible from the outside of the establishment, in any location that is within a 1,000 foot radius of any public playground, playground area in a public park, elementary school or secondary school; (b) Point-of-sale advertising of cigarettes or smokeless tobacco products any portion of which is placed lower than five feet from the floor of any retail establishment which is located within a one thousand foot radius of any public playground, playground area in a public park, elementary school or secondary school, and which is not an adult-only retail establishment." §§ 21.04(5)(a)–(b).

The cigar regulations that are still at issue provide: "(1) Retail Sales Practices. Except as otherwise provided in [§ 22.06(4)], it shall be an unfair or deceptive act or practice for any person who sells or distributes cigars or little cigars directly to consumers within Massachusetts to engage in any of the following practices: (a) sampling of cigars or little cigars or promotional give-aways of cigars or little cigars." § 21.06(1)(a).

"(2) Retail Outlet Sales Practices. [The Court recited practices parallelling those applicable to cigarettes and smokeless tobacco]."

II. [The Court concluded that the Federal Cigarette Labeling and Advertising Act of 1965 as amended, prevented states and localities from regulating the location of cigarette advertising.]

III. By its terms, the FCLAA's pre-emption provision only applies to cigarettes. Accordingly, we must evaluate the smokeless tobacco and cigar petitioners' First Amendment challenges to the State's outdoor and point-of-sale advertising regulations. The cigarette petitioners did not raise a pre-emption challenge to the sales practices regulations. Thus, we must analyze the cigarette as well as the smokeless tobacco and cigar petitioners' claim that certain sales practices regulations for tobacco products violate the First Amendment.

A. [Petitioners] urge us to reject the *Central Hudson* analysis and apply strict scrutiny. [S]everal Members of the Court have expressed doubts about the *Central Hudson* analysis and whether it should apply in particular cases. See, e.g., *44 Liquormart, Inc. v. Rhode Island*, 517 U.S. 484, 501, 510–514, 116 S.Ct. 1495, 134 L.Ed.2d 711 (1996) (joint opinion of Stevens, Kennedy, and Ginsburg, JJ.)(Scalia, J. concurring in part and concurring in judgment)(Thomas, J., concurring in part and concurring in judgment). [But] we see "no need to break new ground. *Central Hudson*, as applied in our more recent commercial speech cases, provides an adequate basis for decision."

Only the last two steps of *Central Hudson*'s four-part analysis are at issue here. The Attorney General has assumed for purposes of summary judgment that petitioners' speech is entitled to First Amendment protection. With respect to the second step, none of the petitioners contests the importance of the State's interest in preventing the use of tobacco products by minors.

The third step of *Central Hudson* concerns the relationship between the harm that underlies the State's interest and the means identified by the State to advance that interest. It requires that "the speech restriction directly and materially advanc[e] the asserted governmental interest. 'This burden is not satisfied by mere speculation or conjecture; rather, a governmental body seeking to sustain a restriction on commercial speech must demonstrate that the harms it recites are real and that its restriction will in fact alleviate them to a material degree.' " We do not, however, require that "empirical data [come] accompanied by a surfeit of background information. [W]e have permitted litigants to justify speech restrictions by reference to studies and anecdotes pertaining to different locales altogether, or even, in a case applying strict scrutiny, to justify restrictions based solely on history, consensus, and 'simple common sense.' "

The last step of the *Central Hudson* analysis "complements" the third step, "asking whether the speech restriction is not more extensive than necessary to serve the interests that support it." We have made it clear that "the least restrictive means" is not the standard; instead, the case law requires a reasonable " 'fit between the legislature's ends and the means chosen to accomplish those ends, [a] means narrowly tailored to achieve the desired objective.' " Focusing on the third and fourth steps of the Central Hudson analysis, we first address the outdoor advertising and point-of-sale advertising regulations for smokeless tobacco and cigars. We then address the sales practices regulations for all tobacco products.

B. The outdoor advertising regulations prohibit smokeless tobacco or cigar advertising within a 1,000–foot radius of a school or playground. * * *

1. The smokeless tobacco and cigar petitioners [maintain] that although the Attorney General may have identified a problem with underage cigarette smoking, he has not identified an equally severe problem with respect to underage use of smokeless tobacco or cigars. The smokeless tobacco petitioner emphasizes the "lack of parity" between cigarettes and smokeless tobacco. The cigar petitioners catalogue a list of differences between cigars and other tobacco products, including the characteristics of the products and marketing strategies. The petitioners finally contend that the Attorney General cannot prove that advertising has a causal link to tobacco use such that limiting advertising will materially alleviate any problem of underage use of their products.

In previous cases, we have acknowledged the theory that product advertising stimulates demand for products, while suppressed advertising may have the opposite effect. *United States v. Edge Broadcasting Co.*, 509 U.S. 418, 434, 113 S.Ct. 2696, 125 L.Ed.2d 345 (1993). The Attorney General cites numerous studies to support this theory in the case of tobacco products. [Our] review of the record reveals that the Attorney General has provided ample documentation of the problem with underage use of smokeless tobacco and cigars. In addition, we disagree with petitioners' claim that there is no evidence that preventing targeted campaigns and limiting youth exposure to advertising will decrease underage use of smokeless tobacco and cigars. On this record and in the posture of summary judgment, we are unable to conclude that the Attorney General's decision to regulate advertising of smokeless tobacco and cigars in an effort to combat the use of tobacco products by minors was based on mere "speculation [and] conjecture."

2. Whatever the strength of the Attorney General's evidence to justify the outdoor advertising regulations, however, we conclude that the regulations do not satisfy the fourth step of the Central Hudson analysis. The final step of the Central Hudson analysis, the "critical inquiry in this case," requires a reasonable fit between the means and ends of the regulatory scheme. The Attorney General's regulations do not meet this standard. The broad sweep of the regulations indicates that the Attorney General did not "carefully calculat[e] the costs and benefits associated with the burden on speech imposed" by the regulations.

The outdoor advertising regulations prohibit any smokeless tobacco or cigar advertising within 1,000 feet of schools or playgrounds. In the District Court, petitioners maintained that this prohibition would prevent advertising in 87% to 91% of Boston, Worchester, and Springfield. The 87% to 91% figure appears to include not only the effect of the regulations, but also the limitations imposed by other generally applicable zoning restrictions. The Attorney General disputed petitioners' figures but "concede[d] that the reach of the regulations is substantial." Thus, the Court of Appeals concluded that the regulations prohibit advertising in a substantial portion of the major metropolitan areas of Massachusetts. * * *

In some geographical areas, these regulations would constitute nearly a complete ban on the communication of truthful information about smokeless tobacco and cigars to adult consumers. The breadth and scope of the regulations, and the process by which the Attorney General adopted the regulations, do not demonstrate a careful calculation of the speech interests involved.

First, the Attorney General did not seem to consider the impact of the 1,000–foot restriction on commercial speech in major metropolitan areas. The Attorney General apparently selected the 1,000–foot distance based on the FDA's decision to impose an identical 1,000–foot restriction when it attempted to regulate cigarette and smokeless tobacco advertising. But the FDA's 1,000–foot regulation was not an adequate basis for the Attorney General to tailor the Massachusetts regulations. The degree to which speech is suppressed—or alternative avenues for speech remain available—under a particular regulatory scheme tends to be case specific. And a case specific analysis makes sense, for although a State or locality may have common interests and concerns about underage smoking and the effects of tobacco advertisements, the impact of a restriction on speech will undoubtedly vary from place to place. The FDA's regulations would have had widely disparate effects nationwide. Even in Massachusetts, the effect of the Attorney General's speech regulations will vary based on whether a locale is rural, suburban, or urban. The uniformly broad sweep of the geographical limitation demonstrates a lack of tailoring.

In addition, the range of communications restricted seems unduly broad. For instance, it is not clear from the regulatory scheme why a ban on oral communications is necessary to further the State's interest. Apparently that restriction means that a retailer is unable to answer inquiries about its tobacco products if that communication occurs outdoors. Similarly, a ban on all signs of any size seems ill suited to target the problem of highly visible billboards, as opposed to smaller signs. To the extent that studies have identified particular advertising and promotion practices that appeal to youth, tailoring would involve targeting those practices while permitting others. As crafted, the regulations make no distinction among practices on this basis. * * *

The State's interest in preventing underage tobacco use is substantial, and even compelling, but it is no less true that the sale and use of tobacco products by adults is a legal activity. We must consider that tobacco retailers and manufacturers have an interest in conveying truthful information about their products to adults, and adults have a corresponding interest in receiving truthful information about tobacco products. [In] some instances, Massachusetts' outdoor advertising regulations would impose particularly onerous burdens on speech. For example, we disagree with the Court of Appeals' conclusion that because cigar manufacturers and retailers conduct a limited amount of advertising in comparison to other tobacco products, "the relative lack of cigar advertising also means that the burden imposed on cigar advertisers is correspondingly small." If some retailers have relatively small advertising budgets, and use few avenues of communication, then the Attorney General's outdoor advertising regulations potentially place a greater, not lesser, burden on those retailers' speech. Furthermore, to the extent that cigar products and cigar advertising differ from that of other tobacco products, that difference should inform the inquiry into what speech restrictions are necessary.

In addition, a retailer in Massachusetts may have no means of communicating to passersby on the street that it sells tobacco products because alternative forms of advertisement, like newspapers, do not allow that retailer to propose an instant transaction in the way that onsite advertising does. The ban on any indoor advertising that is visible from the outside also presents problems in establishments like convenience stores, which have unique security concerns that counsel in favor of full visibility of the store from the outside. It is these sorts of considerations that the Attorney General failed to incorporate into the regulatory scheme.

C. Massachusetts has also restricted indoor, point-of-sale advertising for smokeless tobacco and cigars. Advertising cannot be "placed lower than five feet from the floor of any retail establishment which is located within a one thousand foot radius of" any school or playground. [We] conclude that the point-of-sale advertising regulations fail both the third and fourth steps of the Central Hudson analysis. [T]he State's goal is to prevent minors from using tobacco products and to curb demand for that activity by limiting youth exposure to advertising. The 5 foot rule does not seem to advance that goal. Not all children are less than 5 feet tall, and those who are certainly have the ability to look up and take in their surroundings.

By contrast to Justice Stevens, we do not believe this regulation can be construed as a mere regulation of conduct under *O'Brien*. Here, Massachusetts' height restriction is an attempt to regulate directly the communicative impact of indoor advertising.

The Court of Appeals recognized that the efficacy of the regulation was questionable, but decided that "[i]n any event, the burden on speech imposed by the provision is very limited." There is no de minimis exception for a speech restriction that lacks sufficient tailoring or justification. We conclude that the restriction on the height of indoor advertising is invalid under *Central Hudson*'s third and fourth prongs.

D. The Attorney General also promulgated a number of regulations that restrict sales practices by cigarette, smokeless tobacco, and cigar manufacturers and retailers. * * *

Petitioners devoted little of their briefing to the sales practices regulations, and our understanding of the regulations is accordingly limited by the parties' submissions. As we read the regulations, they basically require tobacco retailers to place tobacco products behind counters and require customers to have contact with a salesperson before they are able to handle a tobacco product.

[Assuming] that petitioners have a cognizable speech interest in a particular means of displaying their products, cf. *Cincinnati v. Discovery Network, Inc.*, 507 U.S. 410, 113 S.Ct. 1505, 123 L.Ed.2d 99 (1993) (distribution of a magazine through newsracks), these regulations withstand First Amendment scrutiny. Massachusetts' sales practices provisions regulate conduct that may have a communicative component, but Massachusetts seeks to regulate the placement of tobacco products for reasons unrelated to the communication of ideas.

[Unattended] displays of tobacco products present an opportunity for access without the proper age verification required by law. Thus, the State prohibits self-service and other displays that would allow an individual to obtain tobacco products without direct contact with a salesperson. It is clear that the regulations leave open ample channels of communication. The regulations do not significantly impede adult access to tobacco products. Moreover, retailers have other means of exercising any cognizable speech interest in the presentation of their products. We presume that vendors may place empty tobacco packaging on open display, and display actual tobacco products so long as that display is only accessible to sales personnel. As for cigars, there is no indication in the regulations that a customer is unable to examine a cigar prior to purchase, so long as that examination takes place through a salesperson. * * *

The means chosen by the State are narrowly tailored to prevent access to tobacco products by minors, are unrelated to expression, and leave open alternative avenues for vendors to convey information about products and for would-be customers to inspect products before purchase.

IV. We have observed that "tobacco use, particularly among children and adolescents, poses perhaps the single most significant threat to public health in the United States." From a policy perspective, it is understandable for the States to attempt to prevent minors from using tobacco products before they reach an age where they are capable of weighing for themselves the risks and potential benefits of tobacco use, and other adult activities. Federal law, however, places limits on policy choices available to the States.

In this case, Congress enacted a comprehensive scheme to address cigarette smoking and health in advertising and pre-empted state regulation of cigarette advertising that attempts to address that same concern, even with respect to youth. The First Amendment also constrains state efforts to limit advertising of tobacco products, because so long as the sale and use of tobacco is lawful for adults, the tobacco industry has a protected interest in communicating information about its products and adult customers have an interest in receiving that information.

To the extent that federal law and the First Amendment do not prohibit state action, States and localities remain free to combat the problem of underage tobacco use by appropriate means. * * *

Justice KENNEDY, with whom Justice SCALIA joins, concurring in part and concurring in the judgment.

The obvious overbreadth of the outdoor advertising restrictions suffices to invalidate them under the fourth part of the test in *Central Hudson*. [My] continuing concerns that the test gives insufficient protection to truthful, nonmisleading commercial speech require me to refrain from expressing agreement with the Court's application of the third part of *Central Hudson*. With the exception of Part III–B–1, then, I join the opinion of the Court.

JUSTICE THOMAS, concurring in part and concurring in the judgment

I join the opinion of the Court (with the exception of Part III–B–1). * * *

I have observed previously that there is no "philosophical or historical basis for asserting that 'commercial' speech is of 'lower value' than 'noncommercial' speech." Indeed, I doubt whether it is even possible to draw a coherent distinction between commercial and noncommercial speech.[2]

It should be clear that if these regulations targeted anything other than advertising for commercial products—if, for example, they were directed at billboards promoting political candidates—all would agree that the restrictions should be subjected to strict scrutiny. In my view, an asserted government interest in keeping people ignorant by suppressing expression "is per se illegitimate and can

2. Tobacco advertising provides a good illustration. The sale of tobacco products is the subject of considerable political controversy, and not surprisingly, some tobacco advertisements both promote a product and take a stand in this political debate. A recent cigarette advertisement, for example, displayed a brand logo next to text reading, "Why do politicians smoke cigars while taxing cigarettes?"

no more justify regulation of 'commercial' speech than it can justify regulation of 'noncommercial' speech." That is essentially the interest asserted here. * * *

[R]espondents [argue] that the regulations target deceptive and misleading speech. Second, they argue that the regulations restrict speech that promotes an illegal transaction—i.e., the sale of tobacco to minors. Neither theory is properly before the Court. For purposes of summary judgment, respondents were willing to assume "that the tobacco advertisements at issue here are truthful, nonmisleading speech about a lawful activity." [E]ven if we were to entertain these arguments, neither is persuasive. Respondents suggest that tobacco advertising is misleading because "its youthful imagery [and] sheer ubiquity" leads children to believe "that tobacco use is desirable and pervasive." This justification is belied, however, by the sweeping overinclusivity of the regulations. Massachusetts has done nothing to target its prohibition to advertisements appealing to "excitement, glamour, and independence"; the ban applies with equal force to appeals to torpor, homeliness, and servility. It has not focused on "youthful imagery"; smokers depicted on the sides of buildings may no more play shuffleboard than they may ride skateboards. * * *

A direct solicitation of unlawful activity may of course be proscribed, whether or not it is commercial in nature. [Viewed] as an effort to proscribe solicitation to unlawful conduct, these regulations clearly fail the *Brandenburg* test. [Even] if Massachusetts could prohibit advertisements reading, "Hey kids, buy cigarettes here," these regulations sweep much more broadly than that. They cover "[any] statement or representation [the] purpose or effect of which is to promote the use or sale" of tobacco products, whether or not the statement is directly or indirectly addressed to minors. On respondents' theory, all tobacco advertising may be limited because some of its viewers may not legally act on it. It is difficult to see any stopping point to a rule that would allow a State to prohibit all speech in favor of an activity in which it is illegal for minors to engage. Presumably, the State could ban car advertisements in an effort to enforce its restrictions on underage driving. It could regulate advertisements urging people to vote, because children are not permitted to vote. * * *

Underlying many of the arguments of respondents and their amici is the idea that tobacco is in some sense sui generis—that it is so special, so unlike any other object of regulation, that application of normal First Amendment principles should be suspended. [Nevertheless], it seems appropriate to point out that to uphold the Massachusetts tobacco regulations would be to accept a line of reasoning that would permit restrictions on advertising for a host of other products.

Tobacco use is, we are told, "the single leading cause of preventable death in the United States." The second largest contributor to mortality rates in the United States is obesity. It is associated with increased incidence of diabetes, hypertension, and coronary artery disease, and it represents a public health problem that is rapidly growing worse. Although the growth of obesity over the last few decades has had many causes, a significant factor has been the increased availability of large quantities of high-calorie, high-fat foods. Such foods, of course, have been aggressively marketed and promoted by fast food companies.

Respondents say that tobacco companies are covertly targeting children in their advertising. Fast food companies do so openly. Moreover, there is considerable evidence that they have been successful in changing children's eating behavior. The effect of advertising on children's eating habits is significant for two reasons. First, childhood obesity is a serious health problem in its own right. Second, eating preferences formed in childhood tend to persist in adulthood. So even though fast food is not addictive in the same way tobacco is, children's exposure to fast food advertising can have deleterious consequences that are difficult to reverse.

To take another example, the third largest cause of preventable deaths in the United States is alcohol. Alcohol use is associated with tens of thousands of deaths each year from cancers and digestive diseases. And the victims of alcohol use are not limited to those who drink alcohol. In 1996, over 17,000 people were killed, and over 321,000 people were injured, in alcohol-related car accidents. Each year, alcohol is involved in several million violent crimes, including almost 200,000 sexual assaults.

Although every State prohibits the sale of alcohol to those under age 21, much alcohol advertising is viewed by children. Not surprisingly, there is considerable evidence that exposure to alcohol advertising is associated with underage drinking. Like underage tobacco use, underage drinking has effects that cannot be undone later in life. Those who begin drinking early are much more likely to become dependent on alcohol. Indeed, the probability of lifetime alcohol dependence decreases approximately 14 percent with each additional year of age at which alcohol is first used. And obviously the effects of underage drinking are irreversible for the nearly 1,700 Americans killed each year by teenage drunk drivers.

Respondents have identified no principle of law or logic that would preclude the imposition of restrictions on fast food and alcohol advertising similar to those they seek to impose on tobacco advertising. In effect, they seek a "vice" exception to the First Amendment. No such exception exists. If it did, it would have almost no limit, for "any product that poses some threat to public health or public morals might reasonably be characterized by a state legislature as relating to 'vice activity.' "

No legislature has ever sought to restrict speech about an activity it regarded as harmless and inoffensive. Calls for limits on expression always are made when the specter of some threatened harm is looming. The identity of the harm may vary. People will be inspired by totalitarian dogmas and subvert the Republic. They will be inflamed by racial demagoguery and embrace hatred and bigotry. Or they will be enticed by cigarette advertisements and choose to smoke, risking disease. It is therefore no answer for the State to say that the makers of cigarettes are doing harm: perhaps they are. But in that respect they are no different from the purveyors of other harmful products, or the advocates of harmful ideas. When the State seeks to silence them, they are all entitled to the protection of the First Amendment. * * *

JUSTICE SOUTER, concurring in part and dissenting in part.

I join Parts I, II–C, II–D, III–A, III–B–1, III–C, and III–D of the Court's opinion. I join Part I of the opinion of Justice Stevens concurring in the judgment in part and dissenting in part. I respectfully dissent from Part III–B–2 of the opinion of the Court, and like Justice Stevens would remand for trial on the constitutionality of the 1,000–foot limit.

JUSTICE STEVENS, with whom JUSTICE GINSBURG and JUSTICE BREYER join, and with whom JUSTICE SOUTER joins as to Part I, concurring in part, concurring in the judgment in part, and dissenting in part. * * *

I. [Stevens, J., argued that the Federal Cigarette Labeling and Advertising Act of 1965, as amended, did not preclude states and localities from regulating the location of cigarette advertising.]

II. *The 1,000–Foot Rule.* I am in complete accord with the Court's analysis of the importance of the interests served by the advertising restrictions. As the Court lucidly explains, few interests are more "compelling," than ensuring that minors do not become addicted to a dangerous drug before they are able to make a mature and informed decision as to the health risks associated with that substance. Unlike other products sold for human consumption, tobacco products are addictive and ultimately lethal for many long-term users. When that interest is combined with the State's concomitant concern for the effective enforcement of its laws regarding the sale of tobacco to minors, it becomes clear that Massachusetts' regulations serve interests of the highest order and are, therefore, immune from any ends-based challenge, whatever level of scrutiny one chooses to employ. Nevertheless, noble ends do not save a speech-restricting statute whose means are poorly tailored. Such statutes may be invalid for two different reasons. First, the means chosen may be insufficiently related to the ends they purportedly serve. Alternatively, the statute may be so broadly drawn that, while effectively achieving its ends, it unduly restricts communications that are unrelated to its policy aims.

To my mind, the 1,000–foot rule does not present a tailoring problem of the first type. For reasons cogently explained in our prior opinions and in the opinion of the Court, we may fairly assume that advertising stimulates consumption and, therefore, that regulations limiting advertising will facilitate efforts to stem consumption. Furthermore, if the government's intention is to limit consumption by a particular segment of the community—in this case, minors—it is appropriate, indeed necessary, to tailor advertising restrictions to the areas where that segment of the community congregates—in this case, the area surrounding schools and playgrounds.

However, I share the majority's concern as to whether the 1,000–foot rule unduly restricts the ability of cigarette manufacturers to convey lawful information to adult consumers. This, of course, is a question of line-drawing. While a ban on all communications about a given subject would be the most effective way to prevent children from exposure to such material, the state cannot by fiat reduce the level of discourse to that which is "fit for children." On the other hand, efforts to protect children from exposure to harmful material will undoubtedly have some spillover effect on the free speech rights of adults.

Finding the appropriate balance is no easy matter. Though many factors plausibly enter the equation when calculating whether a child-directed location restriction goes too far in regulating adult speech, one crucial question is whether the regulatory scheme leaves available sufficient "alternative avenues of communication." Because I do not think the record contains sufficient information to enable us to answer that question, I would vacate the award of summary judgment upholding the 1,000–foot rule and remand for trial on that issue.

[For example,] depending on the answers to empirical questions on which we lack data, the ubiquity of print advertisements hawking particular brands of cigarettes might suffice to inform adult consumers of the special advantages of the respective brands. Similarly, print advertisements, circulars mailed to people's homes, word of mouth, and general information may or may not be sufficient to imbue the adult population with the knowledge that particular stores, chains of stores, or types of stores sell tobacco products.

I note, moreover, that the alleged "overinclusivity" of the advertising regulations while relevant to whether the regulations are narrowly tailored, does not "beli[e]" the claim that tobacco advertising imagery misleads children into believing that smoking is healthy, glamorous, or sophisticated. For purposes of summary judgment, the State conceded that the tobacco companies' advertising concerns lawful activity and is not misleading. Under the Court's disposition of the case today, the State remains free to proffer evidence that the advertising is in fact misleading.

The Sales Practice and Indoor Advertising Restrictions. [T]he sales practice restrictions are best analyzed as regulating conduct, not speech. While the decision how to display one's products no doubt serves a marginal communicative function, the same can be said of virtually any human activity performed with the hope or intention of evoking the interest of others [I]t seems clear to me that laws requiring that stores maintain items behind counters and prohibiting self-service displays fall squarely on the conduct side of the line. Restrictions as to the accessibility of dangerous or legally-restricted products are a common feature of the regulatory regime governing American retail stores. I see nothing the least bit constitutionally problematic in requiring individuals to ask for the assistance of a salesclerk in order to examine or purchase a handgun, a bottle of penicillin, or a package of cigarettes.

Second, though I admit the question is closer, I would, for similar reasons, uphold the regulation limiting tobacco advertising in certain retail establishments to the space five feet or more above the floor. When viewed in isolation, this provision appears to target speech. Further, to the extent that it does target speech it may well run into constitutional problems, as the connection between the ends the statute purports to serve and the means it has chosen are dubious. Nonetheless, I am ultimately persuaded that the provision is unobjectionable because it is little more than an adjunct to the other sales practice restrictions. As the Commonwealth of Massachusetts can properly legislate the placement of products and the nature of displays in its convenience stores, I would not draw a distinction between such restrictions and height restrictions on related product advertising. I would accord the Commonwealth some latitude in imposing restrictions that can have only the slightest impact on the ability of adults to purchase a poisonous product and may save some children from taking the first step on the road to addiction.

III. Because I strongly disagree with the Court's conclusion on the preemption issue, I dissent from Parts II–A and II–B of its opinion. Though I agree with much of what the Court has to say about the First Amendment, I ultimately disagree with its disposition or its reasoning on each of the regulations before us.[12]

CONCEIVING AND RECONCEIVING THE STRUCTURE OF FIRST AMENDMENT DOCTRINE: HATE SPEECH REVISITED—AGAIN

CON LAW: P. 797, after note 4

AMER CON: P. 759, after note 4

RTS & LIB: P. 724, after note 4

In 1952, Virginia declared it a felony publicly to burn a cross with the intent of intimidating any person or group of persons. In 1968, Virginia added a provision that any such burning shall be prima facie evidence of an intent to intimidate. Barry Black led a Ku Klux Klan rally in which a cross was burned

12. Reflecting my partial agreement with the Court, I join Parts I, II–C, II–D, and III–B–1 and concur in the judgment reflected in Part III–D.

after a series of speeches marked by racial hostility, including one speaker saying that he "would love to take a .30/.30 and just random[ly] shoot the blacks." Forty to fifty cars passed the site during the rally, and eight to ten houses were located in its vicinity. The trial court used a Virginia Model Instruction that "the burning of a cross by itself is sufficient evidence from which you may infer the required intent."

Richard Elliot and Jonathan O'Mara attempted to burn a cross at the residence of an African-American. O'Mara pled guilty of attempted burning, reserving the right to challenge the statute; Elliot was convicted in a trial in which the jury was instructed that the Commonwealth had to show the intent to burn the cross and the intent to intimidate. The trial court did not instruct on the meaning of the prima facie provision of the statute, nor did it give the Model Instruction.

The Virginia Supreme Court declared the statute unconstitutional in light of *R.A.V.* and overturned the convictions of the three defendants. VIRGINIA v. BLACK, 538 U.S. 343, 123 S.Ct. 1536, 155 L.Ed.2d 535 (2003), per O'CONNOR, J., upheld the cross burning with intent to intimidate provision, struck down the prima facie evidence provision as interpreted by the jury instruction in the Black case, and, thereby, affirmed the dismissal of Black's prosecution while vacating and remanding for further proceedings with respect to Elliot and O'Mara: "[T]he First Amendment * * * permits a State to ban a 'true threat.' *Watts.* * * * Intimidation in the constitutionally proscribable sense of the word is a type of true threat [so that the] First Amendment permits Virginia to outlaw cross burnings done with the intent to intimidate because burning a cross is a particularly virulent form of intimidation. Instead of prohibiting all intimidating messages, Virginia may choose to regulate this subset of intimidating messages in light of cross burning's long and pernicious history as a signal of impending violence. Thus, just as a State may regulate only that obscenity which is the most obscene due to its prurient content, so too may a State choose to prohibit only those forms of intimidation that are most likely to inspire fear of bodily harm. A ban on cross burning carried out with the intent to intimidate is fully consistent with our holding in *R.A.V.* and is proscribable under the First Amendment."

In a section of the opinion joined by Rehnquist, C.J., Stevens and Breyer, JJ., O'Connor, J., addressed the prima facie evidence provision: "The Supreme Court of Virginia has not ruled on the meaning of the prima facie evidence provision. It has, however, stated that 'the act of burning a cross alone, with no evidence of intent to intimidate, will nonetheless suffice for arrest and prosecution and will insulate the Commonwealth from a motion to strike the evidence at the end of its case-in-chief.' The jury in the case of Richard Elliott did not receive any instruction on the prima facie evidence provision, and the provision was not an issue in the case of Jonathan O'Mara because he pleaded guilty. The court in Barry Black's case, however, instructed the jury that the provision means: 'The burning of a cross, by itself, is sufficient evidence from which you may infer the required intent.'

"The prima facie evidence provision, as interpreted by the jury instruction, renders the statute unconstitutional. Because this jury instruction is the Model Jury Instruction, and because the Supreme Court of Virginia had the opportunity to expressly disavow the jury instruction, the jury instruction's construction of the prima facie provision 'is a ruling on a question of state law that is as binding on us as though the precise words had been written into' the statute. [As] construed by the jury instruction, the prima facie provision strips away the very reason why a

State may ban cross burning with the intent to intimidate. The prima facie evidence provision permits a jury to convict in every cross-burning case in which defendants exercise their constitutional right not to put on a defense. And even where a defendant like Black presents a defense, the prima facie evidence provision makes it more likely that the jury will find an intent to intimidate regardless of the particular facts of the case. The provision permits the Commonwealth to arrest, prosecute, and convict a person based solely on the fact of cross burning itself.

"The act of burning a cross may mean that a person is engaging in constitutionally proscribable intimidation. But that same act may mean only that the person is engaged in core political speech. The prima facie evidence provision in this statute blurs the line between these two meanings of a burning cross. As interpreted by the jury instruction, the provision chills constitutionally protected political speech because of the possibility that a State will prosecute—and potentially convict—somebody engaging only in lawful political speech at the core of what the First Amendment is designed to protect. * * *

"For these reasons, the prima facie evidence provision, as interpreted through the jury instruction and as applied in Barry Black's case, is unconstitutional on its face. We recognize that the Supreme Court of Virginia has not authoritatively interpreted the meaning of the prima facie evidence provision. Unlike Justice Scalia, we refuse to speculate on whether *any* interpretation of the prima facie evidence provision would satisfy the First Amendment. Rather, all we hold is that because of the interpretation of the prima facie evidence provision given by the jury instruction, the provision makes the statute facially invalid at this point. We also recognize the theoretical possibility that the court, on remand, could interpret the provision in a manner different from that so far set forth in order to avoid the constitutional objections we have described. We leave open that possibility. We also leave open the possibility that the provision is severable, and if so, whether Elliott and O'Mara could be retried * * *.

"With respect to Barry Black, we agree with the Supreme Court of Virginia that his conviction cannot stand, and we affirm the judgment of the Supreme Court of Virginia. With respect to Elliott and O'Mara, we vacate the judgment of the Supreme Court of Virginia, and remand the case for further proceedings."

Scalia, J., joined by Thomas, J., concurring and dissenting, agreed that the cross burning/intimidation portion of the statute was constitutional, but he denied that the prima facie evidence aspect of the statute was constitutional. In a portion of his opinion not joined by Thomas, J., Scalia J., nonetheless concurred with the plurality's view that that the jury instruction was invalid: "I believe the prima-facie-evidence provision in Virginia's cross-burning statute is constitutionally unproblematic. Nevertheless, because the Virginia Supreme Court has not yet offered an authoritative construction of [that provision], I concur in the Court's decision to vacate and remand the judgment with respect to respondents Elliott and O'Mara. I also agree that respondent Black's conviction cannot stand. As noted above, the jury in Black's case was instructed that '[t]he burning of a cross, *by itself,* is sufficient evidence from which you may infer the required intent.' Where this instruction has been given, it is impossible to determine whether the jury has rendered its verdict (as it must) in light of the entire body of facts before it—*including* evidence that might rebut the presumption that the cross burning was done with an intent to intimidate—or, instead, has chosen to ignore such rebuttal evidence and focused exclusively on the fact that the defendant burned a cross. Still, I cannot go along with the Court's decision to affirm the judgment with respect to Black. In that judgment, the Virginia Supreme Court, having erroneously concluded that § 18.2–423 is overbroad, not only vacated Black's conviction, but dismissed the indictment against him as well. Because I believe the constitutional defect in Black's conviction is rooted in a jury instruction and not in the statute itself, I would not dismiss the indictment and would permit the Commonwealth to retry Black if it wishes to do so. It is an interesting question whether the plurality's willingness to let the Virginia Supreme Court resolve the plurality's make-believe facial invalidation of the statute extends as well to the facial invalidation insofar as it supports dismissal of the indictment against Black. Logically, there is no reason why it would not."

SOUTER, J., joined by Kennedy and Ginsburg, JJ., concurring in part and dissenting in part, argued that both the cross burning/intimidation section and the prima facie evidence section were unconstitutional: "I agree with the majority that the Virginia statute makes a content-based distinction within the category of punishable intimidating or threatening expression, the very type of distinction we considered in *R.A.V.* I disagree that any exception should save Virginia's law from unconstitutionality under the holding in *R.A.V.* or any acceptable variation of it. [Because] of the burning cross's extraordinary force as a method of intimidation, the *R.A.V.* exception most likely to cover the statute is the first of the three mentioned there, which the *R.A.V.* opinion called an exception for content discrimination on a basis that 'consists entirely of the very reason the entire class of speech at issue is proscribable.' This is the exception the majority speaks of here as covering statutes prohibiting 'particularly virulent' proscribable expression. [The *RAV*] Court explained that when the subcategory is confined to the most obviously proscribable instances, 'no significant danger of idea or viewpoint discrimination exists,' and the explanation was rounded out with some illustrative examples. None of them, however, resembles the case before us.

"[One example] of permissible distinction is for a prohibition of obscenity unusually offensive 'in its prurience,' with citation to a case in which the Seventh Circuit discussed the difference between obscene depictions of actual people and simulations. As that court noted, distinguishing obscene publications on this basis does not suggest discrimination on the basis of the message conveyed. *Kucharek v. Hanaway,* 902 F.2d 513, 517–518 (7th Cir. 1990). The opposite is true, however, when a general prohibition of intimidation is rejected in favor of a distinct proscription of intimidation by cross burning. The cross may have been selected because of its special power to threaten, but it may also have been singled out because of disapproval of its message of white supremacy, either because a legislature thought white supremacy was a pernicious doctrine or because it found that dramatic, public espousal of it was a civic embarrassment. Thus, there is no kinship between the cross-burning statute and the core prurience example. * * *

"The majority's approach could be taken as recognizing an exception to *R.A.V.* when circumstances show that the statute's ostensibly valid reason for punishing particularly serious proscribable expression probably is not a ruse for message suppression, even though the statute may have a greater (but not exclusive) impact on adherents of one ideology than on others. * * *

"My concern here, in any event, is not with the merit of a pragmatic doctrinal move. For whether or not the Court should conceive of exceptions to *R.A.V.*'s general rule in a more practical way, no content-based statute should survive even under a pragmatic recasting of *R.A.V.* without a high probability that no 'official suppression of ideas is afoot,' I believe the prima facie evidence provision stands in the way of any finding of such a high probability here. * * *

"As I see the likely significance of the evidence provision, its primary effect is to skew jury deliberations toward conviction in cases where the evidence of intent to intimidate is relatively weak and arguably consistent with a solely ideological reason for burning. To understand how the provision may work, recall that the symbolic act of burning a cross, without more, is consistent with both intent to intimidate and intent to make an ideological statement free of any aim to threaten. One can tell the intimidating instance from the wholly ideological one only by reference to some further circumstance. In the real world, of course, and in real-world prosecutions, there will always be further circumstances, and the factfinder will always learn something more than the isolated fact of cross burning. Sometimes those circumstances will show an intent to intimidate, but sometimes they will be at least equivocal, as in cases where a white supremacist group burns a cross at an initiation ceremony or political rally visible to the public. In such a case, if the factfinder is aware of the prima facie evidence provision, as the jury was in respondent, the provision will have the practical effect of tilting the jury's thinking in favor of the prosecution. * * * The provision will thus tend to draw nonthreatening ideological expression within the ambit of the prohibition of intimidating expression. * * *

"To the extent the prima facie evidence provision skews prosecutions, then, it skews the statute toward suppressing ideas. Thus, the appropriate way to consider the statute's prima facie evidence term, in my view, is not as if it were an overbroad statutory definition amenable to severance or a narrowing construction. The question here is not the permissible scope of an arguably overbroad statute, but the claim of a clearly content-based statute to an exception from the general prohibition of content-based proscriptions, an exception that is not warranted if the statute's terms show that suppression of ideas may be afoot. Accordingly, the way to look at the prima facie evidence provision is to consider it for any indication of what is afoot. And if we look at the provision for this purpose, it has a very obvious significance as a mechanism for bringing within the statute's prohibition some expression that is doubtfully threatening though certainly distasteful.

"It is difficult to conceive of an intimidation case that could be easier to prove than one with cross burning, assuming any circumstances suggesting intimidation are present. The provision, apparently so unnecessary to legitimate prosecution of intimidation, is therefore quite enough to raise the question whether Virginia's content-based statute seeks more than mere protection against a virulent form of intimidation. It consequently bars any conclusion that an exception to the general rule of *R.A.V.* is warranted on the ground 'that there is no realistic [or little realistic] possibility that official suppression of ideas is afoot.'

"I conclude that the statute under which all three of the respondents were prosecuted violates the First Amendment, since the statute's content-based distinction was invalid at the time of the charged activities, regardless of whether the prima facie evidence provision was given any effect in any respondent's individual case. In my view, severance of the prima facie evidence provision now could not eliminate the unconstitutionality of the whole statute at the time of the respondents' conduct. I would therefore affirm the judgment of the Supreme Court of Virginia vacating the respondents' convictions and dismissing the indictments. Accordingly, I concur in the Court's judgment as to respondent Black and dissent as to respondents Elliott and O'Mara."

Thomas, J., dissenting, maintained that the statute was constitutional: "Although I agree with the majority's conclusion that it is constitutionally permissible to 'ban ... cross burning carried out with intent to intimidate,' I believe that the majority errs in imputing an expressive component to the activity in question. In my view, whatever expressive value cross burning has, the legislature simply wrote it out by banning only intimidating conduct undertaken by a particular means. A conclusion that the statute prohibiting cross burning with intent to intimidate sweeps beyond a prohibition on certain conduct into the zone of expression overlooks not only the words of the statute but also reality.

" 'The world's oldest, most persistent terrorist organization is not European or even Middle Eastern in origin. Fifty years before the Irish Republican Army was organized, a century before Al Fatah declared its holy war on Israel, the Ku Klux Klan was actively harassing, torturing and murdering in the United States. Today [its] members remain fanatically committed to a course of violent opposition to social progress and racial equality in the United States.' M. Newton & J. Newton, *The Ku Klux Klan: An Encyclopedia* vii (1991). * * *

"As the Solicitor General points out, the association between acts of intimidating cross burning and violence is well documented in recent American history. [Virginia's] experience has been no exception. [In] February 1952, in light of [a] series of cross burnings and attendant reports that the Klan, 'long considered dead in Virginia, is being revitalized in Richmond,' Governor Battle announced that 'Virginia might well consider passing legislation to restrict the activities of the Ku Klux Klan.' [As] newspapers reported at the time, the bill was 'to ban the burning of crosses and other similar evidences of *terrorism*.' * * *

"Strengthening [my] conclusion, that the legislature sought to criminalize terrorizing *conduct* is the fact that at the time the statute was enacted, racial segregation was not only the prevailing practice, but also the law in Virginia. And, just two years after the enactment of this statute, Virginia's General Assembly embarked on a campaign of 'massive resistance' in response to *Brown v. Board of Education*. It strains credulity to suggest that a state legislature that adopted a litany of segregationist laws self-contradictorily intended to squelch the segregationist message. Even for segregationists, violent and terroristic conduct, the Siamese twin of cross burning, was intolerable. The ban on cross burning with intent to intimidate demonstrates that even segregationists understood the difference between intimidating and terroristic conduct and racist expression. It is simply beyond belief that, in passing the statute now under review, the Virginia legislature was concerned with anything but penalizing conduct it must have viewed as particularly vicious.

"Accordingly, this statute prohibits only conduct, not expression. And, just as one cannot burn down someone's house to make a political point and then seek refuge in the First Amendment, those who hate cannot terrorize and intimidate to make their point. In light of my conclusion that the statute here addresses only conduct, there is no need to analyze it under any of our First Amendment tests.

"[Even] assuming that the statute implicates the First Amendment, in my view, the fact that the statute permits a jury to draw an inference of intent to intimidate from the cross burning itself presents no constitutional problems. [The] inference is rebuttable and, as the jury instructions given in this case demonstrate, Virginia law still requires the jury to find the existence of each element, including intent to intimidate, beyond a reasonable doubt."

Notes and Questions

R.A.V. struck the ordinance down on its face, but did not rely on the overbreadth doctrine. The Court interpreted the ordinance to apply only to fighting words; it, therefore, could not have been overbroad. The concurring justices in R.A.V. interpreted the ordinance to sweep beyond fighting words, and maintained that the ordinance should have been invalidated on overbreadth grounds. Does O'Connor, J., rely on overbreadth analysis in *Black?* If so, how would the analysis relate to *Brockett v. Spokane Arcades*? Recall that *Brockett* referred to the "normal rule that partial, rather than facial invalidation" of statutes is to be preferred and observed that: "[A]n individual whose own speech or expressive conduct may validly be prohibited or sanctioned is permitted to challenge a statute on its face because it also threatens others not before the court—those who desire to engage in legally protected expression but who may refrain from doing so rather than risk prosecution or undertake to have the law declared partially invalid. If the overbreadth is 'substantial,' the law may not be enforced against anyone, including the party before the court, until it is narrowed to reach only unprotected activity, whether by legislative action or by judicial construction or partial invalidation.

"It is otherwise where the parties challenging the statute are those who desire to engage in protected speech that the overbroad statute purports to punish, or who seek to publish both protected and unprotected material. There is then no want of a proper party to challenge the statute, no concern that an attack on the statute will be unduly delayed or protected speech discouraged. The statute may forthwith be declared invalid to the extent that it reaches too far, but otherwise left intact."[a] How does Black's activity fit into this scheme? In any event, is the Virginia statute substantially overbroad?

PRIOR RESTRAINTS

FOUNDATION CASES

LICENSING

CON LAW: P. 798, add to note 2

AMER CON: P. 761, add to note 2

RTS & LIB: P. 727, add to note 2

WATCHTOWER BIBLE & TRACT SOCIETY v. STRATTON, per STEVENS, J., struck down a village ordinance requiring door to door advocates or distributors of literature to register with the mayor: "It is offensive—not only to the values protected by the First Amendment, but to the very notion of a free society—that in the context of everyday public discourse a citizen must first inform the government of her desire to speak to her neighbors and then obtain a permit to do

a. After the Court has declared that the statute is invalid to the extent it reaches too far, the remaining portion of the statute will be examined to determine whether that portion is severable. That is, it could well be the intent of the legislature that the statute stands or falls as a single package. To invalidate a part, then, could be to invalidate the whole. Alternatively, the legislature may have intended to salvage whatever it might. The question of severability is regarded as one of legislative intent, but, at least with respect to federal legislation, courts will presume that severability was intended. See, e.g., *Regan v. Time, Inc.,* 468 U.S. 641, 104 S.Ct. 3262, 82 L.Ed.2d 487 (1984). The question of whether a provision of a state statute is severable is one of state law.

so. Even if the issuance of permits by the mayor's office is a ministerial task that is performed promptly and at no cost to the applicant, a law requiring a permit to engage in such speech constitutes a dramatic departure from our national heritage and constitutional tradition."

Stevens, J., argued that required licensing impinged on the speaker's interest in anonymity. In addition, "requiring a permit as a prior condition on the exercise of the right to speak imposes an objective burden on some speech of citizens holding religious or patriotic views. As our World War II-era cases dramatically demonstrate, there are a significant number of persons whose religious scruples will prevent them from applying for such a license. There are no doubt other patriotic citizens, who have such firm convictions about their constitutional right to engage in uninhibited debate in the context of door-to-door advocacy, that they would prefer silence to speech licensed by a petty official.

"[Moreover,] there is a significant amount of spontaneous speech that is effectively banned by the ordinance. A person who made a decision on a holiday or a weekend to take an active part in a political campaign could not begin to pass out handbills until after he or she obtained the required permit. Even a spontaneous decision to go across the street and urge a neighbor to vote against the mayor could not lawfully be implemented without first obtaining the mayor's permission. * * *

"Also central to our conclusion that the ordinance does not pass First Amendment scrutiny is that it is not tailored to the Village's stated interests. Even if the interest in preventing fraud could adequately support the ordinance insofar as it applies to commercial transactions and the solicitation of funds, that interest provides no support for its application to petitioners, to political campaigns, or to enlisting support for unpopular causes. The Village, however, argues that the ordinance is nonetheless valid because it serves the two additional interests of protecting the privacy of the resident and the prevention of crime.

"With respect to the former, it seems clear that § 107 of the ordinance, which provides for the posting of 'No Solicitation' signs and which is not challenged in this case, coupled with the resident's unquestioned right to refuse to engage in conversation with unwelcome visitors, provides ample protection for the unwilling listener. [The] annoyance caused by an uninvited knock on the front door is the same whether or not the visitor is armed with a permit.

"With respect to the latter, it seems unlikely that the absence of a permit would preclude criminals from knocking on doors and engaging in conversations not covered by the ordinance. They might, for example, ask for directions or permission to use the telephone, or pose as surveyers or census takers. Or they might register under a false name with impunity because the ordinance contains no provision for verifying an applicant's identity or organizational credentials. Moreover, the Village did not assert an interest in crime prevention below, and there is an absence of any evidence of a special crime problem related to door-to-door solicitation in the record before us.

"The rhetoric used in the World War II-era opinions that repeatedly saved petitioners' coreligionists from petty prosecutions reflected the Court's evaluation of the First Amendment freedoms that are implicated in this case. The value judgment that then motivated a united democratic people fighting to defend those very freedoms from totalitarian attack is unchanged. It motivates our decision today."

Breyer, J., joined by Souter and Ginsburg, JJ., concurred: "While joining the Court's opinion, I write separately to note that the dissent's 'crime prevention' justification for this ordinance is not a strong one. For one thing, there is no indication that the legislative body that passed the ordinance considered this justification. In the intermediate scrutiny context, the Court ordinarily does not supply reasons the legislative body has not given. That does not mean, as the Chief Justice suggests, that only a government with a 'battery of constitutional lawyers,' could satisfy this burden. It does mean that we expect a government to give its real reasons for passing an ordinance.

"Because Stratton did not rely on the crime prevention justification, because Stratton has not now 'present[ed] more than anecdote and supposition,' and because the relationship between the interest and the ordinance is doubtful, I am unwilling to assume that these conjectured benefits outweigh the cost of abridging the speech covered by the ordinance."

Scalia, J., joined by Thomas, J., concurring in the judgment, agreed with some of the Court's opinion, but did not "agree, for example, that one of the causes of the invalidity of Stratton's ordinance is that some people have a religious objection to applying for a permit, and others (posited by the Court) 'have such firm convictions about their constitutional right to engage in uninhibited debate in the context of door-to-door advocacy, that they would prefer silence to speech licensed by a petty official.'

"If a licensing requirement is otherwise lawful, it is in my view not invalidated by the fact that some people will choose, for religious reasons, to forgo speech rather than observe it. That would convert an invalid free-exercise claim into a valid free-speech claim—and a more destructive one at that. Whereas the free-exercise claim, if acknowledged, would merely exempt Jehovah's Witnesses from the licensing requirement, the free-speech claim exempts everybody, thanks to Jehovah's Witnesses.

"As for the Court's fairy-tale category of 'patriotic citizens,' who would rather be silenced than licensed in a manner that the Constitution (but for their 'patriotic' objection) would permit: If our free-speech jurisprudence is to be determined by the predicted behavior of such crackpots, we are in a sorry state indeed."

Rehnquist, C.J., dissented: "The town had little reason to suspect that the negligible burden of having to obtain a permit runs afoul of the First Amendment . For over 60 years, we have categorically stated that a permit requirement for door-to-door canvassers, which gives no discretion to the issuing authority, is constitutional. The District Court and Court of Appeals, relying on our cases, upheld the ordinance. The Court today, however, abruptly changes course and invalidates the ordinance. [With] respect to the interest in protecting privacy, the Court concludes that '[t]he annoyance caused by an uninvited knock on the front door is the same whether or not the visitor is armed with a permit.' True, but that misses the key point: the permit requirement results in fewer uninvited knocks. Those who have complied with the permit requirement are less likely to visit residences with no trespassing signs, as it is much easier for the authorities to track them down.

"The Court also fails to grasp how the permit requirement serves Stratton's interest in preventing crime. We have approved of permit requirements for those engaging in protected First Amendment activity because of a common-sense recognition that their existence both deters and helps detect wrongdoing. And while some people, intent on committing burglaries or violent crimes, are not likely to be deterred by the prospect of a misdemeanor for violating the permit ordinance, the ordinance's effectiveness does not depend on criminals registering. The ordinance prevents and detects serious crime by making it a crime not to register."

Rehnquist, C.J., referred to a double murder that had taken place in Hanover, New Jersey: "The murderers did not achieve their objective until they visited their fifth home over a period of seven months. If Hanover had a permit requirement, the teens may have been stopped before they achieved their objective. One of the residents they visited may have informed the police that there were two canvassers who lacked a permit. Such neighborly vigilance, though perhaps foreign to those residing in modern day cities, is not uncommon in small towns. Or the police on their own may have discovered that two canvassers were violating the ordinance. Apprehension for violating the permit requirement may well have frustrated the teenagers' objectives; it certainly would have assisted in solving the murders had the teenagers gone ahead with their plan.

"Of course, the Stratton ordinance does not guarantee that no canvasser will ever commit a burglary or violent crime. The Court seems to think this dooms the ordinance, erecting an insurmountable hurdle that a law must provide a fool-proof method of preventing crime. In order to survive intermediate scrutiny, however, a law need not solve the crime problem, it need only further the interest in preventing crime. Some deterrence of serious criminal activity is more than enough to survive intermediate scrutiny."

INJUNCTIONS

CON LAW: P. 803, add to note 1, after 1st sentence of final ¶

AMER CON: P. 764, add to note 1, after 1st sentence of final ¶

RTS & LIB: P. 730, add to note 1, after 1st sentence of final ¶

See *Tory v. Cochran*, ___ U.S. ___, 125 S.Ct. 2108, ___ L.Ed.2d ___ (2005)(death of plaintiff makes it unnecessary to reach question whether first amendment bars permanent injunction in a defamation case where plaintiff is a public figure).

JUSTICE AND NEWSGATHERING

NEWSGATHERING

ACCESS TO PRIVATE SOURCES [NEW SUBSECTION]

CON LAW: P. 791, after Notes and Questions

AMER CON: P. 776, after Notes and Questions

RTS & LIB:

Two ABC television reporters used false resumes to get jobs at Food Lion, Inc. supermarkets and, using concealed mini-cameras, secretly videotaped food handling practices during a brief period of employment. Six months later some of the video footage was used by ABC during sweeps week in a *PrimeTime Live* broadcast that was sharply critical of Food Lion. The broadcast included, for example, videotape appearing to show "Food Lion employees repackaging and redating fish that had passed the expiration date, grinding expired beef with fresh beef, and applying barbeque sauce to chicken past its expiration date in order to mask the smell and sell it as fresh in the gourmet food section. The program included statements by former Food Lion employees alleging even more serious mishandling of meat at Food Lion stores across several states."

Food Lion sued Capital Cities/ABC, Inc., [the producers of] *PrimeTime Live*, and Lynne Dale and Susan Barnett, two reporters for the program * * *. Food Lion did not sue for defamation, but challenged ABC's methods of gathering information, alleging among other things fraud, breach of duty of loyalty, and trespass. In federal district court, Food Lion won a judgment for compensatory damages of $1,400 on its fraud claim, $1 against each of the reporters on the duty of loyalty and trespass claims, and $315,000 in punitive damages on the fraud claim against the producers and ABC.

FOOD LION, INC. v. CAPITAL CITIES/ABC, INC., 194 F.3d 505 (4th Cir.1999), per MICHAEL, J., found no actionable fraud under the relevant state law, but affirmed the judgments for breach of duty of loyalty and trespass against a first amendment attack. The court found no actionable fraud because of the lack of injury resulting from its employment of the two reporters other than damages from the publication which it found were not cognizable under the first amendment. The other claims gave rise to nominal damages, not damages arising from the publication: "Because Dale and Barnett did not compete with Food Lion, misappropriate any of its profits or opportunities, or breach its confidences, ABC argues that the reporters did not engage in any disloyal conduct that is tortious under existing law. [The] interests of the employer (ABC) to whom Dale and Barnett gave complete loyalty were adverse to the interests of Food Lion, the employer to whom they were unfaithful. ABC and Food Lion were not business competitors but they were adverse in a fundamental way. ABC's interest was to expose Food Lion to the public as a food chain that engaged in unsanitary and deceptive practices. Dale and Barnett served ABC's interest, at the expense of Food Lion, by engaging in the taping for ABC while they were on Food Lion's payroll. In doing this, Dale and Barnett did not serve Food Lion faithfully, and their interest (which was the same as ABC's) was diametrically opposed to Food Lion's. In these circumstances, we believe that the highest courts of North and South Carolina would hold that the reporters—in promoting the interests of one master, ABC, to the detriment of a second, Food Lion—committed the tort of disloyalty against Food Lion. * * *

"ABC argues that it was error to allow the jury to hold Dale and Barnett liable for trespass. [We] turn first to whether Dale and Barnett's consent to be in non-public areas of Food Lion property was void from the outset because of the resume misrepresentations. '[C]onsent to an entry is often given legal effect' even though it was obtained by misrepresentation or concealed intentions. Without this result, 'a restaurant critic could not conceal his identity when he ordered a meal, or a browser pretend to be interested in merchandise that he could not afford to buy. Dinner guests would be trespassers if they were false friends who never would have been invited had the host known their true character, and a consumer who in an effort to bargain down an automobile dealer falsely claimed to be able to buy the same car elsewhere at a lower price would be a trespasser in a dealer's showroom.'

"Of course, many cases on the spectrum become much harder than these examples, and the courts of North and South Carolina have not considered the validity of a consent to enter land obtained by misrepresentation. Further, the various jurisdictions and authorities in this country are not of one mind in dealing with the issue. Compare *Restatement (Second) of Torts*, § 892B(2) (1965) ('[i]f the person consenting to the conduct of another [is] induced [to consent] by the other's misrepresentation, the consent is not effective for the unexpected invasion or harm') and *Shiffman v. Empire Blue Cross and Blue Shield,* 256 A.D.2d 131, 681 N.Y.S.2d 511, 512 (App.Div.1998) (reporter who gained entry to medical office by posing as potential patient using false identification and insurance cards could not assert consent as defense to trespass claim 'since consent obtained by misrepresentation or fraud is invalid'), with *Desnick v. American Broadcasting Companies*, 44 F.3d 1345 (7th Cir.1995)(ABC agents with concealed cameras who obtained consent to enter an ophthalmic clinic by pretending to be patients were not trespassers because, among other things, they 'entered offices open to anyone').

"We like *Desnick*'s thoughtful analysis about when a consent to enter that is based on misrepresentation may be given effect. In *Desnick,* ABC sent persons posing as patients needing eye care to the plaintiffs' eye clinics, and the test patients secretly recorded their examinations. Some of the recordings were used in a PrimeTime Live segment that alleged intentional misdiagnosis and unnecessary cataract surgery. *Desnick* held that although the test patients misrepresented their purpose, their consent to enter was still valid because they did not invade 'any of the specific interests [relating to peaceable possession of land] the tort of trespass seeks to protect:' the test patients entered offices 'open to anyone expressing a desire for ophthalmic services' and videotaped doctors engaged in professional discussions with strangers, the testers; the testers did not disrupt the offices or invade anyone's private space; and the testers did not reveal the 'intimate details of anybody's life.' *Desnick* supported its conclusion with the following comparison: 'Testers' who pose as prospective home buyers in order to gather evidence of housing discrimination are not trespassers even if they are private persons not acting under color of law. The situation of [ABC's] 'testers' is analogous. Like testers seeking evidence of violation of anti-discrimination laws, [ABC's] test patients gained entry into the plaintiffs' premises by misrepresenting their purposes (more precisely by a misleading omission to disclose those purposes). But the entry was not invasive in the sense of infringing the kind of interest of the plaintiffs that the law of trespass protects; it was not an interference with the ownership or possession of land. * * *

"Although the consent cases as a class are inconsistent, we have not found any case suggesting that consent based on a resume misrepresentation turns a successful job applicant into a trespasser the moment she enters the employer's premises to begin work. Moreover, if we turned successful resume fraud into trespass, we would not be protecting the interest underlying the tort of trespass—the ownership and peaceable possession of land. Accordingly, we cannot say that North and South Carolina's highest courts would hold that misrepresentation on a job application alone nullifies the consent given to an employee to enter the employer's property, thereby turning the employee into a trespasser. The jury's finding of trespass therefore cannot be sustained on the grounds of resume misrepresentation.

"There is a problem, however, with what Dale and Barnett did after they entered Food Lion's property. The jury also found that the reporters committed trespass by breaching their duty of loyalty to Food Lion 'as a result of pursuing [their] investigation for ABC.' We affirm the finding of trespass on this ground because the breach of duty of loyalty—triggered by the filming in non-public areas, which was adverse to Food Lion—was a wrongful act in excess of Dale and Barnett's authority to enter Food Lion's premises as employees.

"The Court of Appeals of North Carolina has indicated that secretly installing a video camera in someone's private home can be a wrongful act in excess of consent given to enter. In the trespass case of *Miller v. Brooks*, 123 N.C.App. 20, 472 S.E.2d 350, 355 (N.C.Ct.App.1996), the (defendant) wife, who claimed she had consent to enter her estranged husband's (the plaintiff's) house, had a private detective place a video camera in the ceiling of her husband's bedroom. The court noted that '[e]ven an authorized entry can be trespass if a wrongful act is done in excess of and in abuse of authorized entry.' [We] recognize that *Miller* involved a private home, not a grocery store, and that it involved some physical alteration to the plaintiff's property (installation of a camera). Still, we believe the general principle is applicable here, at least in the case of Dale, who worked in a Food Lion store in North Carolina. Although Food Lion consented to Dale's entry to do her job, she exceeded that consent when she videotaped in non-public areas of the store and worked against the interests of her second employer, Food Lion, in doing so. * * *

"Here, both Dale and Barnett became employees of Food Lion with the certain consequence that they would breach their implied promises to serve Food Lion faithfully. They went into areas of the stores that were not open to the public and secretly videotaped, an act that was directly adverse to the interests of their second employer, Food Lion. Thus, they [committed] trespass because Food Lion's consent for them to be on its property was nullified when they tortiously breached their duty of loyalty to Food Lion. * * *

"ABC argues that even if state tort law covers some of Dale and Barnett's conduct, the district court erred in refusing to subject Food Lion's claims to any level of First Amendment scrutiny. ABC makes this argument because Dale and Barnett were engaged in newsgathering for *PrimeTime Live*. It is true that there are 'First Amendment interests in newsgathering.' *Branzburg* ("without some protection for seeking out the news, freedom of the press could be eviscerated."). However, the Supreme Court has said in no uncertain terms that 'generally applicable laws do not offend the First Amendment simply because their enforcement against the press has incidental effects on its ability to gather and report the news.' *Cohen v. Cowles Media*.[a]

"In *Cowles*, Cohen, who was associated with a candidate for governor of Minnesota, gave damaging information about a candidate for another office to two reporters on their promise that his (Cohen's) identity would not be disclosed. Because editors at the reporters' newspapers concluded that the source was an essential part of the story, it was published with Cohen named as the origin.[b] Cohen was fired from his job as a result, and he sued the newspapers for breaking the promise. The question in the Supreme Court was whether the First Amendment barred Cohen from recovering damages under state promissory estoppel law. The newspapers argued that absent 'a need to further a state interest of the highest order,' the First Amendment protected them from liability for publishing truthful information, lawfully obtained, about a matter of public concern. The Supreme Court disagreed, holding that the press 'has no special immunity from

a. For commentary, see Jerome A. Barron, *Cohen v. Cowles Media ands its Significance for First Amendment law and Journalism,* 3 Wm. & Mary Bill Rts. J. 419 (1994); Eric B. Easton, *Two Wrongs Mock a Right: Overcoming the Cohen Maledicta that Bar First Amendment Protection for Newsgathering,* 58 Ohio St. L.J. 1135 (1997); Lili Levi, *Dangerous Liasons: Seduction and Betrayal in Confidential Press–Source Relations,* 43 Rutgers L.Rev. 609 (1991).

b. The newspaper contended that the information provided (which reflected badly upon a political candidate) was misleading and that the source's name was newsworthy because he was associated with the other side in the political campaign.

the application of general laws' and that the enforcement of general laws against the press 'is not subject to stricter scrutiny than would be applied to enforcement against other persons or organizations.'

"The key inquiry in *Cowles* was whether the law of promissory estoppel was a generally applicable law. The Court began its analysis with some examples of generally applicable laws that must be obeyed by the press, such as those relating to copyright, labor, antitrust, and tax. More relevant to us, '[t]he press may not with impunity break and enter an office or dwelling to gather news.' In analyzing the doctrine of promissory estoppel, the Court determined that it was a law of general applicability because it 'does not target or single out the press,' but instead applies 'to the daily transactions of all the citizens of Minnesota.' [The] Court thus refused to apply any heightened scrutiny to the enforcement of Minnesota's promissory estoppel law against the newspapers.

"The torts Dale and Barnett committed, breach of the duty of loyalty and trespass, fit neatly into the *Cowles* framework. Neither tort targets or singles out the press. Each applies to the daily transactions of the citizens of North and South Carolina. If, for example, an employee of a competing grocery chain hired on with Food Lion and videotaped damaging information in Food Lion's non-public areas for later disclosure to the public, these tort laws would apply with the same force as they do against Dale and Barnett here. Nor do we believe that applying these laws against the media will have more than an 'incidental effect' on newsgathering.

"ABC argues that *Cowles* is not to be applied automatically to every 'generally applicable law' because the Supreme Court has since said that 'the enforcement of [such a] law may or may not be subject to heightened scrutiny under the First Amendment.' *Turner Broadcasting System, Inc. v. FCC,* 512 U.S. 622, 640, 114 S.Ct. 2445, 129 L.Ed.2d 497 (1994) (contrasting *Barnes v. Glen Theatre* and *Cowles*). In *Glen Theatre* nude dancing establishments and their dancers challenged a generally applicable law prohibiting public nudity. Because the general ban on public nudity covered nude dancing, which was expressive conduct, the Supreme Court applied heightened scrutiny. [There is an] arguable tension between [*Glen Theatre* and *Cowles*]. The cases are consistent, however, if we view the challenged conduct in *Cowles* to be the breach of promise and not some form of expression. In *Glen Theatre,* on the other hand, an activity directly covered by the law, nude dancing, necessarily involved expression, and heightened scrutiny was applied. Here, as in *Cowles,* heightened scrutiny does not apply because the tort laws (breach of duty of loyalty and trespass) do not single out the press or have more than an incidental effect upon its work.

"For the foregoing reasons, we affirm the judgment that Dale and Barnett breached their duty of loyalty to Food Lion and committed trespass. We likewise affirm the damages award against them for these torts in the amount of $2.00. We have already indicated that the fraud claim against all of the ABC defendants must be reversed. Because Food Lion was awarded punitive damages only on its fraud claim, the judgment awarding punitive damages cannot stand.

"We do not reach the [question whether non-publication damages were proximately caused by the fraud] because an overriding (and settled) First Amendment principle precludes the award of publication damages in this [case].[c] Food Lion attempted to avoid the First Amendment limitations on defamation

c. Food Lion closed 80 stores and laid off more than 1,000 employees as a result of the broadcast.

claims by seeking publication damages under non-reputational tort claims, while holding to the normal state law proof standards for these torts. This is precluded by *Hustler Magazine v. Falwell*.

"Food Lion argues that *Cowles,* and not *Hustler* governs its claim for publication damages. According to Food Lion, *Cowles* allowed the plaintiff to recover—without satisfying the constitutional prerequisites to a defamation action—economic losses for publishing the plaintiff's identity in violation of a legal duty arising from generally applicable law. Food Lion says that its claim for damages is like the plaintiff's in *Cowles,* and not like Falwell's in *Hustler*. This argument fails because the Court in *Cowles* distinguished the damages sought there from those in *Hustler* in a way that also distinguishes Food Lion's case from *Cowles*: 'Cohen is not seeking damages for injury to his reputation or his state of mind. He sought damages [for] breach of a promise that caused him to lose his job and lowered his earning capacity. Thus, this is not a case like *Hustler* [where] we held that the constitutional libel standards apply to a claim alleging that the publication of a parody was a state-law tort of intentional infliction of emotional distress.'

"Food Lion, in seeking compensation for matters such as loss of good will and lost sales, is claiming reputational damages from publication, which the *Cowles* Court distinguished by placing them in the same category as the emotional distress damages sought by Falwell in *Hustler*. In other words, according to *Cowles,* 'constitutional libel standards' apply to damage claims for reputational injury from a publication such as the one here.

"Food Lion also argues that because ABC obtained the videotapes through unlawful acts, that is, the torts of breach of duty of loyalty and trespass, it (Food Lion) is entitled to publication damages without meeting the *New York Times* standard. The Supreme Court has never suggested that it would dispense with the *Times* standard in this situation, and we believe *Hustler* indicates that the Court would not. In *Hustler* the magazine's conduct would have been sufficient to constitute an unlawful act, the intentional infliction of emotional distress, if state law standards of proof had applied. [Notwithstanding] the nature of the underlying act, the Court held that satisfying *New York Times* was a prerequisite to the recovery of publication damages.

"In sum, Food Lion could not bypass the *New York Times* standard if it wanted publication damages. [The] district court therefore reached the correct result when it disallowed these damages, although we affirm on a different ground."[d]

Notes and Questions

1. *Civil disobedience?* Consider Randall P. Bezanson, *Means and Ends and Food Lion: The Tension Between Exemption and Independence in Newsgathering By the Press*, 47 Emory L.J. 895 (1998): "The law's normal response when an individual violates the society's rules for a moral or just end is to give the act a decent name—civil disobedience—and then to hold the law violator to account, on the theory that if the 'end' is very important, it must be important enough to achieve at the price the law exacts. A jury [in *Food Lion*] decided that ABC violated the law, perhaps for a just cause, but the price of doing so is the jury's

d. Niemeyer, J., concurring in part and dissenting in part, maintained that the fraud claim implicated damages other than the publication damages that were sufficient to justify the punitive damages award.

damage award. Jesse Jackson recently went to jail overnight, a price he was willing to pay for taking the law into his own hands in service of his own ends. Whether we agree with him or not, we should respect him for that. We would discount the importance of Jackson's act by ignoring it or excusing it."

2. *A newsgather's privilege?* Suppose a reporter has probable cause to believe that a person or institution's conduct poses a significant threat to the health, safety, or financial well-being of others and that his or her methods of newsgathering were not substantially more intrusive than necessary to obtain documentation of the wrongdoing. Should fraud or trespass be privileged? Would the facts in *Food Lion* meet the test?[e] Should the press be liable for publication damages?[f] Punitive damages?[g]

3. *Anti-paparazzi legislation.* California Civil Code § 1708.8 provides that: "A person is liable for physical invasion of privacy when the defendant knowingly enters onto the land of another without permission or otherwise committed a trespass, in order to physically invade the privacy of the plaintiff with the intent to capture any type of visual image, sound recording, or other physical impression of the plaintiff engaging in a personal or familial activity and the physical invasion occurs in a manner that is offensive to a reasonable person. A person is liable for constructive invasion of privacy when the defendant attempts to capture, in a manner that is offensive to a reasonable person, any type of visual image, sound recording, or other physical impression of the plaintiff engaging in a personal or familial activity under circumstances in which the plaintiff had a reasonable expectation of privacy, through the use of a visual or auditory enhancing device, regardless of whether there is a physical trespass, if this image, sound recording, or other physical impression could not have been achieved without a trespass unless the visual or auditory enhancing device was used.

"A person who commits physical invasion of privacy or constructive invasion of privacy, or both, is liable for up to three times the amount of any general and special damages that are proximately caused by the violation of this section.

"This section shall not be construed to impair or limit any otherwise lawful activities of law enforcement personnel or employees of governmental agencies or other entities, either public or private who, in the course and scope of their employment, and supported by an articulable suspicion, attempt to capture * * * evidence of suspected illegal activity, the suspected violation of any administrative rule or regulation, a suspected fraudulent insurance claim, or any other suspected fraudulent conduct or activity involving a violation of law or pattern of business practices adversely affecting the public health or safety. * * *

" 'Personal and familial activity' includes, but is not limited to, intimate details of the plaintiff's personal life, interactions with the plaintiff's family or significant others, or other aspects of plaintiff's private affairs or concerns. Personal and familial activity does not include illegal or otherwise criminal activity[, but] shall include the activities of victims of crime * * *." Constitution-

e. See generally Lyrissa Barnett Lidsky, *Prying, Spying, and Lying: Intrusive Newsgathering and What the Law should do about it,* 73 Tulane L.Rev 173 (1998). See also Diane Leenheer Zimmerman, *I Spy: The Newsgatherer Under Cover,* 33 U.Rich.L.Rev. 1185 (2000).

f. See Richard A. Epstein, *Privacy, Publication, and the First Amendment,* 52 Stan. L.Rev. 1003 (2000).

g. See Andrew B. Sims, *Food for the Lions: Excessive Damages for Newsgathering Torts and the Limitations of first Amendment Doctrines,* 78 B.U.L.Rev. 507 (1998); Comment, *Balancing, Press Immunity, and the Compatability of Tort Law with the First Amendment,* 82 Minn.L.Rev. 1695 (1998).

al?[h] Consider Recent Legislation, *Anti-Paparazzi Legislation,* 36 Harv. J. Leg. 250 (1999): "Public figures will continue to paint the press as evil and mercenary, but until history unfolds, it can be hard to tell a paparazzo from an investigative news journalist. In order to inform the public, the press needs to be able to behave in a way that is contrary to the wishes of its subjects."

4. *Media ride-alongs.* WILSON v. LAYNE, 526 U.S. 603, 119 S.Ct. 1692, 143 L.Ed.2d 818 (1999), per REHNQUIST, C.J., held that privacy considerations outweighed the interests served by having *Washington Post* reporters accompany police in executing an arrest warrant in the home: "Respondents argue that the presence of the *Washington Post* reporters in the Wilsons' home [served] a number of legitimate law enforcement purposes. They first assert that officers should be able to exercise reasonable discretion about when it would 'further their law enforcement mission to permit members of the news media to accompany them in executing a warrant.' But this claim ignores the importance of the right of residential privacy at the core of the Fourth Amendment. It may well be that media ride-alongs further the law enforcement objectives of the police in a general sense, but that is not the same as furthering the purposes of the search. Were such generalized 'law enforcement objectives' themselves sufficient to trump the Fourth Amendment, the protections guaranteed by that Amendment's text would be significantly watered down.

"Respondents next argue that the presence of third parties could serve the law enforcement purpose of publicizing the government's efforts to combat crime, and facilitate accurate reporting on law enforcement activities. There is certainly language in our opinions interpreting the First Amendment which points to the importance of 'the press' in informing the general public about the administration of criminal justice. *Cox Broadcasting.* [No] one could gainsay the truth of these observations, or the importance of the First Amendment in protecting press freedom from abridgement by the government. But the Fourth Amendment also protects a very important right, and in the present case it is in terms of that right that the media ride-alongs must be judged.

"Surely the possibility of good public relations for the police is simply not enough, standing alone, to justify the ride-along intrusion into a private home."

During the course of a cell phone conversation, the president of a local teacher's union, Kane, told his chief labor negotiator, Bartnicki: "If they're not gonna move for three percent, we're gonna have to go to their, their homes * * * To blow off their front porches, we'll have to do some work on some of those guys. (PAUSES). Really, uh, really and truthfully because this is, you know, this is bad news." The conversation was illegally intercepted by an unknown person and was sent to the head of a local taxpayer's organization, Yocum, who in turn, shared it with school board members and a local broadcaster, Vopper. Vopper played the tape on his radio show. Bartnicki and Kane brought an action against Kane and Vopper invoking state and federal laws prohibiting the disclosure of material known to be unlawfully intercepted.

h. Robert M. O'Neil, *Privacy and Press Freedom: Paparazzi and other Intruders,* 1999 U.Ill.Rev 703; Comment, *Much Ado About Newsgathering: Personal Privacy, Law Enforcement, and the Law of Unintended Consequences for Anti-Paparazzi Legislation,* 147 U.Pa.L.Rev. 1435 (1999); Comment, *Paparazzi Legislation: Policy Arguments and Legal Analysis in Support of their Constitutionality,* 46 UCLA L.Rev. 1633 (1999); Note, *Privacy, Technology, and the California "Anti-Paparazzi Statute,* 112 Harv. L.Rev. 1367 (1999).

BARTNICKI v. VOPPER, 532 U.S. 514, 121 S.Ct. 1753, 149 L.Ed.2d 787 (2001), per STEVENS, J., held the statutes unconstitutional as applied to circumstances in which the defendants played no role in the illegal acquisition of the material, their access to the conversation was obtained lawfully, and the conversation was about a public issue: "We agree with petitioners that 18 U.S.C. § 2511(1)(c), as well as its Pennsylvania analog, is in fact a content-neutral law of general applicability. [In] this case, the basic purpose of the statute at issue is to 'protec[t] the privacy of wire[, electronic,] and oral communications.' S.Rep. No. 1097, 90th Cong., 2d Sess., 66 (1968). The statute does not distinguish based on the content of the intercepted conversations, nor is it justified by reference to the content of those conversations. Rather, the communications at issue are singled out by virtue of the fact that they were illegally intercepted—by virtue of the source, rather than the subject matter.

"On the other hand, the naked prohibition against disclosures is fairly characterized as a regulation of pure speech. Unlike the prohibition against the 'use' of the contents of an illegal interception in § 2511(1)(d), subsection (c) is not a regulation of conduct. It is true that the delivery of a tape recording might be regarded as conduct, but given that the purpose of such a delivery is to provide the recipient with the text of recorded statements, it is like the delivery of a handbill or a pamphlet, and as such, it is the kind of 'speech' that the First Amendment protects.

"[As] a general matter, 'state action to punish the publication of truthful information seldom can satisfy constitutional standards.' *Smith v. Daily Mail Publishing Co.* [The] Government identifies two interests served by the statute—first, the interest in removing an incentive for parties to intercept private conversations, and second, the interest in minimizing the harm to persons whose conversations have been illegally intercepted. We assume that those interests adequately justify the prohibition in § 2511(1)(d) against the interceptor's own use of information that he or she acquired by violating § 2511(1)(a), but it by no means follows that punishing disclosures of lawfully obtained information of public interest by one not involved in the initial illegality is an acceptable means of serving those ends.

"The normal method of deterring unlawful conduct is to impose an appropriate punishment on the person who engages in it. If the sanctions that presently attach to a violation of § 2511(1)(a) do not provide sufficient deterrence, perhaps those sanctions should be made more severe. But it would be quite remarkable to hold that speech by a law-abiding possessor of information can be suppressed in order to deter conduct by a non-law-abiding third party.[a]

"[With] only a handful of exceptions, the violations of § 2511(1)(a) that have been described in litigated cases have been motivated by either financial gain or domestic disputes. In virtually all of those cases, the identity of the person or persons intercepting the communication has been known. Moreover, petitioners cite no evidence that Congress viewed the prohibition against disclosures as a response to the difficulty of identifying persons making improper use of scanners and other surveillance devices and accordingly of deterring such conduct, and there is no empirical evidence to support the assumption that the prohibition against disclosures reduces the number of illegal interceptions.

a. The Court recognized some exceptional cases, but stated the speech implicated was of minimal value, *New York v. Ferber*, Sec. 1, VI, A (child pornography), or did not involve a prohibition of speech (possession or receipt of stolen mail or other property).

"Although this case demonstrates that there may be an occasional situation in which an anonymous scanner will risk criminal prosecution by passing on information without any expectation of financial reward or public praise, surely this is the exceptional case. Moreover, there is no basis for assuming that imposing sanctions upon respondents will deter the unidentified scanner from continuing to engage in surreptitious interceptions. Unusual cases fall far short of a showing that there is a 'need of the highest order' for a rule supplementing the traditional means of deterring antisocial conduct. The justification for any such novel burden on expression must be 'far stronger than mere speculation about serious harms.' Accordingly, the Government's first suggested justification for applying § 2511(1)(c) to an otherwise innocent disclosure of public information is plainly insufficient.[19]

"The Government's second argument, however, is considerably stronger. Privacy of communication is an important interest, [and] the fear of public disclosure of private conversations might well have a chilling effect on private speech. [Accordingly], it seems to us that there are important interests to be considered on both sides of the constitutional calculus. In considering that balance, we acknowledge that some intrusions on privacy are more offensive than others, and that the disclosure of the contents of a private conversation can be an even greater intrusion on privacy than the interception itself. As a result, there is a valid independent justification for prohibiting such disclosures by persons who lawfully obtained access to the contents of an illegally intercepted message, even if that prohibition does not play a significant role in preventing such interceptions from occurring in the first place.

"We need not decide whether that interest is strong enough to justify the application of § 2511(c) to disclosures of trade secrets or domestic gossip or other information of purely private concern. In other words, the outcome of the case does not turn on whether § 2511(1)(c) may be enforced with respect to most violations of the statute without offending the First Amendment. The enforcement of that provision in this case, however, implicates the core purposes of the First Amendment because it imposes sanctions on the publication of truthful information of public concern.

"In this case, privacy concerns give way when balanced against the interest in publishing matters of public importance. [The] months of negotiations over the proper level of compensation for teachers at the Wyoming Valley West High School were unquestionably a matter of public concern, and respondents were clearly engaged in debate about that concern. That debate may be more mundane than the Communist rhetoric that inspired Justice Brandeis' classic opinion in *Whitney v. California*, but it is no less worthy of constitutional protection."

Breyer, J., joined by O'Connor, J., concurred: "I write separately to explain why, in my view, the Court's holding does not imply a significantly broader constitutional immunity for the media.

"[As] a general matter, despite the statutes' direct restrictions on speech, the Federal Constitution must tolerate laws of this kind because of the importance of these privacy and speech-related objectives. [Nonetheless], looked at more specifi-

19. Our holding, of course, does not apply to punishing parties for obtaining the relevant information unlawfully. "It would be frivolous to assert—and no one does in these cases—that the First Amendment, in the interest of securing news or otherwise, confers a license on either the reporter or his news sources to violate valid criminal laws. Although stealing documents or private wiretapping could provide newsworthy information, neither reporter nor source is immune from conviction for such conduct, whatever the impact on the flow of news." *Branzburg*.

cally, the statutes, as applied in these circumstances, do not reasonably reconcile the competing constitutional objectives. Rather, they disproportionately interfere with media freedom. For one thing, the broadcasters here engaged in no unlawful activity other than the ultimate publication of the information another had previously obtained. [For] another thing, the speakers had little or no legitimate interest in maintaining the privacy of the particular conversation. That conversation involved a suggestion about 'blow[ing] off ... front porches' and 'do[ing] some work on some of these guys,' thereby raising a significant concern for the safety of others. Where publication of private information constitutes a wrongful act, the law recognizes a privilege allowing the reporting of threats to public safety. [Even] where the danger may have passed by the time of publication, that fact cannot legitimize the speaker's earlier privacy expectation. Nor should editors, who must make a publication decision quickly, have to determine present or continued danger before publishing this kind of threat.

"Further, the speakers themselves, the president of a teacher's union and the union's chief negotiator, were 'limited public figures,' for they voluntarily engaged in a public controversy. They thereby subjected themselves to somewhat greater public scrutiny and had a lesser interest in privacy than an individual engaged in purely private affairs. [This] is not to say that the Constitution requires anyone, including public figures, to give up entirely the right to private communication, i.e., communication free from telephone taps or interceptions. But the subject matter of the conversation at issue here is far removed from that in situations where the media publicizes truly private matters.

"Thus, in finding a constitutional privilege to publish unlawfully intercepted conversations of the kind here at issue, the Court does not create a 'public interest' exception that swallows up the statutes' privacy-protecting general rule. Rather, it finds constitutional protection for publication of intercepted information of a special kind. Here, the speakers' legitimate privacy expectations are unusually low, and the public interest in defeating those expectations is unusually high."

Rehnquist, C.J., joined by Scalia and Thomas, JJ., dissented: "Technology now permits millions of important and confidential conversations to occur through a vast system of electronic networks. These advances, however, raise significant privacy concerns. We are placed in the uncomfortable position of not knowing who might have access to our personal and business e-mails, our medical and financial records, or our cordless and cellular telephone conversations. In an attempt to prevent some of the most egregious violations of privacy, the United States, the District of Columbia, and 40 States have enacted laws prohibiting the intentional interception and knowing disclosure of electronic communications. The Court holds that all of these statutes violate the First Amendment insofar as the illegally intercepted conversation touches upon a matter of 'public concern,' an amorphous concept that the Court does not even attempt to define. But the Court's decision diminishes, rather than enhances, the purposes of the First Amendment: chilling the speech of the millions of Americans who rely upon electronic technology to communicate each day. * * *

"The Court correctly observes that these are 'content-neutral law[s] of general applicability' which serve recognized interests of the 'highest order': 'the interest in individual privacy [and] in fostering private speech.' It nonetheless subjects these laws to the strict scrutiny normally reserved for governmental attempts to censor different viewpoints or ideas. There is scant support, either in precedent or in reason, for the Court's tacit application of strict scrutiny.

"[Here], Congress and the Pennsylvania Legislature have acted 'without reference to the content of the regulated speech.' *Renton v. Playtime Theatres, Inc.* There is no intimation that these laws seek 'to suppress unpopular ideas or information or manipulate the public debate' or that they 'distinguish favored speech from disfavored speech on the basis of the ideas or views expressed.' The antidisclosure provision is based solely upon the manner in which the conversation was acquired, not the subject matter of the conversation or the viewpoints of the speakers. The same information, if obtained lawfully, could be published with impunity. As the concerns motivating strict scrutiny are absent, these content-neutral restrictions upon speech need pass only intermediate scrutiny.

"[I]t is obvious that the *Daily Mail* cases upon which the Court relies do not address the question presented here. Our decisions themselves made this clear: 'The *Daily Mail* principle does not settle the issue whether, in cases where information has been acquired unlawfully by a newspaper or by a source, the government may ever punish not only the unlawful acquisition, but the ensuing publication as well.' *Florida Star*. [Undaunted], the Court places an inordinate amount of weight upon the fact that the receipt of an illegally intercepted communication has not been criminalized. But this hardly renders those who knowingly receive and disclose such communications 'law-abiding,' and it certainly does not bring them under the *Daily Mail* principle. The transmission of the intercepted communication from the eavesdropper to the third party is itself illegal; and where, as here, the third party then knowingly discloses that communication, another illegal act has been committed. The third party in this situation cannot be likened to the reporters in the *Daily Mail* cases, who lawfully obtained their information through consensual interviews or public documents.

"These laws are content neutral; they only regulate information that was illegally obtained; they do not restrict republication of what is already in the public domain; they impose no special burdens upon the media; they have a scienter requirement to provide fair warning; and they promote the privacy and free speech of those using cellular telephones. It is hard to imagine a more narrowly tailored prohibition of the disclosure of illegally intercepted communications, and it distorts our precedents to review these statutes under the often fatal standard of strict scrutiny. These laws therefore should be upheld if they further a substantial governmental interest unrelated to the suppression of free speech, and they do. * * *

"The 'dry up the market' theory, which posits that it is possible to deter an illegal act that is difficult to police by preventing the wrongdoer from enjoying the fruits of the crime, is neither novel nor implausible. It is a time-tested theory that undergirds numerous laws, such as the prohibition of the knowing possession of stolen goods. See 2 W. LaFave & A. Scott, *Substantive Criminal Law* § 8.10(a), p. 422 (1986) ("Without such receivers, theft ceases to be profitable. It is obvious that the receiver must be a principal target of any society anxious to stamp out theft in its various forms"). We ourselves adopted the exclusionary rule based upon similar reasoning, believing that it would 'deter unreasonable searches,' *Oregon v. Elstad*, 470 U.S. 298, 306, 105 S.Ct. 1285, 84 L.Ed.2d 222 (1985), by removing an officer's 'incentive to disregard [the Fourth Amendment],' *Elkins v. United States*, 364 U.S. 206, 217, 80 S.Ct. 1437, 4 L.Ed.2d 1669 (1960).

"The same logic applies here and demonstrates that the incidental restriction on alleged First Amendment freedoms is no greater than essential to further the interest of protecting the privacy of individual communications. Were there no prohibition on disclosure, an unlawful eavesdropper who wanted to disclose the conversation could anonymously launder the interception through a third party and thereby avoid detection. Indeed, demand for illegally obtained private information would only increase if it could be disclosed without repercussion. The law against interceptions, which the Court agrees is valid, would be utterly ineffectual without these antidisclosure provisions.[8]

"[At] base, the Court's decision to hold these statutes unconstitutional rests upon nothing more than the bald substitution of its own prognostications in place of the reasoned judgment of 41 legislative bodies and the United States Congress. The Court does not explain how or from where Congress should obtain statistical evidence about the effectiveness of these laws, and '[s]ince as a practical matter it is never easy to prove a negative, it is hardly likely that conclusive factual data could ever be assembled.' *Elkins*. Reliance upon the 'dry up the market' theory is both logical and eminently reasonable, and our precedents make plain that it is 'far stronger than mere speculation.'

"These statutes also protect the important interests of deterring clandestine invasions of privacy and preventing the involuntary broadcast of private communications. [These] statutes undeniably protect this venerable right of privacy. [Although] the Court recognizes and even extols the virtues of this right to privacy, these are 'mere words,' W. Shakespeare, *Troilus and Cressida*, act v, sc. 3, overridden by the Court's newfound right to publish unlawfully acquired information of 'public concern.' The Court concludes that the private conversation between Gloria Bartnicki and Anthony Kane is somehow a 'debate * * * worthy of constitutional protection.' Perhaps the Court is correct that '[i]f the statements about the labor negotiations had been made in a public arena—during a bargaining session, for example—they would have been newsworthy.' The point, however, is that Bartnicki and Kane had no intention of contributing to a public 'debate' at all, and it is perverse to hold that another's unlawful interception and knowing disclosure of their conversation is speech 'worthy of constitutional protection.' * * *

"The Constitution should not protect the involuntary broadcast of personal conversations. Even where the communications involve public figures or concern public matters, the conversations are nonetheless private and worthy of protection. Although public persons may have forgone the right to live their lives screened from public scrutiny in some areas, it does not and should not follow that they also have abandoned their right to have a private conversation without fear of it being intentionally intercepted and knowingly disclosed.

"Surely 'the interest in individual privacy,' at its narrowest must embrace the right to be free from surreptitious eavesdropping on, and involuntary broadcast of, our cellular telephone conversations. The Court subordinates that right, not to the claims of those who themselves wish to speak, but to the claims of those who wish to publish the intercepted conversations of others. Congress' effort to balance the above claim to privacy against a marginal claim to speak freely is thereby set at naught."

8. The Court attempts to distinguish *Ferber* and *Osborne* on the ground that they involved low-value speech, but this has nothing to do with the reasonableness of the "dry up the market" theory. The Court also posits that Congress here could simply have increased the penalty for intercepting cellular communications. But the Court's back-seat legislative advice does nothing to undermine the reasonableness of Congress' belief that prohibiting only the initial interception would not effectively protect the privacy interests of cellular telephone users.

PRIOR RESTRAINTS, OBSCENITY, AND COMMERCIAL SPEECH

CON LAW: P. 809, include in note 2

RTS & LIB: P. 736, include in note 2

See also *City of Littleton v. Z.J. Gifts D–4,* 541 U.S. 774, 124 S.Ct. 2219, 159 L.Ed.2d 84 (2004) (*Freedman* standards apply to adult business licensing ordinances including the assurance of speedy court decisions); *Thomas v. Chicago Park Dist.,* 534 U.S. 316, 122 S.Ct. 775, 151 L.Ed.2d 783 (2002) (*Freedman* does not apply to content neutral licensing requirement granting authorities for assemblies involving more than fifty persons in public park even when ordinance as a matter of course grants authorities fourteen days to decide whether permit should be issued).

GOVERNMENT PROPERTY AND THE PUBLIC FORUM

NEW FORUMS

CON LAW: P. 857, add to fn. c

AMER CON: P. 808, add to fn. c

RTS & LIB: 784, add to fn. c

Good News Club v. Milford Central School, 533 U.S. 98, 121 S.Ct. 2093, 150 L.Ed.2d 151 (2001)(viewpoint discrimination to refuse access to elementary school classrooms after school for group engaging in religious instruction and prayer to discuss morals and character while permitting access to groups who would discuss the development of character and morals in other ways).

GOVERNMENT SUPPORT OF SPEECH

SUBSIDIES OF SPEECH

CON LAW: P. 896, after note 4

AMER CON: P. 829 after note 7

RTS & LIB: P. 823 after note 4

The Legal Services Corporation ("LSC") was established by the Legal Services Corporation Act to distribute federal funds to recipients providing, among other things, representation of indigent clients seeking welfare benefits. One of the restrictions was that grantees could not use such funds to amend or challenge the constitutionality or the statutory validity of existing welfare laws. LEGAL SERVICES CORP. v. VELAZQUEZ, 531 U.S. 533, 121 S.Ct. 1043, 149 L.Ed.2d 63 (2001), per KENNEDY, J., invalidated the restriction: "The United States and LSC rely on *Rust* as support for the LSC program restrictions. In *Rust,* Congress established program clinics to provide subsidies for doctors to advise patients on a variety of family planning topics. Congress did not consider abortion to be within its family planning objectives, however, and it forbade doctors employed by the program from discussing abortion with their patients. [We] upheld the law, reasoning that Congress had not discriminated against viewpoints on abortion, but had 'merely chosen to fund one activity to the exclusion of the other.' The restrictions were considered necessary 'to ensure that the limits of the federal program [were] observed.' Title X did not single out a particular idea for suppression because it was dangerous or disfavored; rather, Congress prohibited Title X doctors from counseling that was outside the scope of the project.

"The Court in *Rust* did not place explicit reliance on the rationale that the counseling activities of the doctors under Title X amounted to governmental speech; when interpreting the holding in later cases, however, we have explained *Rust* on this understanding. We have said that viewpoint-based funding decisions can be sustained in instances in which the government is itself the speaker or instances, like *Rust,* in which the government 'used private speakers to transmit information pertaining to its own program.' *Rosenberger*. As we said in *Rosenberger,* '[w]hen the government disburses public funds to private entities to convey a governmental message, it may take legitimate and appropriate steps to ensure that its message is neither garbled nor distorted by the grantee.'

"[Neither] the latitude for government speech nor its rationale applies to subsidies for private speech in every instance, however. As we have pointed out, '[i]t does not follow [that] viewpoint-based restrictions are proper when the [government] does not itself speak or subsidize transmittal of a message it favors but instead expends funds to encourage a diversity of views from private speakers.' *Rosenberger*.

"Although the LSC program differs from the program at issue in *Rosenberger* in that its purpose is not to 'encourage a diversity of views,' the salient point is that, like the program in *Rosenberger,* the LSC program was designed to facilitate private speech, not to promote a governmental message. Congress funded LSC grantees to provide attorneys to represent the interests of indigent clients. In the specific context of § 504(a)(16) suits for benefits, an LSC-funded attorney speaks on the behalf of the client in a claim against the government for welfare benefits. The lawyer is not the government's speaker. The attorney defending the decision to deny benefits will deliver the government's message in the litigation. The LSC lawyer, however, speaks on the behalf of his or her private, indigent client.

"The Government has designed this program to use the legal profession and the established Judiciary of the States and the Federal Government to accomplish its end of assisting welfare claimants in determination or receipt of their benefits. The advice from the attorney to the client and the advocacy by the attorney to the courts cannot be classified as governmental speech even under a generous understanding of the concept. In this vital respect this suit is distinguishable from *Rust.*

"The private nature of the speech involved here, and the extent of LSC's regulation of private expression, are indicated further by the circumstance that the Government seeks to use an existing medium of expression and to control it, in a class of cases, in ways which distort its usual functioning. [The] restriction imposed by the statute here threatens severe impairment of the judicial function. Section 504(a)(16) sifts out cases presenting constitutional challenges in order to insulate the Government's laws from judicial inquiry. If the restriction on speech and legal advice were to stand, the result would be two tiers of cases. In cases where LSC counsel were attorneys of record, there would be lingering doubt whether the truncated representation had resulted in complete analysis of the case, full advice to the client, and proper presentation to the court. The courts and the public would come to question the adequacy and fairness of professional representations when the attorney, either consciously to comply with this statute or unconsciously to continue the representation despite the statute, avoided all reference to questions of statutory validity and constitutional authority. A scheme so inconsistent with accepted separation-of-powers principles is an insufficient basis to sustain or uphold the restriction on speech.

"It is no answer to say the restriction on speech is harmless because, under LSC's interpretation of the Act, its attorneys can withdraw. This misses the point.

The statute is an attempt to draw lines around the LSC program to exclude from litigation those arguments and theories Congress finds unacceptable but which by their nature are within the province of the courts to consider. The restriction on speech is even more problematic because in cases where the attorney withdraws from a representation, the client is unlikely to find other counsel. [This] is in stark contrast to *Rust.* There, a patient could receive the approved Title X family planning counseling funded by the Government and later could consult an affiliate or independent organization to receive abortion counseling. Unlike indigent clients who seek LSC representation, the patient in *Rust* was not required to forfeit the Government-funded advice when she also received abortion counseling through alternative channels. Because LSC attorneys must withdraw whenever a question of a welfare statute's validity arises, an individual could not obtain joint representation so that the constitutional challenge would be presented by a non-LSC attorney, and other, permitted, arguments advanced by LSC counsel. * * *

"Congress was not required to fund an LSC attorney to represent indigent clients; and when it did so, it was not required to fund the whole range of legal representations or relationships. The LSC and the United States, however, in effect ask us to permit Congress to define the scope of the litigation it funds to exclude certain vital theories and ideas. The attempted restriction is designed to insulate the Government's interpretation of the Constitution from judicial challenge. The Constitution does not permit the Government to confine litigants and their attorneys in this manner. We must be vigilant when Congress imposes rules and conditions which in effect insulate its own laws from legitimate judicial challenge. Where private speech is involved, even Congress' antecedent funding decision cannot be aimed at the suppression of ideas thought inimical to the Government's own interest.

"For the reasons we have set forth, the funding condition is invalid. The Court of Appeals considered whether the language restricting LSC attorneys could be severed from the statute so that the remaining portions would remain operative. It reached the reasoned conclusion to invalidate the fragment of § 504(a)(16) found contrary to the First Amendment, leaving the balance of the statute operative and in place. That determination was not discussed in the briefs of either party or otherwise contested here, and in the exercise of our discretion and prudential judgment we decline to address it."

Scalia, J., joined by Rehnquist, C.J., and O'Connor and Thomas, JJ., dissented: "The LSC Act, like the scheme in *Rust* does not create a public forum. Far from encouraging a diversity of views, it has always, as the Court accurately states, 'placed restrictions on its use of funds.' Nor does § 504(a)(16) discriminate on the basis of viewpoint, since it funds neither challenges to nor defenses of existing welfare law. The provision simply declines to subsidize a certain class of litigation, and under *Rust* that decision 'does not infringe the right' to bring such litigation. [No] litigant who, in the absence of LSC funding, would bring a suit challenging existing welfare law is deterred from doing so by § 504(a)(16). *Rust* thus controls these cases and compels the conclusion that § 504(a)(16) is constitutional.

"The Court contends that *Rust* is different because the program at issue subsidized government speech, while the LSC funds private speech. This is so unpersuasive it hardly needs response. If the private doctors' confidential advice to their patients at issue in *Rust* constituted 'government speech,' it is hard to imagine what subsidized speech would *not* be government speech. Moreover, the majority's contention that the subsidized speech in these cases is not government speech because the lawyers have a professional obligation to represent the interests of their clients founders on the reality that the doctors in *Rust* had a professional obligation to serve the interests of their patients. * * *

"The Court further asserts that these cases are different from *Rust* because the welfare funding restriction 'seeks to use an existing medium of expression and to control it [in] ways which distort its usual functioning.' This is wrong on both the facts and the law. It is wrong on the law because there is utterly no precedent for the novel and facially implausible proposition that the First Amendment has anything to do with government funding that—though it does not actually abridge anyone's speech—'distorts an existing medium of expression.' None of the [cases] cited by the Court mentions such an odd principle. In *Rosenberger,* the point critical to the Court's analysis was not, as the Court would have it, that it is part of the 'usual functioning' of student newspapers to 'expres[s] many different points of view,' (it surely is not), but rather *that the spending program itself* had been created 'to encourage a diversity of views from private speakers.' What could not be distorted was *the public forum* that the spending program had created. * * *

"The Court's 'nondistortion' principle is also wrong on the facts, since there is no basis for believing that § 504(a)(16), by causing 'cases [to] be presented by LSC attorneys who [can] not advise the courts of serious questions of statutory validity,' will distort the operation of the courts. It may well be that the bar of § 504(a)(16) will cause LSC-funded attorneys to decline or to withdraw from cases that involve statutory validity. But that means at most that fewer statutory challenges to welfare laws will be presented to the courts because of the unavailability of free legal services for that purpose. So what? The same result would ensue from excluding LSC-funded lawyers from welfare litigation entirely. It is not the mandated, nondistortable function of the courts to inquire into all 'serious questions of statutory validity' in all cases. Courts must consider only those questions of statutory validity *that are presented by litigants,* and if the Government chooses not to subsidize the presentation of some such questions, that in no way 'distorts' the courts' role. * * *

"Finally, the Court is troubled 'because in cases where the attorney withdraws from a representation, the client is unlikely to find other counsel.' That is surely irrelevant, since it leaves the welfare recipient in no *worse* condition than he would have been in had the LSC program never been enacted. Respondents properly concede that even if welfare claimants cannot obtain a lawyer anywhere else, the Government is not required to provide one. It is hard to see how providing free legal services to some welfare claimants (those whose claims do not challenge the applicable statutes) while not providing it to others is beyond the range of legitimate legislative choice.

"The only conceivable argument that can be made for distinguishing *Rust* is that there even patients who wished to receive abortion counseling could receive the nonabortion services that the Government-funded clinic offered, whereas here some potential LSC clients who wish to receive representation on a benefits claim that does not challenge the statutes will be unable to do so because their cases raise a reform claim that an LSC lawyer may not present. This difference, of course, is required by the same ethical canons that the Court elsewhere does not wish to distort. Rather than sponsor 'truncated representation,' Congress chose to subsidize only those cases in which the attorneys it subsidized could work freely. And it is impossible to see how this difference from *Rust* has any bearing upon the First Amendment question, [which] is whether the funding scheme is manipulated to have a coercive effect on those who do not hold the subsidized position. *Finley*. It could be claimed to have such an effect if the client in a case ineligible for LSC representation could eliminate the ineligibility by waiving the claim that the statute is invalid; but he cannot. No *conceivable* coercive effect exists.

"This has been a very long discussion to make a point that is embarrassingly simple: The LSC subsidy neither prevents anyone from speaking nor coerces anyone to change speech, and is indistinguishable in all relevant respects from the subsidy upheld in *Rust*. There is no legitimate basis for declaring § 504(a)(16) facially unconstitutional."[a]

GOVERNMENT AS EDUCATOR AND EDITOR

CON LAW: P. 913, after note 3

AMER CON: P. 841, after note 3

RTS & LIB: P. 840, after note 3

UNITED STATES V. AMERICAN LIBRARY ASSOCIATION, INC.

539 U.S. 194, 123 S.Ct. 2297, 156 L.Ed.2d 221 (2003).

CHIEF JUSTICE REHNQUIST announced the judgment of the Court and delivered an opinion, in which JUSTICE O'CONNOR, JUSTICE SCALIA, and JUSTICE THOMAS joined.

To address the problems associated with the availability of Internet pornography in public libraries, Congress enacted the Children's Internet Protection Act (CIPA). Under CIPA, a public library may not receive federal assistance to provide Internet access unless it installs software to block images that constitute obscenity or child pornography, and to prevent minors from obtaining access to material that is harmful to them. The District Court held these provisions facially invalid on the ground that they induce public libraries to violate patrons' First Amendment rights. We now reverse. * * *

By connecting to the Internet, public libraries provide patrons with a vast amount of valuable information. But there is also an enormous amount of pornography on the Internet, much of which is easily obtained. The accessibility of this material has created serious problems for libraries, which have found that patrons of all ages, including minors, regularly search for online pornography. Some patrons also expose others to pornographic images by leaving them displayed on Internet terminals or printed at library printers. * * *

Congress [learned] that filtering software that blocks access to pornographic Web sites could provide a reasonably effective way to prevent such uses of library resources. By 2000, before Congress enacted CIPA, almost 17% of public libraries used such software on at least some of their Internet terminals, and 7% had filters on all of them. A library can set such software to block categories of material, such as "Pornography" or "Violence." When a patron tries to view a site that falls within such a category, a screen appears

a. Scalia, J., also objected to the failure to consider whether the statutory restriction was severable and argued that it was not.

indicating that the site is blocked. But a filter set to block pornography may sometimes block other sites that present neither obscene nor pornographic material, but that nevertheless trigger the filter. To minimize this problem, a library can set its software to prevent the blocking of material that falls into categories like "Education," "History," and "Medical." A library may also add or delete specific sites from a blocking category, and anyone can ask companies that furnish filtering software to unblock particular sites.

Responding to this information, Congress enacted CIPA. It provides that a library may not receive [assistance] unless it has "a policy of Internet safety for minors that includes the operation of a technology protection measure [that] protects against access" by all persons to "visual depictions" that constitute "obscen[ity]" or "child pornography," and that protects against access by minors to "visual depictions" that are "harmful to minors." * * *

Congress has wide latitude to attach conditions to the receipt of federal assistance in order to further its policy objectives. But Congress may not "induce" the recipient "to engage in activities that would themselves be unconstitutional." * * *

Just as [public] forum analysis and heightened judicial scrutiny are incompatible with the role of public television stations and the role of the NEA, they are also incompatible with the discretion that public libraries must have to fulfill their traditional missions. Public library staffs necessarily consider content in making collection decisions and enjoy broad discretion in making them.

The public forum principles [are] out of place in the context of this case. Internet access in public libraries is neither a "traditional" nor a "designated" public forum. * * * First, this resource—which did not exist until quite recently—has not "immemorially been held in trust for the use of the public and, time out of mind, [been] used for purposes of assembly, communication of thoughts between citizens, and discussing public questions." We have "rejected the view that traditional public forum status extends beyond its historic confines." The doctrines surrounding traditional public forums may not be extended to situations where such history is lacking.

Nor does Internet access in a public library satisfy our definition of a "designated public forum." To create such a forum, the government must make an affirmative choice to open up its property for use as a public forum. [A] public library does not acquire Internet terminals in order to create a public forum for Web publishers to express themselves, any more than it collects books in order to provide a public forum for the authors of books to speak. It provides Internet access, not to "encourage a diversity of views from private speakers," *Rosenberger*, but for the same reasons it offers other library resources: to facilitate research, learning, and recreational pursuits by furnishing materials of requisite and appropriate quality. As Congress recognized, "[t]he Internet is simply another method for making information available in a school or library." It is "no more than a technological extension of the book stack."

The District Court disagreed because, whereas a library reviews and affirmatively chooses to acquire every book in its collection, it does not review every Web site that it makes available. Based on this distinction, the court reasoned that a public library enjoys less discretion in deciding which Internet materials to make available than in making book selections. We do not find this distinction constitutionally relevant. A library's failure to make quality-based judgments about all the material it furnishes from the Web does not somehow taint the judgments it does make. A library's need to exercise judgment in making collection decisions depends on its traditional role in identifying suitable and worthwhile material; it is no less entitled to play that role when it collects material from the Internet than when it collects material from any other source. Most libraries already exclude pornography from their print collections because they deem it inappropriate for inclusion. We do not subject these decisions to heightened scrutiny; it would make little sense to treat libraries' judgments to block online pornography any differently, when these judgments are made for just the same reason.

Moreover, because of the vast quantity of material on the Internet and the rapid pace at which it changes, libraries cannot possibly segregate, item by item, all the Internet material that is appropriate for inclusion from all that is not. While a library could limit its Internet collection to just those sites it found worthwhile, it could do so only at the cost of excluding an enormous amount of valuable information that it lacks the capacity to review. Given that tradeoff, it is entirely reasonable for public libraries to reject that approach and instead exclude certain categories of content, without making individualized judgments that everything they do make available has requisite and appropriate quality. * * *

Assuming that [erroneous] blocking presents constitutional difficulties, any such concerns are dispelled by the ease with which patrons may have the filtering software disabled. When a patron encounters a blocked site, he need only ask a librarian to unblock it or (at least in the case of adults) disable the filter. As the District Court found, libraries have the capacity to permanently unblock any erroneously blocked site, and the Solicitor General stated at oral argument that a "library [may] eliminate the filtering with respect to specific sites [at] the request of a patron." [The] District Court viewed unblocking and disabling as inadequate because some patrons may be too embarrassed to request them. But the Constitution does not guarantee the right to acquire information at a public library without any risk of embarrassment. * * *

Justice Stevens asserts the premise that "[a] federal statute penalizing a library for failing to install filtering software on every one of its Internet-accessible computers would unquestionably violate [the First] Amendment." But—assuming [that] public libraries have First Amendment rights—CIPA does not "penalize" libraries that choose not to install such software, or deny them the right to provide their patrons with unfiltered Internet access. Rather, CIPA simply reflects Congress' decision not to subsidize their doing so. To the extent that libraries wish to offer unfiltered access, they are free to do so without federal assistance. "A refusal to fund protected activity, without more, cannot be equated with the imposition of a 'penalty' on that activity." "[A] legislature's decision not to subsidize the exercise of a fundamental right does not infringe the right." *Rust.* * * *

Justice Kennedy, concurring in the judgment.

If, on the request of an adult user, a librarian will unblock filtered material or disable the Internet software filter without significant delay, there is little to this case. The Government represents this is indeed the fact.

The District Court, in its "Preliminary Statement," did say that "the unblocking may take days, and may be unavailable, especially in branch libraries, which are often less well staffed than main libraries." That statement, however, does not appear to be a specific finding. It was not the basis for the District Court's decision in any event, as the court assumed that "the disabling provisions permit public libraries to allow a patron access to any speech that is constitutionally protected with respect to that patron."

If some libraries do not have the capacity to unblock specific Web sites or to disable the filter or if it is shown that an adult user's election to view constitutionally protected Internet material is burdened in some other substantial way, that would be the subject for an as-applied challenge, not the facial challenge made in this case. * * *

JUSTICE BREYER, concurring in the judgment. * * *

Due to present technological limitations, [the] software filters both "overblock," screening out some perfectly legitimate material, and "underblock," allowing some obscene material to escape detection by the filter. But no one has presented any clearly superior or better fitting alternatives.

At the same time, the Act contains an important exception that limits the speech-related harm that "overblocking" might cause. As the plurality points out, the Act allows libraries to permit any adult patron access to an "overblocked" Web site; the adult patron need only ask a librarian to unblock the specific Web site or, alternatively, ask the librarian, "Please disable the entire filter."

The Act does impose upon the patron the burden of making this request. But it is difficult to see how that burden (or any delay associated with compliance) could prove more onerous than traditional library practices associated with segregating library materials in, say, closed stacks, or with interlibrary lending practices that require patrons to make requests that are not anonymous and to wait while the librarian obtains the desired materials from elsewhere. Perhaps local library rules or practices could further restrict the ability of patrons to obtain "overblocked" Internet material. But we are not now considering any such local practices. We here consider only a facial challenge to the Act itself.

Given the comparatively small burden that the Act imposes upon the library patron seeking legitimate Internet materials, I cannot say that any speech-related harm that the Act may cause is disproportionate when considered in relation to the Act's legitimate objectives. * * *

JUSTICE STEVENS, dissenting.

"To fulfill their traditional missions, public libraries must have broad discretion to decide what material to provide their patrons." Accordingly, I agree with the plurality that it is neither inappropriate nor unconstitutional for a local library to experiment with filtering software as a means of curtailing children's access to Internet Web sites displaying sexually explicit images. I also agree with the plurality that the 7% of public libraries that decided to use such software on all of their Internet terminals in 2000 did not act unlawfully. Whether it is constitutional for the Congress of the United States to impose that requirement on the other 93%, however, raises a vastly different question. Rather than allowing local decisionmakers to tailor their responses to local problems, the Children's Internet Protection Act (CIPA) operates as a blunt nationwide restraint on adult access to "an enormous amount of valuable information" that individual librarians cannot possibly review. Most of that information is constitutionally protected speech. In my view, this restraint is unconstitutional. * * *

"[T]he search engines that software companies use for harvesting are able to search text only, not images. This is of critical importance, because CIPA, by its own terms, covers only 'visual depictions.' [Given] the quantity and ever-changing character of Web sites offering free sexually explicit material, it is inevitable that a substantial amount of such material will never be blocked. Because of this "underblocking," the statute will provide parents with a false sense of security without really solving the problem that motivated its enactment. Conversely, the software's reliance on words to identify undesirable sites necessarily results in the blocking of thousands of pages that "contain content that is completely innocuous for both adults and minors, and that no rational person could conclude matches the filtering companies' category definitions, such as "pornography' or 'sex.' " In my judgment, a statutory blunderbuss that mandates this vast amount of "overblocking" abridges the freedom of speech protected by the First Amendment.

The effect of the overblocking is the functional equivalent of a host of individual decisions excluding hundreds of thousands of individual constitutionally protected messages from Internet terminals located in public libraries throughout the Nation. Neither the interest in suppressing unlawful speech nor the interest in protecting children from access to harmful materials justifies this overly broad restriction on adult access to protected speech. * * *

Until a blocked site or group of sites is unblocked, a patron is unlikely to know what is being hidden and therefore whether there is any point in asking for the filter to be removed. It is as though the statute required a significant part of every library's reading materials to be kept in unmarked, locked rooms or cabinets, which could be opened only in response to specific requests. Some curious readers would in time obtain access to the hidden materials, but many would not. Inevitably, the interest of the authors of those works in reaching the widest possible audience would be abridged. Moreover, because the procedures that different libraries are likely to adopt to respond to unblocking requests will no doubt vary, it is impossible to measure the aggregate effect of the statute on patrons' access to blocked sites. Unless we assume that the statute is a mere symbolic gesture, we must conclude that it will create a significant prior restraint on adult access to protected speech. * * *

As the plurality recognizes, we have always assumed that libraries have discretion when making decisions regarding what to include in, and exclude from, their collections. [A] federal statute penalizing a library for failing to install filtering software on every one of its Internet-accessible computers would unquestionably violate that Amendment. I think it equally clear that the First Amendment protects libraries from being denied funds for refusing to comply with an identical rule. An abridgment of speech by means of a threatened denial of benefits can be just as pernicious as an abridgment by means of a threatened penalty. * * *

The plurality argues that the controversial decision in *Rust v. Sullivan* requires rejection of appellees' unconstitutional conditions claim. But, as subsequent cases have explained, *Rust* only involved and only applies to instances of governmental speech—that is, situations in which the government seeks to communicate a specific message. The discounts under the E-rate program and funding under the Library Services and Technology Act (LSTA) program involved in this case do not subsidize any message favored by the Government. As Congress made clear, these programs were designed "[t]o help public libraries provide their patrons with Internet access," which in turn "provide[s] patrons with a vast amount of valuable information." These programs thus are designed to provide access, particularly for individuals in low-income communities to a vast amount and wide variety of private speech. They are not designed to foster or transmit any particular governmental message.

Even if we were to construe the passage of CIPA as modifying the E-rate and LSTA programs such that they now convey a governmental message that no " 'visual depictions' that are 'obscene,' 'child pornography,' or in the case of minors, 'harmful to minors,' " should be expressed or viewed, the use of filtering software does not promote that message. [T]he message conveyed by the use of filtering software is not that all speech except that which is prohibited by CIPA is supported by the Government, but rather that all speech that gets through the software is supported by the Government. And the items that get through the software include some visual depictions that are obscene, some that are child pornography, and some that are harmful to minors, while at the same time the software blocks an enormous amount of speech that is not sexually explicit and certainly does not meet CIPA's definitions of prohibited content. As such, since the message conveyed is far from the message the Government purports to promote—indeed, the material permitted past the filtering software does not seem to have any coherent message–*Rust* is inapposite. * * *

JUSTICE SOUTER, with whom JUSTICE GINSBURG joins, dissenting.

I agree in the main with Justice Stevens that the blocking requirements impose an unconstitutional condition on the Government's subsidies to local libraries for providing access to the Internet. I also agree with the library appellees on a further reason to hold the blocking rule invalid in the exercise of the spending power under Article I, § 8: the rule mandates action by recipient libraries that would violate the First Amendment's guarantee of free speech if the libraries took that action entirely on their own. * * *

I [would not] dissent if I agreed with the majority of my colleagues that an adult library patron could, consistently with the Act, obtain an unblocked terminal simply for the asking. [T]he District Court expressly found that "unblocking may take days, and may be unavailable, especially in branch libraries, which are often less well staffed than main libraries." [We] therefore have to take the statute on the understanding that adults will be denied access to a substantial amount of nonobscene material harmful to children but lawful for adult examination, and a substantial quantity of text and pictures harmful to no one. * * *

We likewise have to examine the statute on the understanding that the restrictions on adult Internet access have no justification in the object of protecting children. Children could be restricted to blocked terminals, leaving other unblocked terminals in areas restricted to adults and screened from casual glances. And of course the statute could simply have provided for unblocking at adult request, with no questions asked. The statute could, in other words, have protected children without blocking access for adults or subjecting adults to anything more than minimal inconvenience, just the way (the record shows) many librarians had been dealing with obscenity and indecency before imposition of the federal conditions. * * *

The question for me, then, is whether a local library could itself constitutionally impose these restrictions on the content otherwise available to an adult patron through an Internet connection, at a library terminal provided for public use. The answer is no. A library that chose to block an adult's Internet access to material harmful to children (and whatever else the undiscriminating filter might interrupt) would be imposing a content-based restriction on communication of material in the library's control that an adult could otherwise lawfully see. This would simply be censorship. * * *

The Court's plurality does not treat blocking affecting adults as censorship, but chooses to describe a library's act in filtering content as simply an instance of the kind of selection from available material that every library (save, perhaps, the Library of Congress) must perform. * * *

Public libraries are indeed selective in what they acquire to place in their stacks, as they must be. [At] every significant point, however, the Internet blocking here defies comparison to the process of acquisition. Whereas traditional scarcity of money and space require a library to make choices about what to acquire, and the choice to be made is whether or not to spend the money to acquire something, blocking is the subject of a choice made after the money for Internet access has been spent or committed. Since it makes no difference to the cost of Internet access whether an adult calls up material harmful for children or the Articles of Confederation, blocking (on facts like these) is not necessitated by scarcity of either money or space. In the instance of the Internet, what the library acquires is electronic access, and the choice to block is a choice to limit access that has already been acquired. Thus, deciding against buying a book means there is no book (unless a loan can be obtained), but blocking the Internet is merely blocking access purchased in its entirety and subject to unblocking if the librarian agrees. The proper analogy therefore is not to passing up a book that might have been bought; it is either to buying a book and then keeping it from adults lacking an acceptable "purpose," or to buying an encyclopedia and then cutting out pages with anything thought to be unsuitable for all adults.

[T]here is no preacquisition scarcity rationale to save library Internet blocking from treatment as censorship, and no support for it in the historical development of library practice. [W]e can smell a rat when a library blocks material already in its control, just as we do when a library removes books from its shelves for reasons having nothing to do with wear and tear, obsolescence, or lack of demand. [The] difference between choices to keep out and choices to throw out is [enormous], a perception that underlay the good sense of the plurality's conclusion in *Pico* that removing classics from a school library in response to pressure from parents and school board members violates the Speech Clause.

There is no good reason, then, to treat blocking of adult enquiry as anything different from the censorship it presumptively is. For this reason, I would hold in accordance with conventional strict scrutiny that a library's practice of blocking would violate an adult patron's First and Fourteenth Amendment right to be free of Internet censorship, when unjustified (as here) by any legitimate interest in screening children from harmful material. On that ground, the Act's blocking requirement in its current breadth calls for unconstitutional action by a library recipient, and is itself unconstitutional.

CON LAW: P. 915, add at end of Sec. 7

RTS & LIB: P. 842, add at end of Sec. 7

Missouri voters passed an amendment to their constitution instructing members of the Congressional delegation to take actions leading to a Congressional term limits amendment to the U.S. Constitution. Candidates failing to take a term limit's pledge were to have a DECLINED TO PLEDGE TO SUPPORT TERM LIMITS statement next to their name on the ballot. Senators or Representatives failing to take certain steps to bring about the term limits amendment were to have a DISREGARDED VOTER'S INSTRUCTIONS ON TERM LIMITS statement next to their name on the ballot.

COOK v. GRALIKE, 531 U.S. 510, 121 S.Ct. 1029, 149 L.Ed.2d 44 (2001), per STEVENS, J., held that the ballot notations were not valid regulations under the Elections Clause, noting that they were efforts to "dictate electoral outcomes," not mere regulations.

REHNQUIST, C.J., joined by O'Connor, J., concurring in the judgment, maintained that the ballot notation provision "violates the First amendment right of a political candidate, once lawfully on the ballot, to have his name appear unaccompanied by pejorative language required by the state."[b]

THE ELECTRONIC MEDIA

THE ELECTRONIC MEDIA AND CONTENT REGULATION

CON LAW: P. 961, after note 6

RTS & LIB: P. 888, after note 6

ASHCROFT v. AMERICAN CIVIL LIBERTIES UNION (I), 535 U.S. 564, 122 S.Ct. 1700, 152 L.Ed.2d 771 (2002), per THOMAS, J., held that the Child Online Protection Act's ("COPA") requirement that prurient interest to children and patent offensiveness for children be determined by reference to "community standards" did not by itself render the statute substantially overbroad. The Court did not determine "whether COPA suffers from substantial overbreadth for other reasons, whether the statute is unconstitutionally vague, or whether the District Court correctly concluded that the statute likely will not survive strict scrutiny analysis once adjudication of the case is completed below."

Thomas, J., joined by Rehnquist, C.J., and Scalia, J., argued that community standards need not be defined by reference to a particular geographic area and recognized that inconsistent conclusions might be reached as to what was obscene for minors in different parts of the country even if a juries were instructed to consider the adult population as a whole as the reference group. The same group of justices joined by O'Connor, J., conceded that the community standards component would force speakers on the Web to "abide by the 'most puritan'

b. Kennedy and Thomas, JJ., also filed concurring opinions.

community's standards." Nonetheless, the four justices found this acceptable because unlike the Communications Decency Act, considered in *Reno,* the material covered by COPA was confined to that patently offensive speech: (1) appearing on the Web, thus excluding e-mail; (2) made for commercial purposes; (3) appealing to the prurient interest of children and (4) lacking serious literary, artistic, political, or scientific value for children—the latter to be judged by an objective test not dependent upon variations in community standards. These justices concluded on the basis of the record before them that they had "no reason to believe that the practical effect of varying community standards under COPA, given the statutes definition of material that is harmful to minors, is significantly greater than the practical effect of varying community standards under federal obscenity statutes. It is noteworthy, for example, that respondents fail to point out even a single exhibit in the record as to which coverage under COPA would depend upon which community in the country evaluated the material." The Court remanded for consideration of other aspects of the Act.[a]

KENNEDY, J., joined by Souter and Ginsburg, JJ., concurring, would have remanded with different instructions: "Unlike Justice Thomas, [I] would not assume that the Act is narrow enough to render the national variation in community standards unproblematic. Indeed, if the District Court correctly construed the statute across its other dimensions, then the variation in community standards might well justify enjoining enforcement of the Act. I would leave that question to the Court of Appeals in the first instance. * * * We cannot know whether variation in community standards renders the Act substantially overbroad without first assessing the extent of the speech covered and the variations in community standards with respect to that speech."

STEVENS, J., dissented: "While the objective nature of the inquiry may eliminate any worry that the serious value determination will be made by the least tolerant community, it does not change the fact that, within the subset of images deemed to have no serious value for minors, the decision whether minors and adults throughout the country will have access to that speech will still be made by the most restrictive community."[b]

On remand, the district court in *Ashcroft* issued a preliminary injunction against the enforcement of COPA, finding it likely that the statute was unconstitutional. The Third Circuit found no abuse of discretion in the issuance of the preliminary injunction. ASHCROFT v. AMERICAN CIVIL LIBERTIES UNION (II), 542 U.S. 656, 124 S.Ct. 2783, 159 L.Ed.2d 690 (2004), per KENNEDY, J., affirmed on the ground that plausible less restrictive alternatives appeared to be available: "The purpose of the [less restrictive alternatives test] test is not to consider whether the challenged restriction has some effect in achieving Congress' goal, regardless of the restriction it imposes. The purpose of the test is to ensure that speech is restricted no further than necessary to achieve the goal, for it is

a. O'Connor, J., concurring would have preferred that the majority explicitly adopt a national standard for defining obscenity on the Internet. Breyer, J., concurring, maintained that Congress intended that community standards referred to that nation's adult community as a whole, not local geographic areas.

b. Thomas, J., joined by Rehnquist, C.J., and O'Connor and Scalia, JJ., responded that "Justice Kennedy and Justice Stevens repeatedly imply that COPA banishes from the Web material deemed harmful to minors by reference to community standards, the statute does no such thing. It only requires that such material be placed behind adult identification screens." See note 6 in the Casebook supra.

important to assure that legitimate speech is not chilled or punished. For that reason, the test does not begin with the status quo of existing regulations, then ask whether the challenged restriction has some additional ability to achieve Congress' legitimate interest. Any restriction on speech could be justified under that analysis. Instead, the court should ask whether the challenged regulation is the least restrictive means among available, effective alternatives. * * *

"As the Government bears the burden of proof on the ultimate question of COPA's constitutionality, respondents must be deemed likely to prevail unless the Government has shown that respondents' proposed less restrictive alternatives are less effective than COPA. Applying that analysis, the District Court concluded that respondents were likely to prevail. That conclusion was not an abuse of discretion, because on this record there are a number of plausible, less restrictive alternatives to the statute.

"The primary alternative considered by the District Court was blocking and filtering software. Blocking and filtering software is an alternative that is less restrictive than COPA, and, in addition, likely more effective as a means of restricting children's access to materials harmful to [them.] Filters are less restrictive than COPA. They impose selective restrictions on speech at the receiving end, not universal restrictions at the source. Under a filtering regime, adults without children may gain access to speech they have a right to see without having to identify themselves or provide their credit card information. Even adults with children may obtain access to the same speech on the same terms simply by turning off the filter on their home computers. Above all, promoting the use of filters does not condemn as criminal any category of speech, and so the potential chilling effect is eliminated, or at least much diminished. All of these things are true, moreover, regardless of how broadly or narrowly the definitions in COPA are construed.

"Filters also may well be more effective than COPA. First, a filter can prevent minors from seeing all pornography, not just pornography posted to the Web from America. The District Court noted in its factfindings that one witness estimated that 40% of harmful-to-minors content comes from overseas. COPA does not prevent minors from having access to those foreign harmful materials. That alone makes it possible that filtering software might be more effective in serving Congress' goals. Effectiveness is likely to diminish even further if COPA is upheld, because the providers of the materials that would be covered by the statute simply can move their operations overseas. It is not an answer to say that COPA reaches some amount of materials that are harmful to minors; the question is whether it would reach more of them than less restrictive alternatives. In addition, the District Court found that verification systems may be subject to evasion and circumvention, for example by minors who have their own credit cards. Finally, filters also may be more effective because they can be applied to all forms of Internet communication, including e-mail, not just communications available via the World Wide Web. * * *

"Filtering software, of course, is not a perfect solution to the problem of children gaining access to harmful-to-minors materials. It may block some materials that are not harmful to minors and fail to catch some that are. Whatever the deficiencies of filters, however, the Government failed to introduce specific evidence proving that existing technologies are less effective than the restrictions in COPA. [In] the absence of a showing as to the relative effectiveness of COPA and the alternatives proposed by respondents, it was not an abuse of discretion for the District Court to grant the preliminary injunction. * * *

"One argument to the contrary is worth mentioning—the argument that filtering software is not an available alternative because Congress may not require it to be used. That argument carries little weight, because Congress undoubtedly may act to encourage the use of filters. We have held that Congress can give strong incentives to schools and libraries to use them. It is incorrect, for that reason, to say that filters are part of the current regulatory status quo.

"[But] this opinion does not foreclose the District Court from concluding, upon a proper showing by the Government that meets the Government's constitutional burden as defined in this opinion, that COPA is the least restrictive alternative available to accomplish Congress' goal."

STEVENS, J., joined by Ginsburg, J., concurred: "In registering my agreement with the Court's less-restrictive-means analysis, I wish to underscore just how restrictive COPA is. COPA is a content-based restraint on the dissemination of constitutionally protected speech. It enforces its prohibitions by way of the criminal law, threatening noncompliant Web speakers with a fine of as much as $50,000, and a term of imprisonment as long as six months, for each offense. Speakers who 'intentionally' violate COPA are punishable by a fine of up to $50,000 for each day of the violation. And because implementation of the various adult-verification mechanisms described in the statute provides only an affirmative defense, § 231(c)(1), even full compliance with COPA cannot guarantee freedom from prosecution. Speakers who dutifully place their content behind age screens may nevertheless find themselves in court, forced to prove the lawfulness of their speech on pain of criminal conviction.

"Criminal prosecutions are, in my view, an inappropriate means to regulate the universe of materials classified as 'obscene,' since 'the line between communications which 'offend' and those which do not is too blurred to identify criminal conduct.' COPA's creation of a new category of criminally punishable speech that is 'harmful to minors' only compounds the problem.

"[O]ur cases have recognized a compelling interest in protecting minors from exposure to sexually explicit materials. As a parent, grandparent, and great-grandparent, I endorse that goal without reservation. As a judge, however, I must confess to a growing sense of unease when the interest in protecting children from prurient materials is invoked as a justification for using criminal regulation of speech as a substitute for, or a simple backup to, adult oversight of children's viewing habits."

SCALIA, J., dissented: "I agree with Justice Breyer's conclusion that COPA is constitutional. Both the Court and Justice Breyer err, however, in subjecting COPA to strict scrutiny. Nothing in the First Amendment entitles the type of material covered by COPA to that exacting standard of review. 'We have recognized that commercial entities which engage in "the sordid business of pandering" by "deliberately emphasiz[ing] the sexually provocative aspects of [their nonobscene products], in order to catch the salaciously disposed," engage in constitutionally unprotected behavior.' *Playboy Entertainment Group* (Scalia, J., dissenting) (quoting *Ginzburg v. United States*).

"There is no doubt that the commercial pornography covered by COPA fits this description. [Since] this business could, consistent with the First Amendment, be banned entirely, COPA's lesser restrictions raise no constitutional concern."

BREYER, J., joined by Rehnquist, C.J., and O'Connor, J., dissented: "The only significant difference between the present statute and *Miller's* definition consists of the addition of the words 'with respect to minors,' and 'for minors'. But the addition of these words to a definition that would otherwise cover only obscenity expands the statute's scope only slightly. That is because the material in question (while potentially harmful to young children) must, first, appeal to the 'prurient interest' of, i.e., seek a sexual response from, some group of adolescents or postadolescents (since young children normally do not so respond). And material that appeals to the 'prurient interest[s]' of some group of adolescents or postadolescents will almost inevitably appeal to the 'prurient interest[s]' of some group of adults as well.

"The 'lack of serious value' requirement narrows the statute yet further—despite the presence of the qualification 'for minors.' That is because one cannot easily imagine material that has serious literary, artistic, political, or scientific value for a significant group of adults, but lacks such value for any significant group of minors. Thus, the statute, read literally, insofar as it extends beyond the legally obscene, could reach only borderline cases. And to take the words of the statute literally is consistent with Congress' avowed objective in enacting this law; namely, putting material produced by professional pornographers behind screens that will verify the age of the viewer. [Other] qualifying phrases, such [as] 'for commercial purposes' limit the statute's scope still [more]. In sum, the Act's definitions limit the statute's scope to commercial pornography. It affects unprotected obscene material. Given the inevitable uncertainty about how to characterize close-to-obscene material, it could apply to (or chill the production of) a limited class of borderline material that courts might ultimately find is protected.

"The Act does not censor the material it covers. Rather, it requires providers of the 'harmful to minors' material to restrict minors' access to it by verifying age. They can do so by inserting screens that verify age using a credit card, adult personal identification number, or other similar technology. In this way, the Act requires creation of an internet screen that minors, but not adults, will find difficult to bypass.

"I recognize that the screening requirement imposes some burden on adults who seek access to the regulated material, as well as on its providers. The cost is, in part, monetary. The parties agreed that a Web site could store card numbers or passwords at between 15 and 20 cents per number. And verification services provide free verification to Web site operators, while charging users less than $20 per year. According to the trade association for the commercial pornographers who are the statute's target, use of such verification procedures is 'standard practice' in their online operations. * * *

"Conceptually speaking, the presence of filtering software is not an *alternative* legislative approach to the problem of protecting children from exposure to commercial pornography. Rather, it is part of the status quo, i.e., the backdrop against which Congress enacted the present statute. It is always true, by definition, that the status quo is less restrictive than a new regulatory law. It is always less restrictive to do *nothing* than to do *something*. But 'doing nothing' does not address the problem Congress sought to address—namely that, despite the availability of filtering software, children were still being exposed to harmful material on the Internet.

"Thus, the relevant constitutional question is not the question the Court asks: Would it be less restrictive to do nothing? Of course it would be. Rather, the relevant question posits a comparison of (a) a status quo that includes filtering software with (b) a change in that status quo that adds to it an age-verification screen requirement. * * * Filtering software, as presently available, does not solve the 'child protection' problem. It suffers from four serious inadequacies that prompted Congress to pass legislation instead of relying on its voluntary use. First, its filtering is faulty, allowing some pornographic material to pass through without hindrance. [Second,] filtering software costs money. Not every family has the $40 or so necessary to install it. [Third,] filtering software depends upon parents willing to decide where their children will surf the Web and able to enforce that decision. As to millions of American families, that is not a reasonable possibility. More than 28 million school age children have both parents or their sole parent in the work force, at least 5 million children are left alone at home without supervision each week, and many of those children will spend afternoons and evenings with friends who may well have access to computers and more lenient parents. Fourth, software blocking lacks precision, with the result that those who wish to use it to screen out pornography find that it blocks a great deal of material that is valuable. * * *

"The Court proposes [that] the Government might 'act to encourage' the use of blocking and filtering software. * * * Obviously, the Government could give all parents, schools, and Internet cafes free computers with filtering programs already installed, hire federal employees to train parents and teachers on their use, and devote millions of dollars to the development of better software. The result might be an alternative that is extremely effective.

"But the Constitution does not, because it cannot, require the Government to disprove the existence of magic solutions, i.e., solutions that, put in general terms, will solve any problem less restrictively but with equal effectiveness. Otherwise, 'the undoubted ability of lawyers and judges,' who are not constrained by the budgetary worries and other practical parameters within which Congress must operate, 'to imagine *some* kind of slightly less drastic or restrictive an approach would make it impossible to write laws that deal with the harm that called the statute into being.'

"My conclusion is that the Act, as properly interpreted, risks imposition of minor burdens on some protected material—burdens that adults wishing to view the material may overcome at modest cost. At the same time, it significantly helps to achieve a compelling congressional goal, protecting children from exposure to commercial pornography. There is no serious, practically available 'less restrictive' way similarly to further this compelling interest."

THE RIGHT NOT TO SPEAK, THE RIGHT TO ASSOCIATE, AND THE RIGHT NOT TO ASSOCIATE

THE RIGHT NOT TO BE ASSOCIATED WITH PARTICULAR IDEAS

CON LAW: P. 967, add to fn. i

AMER CON: P. 868, add to fn. i

RTS & LIB: P. 894, add to fn. i

But cf. *Illinois ex rel. Madigan v. Telemarketing Associates, Inc.*, 538 U.S. 600, 123 S.Ct. 1829, 155 L.Ed.2d 793 (2003)(fraud action cognizable when solicitor represents that a significant amount will go to charity when only 15 cents per dollar would be distributed for such purpose).

FREEDOM OF ASSOCIATION AND EMPLOYMENT

CON LAW: P. 980, add to fn. f

RTS & LIB: P. 907, add to fn. f

See also *San Diego v. Roe*, ___ U.S. ___, 125 S.Ct. 521, 160 L.Ed.2d 410 (2005)(discharge of police officer, for selling home-made sexually explicit videos in which he strips off generic police uniform, was sufficiently "linked to his status as a police officer and designed to exploit his employer's image" that denial of first amendment claim was warranted).

CON LAW: p. 986, at bottom

RTS & LIB: P. 913, at bottom

The Mushroom Promotion, Research, and Consumer Information Act requires fresh mushroom handlers to pay assessments used primarily to fund advertisements promoting mushroom sales. UNITED STATES v. UNITED FOODS, INC., 533 U.S. 405, 121 S.Ct. 2334, 150 L.Ed.2d 438 (2001), per KENNEDY, J., distinguishing *Glickman*, invalidated the assessment requirement: "In *Glickman* the mandated assessments for speech were ancillary to a more comprehensive program restricting marketing autonomy. Here, for all practical purposes, the advertising itself, far from being ancillary, is the principal object of the regulatory scheme. The producers of tree fruit who were compelled to contribute funds [in *Glickman*] for use in cooperative advertising 'd[id] so as a part of a broader collective enterprise in which their freedom to act independently [was] already constrained by the regulatory scheme.' [T]he producers were bound together and required by the statute to market their products according to cooperative rules. To that extent, their mandated participation in an advertising program with a particular message was the logical concomitant of a valid scheme of economic regulation. [I]n the case now before us [, b]eyond the collection and disbursement of advertising funds, there are no marketing orders that regulate how mushrooms may be produced and sold, no exemption from the antitrust laws, and nothing preventing individual producers from making their own marketing decisions."[a]

BREYER, J., joined by Ginsburg and O'Connor, JJ.,[b] dissented: "It is difficult to see why a Constitution that seeks to protect individual freedom would consider the absence of 'heavy regulation' to amount to a special, determinative reason for refusing to permit this less intrusive program. If the Court classifies the former, more comprehensive regulatory scheme as 'economic regulation' for First Amendment purposes, it should similarly classify the latter, which does not differ significantly but for the comparatively greater degree of freedom that it allows."

Pursuant to the Beef Promotion and Research Act, the Secretary of Agriculture established a beef promotion and research board funded by government compelled contributions from the sales and importation of cattle. More than one billion dollars has been collected, much of it used to promote the sale of beef employing the slogan, "Beef: It's What's for Dinner." Many of the promotional messages state that they are funded by America's beef producers. Plaintiffs brought suit maintaining that compelled financial sup-

a. Stevens and Thomas JJ., filed concurring opinions.

b. O'Connor, J., did not join a portion of Breyer, J.'s opinion that argued the program should be classified as a form of economic regulation not subject to special first amendment scrutiny.

port of generic advertisements for beef impeded their efforts to promote the superiority of American beef, grain-fed beef, or certified Angus or Hereford beef, and violated the first amendment.

JOHANNS v. LIVESTOCK MARKETING ASS'N, ___ U.S. ___, 125 S.Ct. 2055, ___ L.Ed.2d ___ (2005), per SCALIA, J., concluded that the beef promotional messages were government speech: "We have sustained First Amendment challenges to allegedly compelled expression in two categories of cases: true "compelled speech" cases, in which an individual is obliged personally to express a message he disagrees with, imposed by the government; and 'compelled subsidy' cases, in which an individual is required by the government to subsidize a message he disagrees with, expressed by a private entity. We have not heretofore considered the First Amendment consequences of government-compelled subsidy of the government's own speech.

"Our compelled-subsidy cases have consistently respected the principle that '[c]ompelled support of a private association is fundamentally different from compelled support of government.' ['The] government, as a general rule, may support valid programs and policies by taxes or other exactions binding on protesting parties. Within this broader principle it seems inevitable that funds raised by the government will be spent for speech and other expression to advocate and defend its own policies.' We have generally assumed, though not yet squarely held, that compelled funding of government speech does not alone raise First Amendment concerns. * * *

"Respondents [assert] that the challenged promotional campaigns differ dispositively from the type of government speech that, our cases suggest, is not susceptible to First Amendment challenge. They point to the role of the Beef Board and its Operating Committee in designing the promotional campaigns, and to the use of a mandatory assessment on beef producers to fund the advertising. * * *

"The Secretary of Agriculture does not write ad copy himself. Rather, the Beef Board's promotional campaigns are designed by the Beef Board's Operating Committee. [Nonetheless,] [t]he message set out in the beef promotions is from beginning to end the message established by the Federal Government.[5]

"Congress has directed the implementation of a 'coordinated program' of promotion, 'including paid advertising, to advance the image and desirability of beef and beef [products.'] Congress and the Secretary have set out the overarching message and some of its elements, and they have left the development of the remaining details to an entity whose members are answerable to the Secretary (and in some cases appointed by him as well).

"Moreover, the record demonstrates that the Secretary exercises final approval authority over every word used in every promotional campaign. All proposed promotional messages are reviewed by Department officials both for substance and for wording, and some proposals are rejected or rewritten by the Department. * * *

5. The principal dissent suggests that if this is so, then the Government has adopted at best a mixed message, because it also promulgates dietary guidelines that, if followed, would discourage excessive consumption of beef. Even if we agreed that the protection of the government-speech doctrine must be forfeited whenever there is inconsistency in the message, we would nonetheless accord the protection here. The beef promotions are perfectly compatible with the guidelines' message of moderate consumption—the ads do not insist that beef is also What's for Breakfast, Lunch, and Midnight Snack.

"The compelled-*subsidy* analysis is altogether unaffected by whether the funds for the promotions are raised by general taxes or through a targeted assessment. Citizens may challenge compelled support of private speech, but have no First Amendment right not to fund government speech. And that is no less true when the funding is achieved through targeted assessments devoted exclusively to the program to which the assessed citizens object.

"[R]espondents' contend that crediting the advertising to 'America's Beef Producers' impermissibly uses not only their money but also their seeming endorsement to promote a message with which they do not agree. Communications cannot be 'government speech,' they argue, if they are attributed to someone other than the government; and the person to whom they are attributed, when he is, by compulsory funding, made the unwilling instrument of communication, may raise a First Amendment objection.

"We need not determine the validity of this argument—which relates to compelled *speech* rather than compelled *subsidy*—with regard to respondents' facial challenge. Since neither the Beef Act nor the Beef Order requires attribution, neither can be the cause of any possible First Amendment harm. The District Court's order enjoining the enforcement of the Act and the Order thus cannot be sustained on this theory.

[This] theory might [form] the basis for an as-applied challenge—if it were established, that is, that individual beef advertisements were attributed to respondents. [Whether] the *individual* respondents who are beef producers would be associated with speech labeled as coming from 'America's Beef Producers' is a question on which the trial record is altogether silent. We have only the funding tagline itself, a trademarked term that, standing alone, is not sufficiently specific to convince a reasonable factfinder that any particular beef producer, or all beef producers, would be tarred with the content of each trademarked ad."

Breyer, J., concurred: "The beef checkoff program in these cases is virtually identical to the mushroom checkoff program in which the Court struck down on First Amendment grounds. The 'government speech' theory the Court adopts today was not before us in [*United Foods*.] I dissented in *United Foods,* based on my view that the challenged assessments involved a form of economic regulation, not speech. * * *

"I remain of the view that the assessments in these cases are best described as a form of economic regulation. However, I recognize that a majority of the Court does not share that view. Now that we have had an opportunity to consider the 'government speech' theory, I accept it as a solution to the problem presented by these cases."

Ginsburg, J., concurred in the judgment: "I resist ranking the promotional messages funded under the Beef Promotion and Research Act of 1985 as government speech, given the message the Government conveys in its own name [discouraging the consumption of trans fatty acids found in cattle and sheep]. I remain persuaded, however, that the assessments in these cases qualify as permissible economic regulation."

Souter, J., joined by Stevens and Kennedy, JJ., dissented: "I take the view that if government relies on the government-speech doctrine to compel specific groups to fund speech with targeted taxes, it must make itself politically accountable by indicating that the content actually is a government message, not just the statement of one self-interested group the government is currently willing to invest with power. Sometimes, as in these very cases, government can make an effective disclosure only by explicitly labeling the speech as its own.

"[T]he requirement of effective public accountability means the ranchers ought to prevail, it being clear that the Beef Act does not establish an advertising scheme subject to effective democratic checks. The reason for this is simple: the ads are not required to show any sign of being speech by the Government, and experience under the Act demonstrates how effectively the Government has masked its role in producing the ads. Most obviously, many of them include the tag line, '[f]unded by America's Beef Producers,' which all but ensures that no one reading them will suspect that the message comes from the National Government. But the tag line just underscores the point that would be true without it, that readers would most naturally think that ads urging people to have beef for dinner were placed and paid for by the beef producers who stand to profit when beef is on the table. No one hearing a commercial for Pepsi or Levi's thinks Uncle Sam is the man talking behind the curtain. Why would a person reading a beef ad think Uncle Sam was trying to make him eat more steak? Given the circumstances, it is hard to see why anyone would suspect the Government was behind the message unless the message came out and said so."[a]

POLITICAL ASSOCIATION AND POLITICAL PARTIES

CON LAW: P. 1000, add to fn c

RTS & LIB: P. 927, add to fn c

Clingman v. Beaver, ___ U.S. ___, 125 S.Ct. 2029, ___ L.Ed.2d ___ (2005) upheld an Oklahoma statute that prohibited parties from allowing members of other parties to vote in their primaries.

WEALTH AND THE POLITICAL PROCESS: CONCERNS FOR EQUALITY

CON LAW: P. 1018, add to note 4

AMER CON: P. 895, add to note 4

RTS & LIB: P. 945, add to note 4

FEC v. COLORADO REPUBLICAN FEDERAL CAMPAIGN COMM., 533 U.S. 431, 121 S.Ct. 2351, 150 L.Ed.2d 461 (2001), per Souter, J., held that the Federal Election Campaign Act's prohibition of expenditures coordinated with the candidate was constitutional: "Coordinated expenditures of money donated to a party are tailor-made to undermine contribution limits."

Thomas, J., joined by Scalia and Kennedy, JJ., and, in part, by Rehnquist, C.J., argued that there was insufficient evidence that contribution limits would be undermined by coordinated expenditures and suggested that parties should be able to confer with candidates about matters such as the best time placement for advertisements: "I remain baffled that this Court has extended the most generous First Amendment safeguards to filing lawsuits, wearing profane jackets, and

a. Thomas, J., also concurred, and Kennedy, J., also dissented.

exhibiting drive-in movies with nudity, but has offered only tepid protection to the core speech and associational rights that our Founders sought to defend."[a]

CON LAW: P. 1020, after note 5, substitute for pp. 1020–1032

AMER CON: P. 898, after note 5, substitute for pp. 898–909

RTS & LIB: P. 947, after note 5, substitute for pp. 947–959

The Bipartisan Campaign Reform Act of 2002 ("BCRA") was primarily crafted to plug two loopholes in the Federal Election Campaign Act of 1971 ("FECA").[a] FECA was designed to moderate the impact of wealth in the political process. As interpreted, FECA distinguished between hard and soft money. Hard money is contributed money that falls at or under the specified contribution limits and complies with certain source limitations. Soft money encompassed contributions not subject to those restrictions which were for the most part ostensibly designed to encourage party-building activities benefitting the political parties in general, but not specific candidates. Under FECA, as interpreted, however, wealthy donors were able to circumvent the restrictions by, for example, (1) giving money directly or indirectly for get-out-the-vote drives benefitting federal candidates; (2) giving unlimited and unregulated funds to support campaign advertising often in the form of attack ads that were intended to support and oppose a particular federal candidate so long as the advertising did not use wording that specifically asked for a vote in one direction or another ("issue ads").

BCRA forbids national party committees from soliciting, receiving, or directing the use of soft-money; it prohibits state and local party committees from using soft money (although it permits their use of hard money and some additional funding) for activities affecting federal elections, including voter registration activity during the 120 days before a federal election and get-out-the-vote drives conducted in connection with an election in which a federal candidate appears on the ballot; it forbids the use of soft money by state and local party committees or state and local candidates and officeholders for any public communication that supports or attacks a federal candidate, whether or not the communication specifically asks for a vote for or against a particular candidate; and it forbids the use of general treasury funds by non-media business corporations, certain non-profit corporations, and unions for "electioneering communications": those communications by broadcast, cable, or satellite that refer to a clearly identified candidate for public office and are made within a time period close to a primary or election involving that candidate.[b]

McCONNELL v. FEDERAL ELECTION COMMISSION, 540 U.S. 93, 124 S.Ct. 619, 157 L.Ed.2d 491 (2003), per STEVENS and O'CONNOR, JJ., joined by Souter, Ginsburg, and Breyer, JJ. (the "Joint Opinion"), upheld the main features of these provisions against a facial constitutional challenge: "Of the two major parties' total spending, soft money accounted for 5% ($21.6 million) in 1984, 11% ($45 million) in 1988, 16% ($80 million) in 1992, 30% ($272 million) in 1996, and 42% ($498 million) in 2000. The national parties transferred large amounts of

a. Rehnquist, C.J., did not join this section of the opinion which argued that *Buckley* wrongly invalidated contribution limitations.

a. BCRA contained many complex provisions and *McConnell* required several opinions of the Court to resolve the issues presented. This edited version seeks briefly to focus on the issues of primary first amendment importance.

b. BCRA prohibited individuals 17 years old and younger from making contributions to candidates or political parties. Rehnquist, C.J., joined by O'Connor, Scalia, Souter, Stevens, and Breyer, JJ., invalidated this provision: "Minors enjoy the protection of the First Amendment."

their soft money to the state parties, which were allowed to use a larger percentage of soft money to finance mixed-purpose activities under FEC rules. In the year 2000, for example, the national parties diverted $280 million—more than half of their soft money—to state parties.

"Many contributions of soft money were dramatically larger than the contributions of hard money permitted by FECA. For example, in 1996 the top five corporate soft-money donors gave, in total, more than $9 million in nonfederal funds to the two national party committees. In the most recent election cycle the political parties raised almost $300 million—60% of their total soft-money fundraising—from just 800 donors, each of which contributed a minimum of $120,000. Moreover, the largest corporate donors often made substantial contributions to both parties. Such practices corroborate evidence indicating that many corporate contributions were motivated by a desire for access to candidates and a fear of being placed at a disadvantage in the legislative process relative to other contributors, rather than by ideological support for the candidates and parties. * * * Corporations and unions spent hundreds of millions of dollars of their general funds to pay for ads [intended to affect election results], and those expenditures, like soft-money donations to the political parties, were unregulated under FECA. Indeed, the ads were attractive to organizations and candidates precisely because they were beyond FECA's reach, enabling candidates and their parties to work closely with friendly interest groups to sponsor so-called issue ads when the candidates themselves were running out of money."

Despite the fact that many of the soft money restrictions regulated spending, the Joint Opinion concluded that the less than strict scrutiny applied to the contribution limits in *Buckley* was appropriately applied to the soft money restrictions: "The relevant inquiry is whether the mechanism adopted to implement the contribution limit, or to prevent circumvention of that limit, burdens speech in a way that a direct restriction on the contribution itself would not. That is not the case here." Applying the *Buckley* contribution limits standard, it concluded that the soft money restrictions were "closely drawn to match the important governmental interests of preventing corruption and the appearance of corruption"[c]: "Justice Kennedy would limit Congress' regulatory interest *only* to the prevention of the actual or apparent quid pro quo corruption 'inherent in' contributions made directly to, contributions made at the express behest of, and expenditures made in coordination with, a federal officeholder or candidate. Regulation of any other donation or expenditure—regardless of its size, the recipient's relationship to the candidate or officeholder, its potential impact on a candidate's election, its value to the candidate, or its unabashed and explicit intent to purchase influence—would, according to Justice Kennedy, simply be out of bounds. This crabbed view of corruption, and particularly of the appearance of corruption, ignores precedent, common sense, and the realities of political fundraising exposed by the record in this litigation.

"Justice Kennedy's interpretation of the First Amendment would render Congress powerless to address more subtle but equally dispiriting forms of corruption. Just as troubling to a functioning democracy as classic *quid pro quo* corruption is the danger that officeholders will decide issues not on the merits or the desires of their constituencies, but according to the wishes of those who have made large financial contributions valued by the officeholder. Even if it occurs

c. The Joint Opinion argued that the application of soft money restrictions to minor parties was permissible because the corruption and appearance of corruption interests were not a function of the number of legislators elected and that an as-applied challenge could be brought if the act prevented the massing of sufficient resources for effective advocacy.

only occasionally, the potential for such undue influence is manifest. And unlike straight cash-for-votes transactions, such corruption is neither easily detected nor practical to criminalize. The best means of prevention is to identify and to remove the temptation. * * *

"Justice Kennedy likewise takes too narrow a view of the appearance of corruption. He asserts that only those transactions with 'inherent corruption potential,' which he again limits to contributions directly to candidates, justify the inference 'that regulating the conduct will stem the appearance of real corruption.' In our view, however, Congress is not required to ignore historical evidence regarding a particular practice or to view conduct in isolation from its context. To be sure, mere political favoritism or opportunity for influence alone is insufficient to justify regulation. As the record demonstrates, it is the manner in which parties have *sold* access to federal candidates and officeholders that has given rise to the appearance of undue influence. Implicit (and, as the record shows, sometimes explicit) in the sale of access is the suggestion that money buys influence. It is no surprise then that purchasers of such access unabashedly admit that they are seeking to purchase just such influence. It was not unwarranted for Congress to conclude that the selling of access gives rise to the appearance of corruption."

With respect to the use of soft money for "issue ads" by state and local parties and candidates, the Joint Opinion concluded: " 'Public communications' that promote or attack a candidate for federal office [also] undoubtedly have a dramatic effect on federal elections. Such ads were a prime motivating force behind BCRA's passage. See 3 1998 Senate Report 4535 (additional views of Sen. Collins) ('[T]he hearings provided overwhelming evidence that the twin loopholes of soft money and bogus issue advertising have virtually destroyed our campaign finance laws, leaving us with little more than a pile of legal rubble'). [A]ny public communication that promotes or attacks a clearly identified federal candidate directly affects the election in which he is participating. The record on this score could scarcely be more abundant. Given the overwhelming tendency of public communications, [we] hold that application of § 323(b)'s contribution caps to such communications is also closely drawn to the anticorruption interest it is intended to address."[d]

In upholding the restrictions on the use of corporate and union treasury funds, the Joint Opinion observed that "under BCRA, corporations and unions may not use their general treasury funds to finance electioneering communications, but they remain free to organize and administer segregated funds, or PACs, for that purpose. Because corporations can still fund electioneering communications with PAC money, it is 'simply wrong' to view the provision as a 'complete ban' on expression rather than a regulation. 'The PAC option allows corporate political participation without the temptation to use corporate funds for political influence, quite possibly at odds with the sentiments of some shareholders or members, and it lets the government regulate campaign activity through registration and disclosure.' * * *

"We have repeatedly sustained legislation aimed at 'the corrosive and distorting effects of immense aggregations of wealth that are accumulated with the help of the corporate form and that have little or no correlation to the public's support for the corporation's political ideas.' Moreover, recent cases have recognized that

d. The Joint Opinion rejected the argument that words like "promote," "oppose," "attack," and "support" were unconstitutionally vague. Later in the opinion, it dismissed seemingly contrary language in *Buckley* as merely a statutory interpretation.

certain restrictions on corporate electoral involvement permissibly hedge against 'circumvention of [valid] contribution limits.' * * *

"Plaintiffs [argue] that FECA § 316(b)(2)'s segregated-fund requirement for electioneering communications is underinclusive because it does not apply to advertising in the print media or on the Internet. The records developed in this litigation and by the Senate Committee adequately explain the reasons for this legislative choice. Congress found that corporations and unions used soft money to finance a virtual torrent of televised election-related ads during the periods immediately preceding federal elections, and that remedial legislation was needed to stanch that flow of money. * * *

"In addition to arguing that [the] segregated-fund requirement is underinclusive, some plaintiffs contend that it unconstitutionally discriminates in favor of media companies. FECA § 304(f)(3)(B)(i) excludes from the definition of electioneering communications any 'communication appearing in a news story, commentary, or editorial distributed through the facilities of any broadcasting station, unless such facilities are owned or controlled by any political party, political committee, or candidate.' Plaintiffs argue this provision gives free rein to media companies to engage in speech without resort to PAC money. [The] effect, however, is much narrower than plaintiffs suggest. The provision excepts news items and commentary only; it does not afford carte blanche to media companies generally to ignore FECA's provisions. The statute's narrow exception is wholly consistent with First Amendment principles. 'A valid distinction ... exists between corporations that are part of the media industry and other corporations that are not involved in the regular business of imparting news to the public.' * * *

"Section 204 of BCRA [applies] the prohibition on the use of general treasury funds to pay for electioneering communications to not-for-profit corporations. Prior to the enactment of BCRA, FECA required such corporations, like business corporations, to pay for their express advocacy from segregated funds rather than from their general treasuries. Our recent decision in *Federal Election Comm'n v. Beaumont*, 539 U. S. 146 , 123 S.Ct. 2200, 156 L.Ed.2d 179 (2003), confirmed that the requirement was valid except insofar as it applied to a sub-category of corporations described as 'MCFL organizations,' as defined by our decision in *MCFL*, 479 U.S. 238, 107 S.Ct. 616, 93 L.Ed. 2d 539 (1986). The constitutional objection to applying FECA's segregated-fund requirement to so-called MCFL organizations necessarily applies with equal force to [section 204].

"Our decision in *MCFL* related to a carefully defined category of entities. We identified three features of the organization at issue in that case that were central to our holding: 'First, it was formed for the express purpose of promoting political ideas, and cannot engage in business activities. If political fundraising events are expressly denominated as requests for contributions that will be used for political purposes, including direct expenditures, these events cannot be considered business activities. This ensures that political resources reflect political support. Second, it has no shareholders or other persons affiliated so as to have a claim on its assets or earnings. This ensures that persons connected with the organization will have no economic disincentive for disassociating with it if they disagree with its political activity. Third, MCFL was not established by a business corporation or a labor union, and it is its policy not to accept contributions from such entities. This prevents such corporations from serving as conduits for the type of direct spending that creates a threat to the political marketplace.'" The Joint Opinion interpreted section 204 not to apply to MCFL organizations and upheld the section on that understanding.

Finally, the Joint Opinion rejected arguments that the act wrongly discriminates against political parties in favor of special interest groups: "BCRA imposes numerous restrictions on the fundraising abilities of political parties, of which the soft-money ban is only the most prominent. Interest groups, however, remain free to raise soft money to fund voter registration, GOTV activities, mailings, and broadcast advertising (other than electioneering communications). * * * Congress is fully entitled to consider the real-world differences between political parties and interest groups when crafting a system of campaign finance regulation. Interest groups do not select slates of candidates for elections. Interest groups do not determine who will serve on legislative committees, elect congressional leadership, or organize legislative caucuses. Political parties have influence and power in the legislature that vastly exceeds that of any interest group. As a result, it is hardly surprising that party affiliation is the primary way by which voters identify candidates, or that parties in turn have special access to and relationships with federal officeholders. [Taken] seriously, appellants' equal protection arguments would call into question not just Title I of BCRA, but much of the pre-existing structure of FECA as well."

Scalia, J., dissented from the those parts of the judgment upholding the soft money, issue ad, and corporate/union treasury restrictions: "This is a sad day for the freedom of speech. Who could have imagined that the same Court which, within the past four years, has sternly disapproved of restrictions upon such inconsequential forms of expression as virtual child pornography, tobacco advertising, dissemination of illegally intercepted communications, sexually explicit cable programming would smile with favor upon a law that cuts to the heart of what the First Amendment is meant to protect: the right to criticize the government. For that is what the most offensive provisions of this legislation are all about. We are governed by Congress, and this legislation prohibits the criticism of Members of Congress by those entities most capable of giving such criticism loud voice: national political parties and corporations, both of the commercial and the not-for-profit sort. It forbids pre-election criticism of incumbents by corporations, even not-for-profit corporations, by use of their general funds; and forbids national-party use of 'soft' money to fund 'issue ads' that incumbents find so offensive. * * *

"Beyond that, however, the present legislation *targets* for prohibition certain categories of campaign speech that are particularly harmful to incumbents. Is it accidental, do you think, that incumbents raise about three times as much 'hard money'—the sort of funding generally not restricted by this legislation—as do their challengers? [This] is not to say that *any* regulation of money is a regulation of speech. The government may apply general commercial regulations to those who use money for speech if it applies them evenhandedly to those who use money for other purposes. But where the government singles out money used to fund speech as its legislative object, it is acting against speech as such, no less than if it had targeted the paper on which a book was printed or the trucks that deliver it to the bookstore. * * *

"Nor is there any basis in reason why First Amendment rights should not attach to corporate associations—and we have said so. In *First Nat. Bank of Boston v. Bellotti*, 435 U. S. 765, 98 S.Ct 1407, 55 L.Ed.2d 707 (1978), we held unconstitutional a state prohibition of corporate speech designed to influence the vote on referendum proposals. [The] Court changed course in *Austin v. Michigan*

Chamber of Commerce, 494 U. S. 652, 110 S.Ct. 1391, 108 L.Ed.2d 562 (1990), upholding a state prohibition of an independent corporate expenditure in support of a candidate for state office. I dissented in that case, and remain of the view that it was error. In the modern world, giving the government power to exclude corporations from the political debate enables it effectively to muffle the voices that best represent the most significant segments of the economy and the most passionately held social and political views. People who associate—who pool their financial resources—for purposes of economic enterprise overwhelmingly do so in the corporate form; and with increasing frequency, incorporation is chosen by those who associate to defend and promote particular ideas—such as the American Civil Liberties Union and the National Rifle Association, parties to these cases. Imagine, then, a government that wished to suppress nuclear power—or oil and gas exploration, or automobile manufacturing, or gun ownership, or civil liberties—and that had the power to prohibit corporate advertising against its proposals. To be sure, the individuals involved in, or benefited by, those industries, or interested in those causes, could (given enough time) form political action committees or other associations to make their case. But the organizational form in which those enterprises already exist, and in which they can most quickly and most effectively get their message across, is the corporate form. The First Amendment does not in my view permit the restriction of that political speech. * * *

"But what about the danger to the political system posed by 'amassed wealth'? The most direct threat from that source comes in the form of undisclosed favors and payoffs to elected officials—which have already been criminalized, and will be rendered no more discoverable by the legislation at issue here. The use of corporate wealth (like individual wealth) to speak to the electorate is unlikely to 'distort' elections—*especially* if disclosure requirements *tell* the people where the speech is coming from. The premise of the First Amendment is that the American people are neither sheep nor fools, and hence fully capable of considering both the substance of the speech presented to them and its proximate and ultimate source. If that premise is wrong, our democracy has a much greater problem to overcome than merely the influence of amassed wealth. * * *

"It cannot be denied, however, that corporate (like noncorporate) allies will have greater access to the officeholder, and that he will tend to favor the same causes as those who support him (which is usually *why* they supported him). That is the nature of politics—if not indeed human nature—and how this can properly be considered 'corruption' (or 'the appearance of corruption') with regard to corporate allies and not with regard to other allies is beyond me. If the Bill of Rights had intended an exception to the freedom of speech in order to combat this malign proclivity of the officeholder to agree with those who agree with him, and to speak more with his supporters than his opponents, it would surely have said so. It did not do so, I think, because the juice is not worth the squeeze. Evil corporate (and private affluent) influences are well enough checked (so long as adequate campaign-expenditure disclosure rules exist) by the politician's fear of being portrayed as "in the pocket" of so-called moneyed interests. The incremental benefit obtained by muzzling corporate speech is more than offset by loss of the information and persuasion that corporate speech can contain. That, at least, is the assumption of a constitutional guarantee which prescribes that Congress shall make no law abridging the freedom of speech."

THOMAS, J., joined in part by Scalia, J., also dissented from those parts of the judgment upholding the soft money, issue ad, and corporate/union treasury restrictions: "[T]he Court today upholds what can only be described as the most significant abridgment of the freedoms of speech and association since the Civil

War." Thomas, J., argued that insufficient scrutiny was applied to the act's "expanding the anticircumvention rationale beyond reason." He maintained that expanded bribery laws would be a less restrictive alternative and that the evidence of "quid pro quo corruption was exceedingly weak": "The joint opinion also places a substantial amount of weight on the fact that 'in 1996 and 2000, more than half of the top 50 soft-money donors gave substantial sums to both major national parties,' and suggests that this fact 'leav[es] room for no other conclusion but that these donors were seeking influence, or avoiding retaliation, rather than promoting any particular ideology.' But that is not necessarily the case. The two major parties are not perfect ideological opposites, and supporters or opponents of certain policies or ideas might find substantial overlap between the two parties. If donors feel that both major parties are in general agreement over an issue of importance to them, it is unremarkable that such donors show support for both parties. This commonsense explanation surely belies the joint opinion's too-hasty conclusion drawn from a relatively innocent fact. * * *

"In *Austin*, the Court recognized a 'different type of corruption' from the 'financial quid pro quo': the 'corrosive and distorting effects of immense aggregations of wealth that are accumulated with the help of the corporate form and that have little or no correlation to the public's support for the corporation's political ideas.' The only effect, however, that the 'immense aggregations' of wealth will have (in the context of independent expenditures) on an election is that they might be used to fund communications to convince voters to select certain candidates over others. In other words, the 'corrosive and distorting effects' described in *Austin* are that corporations, on behalf of their shareholders, will be able to convince voters of the correctness of their ideas. * * *

"*Austin's* definition of 'corruption' is incompatible with the First Amendment [a]nd the shareholder protection rationale is equally unavailing. The 'shareholder invests in a corporation of his own volition and is free to withdraw his investment at any time and for any reason,' "

Thomas, J., also argued that the Court could not distinguish media corporations from other business corporations: "The chilling endpoint of the Court's reasoning is not difficult to foresee: outright regulation of the press. None of the rationales offered by the defendants, and none of the reasoning employed by the Court, exempts the press. [Candidates] can be just as grateful to media companies as they can be to corporations and unions. In terms of 'the corrosive and distorting effects' of wealth accumulated by corporations that has 'little or no correlation to the public's support for the corporation's political ideas,' there is no distinction between a media corporation and a nonmedia corporation. [W]hat is to stop a future Congress from concluding that the availability of unregulated media corporations creates a loophole that allows for easy 'circumvention' of the limitations of the current campaign finance laws? [Although] today's opinion does not expressly strip the press of First Amendment protection, there is no principle of law or logic that would prevent the application of the Court's reasoning in that setting."

KENNEDY, J., joined by Rehnquist, C.J., and in part by Scalia and Thomas, JJ., also dissented from those parts of the judgment upholding issue ad, and corporate/union treasury restrictions and from the main features of the judgment upholding the soft money restrictions: "[Although] *Buckley* subjected expenditure limits to strict scrutiny and contribution limits to less exacting review, it held neither could withstand constitutional challenge unless it was shown to advance the anticorruption interest. * * * *Buckley* made clear, by its express language and its context, that the corruption interest only justifies regulating candidates' and officeholders' receipt of what we can call the 'quids' in the quid pro quo formulation. The Court rested its decision on the principle that campaign finance regulation that restricts speech without requiring proof of particular corrupt action withstands constitutional challenge only if it regulates conduct posing a demonstrable quid pro quo danger: [Placing] *Buckley's* anticorruption rationale in the context of the federal legislative power yields the following rule: Congress' interest in preventing corruption provides a basis for regulating federal candidates' and officeholders' receipt of quids, whether or not the candidate or officeholder corruptly received them. Conversely, the rule requires the Court to strike down campaign finance regulations when they do not add regulation to 'actual or apparent quid pro quo arrangements.' * * *

"To ignore the fact that in *Buckley* the money at issue was given to candidates, creating an obvious quid pro quo danger as much as it led to the candidates also providing access to the donors, is to ignore the Court's comments in *Buckley* that show quid pro quo was of central importance to the analysis. The majority also ignores that in *Buckley*, and ever since, those party contributions that have been subject to congressional limit were not general party-building contributions but were only contributions used to influence particular elections. That is, they were contributions that flowed to a particular candidate's benefit, again posing a quid pro quo danger. And it ignores that in *Colorado II*, the party spending was that which was coordinated with a particular candidate, thereby implicating quid pro quo dangers. In all of these ways the majority breaks the necessary tether between quid and access and assumes that access, all by itself, demonstrates corruption and so can support regulation. * * *

"Access in itself, however, shows only that in a general sense an officeholder favors someone or that someone has influence on the officeholder. There is no basis, in law or in fact, to say favoritism or influence in general is the same as corrupt favoritism or influence in particular. [Though] the majority cites common sense as the foundation for its definition of corruption, in the context of the real world only a single definition of corruption has been found to identify political corruption successfully and to distinguish good political responsiveness from bad—that is quid pro quo. Favoritism and influence are not, as the Government's theory suggests, avoidable in representative politics. It is in the nature of an elected representative to favor certain policies, and, by necessary corollary, to favor the voters and contributors who support those policies. It is well understood that a substantial and legitimate reason, if not the only reason, to cast a vote for, or to make a contribution to, one candidate over another is that the candidate will respond by producing those political outcomes the supporter favors. Democracy is premised on responsiveness. Quid pro quo corruption has been, until now, the only agreed upon conduct that represents the bad form of responsiveness and presents a justiciable standard with a relatively clear limiting principle: Bad responsiveness may be demonstrated by pointing to a relationship between an official and a quid. * * *

"Independent party activity, which by definition includes independent receipt and spending of soft money, lacks a possibility for quid pro quo corruption of federal officeholders. This must be all the more true of a party's independent receipt and spending of soft money donations neither directed to nor solicited by a candidate.

"The Government's premise is also unsupported by the record before us. The record confirms that soft money party contributions, without more, do not create quid pro quo corruption potential. As a conceptual matter, generic party contributions may engender good will from a candidate or officeholder. [Still], no Member of Congress testified this favoritism changed voting behavior.''

Rehnquist, C.J., joined by Scalia and Kennedy, JJ., dissented from that part of the judgment upholding the main features of the soft money restrictions: ''The lynchpin of Title I, new FECA § 323(a), prohibits national political party committees from 'solicit[ing],' 'receiv[ing],' 'direct[ing] to another person,' and 'spend[ing]' *any* funds not subject to federal regulation, even if those funds are used for nonelection related activities. The Court concludes that such a restriction is justified because under FECA, 'donors have been free to contribute substantial sums of soft money to the national parties, which the parties can spend for the specific purpose of influencing a particular candidate's federal election.'Accordingly, '[i]t is not only plausible, but likely, that candidates would feel grateful for such donations and that donors would seek to exploit that gratitude.'. But the Court misses the point. Certainly 'infusions of money into [candidates'] campaigns,' can be regulated, but § 323(a) does not regulate only donations given to influence a particular federal election; it regulates *all donations* to national political committees, no matter the use to which the funds are put.

''The Court attempts to sidestep the unprecedented breadth of this regulation by stating that the 'close relationship between federal officeholders and the national parties' makes all donations to the national parties 'suspect.' But a close association with others, especially in the realm of political speech, is not a surrogate for corruption; it is one of our most treasured First Amendment rights. * * *

''BCRA's overinclusiveness is not limited to national political parties. To prevent the circumvention of the ban on the national parties' use of nonfederal funds, BCRA extensively regulates state parties, primarily state elections, and state candidates. For example, new FECA § 323(b), by reference to new FECA §§ 301(20)(A)(i)-(ii), prohibits state parties from using nonfederal funds for general partybuilding activities such as voter registration, voter identification, and get out the vote for state candidates even if federal candidates are not mentioned. New FECA § 323(d) prohibits state and local political party committees, like their national counterparts, from soliciting and donating 'any funds' to nonprofit organizations such as the National Rifle Association or the National Association for the Advancement of Colored People (NAACP). And, new FECA § 323(f) requires a state gubernatorial candidate to abide by federal funding restrictions when airing a television ad that tells voters that, if elected, he would oppose the President's policy of increased oil and gas exploration within the State because it would harm the environment. See 2 U. S. C. A. §§ 441i(f), 431(20)(A)(iii) (regulating 'public communication[s] that refe[r] to a clearly identified candidate for Federal office (regardless of whether a candidate for State or local office is also mentioned or identified) and that ... attacks or opposes a candidate for that office').

''Although these provisions are more focused on activities that may *affect* federal elections, there is scant evidence in the record to indicate that federal candidates or officeholders are corrupted or would appear corrupted by donations for these activities.''

FREEDOM OF RELIGION

ESTABLISHMENT CLAUSE

AID TO RELIGION

CON LAW: P. 1055, after note 3

AMER CON: P. 928, after note 2

RTS & LIB: P. 982, after note 3

ZELMAN v. SIMMONS–HARRIS

536 U.S. 639, 122 S.Ct. 2460, 153 L.Ed.2d 604 (2002).

CHIEF JUSTICE REHNQUIST delivered the opinion of the Court.

* * * Cleveland's public schools have been among the worst performing public schools in the Nation. In 1995, a Federal District Court declared a "crisis of magnitude" and placed the entire Cleveland school district under state control. Shortly thereafter, the state auditor found that Cleveland's public schools [had] failed to meet any of the 18 state standards for minimal acceptable performance. Only 1 in 10 ninth graders could pass a basic proficiency examination, and students at all levels performed at a dismal rate compared with students in other Ohio public schools. More than two-thirds of high school students either dropped or failed out before graduation. Of those students who managed to reach their senior year, one of every four still failed to graduate. Of those students who did graduate, few could read, write, or compute at levels comparable to their counterparts in other cities.

It is against this backdrop that Ohio enacted, among other initiatives, its Pilot Project Scholarship Program [which] provides financial assistance to families in any Ohio school district that is or has been "under federal court order requiring supervision and operational management of the district by the state superintendent." Cleveland is the only Ohio school district to fall within that category.

[First,] the program provides tuition aid for students [to] attend a participating public or private school of their parent's choosing. Second, the program provides tutorial aid for students who choose to remain enrolled in public school.

[Any] private school, whether religious or nonreligious, may participate in the tuition aid portion of [the] program and accept program students so long as the school is located within the boundaries of a covered district and meets statewide educational standards. Participating private schools must agree not to discriminate on the basis of race, religion, or ethnic background, or to "advocate or foster unlawful behavior or teach hatred of any person or group on the basis of race, ethnicity, national origin, or religion." Any public school located in a school district adjacent to the covered district may also participate in the program. Adjacent public schools are eligible to receive a $2,250 tuition grant for each program student accepted in addition to the full amount of per-pupil state funding attributable to each additional student.

Tuition aid is distributed to parents according to financial need. Families with incomes below 200% of the poverty line are given priority and are eligible to receive 90% of private school tuition up to $2,250. For these lowest-income families, participating private schools may not charge a parental co-payment greater than $250. For all other families, the program pays 75% of tuition costs, up to $1,875, with no co-payment cap. [If] parents choose a private school, checks are made payable to the parents who then endorse the checks over to the chosen school.

[In] the 1999–2000 school year, 56 private schools participated in the program, 46 (or 82%) of which had a religious affiliation. None of the public schools in districts adjacent to Cleveland have elected to participate. More than 3,700 students participated in the scholarship program, most of whom (96%) enrolled in religiously affiliated schools. Sixty percent of these students were from families at or below the poverty line. * * *

The program is part of a broader undertaking by the State to enhance the educational options of Cleveland's schoolchildren in response to the 1995 takeover. That undertaking includes programs governing community and magnet schools. Community schools are funded under state law but are run by their own school boards, not by local school districts. These schools enjoy academic independence to hire their own teachers and to determine their own curriculum. They can have no religious affiliation and are required to accept students by lottery. During the 1999–2000 school year, there were 10 start-up community schools in the Cleveland City School District with more than 1,900 students enrolled. For each child enrolled in a community school, the school receives state funding of $4,518, twice the funding a participating program school may receive.

Magnet schools are public schools operated by a local school board that emphasize a particular subject area, teaching method, or service to students. For each student enrolled in a magnet school, the school district receives $7,746, including state funding of $4,167, the same amount received per student enrolled at a traditional public school. As of 1999, parents in Cleveland were able to choose from among 23 magnet schools, which together enrolled more than 13,000 students in kindergarten through eighth grade. These schools provide specialized teaching methods, such as Montessori, or a particularized curriculum focus, such as foreign language, computers, or the arts.

[There] is no dispute that the program challenged here was enacted for the valid secular purpose of providing educational assistance to poor children in a demonstrably failing public school system. Thus, the question presented is whether the Ohio program nonetheless has the forbidden "effect" of advancing or inhibiting religion.

To answer that question, our decisions have drawn a consistent distinction between government programs that provide aid directly to religious schools, and programs of true private choice, in which government aid reaches religious schools only as a result of the genuine and independent choices of private individuals. * * *

Mueller, *Witters*, and *Zobrest* [make] clear that [the latter kind of] government aid program [is] not readily subject to challenge under the Establishment Clause. [The] incidental advancement of a religious mission, or the perceived endorsement of a religious message, is reasonably attributable to the individual recipient, not to the government, whose role ends with the disbursement of benefits. [It] is precisely for these reasons that we have never found a program of true private choice to offend the Establishment Clause.

We believe that the program challenged here is a program of true private choice. [It] is neutral in all respects toward religion. It is part of a general and multifaceted undertaking by the State of Ohio to provide educational opportunities to the children of a failed school district. It confers educational assistance directly to a broad class of individuals defined without reference to religion. [The] program permits the participation of all schools within the district, religious or nonreligious. Adjacent public schools also may participate and have a financial incentive to do so. Program benefits are available to participating families on neutral terms, with no reference to religion. The only preference stated anywhere in the program is a preference for low-income families, who receive greater assistance and are given priority for admission at participating schools.

There are no "financial incentive[s]" that "ske[w]" the program toward religious schools. *Witters*. Such incentives "[are] not present [where] the aid is allocated on the basis of neutral, secular criteria that neither favor nor disfavor religion, and is made available to both religious and secular beneficiaries on a nondiscriminatory basis." *Agostini*. The program here in fact creates financial disincentives for religious schools, with private schools receiving only half the government assistance given to community schools and one-third the assistance given to magnet schools. Adjacent public schools, should any choose to accept program students, are also eligible to receive two to three times the state funding of a private religious [school]. Parents that choose to participate in the scholarship program and then to enroll their children in a private school (religious or nonreligious) must copay a portion of the school's tuition. Families that choose a community school, magnet school, or traditional public school pay nothing. Although such features of the program are not necessary to its constitutionality, they clearly dispel the claim that the program "creates * * * financial incentive[s] for parents to choose a sectarian school." *Zobrest*.[3]

[Any] objective observer familiar with the full history and context of the Ohio program would reasonably view it as one aspect of a broader undertaking to assist poor children in failed schools, not as an endorsement of religious schooling in general.

There also is no evidence that the program fails to provide genuine opportunities for Cleveland parents to select secular educational options for their school-age children. Cleveland schoolchildren enjoy a range of educational choices: They may remain in public school as before, remain in public school with publicly funded tutoring aid, obtain a scholarship and choose a religious school, obtain a scholarship and choose a nonreligious private school, enroll in a community school, or enroll in a magnet school. That 46 of the 56 private schools now participating in

3. Justice Souter suggests the program is not "neutral" because program students cannot spend scholarship vouchers at traditional public schools. This objection is mistaken: Public schools in Cleveland already receive $7,097 in public funding per pupil—$4,167 of which is attributable to the State. Program students who receive tutoring aid and remain enrolled in traditional public schools therefore direct almost twice as much state funding to their chosen school as do program students who receive a scholarship and attend a private school.* * *

the program are religious schools does not condemn it as [t]he Establishment Clause question is whether Ohio is coercing parents into sending their children to religious schools, and that question must be answered by evaluating all options * * *.

Justice Souter speculates that because more private religious schools currently participate in the program, the program itself must somehow discourage the participation of private nonreligious schools.[4] But Cleveland's preponderance of religiously affiliated private schools certainly did not arise as a result of the program; it is a phenomenon common to many American cities. Indeed, by all accounts the program has captured a remarkable cross-section of private schools, religious and nonreligious. It is true that 82% of Cleveland's participating private schools are religious schools, but it is also true that 81% of private schools in Ohio are religious schools. To attribute constitutional significance to this figure, moreover, would lead to the absurd result that a neutral school-choice program might [be] constitutional in some States, such as Maine or Utah, where less than 45% of private schools are religious schools, but not in other States, such as Nebraska or Kansas, where over 90% of private schools are religious schools.

Respondents and Justice Souter claim [that] we should attach constitutional significance to the fact that 96% of scholarship recipients have enrolled in religious schools. They claim that this alone proves parents lack genuine choice, even if no parent has ever said so. We need not consider this argument in detail, since it was flatly rejected in *Mueller*, where we found it irrelevant that 96% of parents taking deductions for tuition expenses paid tuition at religious schools. [The] constitutionality of a neutral educational aid program simply does not turn on whether and why, in a particular area, at a particular time, most private schools are run by religious organizations, or most recipients choose to use the aid at a religious school. As we said in *Mueller*, "[s]uch an approach would scarcely provide the certainty that this field stands in need of, nor can we perceive principled standards by which such statistical evidence might be evaluated."

This point is aptly illustrated here. The 96% figure upon which respondents and Justice Souter rely discounts entirely (1) the more than 1,900 Cleveland children enrolled in alternative community schools, (2) the more than 13,000 children enrolled in alternative magnet schools, and (3) the more than 1,400 children enrolled in traditional public schools with tutorial assistance. Including some or all of these children in the denominator of children enrolled in nontraditional schools during the 1999–2000 school year drops the percentage enrolled in

4. Justice Souter appears to base this claim on the unfounded assumption that capping the amount of tuition charged to low-income students (at $2,500) favors participation by religious schools. [But] the record [shows] that nonreligious private schools operating in Cleveland also seek and receive substantial third-party contributions. Indeed, the actual operation of the program refutes Justice Souter's argument that few but religious schools can afford to participate: Ten secular private schools operated within the Cleveland City School District when the program was adopted. All 10 chose to participate in the program and have continued to participate to this day. And while no religious schools have been created in response to the program, several nonreligious schools have been created in spite of the fact that a principal barrier to entry of new private schools is the uncertainty caused by protracted litigation which has plagued the program since its inception. See also 234 F.3d 945, 970 (CA6 2000) ("There is not a scintilla of evidence in this case that any school, public or private, has been discouraged from participating in the school voucher program because it cannot 'afford' to do so") (Ryan, J., concurring in part and dissenting in part). Similarly mistaken is Justice Souter's reliance on the low enrollment of scholarship students in nonreligious schools during the 1999–2000 school year. These figures ignore the fact that the number of program students enrolled in nonreligious schools has widely varied from year to year, underscoring why the constitutionality of a neutral choice program does not turn on annual tallies of private decisions made in any given year by thousands of individual aid recipients.

religious schools from 96% to under 20%. The 96% figure also represents but a snapshot of one particular school year. In the 1997–1998 school year, by contrast, only 78% of scholarship recipients attended religious schools. The difference was attributable to two private nonreligious schools that had accepted 15% of all scholarship students electing instead to register as community schools, in light of larger per-pupil funding for community schools and the uncertain future of the scholarship program generated by this litigation.[5] Many of the students enrolled in these schools as scholarship students remained enrolled as community school students, thus demonstrating the arbitrariness of counting one type of school but not the other to assess primary [effect].[6]

Respondents finally claim that we should look to *Committee for Public Ed. & Religious Liberty v. Nyquist* to decide these cases. We disagree for two reasons. First, the program in *Nyquist* was quite different from the program challenged [here.] Although the program was enacted for ostensibly secular purposes, we found that its "function" was "unmistakably to provide desired financial support for nonpublic, sectarian institutions." Its genesis, we said, was that private religious schools faced "increasingly grave fiscal problems." [It] provided tax benefits "unrelated to the amount of money actually expended by any parent on tuition," ensuring a windfall to parents of children in religious schools. It similarly provided tuition reimbursements designed explicitly to "offe[r] an incentive to parents to send their children to sectarian schools." Indeed, the program flatly prohibited the participation of any public school, or parent of any public school enrollee. Ohio's program shares none of these features.

Second, [we] expressly reserved judgment with respect to "a case involving some form of public assistance (e.g., scholarships) made available generally without regard to the sectarian-nonsectarian, or public-nonpublic nature of the institution benefited." That, of course, is the very question now before us, and it has since been answered [in *Mueller*, *Witters*, and *Zobrest*].[7]

The judgment of the Court of Appeals is reversed.

JUSTICE O'CONNOR, concurring. * * *

These cases are different from prior indirect aid cases in part because a significant portion of the funds appropriated for the voucher program reach religious schools without restrictions on the use of these funds. The share of public resources that reach religious schools is not, however, as significant as

5. The fluctuations seen in the Cleveland program are hardly atypical. Experience in Milwaukee, which since 1991 has operated an educational choice program similar to the Ohio program, demonstrates that the mix of participating schools fluctuates significantly from year to year based on a number of factors, one of which is the uncertainty caused by persistent litigation. Since the Wisconsin Supreme Court declared the Milwaukee program constitutional in 1998, several nonreligious private schools have entered the Milwaukee market, and now represent 32% of all participating schools. [There] are currently 34 nonreligious private schools participating in the Milwaukee program, a nearly a five-fold increase from the 7 nonreligious schools that participated when the program began in 1990. * * *

6. Justice Souter and Justice Stevens claim that community schools and magnet schools are separate and distinct from program schools, simply because the program itself does not include community and magnet school options. But none of the dissenting opinions explain how there is any perceptible difference between scholarship schools, community schools, or magnet schools from the perspective of Cleveland parents looking to choose the best educational option for their school-age children.* * *

7. Justice Breyer would raise the invisible specters of "divisiveness" and "religious strife" to find the program unconstitutional [but] the program has ignited no "divisiveness" or "strife" other than this litigation. * * * We quite rightly have rejected the claim that some speculative potential for divisiveness bears on the constitutionality of educational aid programs. *Mitchell*.

respondents suggest. [Even] if one assumes that all voucher students came from low-income families and that each voucher student used up the entire $2,250 voucher, at most $8.2 million of public funds flowed to religious schools under the voucher program in 1999–2000. Although just over one-half as many students attended community schools as religious private schools on the state fisc, the State spent over $1 million more—$9.4 million—on students in community schools than on students in religious private schools because per-pupil aid to community schools is more than double the per-pupil aid to private schools under the voucher program. Moreover, the amount spent on religious private schools is minor compared to the $114.8 million the State spent on students in the Cleveland magnet schools.

Although $8.2 million is no small sum, it pales in comparison to the amount of funds that federal, state, and local governments already provide religious institutions. Religious organizations may qualify for exemptions from the federal corporate income tax, the corporate income tax in many States, and property taxes in all 50 States, and clergy qualify for a federal tax break on income used for housing expenses. In addition, the Federal Government provides individuals, corporations, trusts, and estates a tax deduction for charitable contributions to qualified religious groups. Finally, the Federal Government and certain state governments provide tax credits for educational expenses, many of which are spent on education at religious schools.

[The] state property tax exemptions for religious institutions alone amount to very large sums annually. For example, available data suggest [that] Wisconsin's exemption lowers revenues by approximately $122 million. [As] for the Federal Government, the tax deduction for charitable contributions reduces federal tax revenues by nearly $25 billion annually, and it is reported that over 60 percent of household charitable contributions go to religious charities * * *.

[Federal] dollars also reach religiously affiliated organizations through public health programs such as Medicare and Medicaid, through educational programs such as the Pell Grant program and the G. I. Bill of Rights, and through child care programs such as the Child Care and Development Block Grant Program. * * *

A significant portion of the funds appropriated for these programs reach religiously affiliated institutions, typically without restrictions on its subsequent use.[a]

JUSTICE SOUTER, with whom JUSTICE STEVENS, JUSTICE GINSBURG, and JUSTICE BREYER join, dissenting.

[In] the city of Cleveland the overwhelming proportion of large appropriations for voucher money must be spent on religious schools if it is to be spent at all, and will be spent in amounts that cover almost all of tuition. The money will thus pay for eligible students' instruction not only in secular subjects but in religion as well, in schools that can fairly be characterized as founded to teach religious doctrine and to imbue teaching in all subjects with a religious dimension.[2] * * *

a. The concurring opinion of Thomas, J.—questioning whether the Establishment Clause should be applied to the states, and rejecting use of the fourteenth amendment "to oppose neutral programs of school choice through the incorporation of the Establishment Clause"—is omitted.

2. See, e.g., App. (Saint Jerome School Parent and Student Handbook 1999–2000, p. 1) ("FAITH must dominate the entire educational process so that the child can make decisions according to Catholic values and choose to lead a Christian life"); id., (Westside Baptist Christian School Parent–Student Handbook, p. 7) ("Christ is the basis of all learning. All subjects will be taught from the Biblical perspective that all truth is God's truth").

The majority's statements of Establishment Clause doctrine cannot be appreciated without some historical perspective on the Court's announced limitations on government aid to religious education, and its repeated repudiation of limits previously set. My object here [is] to set out the broad doctrinal stages covered in the modern era, and to show that doctrinal bankruptcy has been reached today.

Viewed with the necessary generality, the cases can be categorized in three groups. In the period from 1947 to 1968, the basic principle of no aid to religion through school benefits was unquestioned. Thereafter for some 15 years, the Court termed its efforts as attempts to draw a line against aid that would be divertible to support the religious, as distinct from the secular, activity of an institutional beneficiary. Then, starting in 1983, concern with divertibility was gradually lost in favor of approving aid in amounts unlikely to afford substantial benefits to religious schools, when offered evenhandedly without regard to a recipient's religious character, and when channeled to a religious institution only by the genuinely free choice of some private individual. Now, the three stages are succeeded by a fourth, in which the substantial character of government aid is held to have no constitutional significance, and the espoused criteria of neutrality in offering aid, and private choice in directing it, are shown to be nothing but examples of verbal formalism.

[If] regular, public schools (which can get no voucher payments) "participate" in a voucher scheme with schools that can, and public expenditure is still predominantly on public schools, then the majority's reasoning would find neutrality in a scheme of vouchers available for private tuition in districts with no secular private schools at all. "Neutrality" as the majority employs the term is, literally, verbal and nothing more. * * *

The majority addresses the issue of choice the same way it addresses neutrality, by asking whether recipients or potential recipients of voucher aid have a choice of public schools among secular alternatives to religious schools. Again, however, the majority asks the wrong question and misapplies the criterion. [The] majority's view that all educational choices are comparable for purposes of choice thus ignores the whole point of the choice test: it is a criterion for deciding whether indirect aid to a religious school is legitimate because it passes through private hands that can spend or use the aid in a secular school. [The] majority now has transformed this question about private choice in channeling aid into a question about selecting from examples of state spending (on education) including direct spending on magnet and community public schools that goes through no private hands and could never reach a religious school under any circumstance. [And] because it is unlikely that any participating private religious school will enroll more pupils than the generally available public system, it will be easy to generate numbers suggesting that aid to religion is not the significant intent or effect of the voucher scheme.* * *

If, contrary to the majority, we ask the right question about genuine choice to use the vouchers, the answer shows that something is influencing choices in a way that aims the money in a religious direction: * * * 96.6% of all voucher recipients go to religious schools, only 3.4% to nonreligious [ones.] One answer to these statistics, for example, which would be consistent with the genuine choice claimed to be operating, might be that 96.6% of families choosing to avail themselves of vouchers choose to educate their children in schools of their own religion. This would not, in my view, render the scheme constitutional, but it would speak to the majority's choice criterion. Evidence shows, however, that almost two out of three families using vouchers to send their children to religious schools did not embrace the religion of those schools. The families made it clear they had not chosen the schools because they wished their children to be proselytized in a religion not their own, or in any religion, but because of educational opportunity.

Even so, the fact that some 2,270 students chose to apply their vouchers to schools of other religions might be consistent with true choice if the students "chose" their religious schools over a wide array of private nonreligious options, or if it could be shown generally that Ohio's program had no effect on educational choices and thus no impermissible effect of advancing religious education. But both possibilities are contrary to fact. First, even if all existing nonreligious private schools in Cleveland were willing to accept large numbers of voucher students, only a few more than the 129 currently enrolled in such schools would be able to attend, as the total enrollment at all nonreligious private schools in Cleveland for kindergarten through eighth grade is only 510 children, and there is no indication that these schools have many open seats.[13] Second, the $2,500 cap that the program places on tuition for participating low-income pupils has the effect of curtailing the participation of nonreligious schools: "nonreligious schools with higher tuition (about $4,000) stated that they could afford to accommodate just a few voucher students."[14] By comparison, the average tuition at participating Catholic schools in Cleveland in 1999–2000 was $1,592, almost $1,000 below the cap.[15]

Of course, the obvious fix would be to increase the value of vouchers so that existing nonreligious private and non-Catholic religious schools would be able to enroll more voucher students, and to provide incentives for educators to create new such schools given that few presently exist. [But] it is simply unrealistic to presume that parents of elementary and middle schoolchildren in Cleveland will have a range of secular and religious choices even arguably comparable to the statewide program for vocational and higher education in *Witters*. And to get to that hypothetical point would require that such massive financial support be made available to religion as to disserve every objective of the Establishment Clause even more than the present scheme does.

13. Justice O'Connor points out that "there is no record evidence that any voucher-eligible student was turned away from a nonreligious private school in the voucher program." But there is equally no evidence to support her assertion that "many parents with vouchers selected nonreligious private schools over religious alternatives," and in fact the evidence is to the contrary, as only 129 students used vouchers at private nonreligious schools.

14. Of the 10 nonreligious private schools that "participate" in the Cleveland voucher program, 3 currently enroll no voucher students. And of the remaining seven schools, one enrolls over half of the 129 students that attend these nonreligious schools, while only two others enroll more than 8 voucher students. Such schools can charge full tuition to students whose families do not qualify as "low income," but unless the number of vouchers are drastically increased, it is unlikely that these students will constitute a large fraction of voucher recipients, as the program gives preference in the allocation of vouchers to low-income children.

15. * * * Justice O'Connor argues that nonreligious private schools can compete with Catholic and other religious schools below the $2,500 tuition cap. The record does not support this assertion, as only three secular private schools in Cleveland enroll more than eight voucher students. See n. 14. Nor is it true, as she suggests, that our national statistics are spurious because secular schools cater to a different market from Catholic or other religious schools: while there is a spectrum of nonreligious private schools, there is likely a commensurate range of low-end and high-end religious schools. My point is that at each level, the religious schools have a comparative cost advantage due to church subsidies, donations of the faithful, and the like. The majority says that nonreligious private schools in Cleveland derive similar benefits from "third-party contributions," n. 4, but the one affidavit in the record that backs up this assertion with data concerns a private school for "emotionally disabled and developmentally delayed children" that received 11% of its budget from the United Way organization, a large proportion to be sure, but not even half of the 24.1% of budget that Catholic schools on average receive in parish subsidies alone.

[And] contrary to the majority's assertion, public schools in adjacent districts hardly have a financial incentive to participate in the Ohio voucher program, and none has.[17] [It] is entirely irrelevant that the State did not deliberately design the network of private schools for the sake of channeling money into religious institutions. The criterion is one of genuinely free choice on the part of the private individuals who choose, and a Hobson's choice is not a choice, whatever the reason for being Hobsonian. * * *

The scale of the aid to religious schools approved today is unprecedented, both in the number of dollars and in the proportion of systemic school expenditure supported. [In] paying for practically the full amount of tuition for thousands of qualifying students, the scholarships purchase everything that tuition purchases, be it instruction in math or indoctrination in faith. [T]he majority makes no pretense that substantial amounts of tax money are not systematically underwriting religious practice and indoctrination.

It is virtually superfluous to point out that every objective underlying the prohibition of religious establishment is betrayed by this scheme, but something has to be said about the enormity of the violation. [The first objective is] respect for freedom of conscience. Jefferson described it as the idea that no one "shall be compelled [to] support any religious worship, place, or ministry whatsoever."

As for the second objective, to save religion from its own corruption, [t]he risk is already being realized. In Ohio, for example, a condition of receiving government money under the program is that [the] school may not give admission preferences to children who are members of the patron faith; children of a parish are generally consigned to the same admission lotteries as non-believers. [Nor] is the State's religious antidiscrimination restriction limited to student admission policies: by its terms, a participating religious school may well be forbidden to choose a member of its own clergy to serve as teacher or principal over a layperson of a different religion claiming equal qualification for the job. Indeed, a separate condition that "[t]he school [not] teach hatred of any person or group on the basis [of] religion," could be understood (or subsequently broadened) to prohibit religions from teaching traditionally legitimate articles of faith as to the error, sinfulness, or ignorance of [others].

For perspective on this foot-in-the-door of religious regulation, it is well to remember that the money has barely begun to flow. [T]here is no question that religious schools in Ohio are on the way to becoming bigger businesses with budgets enhanced to fit their new stream of tax-raised income. See, e.g., People for the American Way Foundation, A Painful Price 5, 9, 11 (Feb. 14, 2002) (of 91 schools participating in the Milwaukee program, 75 received voucher payments in excess of tuition, 61 of those were religious and averaged $185,000 worth of overpayment per school, justified in part to "raise low salaries"). The administrators of those same schools are also no doubt following the politics of a move in the Ohio State Senate to raise the current maximum value of a school voucher from $2,250 to the base amount of current state spending on each public school student ($4,814 for the 2001 fiscal year). Ohio, in fact, is merely replicating the experience in Wisconsin, where a similar increase in the value of educational vouchers in Milwaukee has induced the creation of some 23 new private schools, some of which, we may safely surmise, are religious. New schools have presumably pegged

17. As the Court points out, an out-of-district public school that participates will receive a $2,250 voucher for each Cleveland student on top of its normal state funding. The basic state funding, though, is a drop in the bucket as compared to the cost of educating that student, as much of the cost (at least in relatively affluent areas with presumptively better academic standards) is paid by local income and property taxes. * * *

their financial prospects to the government from the start, and the odds are that increases in government aid will bring the threshold voucher amount closer to the tuition at even more expensive religious schools.

When government aid goes up, so does reliance on it; the only thing likely to go down is independence. [As] appropriations for religious subsidy rise, competition for the money will tap sectarian religion's capacity for discord. * * *

Justice Breyer has addressed this issue in his own dissenting opinion, which I join, and here it is enough to say that the intensity of the expectable friction can be gauged by realizing that the scramble for money will energize not only contending sectarians, but taxpayers who take their liberty of conscience seriously. * * *

JUSTICE BREYER, with whom JUSTICE STEVENS and JUSTICE SOUTER join, dissenting.

[T]he Court's 20th century Establishment Clause cases—both those limiting the practice of religion in public schools and those limiting the public funding of private religious education—focused directly upon social conflict, potentially created when government becomes involved in religious education. [The] Court appreciated the religious diversity of contemporary American society. [It] understood the Establishment Clause to prohibit (among other things) [favoring some religions at the expense of others]. Yet *how* did the Clause achieve that objective? Did it simply require the government to give each religion an equal chance to introduce religion into the primary schools—a kind of "equal opportunity" approach to the interpretation of the Establishment Clause? [T]he Court concluded that the Establishment Clause required "separation," in part because an "equal opportunity" approach was not workable. With respect to religious activities in the public schools, how could the Clause require public primary and secondary school teachers, when reading prayers or the Bible, *only* to treat all religions alike? In many places there were too many religions, too diverse a set of religious practices, too many whose spiritual beliefs denied the virtue of formal religious training. * * *

With respect to government aid to private education, did not history show that efforts to obtain equivalent funding for the private education of children whose parents did not hold popular religious beliefs only exacerbated religious strife? * * *

The principle underlying these cases—avoiding religiously based social conflict—remains of great concern. As religiously diverse as America had become when the Court decided its major 20th century Establishment Clause cases, we are exponentially more diverse today. America boasts more than 55 different religious groups and subgroups with a significant number of members. * * * School voucher programs finance the religious education of the young. And, if widely adopted, they may well provide billions of dollars that will do so. Why will different religions not become concerned about, and seek to influence, the criteria used to channel this money to religious schools? Why will they not want to examine the implementation of the programs that provide this money—to determine, for example, whether implementation has biased a program toward or against particular sects, or whether recipient religious schools are adequately fulfilling a program's criteria? If so, just how is the State to resolve the resulting controversies without provoking legitimate fears of the kinds of religious favoritism that, in so religiously diverse a Nation, threaten social dissension? * * *

I concede that the Establishment Clause currently permits States to channel various forms of assistance to religious schools, for example, transportation costs for students, computers, and secular texts.

School voucher programs differ, however, in both *kind* and *degree* from aid programs upheld in the past. They differ in kind because they direct financing to a core function of the church: the teaching of religious truths to young children. For that reason the constitutional demand for "separation" is of particular constitutional concern. * * * History suggests, not that such private school teaching of religion is undesirable, but that *government funding* of this kind of religious endeavor is far more contentious than providing funding for secular textbooks, computers, vocational training, or even funding for adults who wish to obtain a college education at a religious university. [H]istory also shows that government involvement in religious primary education is far more divisive than state property tax exemptions for religious institutions or tax deductions for charitable contributions, both of which come far closer to exemplifying the neutrality that distinguishes, for example, fire protection on the one hand from direct monetary assistance on the other. * * *

I do not believe that the "parental choice" aspect of the voucher program sufficiently offsets the concerns I have mentioned. Parental choice cannot help the taxpayer who does not want to finance the religious education of children. It will not always help the parent who may see little real choice between inadequate nonsectarian public education and adequate education at a school whose religious teachings are contrary to his own. It will not satisfy religious minorities unable to participate because they are too few in number to support the creation of their own private schools. It will not satisfy groups whose religious beliefs preclude them from participating in a government-sponsored program, and who may well feel ignored as government funds primarily support the education of children in the doctrines of the dominant religions. And it does little to ameliorate the entanglement problems or the related problems of social division * * *.[b]

RELIGION AND PUBLIC SCHOOLS

CON LAW: P. 1070, add at end

AMER CON: P. 944, add at end of Part III

RTS & LIB: P. 997, add at end

GOOD NEWS CLUB v. MILFORD CENTRAL SCHOOL, p. 135 of this Supplement, per THOMAS, J., used similar analysis to find no establishment clause violation for a public school's permitting a Christian organization to use schoolrooms for weekly after school meetings, which involved religious instruction and worship, when the school allowed such use by other groups for "the moral and character development of children": "As in *Lamb's Chapel*, the Club's meetings were held after school hours, not sponsored by the school, and open to any student who obtained parental consent, not just to Club members. As in *Widmar*, Milford made its forum available to other organizations. * * *

"Milford attempts to distinguish *Lamb's Chapel* and *Widmar* by emphasizing that Milford's policy involves elementary school children. [This] is unpersuasive.

b. Stevens, J.'s brief separate dissent, stating that "whenever we remove a brick from the wall that was designed to separate religion and government, we increase the risk of religious strife and weaken the foundation of our democracy," is omitted.

"First, we have held that 'a significant factor in upholding governmental programs in the face of Establishment Clause attack is their *neutrality* towards religion.' *Rosenberger*. * * *

"Second, to the extent we consider whether the community would feel coercive pressure to engage in the Club's activities, [i]t is the parents who choose whether their children will attend the Good News Club meetings. Because the children cannot attend without their parents' permission, they cannot be coerced into engaging in the Good News Club's religious activities.

"[Third, here], where the school facilities are being used for a nonschool function and there is no government sponsorship of the Club's activities, *Lee v. Weisman*, [Part IV infra, involving prayer at graduation exercises,] is inapposite. * * *

"Fourth, even if we were to consider the possible misperceptions by schoolchildren in deciding whether Milford's permitting the Club's activities would violate the Establishment Clause, the facts of this case simply do not support Milford's conclusion. [The] meetings were held in a combined high school resource room and middle school special education room, not in an elementary school classroom. The instructors are not schoolteachers. And the children in the group are not all the same age as in the normal classroom setting; their ages range from 6 to 12. In sum, these circumstances simply do not support the theory that small children would perceive endorsement here."

Scalia, J., concurred to emphasize his view, expressed in *Lamb's Chapel*, that "perceptions of endorsement [do] not count [when] giving [a private religious group] nondiscriminatory access to school facilities." In contrast, Breyer, J., concurred to emphasize his view that "the government's 'neutrality' in respect to religion is one, but only one, of the considerations relevant to deciding whether a public school's policy violates the Establishment Clause. See, e.g., *Mitchell* (O'Connor, J., concurring). As this Court previously has indicated, a child's perception that the school has endorsed a particular religion or religion in general may also prove critically important. [Today's opinion holds only] that the school was not entitled to summary judgment [and] both parties, if they so desire, should have a fair opportunity to fill the evidentiary gap."[a]

OFFICIAL ACKNOWLEDGEMENT OF RELIGION

CON LAW: P. 1084, end of note 1
AMER CON: P. 953, end of note 1
RTS & LIB: P. 1011, end of note 1

Two cases in 2005 involving the Ten Commandments considered the issues of whether the establishment clause test required a secular purpose and, if so, how it may be proven and whether it must be the exclusive purpose or something less. *McCreary*, below, was the first to invalidate a public acknowledgment of religion outside the context of the public schools.

McCREARY COUNTY v. ACLU, ___ U.S. ___, 125 S.Ct. 2722, ___ L.Ed.2d ___ (2005), per Souter, J. held that posting copies of the Ten Commandments in two

a. Souter, J., dissented on this ground, because of "the majority's refusal to remand," adding that "there is a good case that Good News's exercises blur the line between public classroom instruction and private religious indoctrination, leaving a reasonable elementary school pupil unable to appreciate that the former instruction is the business of the school while the latter evangelism is not." Stevens, J., dissented on free speech grounds, see p. 135 of this Supplement.

Kentucky county courthouses violated the establishment clause because of a "predominantly religious purpose": "Ever since [*Lemon,*] a secular legislative purpose" has been a common, albeit seldom dispositive, element of our cases. [When] government acts with the ostensible and predominant purpose of advancing religion, it violates that central Establishment Clause value of official religious neutrality, [even though] given its generality as a principle, an appeal to neutrality alone cannot possibly lay every issue to rest, or tell us what issues on the margins are substantial enough for constitutional significance * * *.

"Examination of purpose is a staple of statutory interpretation that makes up the daily fare of every appellate court in the country, [and] governmental purpose is a key element of a good deal of constitutional doctrine, e.g., *Washington v. Davis*, (discriminatory purpose required for Equal Protection violation); *Hunt v. Washington State Apple Advertising Comm'n,* (discriminatory purpose relevant to dormant Commerce Clause claim); *Church of Lukumi Babalu Aye, Inc. v. Hialeah,* (discriminatory purpose raises level of scrutiny required by free exercise claim). [S]crutinizing purpose does make practical sense, [where] an understanding of official objective emerges from readily discoverable fact, without any judicial psychoanalysis of a drafter's heart of hearts [, and when "openly available data supported a commonsense conclusion that a religious objective permeated the government's action."] The eyes that look to purpose belong to an 'objective observer,' one who takes account of the traditional external signs that show up in the 'text, legislative history, and implementation of the statute,' or comparable official act. *Santa Fe Ind. School Dist.* [infra]. [A]lthough a legislature's stated reasons will generally get deference, the secular purpose required has to be genuine, not a sham, and not merely secondary to a religious objective.[13]"

The Court's detailed examination of the record showed that the counties first posted only the Ten Commandments. When suit was filed, the counties adopted "resolutions reciting that the Ten Commandments are 'the precedent legal code upon which the civil and criminal codes [of] Kentucky are founded,' and stating several grounds for taking that position," most of which were related to religion. The displays were expanded to include "eight other documents in smaller frames, each either having a religious theme or excerpted to highlight a religious element," including the Preamble to the Constitution, the Mayflower Compact, and Presidential Proclamations. After a preliminary injunction was issued, the counties installed another display, "the third within a year," entitled "The Foundations of American Law and Government Display," made up "of nine framed documents of equal size" including the Bill of Rights and a picture of Lady Justice, all nine accompanied by statements about their historical and legal significance.

"[T]he Commandments 'are undeniably a sacred text in the Jewish and Christian faiths' [*Stone v. Graham*]. This is not to deny that the Commandments have had influence on civil or secular law; [but where] the text is set out, the insistence of the religious message is hard to avoid in the absence of a context plausibly suggesting a message going beyond an excuse to promote the religious point of view.[a] [W]e do not decide that the Counties' past actions forever taint any

13. The dissent nonetheless maintains that the purpose test is satisfied so long as any secular purpose for the government action is apparent. [While] heightened deference to legislatures is appropriate for the review of economic legislation, an approach that credits any valid purpose, no matter how trivial, has not been the way the Court has approached government action that implicates establishment.

a. As for *Marsh* and *Lynch*, "créches placed with holiday symbols and prayers by legislators do not insistently call for religious action on the part of citizens; the history of posting the Commandments expressed a purpose to urge citizens to act in prescribed ways as a personal response to divine authority."

effort on their part to deal with the subject matter. [But] a conclusion that centuries-old purposes may no longer be operative says nothing about the relevance of recent evidence of purpose. [Nor] do we have occasion here to hold that a sacred text can never be integrated constitutionally into a governmental display on the subject of law, or American history. * * *

"The dissent, however, puts forward a limitation on the application of the neutrality principle [to] show that the Framers understood the ban on establishment of religion as sufficiently narrow to allow the government to espouse submission to the divine will [and] that government may espouse a tenet of traditional monotheism. [This] apparently means that government should be free to approve the core beliefs of a favored religion over the tenets of others, a view that should trouble anyone who prizes religious liberty. [But] there is also evidence supporting the proposition that the Framers intended the Establishment Clause to require governmental neutrality in matters of religion, including neutrality in statements acknowledging religion."

Scalia, joined by Rehnquist, C.J. and Kennedy and Thomas, JJ., dissented: "[B]oth historical fact [pointing to actions beginning with President Washington and the First Congress to Congress's unanimous action in 2002 about "under God" in the Pledge of Allegiance] and current practice ["federal, state and local governments across the Nation" have displayed the Ten Commandments] [contradict] the demonstrably false principle that the government cannot favor religion over irreligion. [T]he principle that the government cannot favor one religion over another [is] indeed a valid principle where public aid or assistance to religion is concerned, or where the free exercise of religion is at issue, but it necessarily applies in a more limited sense to public acknowledgment of the Creator. [Nothing] stands behind the Court's assertion that governmental affirmation of the society's belief in God is unconstitutional except the Court's own say-so, citing as support only the unsubstantiated say-so of earlier Courts going back no farther than the mid–20th century. * * * Publicly honoring the Ten Commandments cannot be reasonably understood as a government endorsement of a particular religious viewpoint. [We must] recognize that in the context of public acknowledgments of God there are legitimate *competing* interests: On the one hand, the interest of that minority in not feeling 'excluded'; but on the other, the interest of the overwhelming majority of religious believers in being able to give God thanks and supplication *as a people,* and with respect to our national endeavors. [T]he legitimacy of a government action with a wholly secular effect [cannot] turn on the *misperception* of an imaginary observer that the government officials behind the action had the intent to advance religion.

"[The] constitutional problem, the Court says, is with the Counties' *purpose* in erecting the Foundations Displays, not the displays themselves. The Court adds in a footnote: 'One consequence of taking account of the purpose underlying past actions is that the same government action may be constitutional if taken in the first instance and unconstitutional if it has a sectarian heritage.' This inconsistency may be explicable in theory, but I suspect that the 'objective observer' with whom the Court is so concerned will recognize its absurdity in practice. * * * Displays erected in silence (and under the direction of good legal advice) are permissible, while those hung after discussion and debate are deemed unconstitutional. Reduction of the Establishment Clause to such minutiae trivializes the Clause's protection against religious establishment; indeed, it may inflame religious passions by making the passing comments of every government official the subject of endless litigation.

"In any event, the Court's conclusion that the Counties exhibited the Foundations Displays with the purpose of promoting religion is doubtful. [If,] as discussed above, the Commandments have a proper place in our civic history, even placing them by themselves can be civically motivated—especially when they are placed [in] a courthouse. [What] Justice Kennedy said of the crèche in *Allegheny County* is equally true of the Counties' original Ten Commandments displays [quoting CON LAW p. 1078, middle ¶; AMER CON p. 948, 2d ¶; RTS & LIB p. 1005, middle ¶]. [They] are assuredly a religious symbol, but they are not so closely associated with a single religious belief that their display can reasonably be understood as preferring one religious sect over another. The Ten Commandments are recognized by Judaism, Christianity, and Islam alike as divinely given. [The] Court may well be correct in identifying the third displays as the fruit of a desire to display the Ten Commandments, but neither our cases nor our history support its assertion that such a desire renders the fruit poisonous."

VAN ORDEN v. PERRY, 545 U.S. ___, 125 S.Ct. 2854, ___ L.Ed.2d ___ (2005), upheld the display of a monument, donated by the Eagles, inscribed with the Ten Commandments on the Texas State Capitol grounds "between the Capitol and the Supreme Court building. [The] 22 acres contain 17 monuments and 21 historical markers commemorating the 'people, ideals, and events that compose Texan identity.'[1] [A]n eagle grasping the American flag, an eye inside of a pyramid, and two small tablets with what appears to be an ancient script are carved above the text of the Ten Commandments. Below the text are two Stars of David and the superimposed Greek letters Chi and Rho, which represent Christ. The bottom of the monument bears the inscription 'PRESENTED TO THE PEOPLE AND YOUTH OF TEXAS BY THE FRATERNAL ORDER OF EAGLES OF TEXAS 1961.'" REHNQUIST, C.J., joined by Scalia, Kennedy, and Thomas, JJ. wrote the plurality opinion: "Our institutions presuppose a Supreme Being, yet these institutions must not press religious observances upon their citizens. Reconciling [these] requires that we neither abdicate our responsibility to maintain a division between church and state nor evince a hostility to religion by disabling the government from in some ways recognizing our religious heritage. * * *

"Whatever may be the fate of the *Lemon* test in the larger scheme of Establishment Clause jurisprudence, we think it not useful in dealing with the sort of passive monument that Texas has erected on its Capitol grounds. Instead, our analysis is driven both by the nature of the monument and by our Nation's history. As we explained in *Lynch,* 'There is an unbroken history of official acknowledgment by all three branches of government of the role of religion in American life from at least 1789.' * * * Recognition of the role of God in our Nation's heritage has also been reflected in our decisions. We have acknowledged, for example, that 'religion has been closely identified with our history and government,' *Schempp,* and that '[t]he history of man is inseparable from the

1. The monuments are: Heroes of the Alamo, Hood's Brigade, Confederate Soldiers, Volunteer Fireman, Terry's Texas Rangers, Texas Cowboy, Spanish–American War, Texas National Guard, Ten Commandments, Tribute to Texas School Children, Texas Pioneer Woman, The Boy Scouts' Statue of Liberty Replica, Pearl Harbor Veterans, Korean War Veterans, Soldiers of World War I, Disabled Veterans, and Texas Peace Officers.

history of religion,' *Engel*. This recognition has led us to hold that the Establishment Clause permits a state legislature to open its daily sessions with a prayer by a chaplain paid by the State. *Marsh*.[8] Such a practice, we thought, was 'deeply embedded in the history and tradition of this country.' [In] this case we are faced with a display of the Ten Commandments on government property outside the Texas State Capitol. [Similar] acknowledgments can be seen throughout a visitor's tour of our Nation's Capital. * * *

"Of course, the Ten Commandments are religious—they were so viewed at their inception and so remain. The monument, therefore, has religious significance. According to Judeo–Christian belief, the Ten Commandments were given to Moses by God on Mt. Sinai. But Moses was a lawgiver as well as a religious leader. And the Ten Commandments have an undeniable historical meaning, as the foregoing examples demonstrate. Simply having religious content or promoting a message consistent with a religious doctrine does not run afoul of the Establishment Clause. There are, of course, limits to the display of religious messages or symbols. For example, we held unconstitutional a Kentucky statute requiring the posting of the Ten Commandments in every public schoolroom. [*Stone*] stands as an example of the fact that we have 'been particularly vigilant in monitoring compliance with the Establishment Clause in elementary and secondary schools.' [The] placement of the Ten Commandments monument on the Texas State Capitol grounds is a far more passive use of those texts than was the case in *Stone,* where the text confronted elementary school students every day."

Scalia, J. also concurred briefly: "I would prefer to reach the same result by adopting an Establishment Clause jurisprudence that is in accord with our Nation's past and present practices, and that can be consistently applied—the central relevant feature of which is that there is nothing unconstitutional in a State's favoring religion generally, honoring God through public prayer and acknowledgment, or, in a nonproselytizing manner, venerating the Ten Commandments. See *McCreary* (Scalia, J., dissenting)."

Thomas, J., also concurred because "in a seeming attempt to balance out its willingness to consider almost any acknowledgment of religion an establishment, in other cases Members of this Court have concluded that the term or symbol at issue has no religious meaning by virtue of its ubiquity or rote ceremonial invocation. [Even] when this Court's precedents recognize the religious meaning of symbols or words, that recognition fails to respect fully religious belief or disbelief. [R]ather than trying to suggest meaninglessness where there is meaning, the Chief Justice rightly recognizes that the monument has 'religious significance.'" Preferably, however, the Court should "return to the views of the Framers" and hold that establishment clause does not apply to the states, or even if it does, the Court should "adopt coercion as the touchstone for our Establishment Clause inquiry." See Thomas, J.'s concurrence in *Elk Grove*, infra.

Breyer, J. concurred only in the judgment: "[T]he Establishment Clause does not compel the government to purge from the public sphere all that in any way partakes of the religious. Such absolutism is not only inconsistent with our national traditions, but would also tend to promote the kind of social conflict the Establishment Clause seeks to avoid.

"Thus, [the] Court has found no single mechanical formula that can accurately draw the constitutional line in every case. Where the Establishment Clause is at issue, tests designed to measure 'neutrality' alone are insufficient, both because it

8. Indeed, [i]n *Marsh,* the prayers were often explicitly Christian, but the chaplain removed all references to Christ the year after the suit was filed.

is sometimes difficult to determine when a legal rule is 'neutral,' and because 'untutored devotion to the concept of neutrality can lead to invocation or approval of results which partake not simply of that noninterference and noninvolvement with the religious which the Constitution commands, but of a brooding and pervasive devotion to the secular and a passive, or even active, hostility to the religious.' * * *

"If the relation between government and religion is one of separation, but not of mutual hostility and suspicion, one will inevitably find difficult borderline cases. And in such cases, I see no test-related substitute for the exercise of legal judgment. That judgment is not a personal judgment. Rather, as in all constitutional cases, it must reflect and remain faithful to the underlying purposes of the Clauses, and it must take account of context and consequences measured in light of those purposes. While the Court's prior tests provide useful guideposts—and might well lead to the same result the Court reaches today, no exact formula can dictate a resolution to such fact-intensive cases. * * *

"In certain contexts, a display of the tablets of the Ten Commandments can convey not simply a religious message but also a secular moral message (about proper standards of social conduct). And in certain contexts, a display of the tablets can also convey a historical message (about a historic relation between those standards and the law)—a fact that helps to explain the display of those tablets in dozens of courthouses throughout the Nation, including the Supreme Court of the United States.

"Here [t]he group that donated the monument, the Fraternal Order of Eagles, a private civic (and primarily secular) organization, while interested in the religious aspect of the Ten Commandments, sought to highlight the Commandments' role in shaping civic morality as part of that organization's efforts to combat juvenile delinquency. [The] physical setting of the monument, moreover, suggests little or nothing of the sacred. The monument sits in a large park containing 17 monuments and 21 historical markers, all designed to illustrate the 'ideals' of those who settled in Texas and of those who have lived there since that time. The setting does not readily lend itself to meditation or any other religious activity. But it does provide a context of history and moral ideals. [T]he context suggests that the State intended the display's moral message—an illustrative message reflecting the historical "ideals" of Texans—to predominate. [The] 40 years [that] passed in which the presence of this monument, legally speaking, went unchallenged [suggest] more strongly than can any set of formulaic tests that few individuals, whatever their system of beliefs, are likely to have understood the monument as amounting, in any significantly detrimental way, to a government effort to favor a particular religious sect, primarily to promote religion over nonreligion. [Those] 40 years suggest that the public visiting the capitol grounds has considered the religious aspect of the tablets' message as part of what is a broader moral and historical message reflective of a cultural heritage. [This] case also differs from *McCreary County*, where the short (and stormy) history of the courthouse Commandments' displays demonstrates the substantially religious objectives of those who mounted them, and the effect of this readily apparent objective upon those who view them. [This] display has stood apparently uncontested for nearly two generations. That experience helps us understand that as a practical matter of *degree* this display is unlikely to prove divisive. And this matter of degree is, I believe, critical in a borderline case such as this one.

"At the same time, to reach a contrary conclusion [would], I fear, lead the law to exhibit a hostility toward religion that has no place in our Establishment

Clause traditions. Such a holding might well encourage disputes concerning the removal of longstanding depictions of the Ten Commandments from public buildings across the Nation. And it could thereby create the very kind of religiously based divisiveness that the Establishment Clause seeks to avoid."

STEVENS, J., joined by Ginsburg, J., dissented: "Viewed on its face, Texas' display has no purported connection to God's role in the formation of Texas or the founding of our Nation; nor does it provide the reasonable observer with any basis to guess that it was erected to honor any individual or organization. The message transmitted by Texas' chosen display is quite plain: This State endorses the divine code of the 'Judeo–Christian' God. * * *

"In my judgment, at the very least, the Establishment Clause has created a strong presumption against the display of religious symbols on public property. [We] have repeatedly reaffirmed that neither a State nor the Federal Government 'can constitutionally pass laws or impose requirements which aid all religions as against non-believers, and neither can aid those religions based on a belief in the existence of God as against those religions founded on different beliefs.' I do not discount the importance of avoiding an overly strict interpretation of [this principle] so often used to define the reach of the Establishment Clause. [This] Court has often recognized 'an unbroken history of official acknowledgment [of] the role of religion in American life.' [This] case, however, is not about historic preservation or the mere recognition of religion. * * *

"The monolith displayed on Texas Capitol grounds cannot be discounted as a passive acknowledgment of religion, nor can the State's refusal to remove it upon objection be explained as a simple desire to preserve a historic relic. This Nation's resolute commitment to neutrality with respect to religion is flatly inconsistent with the plurality's wholehearted validation of an official state endorsement of the message that there is one, and only one, God.

"When the Ten Commandments monument was donated to the State of Texas in 1961, it was not for the purpose of commemorating a noteworthy event in Texas history. [The] donors were motivated by a desire to 'inspire the youth' and curb juvenile delinquency by providing children with a 'code of conduct or standards by which to govern their actions.' [B]y disseminating the 'law of God'—directing fidelity to God and proscribing murder, theft, and adultery—the Eagles hope that this divine guidance will help wayward youths conform their behavior and improve their lives. In my judgment, the significant secular by-products that are intended consequences of religious instruction—indeed, of the establishment of most religions—are not the type of 'secular' purposes that justify government promulgation of sacred religious messages. [The] State may admonish its citizens not to lie, cheat or steal, to honor their parents and to respect their neighbors' property; and it may do so by printed words, in television commercials, or on granite monuments in front of its public buildings. Moreover, the State may provide its schoolchildren and adult citizens with educational materials that explain the important role that our forebears' faith in God played in their decisions to select America as a refuge from religious persecution, to declare their independence from the British Crown, and to conceive a new Nation. The message at issue in this case, however, is fundamentally different from either a bland admonition to observe generally accepted rules of behavior or a general history lesson. [It] cannot be analogized to an appendage to a common article of commerce ('In God we Trust') or an incidental part of a familiar recital ('God save the United States and this honorable Court'). [Attempts] to secularize what is unquestionably a sacred text defy credibility and disserve people of faith.

"Even if, however, the message of the monument, despite the inscribed text, fairly could be said to represent the belief system of all Judeo–Christians, it would still run afoul of the Establishment Clause by prescribing a compelled code of conduct from one God, namely a Judeo–Christian God, that is rejected by prominent polytheistic sects, such as Hinduism, as well as nontheistic religions, such as Buddhism. * * * Critical examination of the Decalogue's prominent display at the seat of Texas government, rather than generic citation to the role of religion in American life, unmistakably reveals on which side of the 'slippery slope,' (Breyer, J., concurring in judgment), this display must fall. * * *

"The speeches and rhetoric characteristic of the founding era [do] not answer the question before us. [W]hen public officials deliver public speeches, we recognize that their words are not exclusively a transmission from *the* government because those oratories have embedded within them the inherently personal views of the speaker as an individual member of the polity. The permanent placement of a textual religious display on state property is different in kind; it amalgamates otherwise discordant individual views into a collective statement of government approval. [T]here is another critical nuance lost in the plurality's portrayal of history. Simply put, many of the Founders who are often cited as authoritative expositors of the Constitution's original meaning understood the Establishment Clause to stand for a *narrower* proposition than the plurality, for whatever reason, is willing to accept. Namely, many of the Framers understood the word 'religion' in the Establishment Clause to encompass only the various sects of Christianity. [Scalia, J.'s] inclusion of Judaism and Islam [in his *McCreary* dissent] is a laudable act of religious tolerance, but it is one that is unmoored from the Constitution's history and text, and moreover one that is patently arbitrary in its inclusion of some, but exclusion of other (e.g., Buddhism), widely practiced non-Christian religions. * * *

"A reading of the First Amendment dependent on [the] purported original meanings [would] eviscerate the heart of the Establishment Clause. [It] would permit States to construct walls of their own choosing—Baptists inside, Mormons out; Jewish Orthodox inside, Jewish Reform out. [As] we have said in the context of statutory interpretation, legislation 'often [goes] beyond the principal evil [at which the statute was aimed] to cover reasonably comparable evils, and it is ultimately the provisions of our laws rather than the principal concerns of our legislators by which we are governed.' In similar fashion, we have construed the Equal Protection Clause of the Fourteenth Amendment to prohibit segregated schools, even though those who drafted that Amendment evidently thought that separate was not unequal. We have held that the same Amendment prohibits discrimination against individuals on account of their gender, despite the fact that the contemporaries of the Amendment 'doubt[ed] very much whether any action of a State not directed by way of discrimination against the negroes as a class, or on account of their race, will ever be held to come within the purview of this provision,' And we have construed 'evolving standards of decency' to make impermissible practices that were not considered 'cruel and unusual' at the founding. * * *

"The principle that guides my analysis is neutrality.[35] [As] religious pluralism has expanded, so has our acceptance of what constitutes valid belief systems. The

35. Justice Thomas contends that the Establishment Clause [reaches] only the governmental coercion of individual belief or disbelief. In my view, [that] cannot be the full extent of the provision's reach. [Thomas, J.'s] "coercion view," [would] not prohibit explicit state endorsements of religious orthodoxies of particular sects, actions that lie at the heart of what

evil of discriminating today against atheists, "polytheists[,] and believers in unconcerned deities," *McCreary County,* (Scalia, J., dissenting), is in my view a direct descendent of the evil of discriminating among Christian sects. The Establishment Clause thus forbids it and, in turn, forbids Texas from displaying the Ten Commandments monument the plurality so casually affirms."

SOUTER, J., joined by Stevens and Ginsburg, JJ., also dissented:[b] "[T]he Establishment Clause requires neutrality as a general rule. [A] governmental display of an obviously religious text cannot be squared with neutrality, except in a setting that plausibly indicates that the statement is not placed in view with a predominant purpose on the part of government either to adopt the religious message or to urge its acceptance by others.[1]

"[A] pedestrian happening upon the monument at issue here needs no training in religious doctrine to realize that the statement of the Commandments, quoting God himself, proclaims that the will of the divine being is the source of obligation to obey the rules, including the facially secular ones. [To] ensure that the religious nature of the monument is clear to even the most casual passerby, the word 'Lord' appears in all capital letters (as does the word 'am'), so that the most eye-catching segment of the quotation is the declaration 'I AM the LORD thy God.' [It] would therefore be difficult to miss the point that the government of Texas is telling everyone who sees the monument to live up to a moral code because God requires it, with both code and conception of God being rightly understood as the inheritances specifically of Jews and Christians. [It] stands in contrast to any number of perfectly constitutional depictions of [the Commandments], the frieze of our own Courtroom providing a good example, where the figure of Moses stands among history's great lawgivers. While Moses holds the tablets of the Commandments showing some Hebrew text, no one looking at the lines of figures in marble relief is likely to see a religious purpose behind the assemblage or take away a religious message from it. [T]he viewers may just as naturally see the tablets of the Commandments (showing the later ones, forbidding things like killing and theft, but without the divine preface) as background from which the concept of law emerged, ultimately having a secular influence in the history of the Nation. [But] 17 monuments with no common appearance, history, or esthetic role scattered over 22 acres is not a museum, and anyone strolling around the lawn would surely take each memorial on its own terms without any dawning sense that some purpose held the miscellany together more coherently than fortuity and the edge of the grass.[6]

"To be sure, Kentucky's compulsory-education law [in *Stone*] meant that the schoolchildren were forced to see the display every day, whereas many see the monument by choice, and those who customarily walk the Capitol grounds can

the Clause was meant to regulate. The government could, for example, take out television advertisements lauding Catholicism as the only pure religion. Under the reasoning endorsed by Justice Thomas, those programs would not be coercive because the viewer could simply turn off the television or ignore the ad.

Further, [e]nshrining coercion as the Establishment Clause touchstone fails to eliminate the difficult judgment calls regarding "the form that coercion must take." * * *

b. O'Connor, J., dissented, "for essentially the reasons given by Justice Souter."

1. [In] the present case, the religious purpose was evident on the part of the donating organization. [I]t was not just the terms of the moral code, but the proclamation that the terms of the code were enjoined by God, that the Eagles put forward in the monuments they donated.

6. [A]lthough the nativity scene in *Allegheny County* was donated by the Holy Name Society, we concluded that "[n]o viewer could reasonably think that [the scene] occupies [its] location [at the seat of county government] without the support and approval of the government."

presumably avoid it if they choose. But in my judgment (and under our often inexact Establishment Clause jurisprudence, such matters often boil down to judgment (Breyer, J., concurring in judgment)), this distinction should make no difference. The monument in this case sits on the grounds of the Texas State Capitol[,] the civic home of every one of the State's citizens. If neutrality in religion means something, any citizen should be able to visit that civic home without having to confront religious expressions clearly meant to convey an official religious position that may be at odds with his own religion, or with rejection of religion.

"Finally, though this too is a point on which judgment will vary, I do not see a persuasive argument for constitutionality in the plurality's observation that Van Orden's lawsuit comes '[f]orty years after the monument's erection.' [We] have approved framing-era practices because they must originally have been understood as constitutionally permissible, e.g., *Marsh*, and we have recognized that Sunday laws have grown recognizably secular over time, *McGowan*. There is also an analogous argument, not yet evaluated, that ritualistic religious expression can become so numbing over time that its initial Establishment Clause violation becomes at some point too diminished for notice. [But] other explanations may do better in accounting for the late resort to the courts. Suing a State over religion puts nothing in a plaintiff's pocket and can take a great deal out, and even with volunteer litigators to supply time and energy, the risk of social ostracism can be powerfully deterrent. I doubt that a slow walk to the courthouse, even one that took 40 years, is much evidentiary help in applying the Establishment Clause."

CON LAW: P. 1088, after note 3

AMER CON: P. 956, after note 3

RTS & LIB: P. 1015, after note 3

NEWDOW v. U.S. CONGRESS, 292 F.3d 597 (9th Cir. 2002), amended, 321 F.3d 772 (9th Cir.2003), per GOODWIN, J., (2–1), held the congressional addition of the words "under God" to the Pledge of Allegiance by a 1954 federal statute, and the daily recitation in the classroom of the Pledge of Allegiance with the added words by plaintiff's daughter's public school teacher, violated the Establishment Clause: "Newdow is an atheist whose daughter attends public elementary school in the Elk Grove Unified School District ('EGUSD') in California. [The] California Education Code requires that public schools begin each school day with 'appropriate patriotic exercises' and that '[t]he giving of the Pledge of Allegiance to the Flag of the United States of America shall satisfy' this requirement. To implement the California statute, the school district that Newdow's daughter attends has promulgated a policy that states, in pertinent part: 'Each elementary school class [shall] recite the 'pledge of allegiance to the flag once each day.'[2]

"Newdow [claims] that his daughter is injured when she is compelled to 'watch and listen as her state employed teacher in her state-run school leads her classmates in a ritual proclaiming that there is a God, and that our's [sic] is 'one nation under God.' * * *

"Over the last three decades, the Supreme Court has used three interrelated tests to analyze alleged violations of the Establishment Clause in the realm of

2. [On] June 22, 1942, Congress first codified the Pledge as "I pledge allegiance to the flag of the United States of America and to the Republic for which it stands, one Nation indivisible, with liberty and justice for all." On June 14, 1954, Congress amended Section 172 to add the words "under God" after the word "Nation."

public education: the three-prong test set forth in *Lemon*; the 'endorsement' test and the 'coercion' test * * * .

"In the context of the Pledge, the statement that the United States is a nation 'under God' is an endorsement of religion. [The] recitation that ours is a nation 'under God' is not a mere acknowledgment that many Americans believe in a deity. Nor is it merely descriptive of the undeniable historical significance of religion in the founding of the Republic. Rather, [it] is normative. To recite the Pledge is not to describe the United States; instead, it is to swear allegiance to the values for which the flag stands: unity, indivisibility, liberty, justice, and—since 1954—monotheism. The text of the official Pledge, codified in federal law, impermissibly takes a position with respect to the purely religious question of the existence and identity of God. A profession that we are a nation 'under God' is identical, for Establishment Clause purposes, to a profession that we are a nation 'under Jesus,' a nation 'under Vishnu,' a nation 'under Zeus,' or a nation 'under no god,' because none of these professions can be neutral with respect to religion. [Furthermore], the school district's practice of teacher-led recitation of the Pledge aims to inculcate in students a respect for the ideals set forth in the Pledge, and thus amounts to state endorsement of these ideals. Although students cannot be forced to participate in recitation of the Pledge, the school district is nonetheless conveying a message of state endorsement of a religious belief when it requires public school teachers to recite, and lead the recitation of, the current form of the Pledge. * * *

"Similarly, the policy and the Act fail the coercion test. Just as in *Lee*, the policy and the Act place students in the untenable position of choosing between participating in an exercise with religious content or protesting. [Although] the defendants argue that the religious content of 'one nation under God' is minimal, to an atheist or a believer in certain non-Judeo–Christian religions or philosophies, it may reasonably appear to be an attempt to enforce a 'religious orthodoxy' of monotheism, and is therefore impermissible. The coercive effect of this policy is particularly pronounced in the school setting given the age and impressionability of schoolchildren, and their understanding that they are required to adhere to the norms set by their school, their teacher and their fellow students. Furthermore, under *Lee*, the fact that students are not required to participate is no basis for distinguishing *Barnette* from the case at bar because, even without a recitation requirement for each child, the mere fact that a pupil is required to listen every day to the statement 'one nation under God' has a coercive effect. [The] 'subtle and indirect' social pressure which permeates the classroom also renders more acute the message sent to non-believing schoolchildren that they are outsiders. * * *

"Finally we turn to [*Lemon*]. Historically, the primary purpose of the 1954 Act was to advance religion, in conflict with the first prong of the *Lemon* test. The federal defendants 'do not dispute that the words "under God" were intended' 'to recognize a Supreme Being,' at a time when the government was publicly inveighing against atheistic communism. Nonetheless, the federal defendants argue that the Pledge must be considered as a whole when assessing whether it has a secular purpose. They claim that the Pledge has the secular purpose of 'solemnizing public occasions, expressing confidence in the future, and encouraging the recognition of what is worthy of appreciation in society.'

"The flaw in defendants' argument [is] apparent when one considers the Court's analysis in *Wallace*. There, the Court struck down Alabama's statute mandating a moment of silence for 'meditation or voluntary prayer' not because the final version 'as a whole' lacked a primary secular purpose, but because the state legislature had amended the statute specifically and solely to add the words 'or voluntary prayer.'

"[Because] the Act fails the purpose prong of Lemon, we need not examine the other prongs.[12]"

In ELK GROVE UNIFIED SCHOOL DIST. v. NEWDOW, 542 U.S. 1, 124 S.Ct. 2301, 159 L.Ed.2d 98 (2004), the Supreme Court reversed the Ninth Circuit because Newdow did not have standing (see page ___ of this Supplement). Three justices reached the merits and concluded that public school recitation of the Pledge of Allegiance (with the words "under God") did not violate the Establishment Clause. REHNQUIST, C.J., joined by O'Connor, J., noted that the sponsor of the 1954 amendment, which added the words, "said its purpose was to contrast this country's belief in God with the Soviet Union's embrace of atheism. We do not know what other Members of Congress thought about the purpose of the amendment. Following the decision of the Court of Appeals in this case, Congress passed legislation that made extensive findings about the historic role of religion in the political development of the Nation and reaffirmed the text of the Pledge. To the millions of people who regularly recite the Pledge, and who have no access to, or concern with, such legislation or legislative history, 'under God' might mean several different [things]. Examples of patriotic invocations of God and official acknowledgments of religion's role in our Nation's history abound. * * *

"I do not believe that the phrase 'under God' in the Pledge converts its recital into a 'religious exercise' of the sort described in *Lee.* [It is] in no sense a prayer, nor an endorsement of any [religion]. Reciting the Pledge, or listening to others recite it, is a patriotic exercise, not a religious one; participants promise fidelity to our flag and our Nation, not to any particular God, faith, or church."

O'CONNOR, J., added: "For centuries, we have marked important occasions or pronouncements with references to God and invocations of divine assistance. Such references can serve to solemnize an occasion instead of to invoke divine provenance. The reasonable observer [,] fully aware of our national history and the origins of such practices, would not perceive these acknowledgments as signifying a government endorsement of any specific religion, or even of religion over non-religion.

12. We recognize that the Supreme Court has occasionally commented in dicta that the presence of "one nation under God" in the Pledge of Allegiance is constitutional. However, the Court has never been presented with the question directly, and has always clearly refrained from deciding it. Accordingly, it has never applied any of the three tests to the Act or to any school policy regarding the recitation of the Pledge. [The] only other United States Court of Appeals to consider the issue [upheld it] in *Sherman v. Community Consolidated School District 21*, 980 F.2d 437 (7th Cir. 1992). [The] *Sherman* court first stated that: If as *Barnette* holds no state may require anyone to recite the Pledge, and if as the prayer cases hold the recitation by a teacher or rabbi of unwelcome words is coercion, then the Pledge of Allegiance becomes unconstitutional under all circumstances, just as no school may read from a holy scripture at the start of class. It then concludes, however, that this reasoning is flawed because the First Amendment "[does] not establish general rules about speech or schools; [it] call[s] for religion to be treated differently." We have some difficulty understanding this statement; we do not believe that the Constitution prohibits compulsory patriotism as in *Barnette*, but permits compulsory religion as in this case. If government-endorsed religion is to be treated differently from government-endorsed patriotism, the treatment must be less favorable, not more. * * *

"There are no de minimis violations of the Constitution—no constitutional harms so slight that the courts are obliged to ignore them. Given the values that the Establishment Clause was meant to serve, however, I believe that government can, in a discrete category of cases, acknowledge or refer to the divine without offending the Constitution. This category of 'ceremonial deism' most clearly encompasses such things as the national motto ("In God We Trust"), religious references in traditional patriotic songs such as the Star–Spangled Banner, and the words with which the Marshal of this Court opens each of its sessions. See *Allegheny* (opinion of O'Connor, J.). * * *

"This case requires us to determine whether the appearance of the phrase 'under God' in the Pledge of Allegiance constitutes an instance of such ceremonial deism. Although it is a close question, I conclude that it [does.]

"The Pledge complies with [the] requirement [that "no religious acknowledgment could claim to be an instance of ceremonial deism if it explicitly favored one particular religious belief system over another"]. It does not refer to a nation 'under Jesus' or 'under Vishnu,' but instead acknowledges religion in a general way: a simple reference to a generic 'God.' Of course, some religions—Buddhism, for instance—are not based upon a belief in a separate Supreme Being. But one would be hard pressed to imagine a brief solemnizing reference to religion that would adequately encompass every religious belief expressed by any citizen of this Nation."

Thomas, J., also concurred: "Adherence to *Lee* would require us to strike down the Pledge policy, which, in most respects, poses more serious difficulties than the prayer at issue in *Lee.* * * * I believe, however, that *Lee* was wrongly decided. [The] kind of coercion implicated by the Religion Clauses is that accomplished "*by force of law and threat of penalty.*" *Lee* (Scalia, J., dissenting). Peer pressure, unpleasant as it may be, is not coercion.

"[The] text and history of the Establishment Clause strongly suggest that it is a federalism provision intended to prevent Congress from interfering with state establishments. Thus, unlike the Free Exercise Clause, which does protect an individual right, it makes little sense to incorporate the Establishment Clause. In any case, I do not believe that the Pledge policy infringes any religious liberty right that would arise from incorporation of the Clause. Because the Pledge policy also does not infringe any free-exercise rights, I conclude that it is constitutional."

CON LAW: P. 1090, at end of note (b)

AMER CON: P. 958, at end of note (b)

RTS & LIB: P. 1017, at end of note (b)

Concurring in *Van Orden v. Perry*, p. 179 of this Supplement, Thomas, J., argued: "The ['reasonable observer'] analysis is not fully satisfying to either nonadherents or adherents. For the nonadherent, who may well be more sensitive than the hypothetical 'reasonable observer,' or who may not know all the facts, this test fails to capture completely the honest and deeply felt offense he takes from the government conduct. For the adherent, this analysis takes no account of the message sent by removal of the sign or display, which may well appear to him to be an act hostile to his religious faith. The Court's foray into religious meaning either gives insufficient weight to the views of nonadherents and adherents alike, or it provides no principled way to choose between those views. In sum, this Court's effort to assess religious meaning is fraught with futility."

FREE EXERCISE CLAUSE AND RELATED PROBLEMS

CONFLICT WITH STATE REGULATION

CON LAW: P. 1110, at end of note 1

AMER CON: P. 972, at end of note 1

RTS & LIB: P. 1037, at end of note 1

(c) LOCKE v. DAVEY, 540 U.S. 712, 124 S.Ct. 1307, 158 L.Ed.2d 1 (2004), per REHNQUIST, C.J., held that the exclusion (as required by the state constitution) from Washington's postsecondary education Promise Scholarship Program to assist academically gifted students, of pursuit of a devotional theology degree, did not violate the free exercise clause: "[W]e have long said that 'there is room for play in the points' between [the religion clauses]. *Walz.* In other words, there are some state actions permitted by the Establishment Clause but not required by the Free Exercise Clause. [And] there is no doubt that the State could, consistent with the Federal Constitution, permit Promise Scholars to pursue a degree in devotional theology, see *Witters* * * *.

"[Respondent] contends that under the rule we enunciated in *Lukumi*, the program is presumptively unconstitutional because it is not facially neutral with respect to religion. [But in] the present case, the State's disfavor of religion (if it can be called that) is of a far milder kind [than in *Lukumi*]. It imposes neither criminal nor civil sanctions on any type of religious service or rite. It does not deny to ministers the right to participate in the political affairs of the community. See *McDaniel*. And it does not require students to choose between their religious beliefs and receiving a government benefit.[4] See *Hobbie*; *Sherbert*. The State has merely chosen not to fund a distinct category of instruction.

"[M]ajoring in devotional theology is akin to a religious calling as well as an academic pursuit. [That] a State would deal differently with religious education for the ministry than with education for other callings is a product of these views, not evidence of hostility toward religion.

"[T]he interest that [the Washington constitution] seeks to further is scarcely novel. In fact, we can think of few areas in which a State's antiestablishment interests come more into play.[5] Since the founding of our country, there have been popular uprisings against procuring taxpayer funds to support church leaders, which was one of the hallmarks of an 'established' religion. * * *

Most States that sought to avoid such an establishment around the time of the founding placed in their constitutions formal prohibitions against using tax funds to support the ministry. [T]hat early state constitutions saw no problem in explicitly excluding *only* the ministry from receiving state dollars reinforces the conclusion that religious instruction is of a different ilk.

"Far from evincing the hostility toward religion which was manifest in *Lukumi,* we believe that the entirety of the Promise Scholarship Program goes a long way toward including religion in its benefits.[8] The program permits students

4. Promise Scholars may still use their scholarship to pursue a secular degree at a different institution from where they are studying devotional theology.

5. Justice Scalia notes that the State's "philosophical preference" to protect individual conscience is potentially without limit; however, the only interest at issue here is the State's interest in not funding the religious training of clergy. * * *

8. Washington has also been solicitous in ensuring that its constitution is not hostile towards religion, and at least in some respects, its constitution provides greater protection of

to attend pervasively religious schools, so long as they are accredited [and] students are still eligible to take devotional theology courses."

SCALIA, J., joined by Thomas, J., dissented, finding *Lukumi* "irreconcilable with today's decision": "When the State makes a public benefit generally available, that benefit becomes part of the baseline against which burdens on religion are measured; and when the State withholds that benefit from some individuals solely on the basis of religion, it violates the Free Exercise Clause no less than if it had imposed a special tax.

"[No] field of study but religion is singled out for disfavor. [The history relied on by the Court] involved not the inclusion of religious ministers in public benefits programs like the one at issue here, but laws that singled them out for financial aid. [No] one would seriously contend, for example, that the Framers would have barred ministers from using public roads on their way to church.[1]

"[T]he State already has all the play in the joints it needs. There are any number of ways it could respect both its unusually sensitive concern for the conscience of its taxpayers *and* the Federal Free Exercise Clause. It could make the scholarships redeemable only at public universities (where it sets the curriculum), or only for select courses of study. Either option would replace a program that facially discriminates against religion with one that just happens not to subsidize it.

"[T]he interest to which the Court defers is not fear of a conceivable Establishment Clause violation, budget constraints, avoidance of endorsement, or substantive neutrality—none of these. It is a pure philosophical preference: the State's opinion that it would violate taxpayers' freedom of conscience *not* to discriminate against candidates for the ministry. This sort of protection of 'freedom of conscience' has no logical limit and can justify the singling out of religion for exclusion from public programs in virtually any context. The Court never says whether it deems this interest compelling (the opinion is devoid of any mention of standard of review) but, self-evidently, it is not.[2]

"The Court makes no serious attempt to defend the program's neutrality, and instead identifies two features thought to render its discrimination less offensive. The first is the lightness of Davey's burden. The Court offers no authority for approving facial discrimination against religion simply because its material consequences are not severe. I might understand such a test if we were still in the business of reviewing facially neutral laws that merely happen to burden some individual's religious exercise, but we are not. See *Smith*. Discrimination *on the face of a statute* is something else. The indignity of being singled out for special burdens on the basis of one's religious calling is so profound that the concrete harm produced can never be dismissed as insubstantial. The Court has not required proof of 'substantial' concrete harm with other forms of discrimination, see, e.g., *Brown v. Board of Education,* and it should not do so here. * * *

religious liberties than the Free Exercise Clause (rejecting standard in *Smith*) * * *.

1. No State [with] a constitutional provision [that] prohibited the use of tax funds to support the ministry [has,] so far as I know, ever prohibited the hiring of public employees who use their salary to conduct ministries, or excluded ministers from generally available disability or unemployment benefits. * * *

2. [If] religious discrimination required only a rational basis, the Free Exercise Clause would impose no constraints other than those the Constitution already imposes on all government action. The question is not whether theology majors are different, but whether the differences are substantial enough to justify a discriminatory financial penalty that the State inflicts on no other major. Plainly they are not. * * *

"The other reason the Court thinks this particular facial discrimination less offensive is that the scholarship program was not motivated by animus toward religion. [If] a State deprives a citizen of trial by jury or passes an ex post facto law, we do not pause to investigate whether it was actually trying to accomplish the evil the Constitution prohibits. It is sufficient that the citizen's rights have been infringed. [We] do sometimes look to legislative intent to smoke out more subtle instances of discrimination, but we do so as a *supplement* to the core guarantee of facially equal treatment, not as a replacement for it.

"[This] case is about discrimination against a religious minority. Most citizens of this country identify themselves as professing some religious belief, but the State's policy poses no obstacle to practitioners of only a tepid, civic version of faith. Those the statutory exclusion actually affects—those whose belief in their religion is so strong that they dedicate their study and their lives to its ministry—are a far narrower set. One need not delve too far into modern popular culture to perceive a trendy disdain for deep religious conviction."

(d) After *Locke*, may a state exclude church related elementary and secondary schools (or colleges and universities)—at least those that are "pervasively religious"—from a generally available program of state aid to education?

CONFLICT BETWEEN THE CLAUSES

CON LAW: P. 1136, before note 4

AMER CON: P. 992, before note 4

RTS & LIB: P. 1063, before note 4

CUTTER v. WILKINSON, ___ U.S. ___, 125 S.Ct. 2113, ___ L. Ed.2d ___ (2005), per GINSBURG, J., relying on *Amos* and language in *Smith*, held that the Religious Land Use and Institutionalized Persons Act of 2000—which provides, "No government shall impose a substantial burden on the religious exercise of a person residing in or confined to an institution," unless the burden furthers "a compelling governmental interest," and does so by "the least restrictive means"—does not violate the establishment clause:

RLUIPA "does not, on its face, exceed the limits of permissible government accommodation of religious practices [because] it alleviates exceptional government-created burdens on private religious exercise. [Furthermore], the Act on its face does not founder on shoals the Court's prior decisions have identified: Properly applying RLUIPA, courts must take adequate account of the burdens a requested accommodation may impose on nonbeneficiaries, see *Caldor*, and they must be satisfied that the Act's prescriptions are and will be administered neutrally among different faiths, see *Kiryas Joel*.[8] [It] covers state-run institutions—mental hospitals, prisons, and the like—in which the government exerts a degree of control unparalleled in civilian society and severely disabling to private religious exercise.[9] * * *[10] * * *

8. Directed at obstructions institutional arrangements place on religious observances, RLUIPA does not require a State to pay for an inmate's devotional accessories. See, e.g., *Charles v. Verhagen*, 348 F.3d 601, 605 (C.A.7 2003) (overturning prohibition on possession of Islamic prayer oil but leaving inmate-plaintiff with responsibility for purchasing the oil).

9. See, e.g., ibid. (prison's regulation prohibited Muslim prisoner from possessing ritual cleansing oil); *Young v. Lane*, 922 F.2d 370, 375–376 (C.A.7 1991) (prison's regulation restricted wearing of yarmulkes); *Hunafa v. Murphy*, 907 F.2d 46, 47–48 (C.A.7 1990) (noting instances in which Jewish and Muslim prisoners were served pork, with no substitute available).

10. Respondents argue [that RLUIPA] advances religion by encouraging prisoners to

"We have no cause to believe that RLUIPA would not be applied in an appropriately balanced way, with particular sensitivity to security concerns. [Its sponsors] anticipated that courts would apply the Act's standard with 'due deference to the experience and expertise of prison and jail administrators in establishing necessary regulations and procedures to maintain good order, security and discipline, consistent with consideration of costs and limited resources.' "[a]

"get religion," and thereby gain accommodations afforded under RLUIPA. While some accommodations of religious observance, notably the opportunity to assemble in worship services, might attract joiners seeking a break in their closely guarded day, we doubt that all accommodations would be perceived as "benefits." For example, congressional hearings on RLUIPA revealed that one state corrections system served as its kosher diet "a fruit, a vegetable, a granola bar, and a liquid nutritional supplement—each and every meal." The argument, in any event, founders on the fact that Ohio already facilitates religious services for mainstream faiths. The State provides chaplains, allows inmates to possess religious items, and permits assembly for worship.

a. Thomas, J., who joined the Court's opinion, concurred "to explain why a proper historical understanding of the Clause as a federalism provision leads to the same conclusion." See his opinion in *Elk Grove*, p. 188 of this Supplement.

EQUAL PROTECTION

TRADITIONAL APPROACH

CON LAW: P. 1143, after note 4

AMER CON: P. 1000, after note 4

RTS & LIB: P. 1071, after note 4

Fitzgerald v. Racing Ass'n, 539 U.S. 103, 123 S.Ct. 2156, 156 L.Ed.2d 99 (2003), unanimously rejected an equal protection attack on a state statute imposing a higher tax on revenue from slot machines at race tracks than on revenues from slot machines at riverboat casinos. Although the state had permitted slot machines at race tracks in order to save the tracks from economic distress, it was not irrational to tax the race track machines at a higher rate than the riverboat machines, because the legislature may have had independent reasons to want to promote the financial viability of riverboats: "[T]he Iowa law, like most laws, might predominantly serve one general objective, say, helping the racetracks, while containing subsidiary provisions that seek to achieve other desirable (perhaps even contrary) ends as well, thereby producing a law that balances objectives but still serves the general objective when seen as a whole."

RACE AND ETHNIC ANCESTRY

DISCRIMINATION AGAINST RACIAL AND ETHNIC MINORITIES

CON LAW: P. 1167, at end of note 3

AMER CON: P. 1019, at the end of note 2

RTS & LIB: P. 1095, at the end of note 3

4. *The Endo case.* As is emphasized in Patrick O. Gudridge, *Remember Endo?*, 116 Harv.L.Rev. 1933 (2003), *Korematsu* came down the same day as a companion case, *Ex parte Endo*, 323 U.S. 283, 65 S.Ct. 208, 89 L.Ed. 243 (1944). *Endo* held that neither the Executive Order authorizing the exclusion from the West Coast nor the statute that ratified it empowered the War Relocation Authority to detain in a relocation center a person, such as Endo, who was conceded by the government to be "loyal" to the United States. The Court therefore ordered Endo's release. According to Gudridge at 1934, Black, J.'s *Korematsu* opinion, "read closely, tries hard to persuade its readers that *Korematsu* is not an important case. The important case, we are supposed to conclude, is [*Endo*]." *Endo*, however, did not rest on expressly constitutional grounds, nor did it hold forced confinement in relocation centers to be categorically impermissible, as explained by Jackson, J., in a draft concurrence that he ultimately decided not

to publish: "This decision and that in Korematsu's case are separated by a wide chasm, and the real question in this case seems to have fallen therein. In Korematsu's case the Court [formally approves only an exclusion order commanding persons of Japanese ancestry to leave designated West Coast areas and] stops short of the question whether an American citizen may be detained in camps without conviction of crime. In Endo's case the Court is careful to start beyond it and to hold no more than that such a citizen may not be held after the government confesses that it has no security reason for holding her. [The] difference in grounds is substantial. No one may as a right obtain a certification of loyalty. [Anyone] bent on keeping another in custody may say [that] it cannot be known that his prisoner would not commit a crime if he were at large. So the grounds taken by the Court is one available to but few and favored ones." Quoted in Gudridge at 1969. Murphy, J., who dissented in *Korematsu*, concurred in the judgment but not the Court's opinion in *Endo*. His brief opinion noted that Endo wished to return to Sacramento, California, from which she continued to be excluded by military orders upheld in *Korematsu*.

CON LAW: P. 1179, add after note 4

AMER CON: P. 1029, add after note 4

RTS & LIB: P. 1107, add after note 4

JOHNSON v. CALIFORNIA, ___ U.S. ___, 125 S.Ct. 1141, 160 L.Ed.2d 949 (2005), held that the "strict scrutiny" test developed in prior race discrimination cases (under which racial classifications will be upheld only if proven to be "narrowly tailored" to further "compelling governmental interests") applied to a policy of the California Department of Corrections (CDC) to assign newly arrived prisoners to temporary cells "based on a number of factors, [but] predominantly race." The Court, per O'Connor, J., rejected arguments for applying "the deferential standard of review articulated in *Turner v. Safley*, 482 U.S. 78, 107 S.Ct. 2254, 96 L.Ed.2d 64 (1987), under which courts will ordinarily uphold any prison regulation that is "reasonably related" to "legitimate penological interests." Unlike burdens on prisoners' rights to privacy, speech, and religion, "the right not to be discriminated against based on one's race is not susceptible to the logic of *Turner*. It is not a right that need necessarily be compromised for the sake of proper prison administration."

Although Stevens, J., agreed about the applicable standard of review, he dissented from the Court's remand of the case to the district court to apply the compelling interest test and would have held squarely that the challenged policy violated the Equal Protection Clause. Thomas, J., joined by Scalia, J., dissented. In light of the threats of race-based prison violence and the general needs of prison administration, they would have upheld the CDC's policy on the basis of *Turner*.

AFFIRMATIVE ACTION AND "BENIGN" DISCRIMINATION

CON LAW: P.1221, omit pp. 1221–1241 of Sec. VI

AMER CON: P. 1047, omit pp. 1047–1057 of Sec. V

RTS & LIB: P. 1149, omit pp. 1149–1169 of Sec. VI

[Begin the section with *Richmond v. J.A. Croson Co.*]

CON LAW: P. 1261, end of section 2

AMER CON: P. 1076, end of section 2

RTS & LIB: p. 1189, end of section 2

GRUTTER v. BOLLINGER

539 U.S. 306, 123 S.Ct. 2325, 156 L.Ed.2d 304 (2003).

JUSTICE O'CONNOR delivered the opinion of the Court.

This case requires us to decide whether the use of race as a factor in student admissions by the University of Michigan Law School (Law School) is unlawful.

I A. The Law School ranks among the Nation's top law schools. It receives more than 3,500 applications each year for a class of around 350 students. The hallmark of [the Law School's admission] policy is its focus on academic ability coupled with a flexible assessment of applicants' talents, experiences, and potential "to contribute to the learning of those around them." [In] reviewing an applicant's file, admissions officials must consider the applicant's undergraduate grade point average (GPA) and Law School Admissions Test (LSAT) score because they are important (if imperfect) predictors of academic success in law school. The policy stresses that "no applicant should be admitted unless we expect that applicant to do well enough to graduate with no serious academic problems." The policy makes clear, however, that even the highest possible score does not guarantee admission to the Law School. Nor does a low score automatically disqualify an applicant. [S]o-called "soft variables" such as "the enthusiasm of recommenders, the quality of the undergraduate institution, the quality of the applicant's essay, and the areas and difficulty of undergraduate course selection" are all brought to bear in assessing an "applicant's likely contributions to the intellectual and social life of the institution."

The policy aspires to "achieve that diversity which has the potential to enrich everyone's education and thus make a law school class stronger than the sum of its parts." The policy does not restrict the types of diversity contributions eligible for "substantial weight" in the admissions process, but [it reaffirms] the Law School's longstanding commitment to "one particular type of diversity," that is, "racial and ethnic diversity with special reference to the inclusion of students from groups which have been historically discriminated against, like African-Americans, Hispanics and Native Americans, who without this commitment might not be represented in our student body in meaningful numbers." By enrolling a "critical mass of [underrepresented] minority students," the Law School seeks to "ensur[e] their ability to make unique contributions to the character of the Law School."

B. Petitioner Barbara Grutter is a white Michigan resident who applied to the Law School in 1996 with a 3.8 grade point average and 161 LSAT score. The Law School initially placed petitioner on a waiting list, but subsequently rejected her application. [She then filed suit alleging that University officials] discriminated against her on the basis of race in violation of the Fourteenth Amendment [and civil rights statutes including the 1964 Civil Rights Act].

[During] the 15-day bench trial, the parties introduced extensive evidence concerning the Law School's use of race in the admissions process. [A former admission directory] testified that at the height of the admissions season, he would frequently consult the so-called "daily reports" that kept track of the racial and ethnic composition of the class (along with other information such as residency status and gender). This was done, [he] testified, to ensure that a critical mass of underrepresented minority students would be reached so as to realize the educational benefits of a diverse student body. [The current admissions director Erica Munzel] testified that "critical mass" means "meaningful numbers" or "meaningful representation," which she understood to mean a number that encourages underrepresented minority students to participate in the classroom and not feel isolated. Munzel stated there is no number, percentage, or range of numbers or percentages that constitute critical mass. Munzel also asserted that she must consider the race of applicants because a critical mass of underrepresented minority students could not be enrolled if admissions decisions were based primarily on undergraduate GPAs and LSAT scores.

[An expert witness of the Law School,] Dr. Stephen Raudenbush, [testified] that in 2000, [when] 35 percent of underrepresented minority applicants were admitted, [if] race were not considered, only 10 percent of those applicants would have been admitted. Under this scenario, underrepresented minority students would have comprised 4 percent of the entering class in 2000 instead of the actual figure of 14.5 percent.

II A. We last addressed the use of race in public higher education over 25 years ago. In the landmark case of *Regents of Univ. of California v. Bakke*, 438 U.S. 265, 98 S.Ct. 2733, 57 L.Ed.2d 750 (1978), we reviewed a racial set-aside program that reserved 16 out of 100 seats in a medical school class for members of certain minority groups. The decision produced six separate opinions, none of which commanded a majority of the Court. Four Justices would have upheld the program against all attack on the ground that the government can use race to "remedy disadvantages cast on minorities by past racial prejudice." ([See] joint opinion of Brennan, White, Marshall, and Blackmun, JJ., concurring in judgment in part and dissenting in part). [These Justices thought that race-based affirmative action programs were categorically different in kind from race-based classifications adopted to exclude, stigmatize, or demean. They would therefore not have subjected race-based affirmative action programs to "strict" judicial scrutiny, but would have assessed them under intermediate scrutiny, under which "racial classifications designed to further remedial purposes 'must serve important governmental objectives and must be substantially related to the achievement of those objectives.' "] Four other Justices avoided the constitutional question altogether and struck down the program on statutory grounds. ([See the] opinion of Stevens, J., joined by Burger, C.J., and Stewart and Rehnquist, JJ., concurring in judgment in part and dissenting in part). Justice Powell provided a fifth vote not only for invalidating the set-aside program, but also for reversing the state court's injunction against any use of race whatsoever. [Although Justice Powell thought that affirmative action programs should be subject to strict judicial scrutiny, he concluded that a properly tailored program could pass that test in the field of education.] The only holding for the Court in *Bakke* was that a "State has a substantial interest that legitimately may be served by a properly devised admissions program involving the competitive consideration of race and ethnic origin."

[Since] this Court's splintered decision in *Bakke*, Justice Powell's opinion announcing the judgment of the Court has served as the touchstone for constitutional analysis of race-conscious admissions policies. Public and private universities across the Nation have modeled their own admissions programs on Justice Powell's views on permissible race-conscious policies. We therefore discuss Justice Powell's opinion in some detail. Justice Powell began by stating that "[t]he guarantee of equal protection cannot mean one thing when applied to one individual and something else when applied to a person of another color. If both are not accorded the same protection, then it is not equal." In Justice Powell's view, when governmental decisions "touch upon an individual's race or ethnic background, he is entitled to a judicial determination that the burden he is asked to bear on that basis is precisely tailored to serve a compelling governmental interest." Under this exacting standard, only one of the interests asserted by the university survived Justice Powell's scrutiny. First, Justice Powell rejected an interest in "reducing the historic deficit of traditionally disfavored minorities in medical schools and in the medical profession" as an unlawful interest in racial balancing.[a] Second, Justice Powell rejected an interest in remedying societal discrimination because such measures would risk placing unnecessary burdens on innocent third parties "who bear no responsibility for whatever harm the beneficiaries of the special admissions program are thought to have suffered." Third, Justice Powell rejected an interest in "increasing the number of physicians who will practice in communities currently underserved," concluding that even if such an interest could be compelling in some circumstances the program under review was not "geared to promote that goal."

Justice Powell approved the university's use of race to further only one interest: "the attainment of a diverse student body." With the important proviso that "constitutional limitations protecting individual rights may not be disregarded," Justice Powell grounded his analysis in the academic freedom that "long has been viewed as a special concern of the First Amendment." Justice Powell emphasized that nothing less than the "nation's future

a. On this point, Powell, J., differed sharply with the joint opinion of Brennan, White, Marshall, and Blackmun, JJ, who believed that the "purpose of remedying the effects of past societal discrimination is [sufficiently] important to justify the use of race-conscious admissions programs where there is a sound basis for concluding that minority underrepresentation is substantial and chronic, and that the handicap of past discrimination is impeding access of minorities." In *Grutter*, the University of Michigan apparently accepted it as settled by prior Supreme Court decisions that it could not justify its affirmative action program as a remedy for past *societal* discrimination (as opposed to past discrimination by the University itself). Does the University's interest in race as an element of relevant diversity depend on the existence of past societal (or present) societal discrimination on the basis of race?

depends upon leaders trained through wide exposure" to the ideas and mores of students as diverse as this Nation of many peoples." In seeking the "right to select those students who will contribute the most to the 'robust exchange of ideas,'" a university seeks "to achieve a goal that is of paramount importance in the fulfillment of its mission."

Justice Powell was, however, careful to emphasize that in his view race "is only one element in a range of factors a university properly may consider in attaining the goal of a heterogeneous student body." For Justice Powell, "[i]t is not an interest in simple ethnic diversity, in which a specified percentage of the student body is in effect guaranteed to be members of selected ethnic groups," that can justify the use of race. Rather, "[t]he diversity that furthers a compelling state interest encompasses a far broader array of qualifications and characteristics of which racial or ethnic origin is but a single though important element."

B. [Because] the Fourteenth Amendment "protect[s] persons, not groups," all "governmental action based on race—a group classification long recognized as in most circumstances irrelevant and therefore prohibited—should be subjected to detailed judicial inquiry to ensure that the personal right to equal protection of the laws has not been infringed." *Adarand*. We have held that all racial classifications imposed by government "must be analyzed by a reviewing court under strict scrutiny." [We] apply strict scrutiny to all racial classifications to " 'smoke out' illegitimate uses of race by assuring that [government] is pursuing a goal important enough to warrant use of a highly suspect tool." *Croson*. Strict scrutiny is not "strict in theory, but fatal in fact." *Adarand*. [When] race-based action is necessary to further a compelling governmental interest, such action does not violate the constitutional guarantee of equal protection so long as the narrow-tailoring requirement is also satisfied.

III A. [R]espondents assert only one justification for their use of race in the admissions process: obtaining "the educational benefits that flow from a diverse student body." We first wish to dispel the notion that the Law School's argument has been foreclosed, either expressly or implicitly, by our affirmative-action cases decided since *Bakke*. It is true that some language in those opinions might be read to suggest that remedying past discrimination is the only permissible justification for race-based governmental action. But we have never held that the only governmental use of race that can survive strict scrutiny is remedying past discrimination.

[Today], we hold that the Law School has a compelling interest in attaining a diverse student body. The Law School's educational judgment that such diversity is essential to its educational mission is one to which we defer. [We] have long recognized that, given the important purpose of public education and the expansive freedoms of speech and thought associated with the university environment, universities occupy a special niche in our constitutional tradition. In announcing the principle of student body diversity as a compelling state interest, Justice Powell invoked our cases recognizing a constitutional dimension, grounded in the First Amendment, of educational autonomy: [Our] conclusion that the Law School has a compelling interest in a diverse student body is informed by our view that attaining a diverse student body is at the heart of the Law School's proper institutional mission, and that "good faith" on the part of a university is "presumed" absent "a showing to the contrary."

As part of its goal of "assembling a class that is both exceptionally academically qualified and broadly diverse," the Law School seeks to "enroll a 'critical mass' of minority students." The Law School's interest is not simply "to assure within its student body some specified percentage of a particular group merely because of its race or ethnic origin." That would amount to outright racial balancing, which is patently unconstitutional. Rather, the Law School's concept of critical mass is defined by reference to the educational benefits that diversity is designed to produce. These benefits are substantial. As the District Court emphasized, the Law School's admissions policy promotes "cross-racial understanding," helps to break down racial stereotypes, and "enables [students] to better understand persons of different races." These benefits are "important and laudable," because "classroom discussion is livelier, more spirited, and simply more enlightening and interesting" when the students have "the greatest possible variety of backgrounds." [Numerous] studies show that student body diversity promotes learning outcomes, and "better prepares students for an increasingly diverse workforce and society, and better prepares them as professionals." Brief for American Educational Research Association et al. as Amici Curiae 3; see, e.g., W. Bowen & D. Bok, *The Shape of the River* (1998); *Diversity Challenged: Evidence on the Impact of Affirmative Action* (G. Orfiel & M. Kurlaender eds. 2001); *Compelling Interest: Examining the Evidence on Racial Dynamics in Colleges and Universities* (M. Chang, D. Witt, J. Jones, & K. Hakuta eds. 2003).

These benefits are not theoretical but real, as major American businesses have made clear that the skills needed in today's increasingly global marketplace can only be developed through exposure to widely diverse people, cultures, ideas, and viewpoints. What is more, high-ranking retired officers and civilian leaders of the United States military assert that, "[b]ased on [their] decades of experience," a "highly qualified, racially diverse officer corps [is] essential to the military's ability to fulfill its principle mission to provide national security." Brief for Julius W. Becton, Jr. et al. as Amici Curiae 27. The primary sources for the Nation's officer corps are the service academies and the Reserve Officers Training Corps (ROTC), the latter comprising students already admitted to participating colleges and universities. At present, "the military cannot achieve an officer corps that is both highly qualified and racially diverse unless the service academies and the ROTC used limited race-conscious recruiting and admissions policies." Ibid. To fulfill its mission, the military "must be selective in admissions for training and education for the officer corps, and it must train and educate a highly qualified, racially diverse officer corps in a racially diverse setting." Ibid. We agree that "[i]t requires only a small step from this analysis to conclude that our country's other most selective institutions must remain both diverse and selective." *Ibid.*

[U]niversities, and in particular, law schools, represent the training ground for a large number of our Nation's leaders. *Sweatt v. Painter*. [In] order to cultivate a set of leaders with legitimacy in the eyes of the citizenry, it is necessary that the path to leadership be visibly open to talented and qualified individuals of every race and ethnicity. All members of our heterogeneous society must have confidence in the openness and integrity of the educational institutions that provide this training. As we have recognized, law schools "cannot be effective in isolation from the individuals and institutions with which the law interacts." See *Sweatt*. Access to legal education (and thus the legal profession) must be inclusive of talented and qualified individuals of every race and ethnicity, so that all members of our heterogeneous society may participate in the educational institutions that provide the training and education necessary to succeed in America.

The Law School does not premise its need for critical mass on "any belief that minority students always (or even consistently) express some characteristic minority viewpoint on any issue." To the contrary, diminishing the force of such stereotypes is both a crucial part of the Law School's mission, and one that it cannot accomplish with only token numbers of minority students. Just as growing up in a particular region or having particular professional experiences is likely to affect an individual's views, so too is one's own, unique experience of being a racial minority in a society, like our own, in which race unfortunately still matters. The Law School has determined, based on its experience and expertise, that a "critical mass" of underrepresented minorities is necessary to further its compelling interest in securing the educational benefits of a diverse student body.

B. Even in the limited circumstance when drawing racial distinctions is permissible to further a compelling state interest, government is still "constrained in how it may pursue that end: [T]he means chosen to accomplish the [government's] asserted purpose must be specifically and narrowly framed to accomplish that purpose." The purpose of the narrow tailoring requirement is to ensure that "the means chosen 'fit' [the] compelling goal so closely that there is little or no possibility that the motive for the classification was illegitimate racial prejudice or stereotype." *Richmond*. [To] be narrowly tailored, a race-conscious admissions program cannot use a quota system—it cannot "insulat[e] each category of applicants with certain desired qualifications from competition with all other applicants." *Bakke* (opinion of Powell, J.). Instead, a university may consider race or ethnicity only as a " 'plus' in a particular applicant's file," without "insulat[ing] the individual from comparison with all other candidates for the available seats." In other words, an admissions program must be "flexible enough to consider all pertinent elements of diversity in light of the particular qualifications of each applicant, and to place them on the same footing for consideration, although not necessarily according them the same weight."

We find that the Law School's admissions program bears the hallmarks of a narrowly tailored plan.[The] the Law School's admissions program does not operate as a quota. Properly understood, a "quota" is a program in which a certain fixed number or proportion of opportunities are "reserved exclusively for certain minority groups." In contrast, "a permissible goal [requires] only a good-faith effort [to] come within a range demarcated by the goal itself."

[The] Law School's goal of attaining a critical mass of underrepresented minority students does not transform its program into a quota. [Nor] does the Law School's consultation of the "daily reports," which keep track of the racial and ethnic composition of the class (as well as of residency and gender), "suggest [ ] there was no further attempt at individual review save for race itself" during the final stages of the admissions process. To the contrary, the

Law School's admissions officers testified without contradiction that they never gave race any more or less weight based on the information contained in these reports. Moreover, between 1993 and 2000, the number of African–American, Latino, and Native–American students in each class at the Law School varied from 13.5 to 20.1 percent, a range inconsistent with a quota.

[That] a race-conscious admissions program does not operate as a quota does not, by itself, satisfy the requirement of individualized consideration. When using race as a "plus" factor in university admissions, a university's admissions program must remain flexible enough to ensure that each applicant is evaluated as an individual and not in a way that makes an applicant's race or ethnicity the defining feature of his or her application. [Here], the Law School engages in a highly individualized, holistic review of each applicant's file, giving serious consideration to all the ways an applicant might contribute to a diverse educational environment. The Law School affords this individualized consideration to applicants of all races.

[Petitioner] and the United States argue that the Law School's plan is not narrowly tailored because race-neutral means exist to obtain the educational benefits of student body diversity that the Law School seeks. We disagree. Narrow tailoring does not require exhaustion of every conceivable race-neutral alternative. Nor does it require a university to choose between maintaining a reputation for excellence or fulfilling a commitment to provide educational opportunities to members of all racial groups. [The] District Court took the Law School to task for failing to consider race-neutral alternatives such as "using a lottery system" or "decreasing the emphasis for all applicants on undergraduate GPA and LSAT scores." But these alternatives would require a dramatic sacrifice of diversity, the academic quality of all admitted students, or both. [Because] a lottery would make [nuanced] judgment impossible, it would effectively sacrifice all other educational values, not to mention every other kind of diversity. So too with the suggestion that the Law School simply lower admissions standards for all students, a drastic remedy that would require the Law School to become a much different institution and sacrifice a vital component of its educational mission.

The United States advocates "percentage plans," recently adopted by public undergraduate institutions in Texas, Florida, and California to guarantee admission to all students above a certain class-rank threshold in every high school in the State. The United States does not, however, explain how such plans could work for graduate and professional schools. Moreover, even assuming such plans are race-neutral, they may preclude the university from conducting the individualized assessments necessary to assemble a student body that is not just racially diverse, but diverse along all the qualities valued by the university.

We acknowledge that "there are serious problems of justice connected with the idea of preference itself." To be narrowly tailored, a race-conscious admissions program must not "unduly burden individuals who are not members of the favored racial and ethnic groups." We are satisfied that the Law School's admissions program does not. As Justice Powell recognized in *Bakke*, so long as a race-conscious admissions program uses race as a "plus" factor in the context of individualized consideration, a rejected applicant "will not have been foreclosed from all consideration for that seat simply because he was not the right color or had the wrong surname. [His] qualifications would have been weighed fairly and competitively, and he would have no basis to complain of unequal treatment under the Fourteenth Amendment."

We are mindful, however, that "[a] core purpose of the Fourteenth Amendment was to do away with all governmentally imposed discrimination based on race." Accordingly, race-conscious admissions policies must be limited in time. This requirement reflects that racial classifications, however compelling their goals, are potentially so dangerous that they may be employed no more broadly than the interest demands. In the context of higher education, the durational requirement can be met by sunset provisions in race-conscious admissions policies and periodic reviews to determine whether racial preferences are still necessary to achieve student body diversity. [We] take the Law School at its word that it would "like nothing better than to find a race-neutral admissions formula" and will terminate its race-conscious admissions program as soon as practicable. It has been 25 years since Justice Powell first approved the use of race to further an interest in student body diversity in the context of public higher education. Since that time, the number of minority applicants with high grades and test scores has indeed increased. We expect that 25 years from now, the use of racial preferences will no longer be necessary to further the interest approved today.

IV. In summary, the Equal Protection Clause does not prohibit the Law School's narrowly tailored use of race in admissions decisions to further a compelling interest in obtaining the educational benefits that flow from a diverse student body. Consequently, petitioner's statutory claims based [also] fail [under cases holding .the relevant statutory prohibitions to sweep no more broadly than the Equal Protection Clause].

JUSTICE GINSBURG, with whom JUSTICE BREYER joins, concurring.

[It] was only 25 years before *Bakke* that this Court declared public school segregation unconstitutional, a declaration that, after prolonged resistance, yielded an end to a law-enforced racial caste system, itself the legacy of centuries of slavery. [Today, it] is well documented that conscious and unconscious race bias, even rank discrimination based on race, remain alive in our land, impeding realization of our highest values and ideals. As to public education, data for the years 2000–2001 show that 71.6% of African-American children and 76.3% of Hispanic children attended a school in which minorities made up a majority of the student body. And schools in predominantly minority communities lag far behind others measured by the educational resources available to them. Despite these inequalities, some minority students are able to meet the high threshold requirements set for admission to the country's finest undergraduate and graduate educational institutions. As lower school education in minority communities improves, an increase in the number of such students may be anticipated. From today's vantage point, one may hope, but not firmly forecast, that over the next generation's span, progress toward nondiscrimination and genuinely equal opportunity will make it safe to sunset affirmative action.

CHIEF JUSTICE REHNQUIST, with whom JUSTICE SCALIA, JUSTICE KENNEDY, and JUSTICE THOMAS join, dissenting.

I agree with the Court that, "in the limited circumstance when drawing racial distinctions is permissible," the government must ensure that its means are narrowly tailored to achieve a compelling state interest. I do not believe, however, that the University of Michigan Law School's (Law School) means are narrowly tailored to the interest it asserts. The Law School claims it must take the steps it does to achieve a "critical mass" of underrepresented minority students. But its actual program bears no relation to this asserted goal. Stripped of its "critical mass" veil, the Law School's program is revealed as a naked effort to achieve racial balancing.

[Before] the Court's decision today, we consistently applied the same strict scrutiny analysis regardless of the government's purported reason for using race and regardless of the setting in which race was being used. [Today, although] the Court recites the language of our strict scrutiny analysis, its application of that review is unprecedented in its deference.

In practice, the Law School's program bears little or no relation to its asserted goal of achieving "critical mass." From 1995 through 2000, the Law School admitted between 1,130 and 1,310 students. Of those, between 13 and 19 were Native American, between 91 and 108 were African–Americans, and between 47 and 56 were Hispanic. If the Law School is admitting between 91 and 108 African–Americans in order to achieve "critical mass," thereby preventing African–American students from feeling "isolated or like spokespersons for their race," one would think that a number of the same order of magnitude would be necessary to accomplish the same purpose for Hispanics and Native Americans. Similarly, even if all of the Native American applicants admitted in a given year matriculate, which the record demonstrates is not at all the case,[7] how can this possibly constitute a "critical mass" of Native Americans in a class of over 350 students? In order for this pattern of admission to be consistent with the Law School's explanation of "critical mass," one would have to believe that the objectives of "critical mass" offered by respondents are achieved with only half the number of Hispanics and one-sixth the number of Native Americans as compared to African-Americans. But respondents offer no race-specific reasons for such disparities. Instead, they simply emphasize the importance of achieving "critical mass," without any explanation of why that concept is applied differently among the three underrepresented minority groups.

These different numbers, moreover, come only as a result of substantially different treatment among the three underrepresented minority groups. [For] example, in 2000, 12 Hispanics who scored between a 159–160 on the LSAT and earned a GPA of 3.00 or higher applied for admission and only 2 were admitted. Meanwhile, 12 African–Americans in the same range of qualifications applied for admission and all 12 were admitted. Likewise, that same year, 16 Hispanics who scored between a 151–153 on the LSAT and earned a 3.00 or higher applied for admission and only 1 of those applicants was admitted. Twenty-three similarly qualified African–Americans applied for admission and 14 were admitted.

Only when the "critical mass" label is discarded does a likely explanation for these numbers emerge. [The] correlation between the percentage of the Law School's pool of applicants who are members of the three minority groups

7. Indeed, during this 5-year time period, enrollment of Native American students dropped to as low as three such students. Any assertion that such a small group constituted a "critical mass" of Native Americans is simply absurd.

and the percentage of the admitted applicants who are members of these same groups is far too precise to be dismissed as merely the result of the school paying "some attention to [the] numbers." As the tables below show, from 1995 through 2000 the percentage of admitted applicants who were members of these minority groups closely tracked the percentage of individuals in the school's applicant pool who were from the same groups. [The Chief Justice here included a table showing that in 1995, 9.7% of the Law Schools's applicants were African–American, as were 9.4% of its admittees, and that for the following years the corresponding numbers were, respectively 9.3% and 9.2% in 1996; 9.3% and 8.3% in 1997; 8.6% and 7.9% in 1998; 7.3% and 7.1% in 1999; and 7.5% and 7.3% in 2000. For Hispanics, the parallel numbers of applicants and admittees for the same years were 5.1% and 5.0% in 1995; 5.1% and 4.6% in 1996; 4.8% and 3.9% in 1997; 4.2% and 4.2% in 1998; 4.5% and 3.8% in 1999; and 4.9% and 4.2% in 2000. During the same period, Native American applicants ranged between 0.7% and 1.1% of the total applicant pool, and the number of admitted students ran between 1.1% and 1.6%.]

For example, in 1995, when 9.7% of the applicant pool was African–American, 9.4% of the admitted class was African–American. By 2000, only 7.5% of the applicant pool was African–American, and 7.3% of the admitted class was African–American. [The] tight correlation between the percentage of applicants and admittees of a given race, therefore, must result from careful race based planning by the Law School. It suggests a formula for admission based on the aspirational assumption that all applicants are equally qualified academically, and therefore that the proportion of each group admitted should be the same as the proportion of that group in the applicant pool. [This] is precisely the type of racial balancing that the Court itself calls "patently unconstitutional."

JUSTICE KENNEDY, dissenting.

The opinion by Justice Powell in *Bakke*, in my view, states the correct rule for resolving this case. The Court, however, does not apply strict scrutiny. By trying to say otherwise, it undermines both the test and its own controlling precedents.

[About] 80 to 85 percent of the places in the entering class are given to applicants in the upper range of Law School Admissions Test scores and grades. An applicant with these credentials likely will be admitted without consideration of race or ethnicity. With respect to the remaining 15 to 20 percent of the seats, race is likely outcome determinative for many members of minority groups. That is where the competition becomes tight and where any given applicant's chance of admission is far smaller if he or she lacks minority status. At this point the numerical concept of critical mass has the real potential to compromise individual review. The Law School has not demonstrated how individual consideration is, or can be, preserved at this stage of the application process given the instruction to attain what it calls critical mass. In fact the evidence shows otherwise. There was little deviation among admitted minority students during the years from 1995 to 1998. The percentage of enrolled minorities fluctuated only by 0.3%, from 13.5% to 13.8%. The number of minority students to whom offers were extended varied by just a slightly greater magnitude of 2.2%, from the high of 15.6% in 1995 to the low of 13.4% in 1998.

[The] narrow fluctuation band raises an inference that the Law School subverted individual determination, and strict scrutiny requires the Law School to overcome the inference. At the very least, the constancy of admitted minority students and the close correlation between the racial breakdown of admitted minorities and the composition of the applicant pool, [require] the Law School either to produce a convincing explanation or to show it has taken adequate steps to ensure individual assessment. The Law School does neither.

The obvious tension between the pursuit of critical mass and the requirement of individual review increased by the end of the admissions season. [The] consultation of daily reports during the last stages in the admissions process suggests there was no further attempt at individual review save for race itself. The admissions officers could use the reports to recalibrate the plus factor given to race depending on how close they were to achieving the Law School's goal of critical mass. The bonus factor of race would then become divorced from individual review; it would be premised instead on the numerical objective set by the Law School. [The] daily consideration of racial breakdown of admitted students is not a feature of affirmative-action programs used by other institutions of higher learning. The Little Ivy League colleges, for instance, do not keep ongoing tallies of racial or ethnic composition of their entering students. See Brief for Amherst College et al. as Amici Curiae 10.

JUSTICE SCALIA, with whom JUSTICE THOMAS joins, concurring in part and dissenting in part.

The "educational benefit" that the University of Michigan seeks to achieve by racial discrimination consists, according to the Court, of "cross-racial understanding," and "better prepar[ation of] students for an increasingly diverse workforce and society," all of which is necessary not only for work, but also for good "citizenship." This is not, of course, an "educational benefit" on which students will be graded on their Law School transcript (Works and Plays Well with Others: B+) or tested by the bar examiners (Q: Describe in 500 words or less your cross-racial understanding). For it is a lesson of life rather than law—essentially the same lesson taught to (or rather learned by, for it cannot be "taught" in the usual sense) people three feet shorter and twenty years younger than the full-grown adults at the University of Michigan Law School, in institutions ranging from Boy Scout troops to public-school kindergartens. If properly considered an "educational benefit" at all, it is surely not one that is either uniquely relevant to law school or uniquely "teachable" in a formal educational setting. And therefore: If it is appropriate for the University of Michigan Law School to use racial discrimination for the purpose of putting together a "critical mass" that will convey generic lessons in socialization and good citizenship, surely it is no less appropriate—indeed, particularly appropriate—for the civil service system of the State of Michigan to do so. There, also, those exposed to "critical masses" of certain races will presumably become better Americans, better Michiganders, better civil servants. And surely private employers cannot be criticized—indeed, should be praised—if they also "teach" good citizenship to their adult employees through a patriotic, all-American system of racial discrimination in hiring. The nonminority individuals who are deprived of a legal education, a civil service job, or any job at all by reason of their skin color will surely understand.

Unlike a clear constitutional holding that racial preferences in state educational institutions are impermissible, or even a clear anticonstitutional holding that racial preferences in state educational institutions are OK, today's [decision in *Grutter*, when coupled with the Court's decision in *Gratz*, which follows immediately,] seems perversely designed to prolong the controversy and the litigation. Some future lawsuits will presumably focus on whether the discriminatory scheme in question contains enough evaluation of the applicant "as an individual,"and sufficiently avoids "separate admissions tracks" [to be constitutionally permissible]. Some will focus on whether a university has gone beyond the bounds of a " 'good faith effort' " and has so zealously pursued its "critical mass" as to make it an unconstitutional de facto quota system, rather than merely " 'a permissible goal.' " Other lawsuits may focus on whether, in the particular setting at issue, any educational benefits flow from racial diversity. (That issue was not contested in *Grutter*; and while the opinion accords "a degree of deference to a university's academic decisions," "deference does not imply abandonment or abdication of judicial review.") Still other suits may challenge the bona fides of the institution's expressed commitment to the educational benefits of diversity that immunize the discriminatory scheme in *Grutter*. (Tempting targets, one would suppose, will be those universities that talk the talk of multiculturalism and racial diversity in the courts but walk the walk of tribalism and racial segregation on their campuses—through minority-only student organizations, separate minority housing opportunities, separate minority student centers, even separate minority-only graduation ceremonies.) And still other suits may claim that the institution's racial preferences have gone below or above the mystical *Grutter*-approved "critical mass." Finally, litigation can be expected on behalf of minority groups intentionally short changed in the institution's composition of its generic minority "critical mass." I do not look forward to any of these cases. The Constitution proscribes government discrimination on the basis of race, and state-provided education is no exception.

JUSTICE THOMAS, with whom JUSTICE SCALIA joins as to Parts I–VII, concurring in part and dissenting in part.

Frederick Douglass, speaking to a group of abolitionists almost 140 years ago, delivered a message lost on today's majority: "[I]n regard to the colored people, there is always more that is benevolent, I perceive, than just, manifested towards us. What I ask for the negro is not benevolence, not pity, not sympathy, but simply *justice*.... And if the negro cannot stand on his own legs, let him fall.... All I ask is, give him a chance to stand on his own legs! Let him alone! ... Your interference is doing him positive injury." [Like] Douglass, I believe blacks can achieve in every avenue of American life without the meddling of university administrators. Because I wish to see all students succeed whatever their color, I share, in some respect, the sympathies of those who sponsor the type of discrimination advanced by the University of Michigan Law School (Law School). The Constitution does not, however, tolerate institutional devotion to the status quo in admissions policies when such devotion ripens into racial discrimination. Nor does the Constitution countenance the unprecedented deference the Court gives to the Law School, an approach inconsistent with the very concept of "strict scrutiny."

The majority upholds the Law School's racial discrimination not by interpreting the people's Constitution, but by responding to a faddish slogan of the cognoscenti. Nevertheless, I concur in part in the Court's opinion. First, I agree with the Court insofar as its decision, which approves of only one racial classification, confirms that further use of race in admissions remains unlawful. Second, I agree with the Court's holding that racial discrimination in higher education admissions will be illegal in 25 years. I respectfully dissent from the remainder of the Court's opinion and the judgment, however, because I believe that the Law School's current use of race violates the Equal Protection Clause and that the Constitution means the same thing today as it will in 300 months. * * *

II. Unlike the majority, I seek to define with precision the interest being asserted by the Law School before determining whether that interest is so compelling as to justify racial discrimination. The Law School maintains that it wishes to obtain "educational benefits that flow from student body diversity." This statement must be evaluated carefully, because it implies that both "diversity" and "educational benefits" are components of the Law School's compelling state interest. [The] Law School [apparently] believes that only a racially mixed student body can lead to the educational benefits it seeks. How, then, is the Law School's interest in these allegedly unique educational "benefits" not simply the forbidden interest in "racial balancing" that the majority expressly rejects? A distinction between these two ideas (unique educational benefits based on racial aesthetics and race for its own sake) is purely sophistic—so much so that the majority uses them interchangeably.

III. Justice Powell's opinion in *Bakke* and the Court's decision today rest on the fundamentally flawed proposition that racial discrimination can be contextualized so that a goal, such as classroom aesthetics, can be compelling in one context but not in another. [Under] the proper standard, there is no pressing public necessity in maintaining a public law school at all and, it follows, certainly not an elite law school. Likewise, marginal improvements in legal education do not qualify as a compelling state interest. * * *

IV. [With] the adoption of different admissions methods, such as accepting all students who meet minimum qualifications, the Law School could achieve its vision of the racially aesthetic student body without the use of racial discrimination. The Law School concedes this, but the Court holds, implicitly and under the guise of narrow tailoring, that the Law School has a compelling state interest in doing what it wants to do. I cannot agree. First, under strict scrutiny, the Law School's assessment of the benefits of racial discrimination and devotion to the admissions status quo are not entitled to any sort of deference, grounded in the First Amendment or anywhere else. Second, even if its "academic selectivity" must be maintained at all costs along with racial discrimination, the Court ignores the fact that other top law schools have succeeded in meeting their aesthetic demands without racial discrimination.

[The] Court bases its unprecedented deference to the Law School—a deference antithetical to strict scrutiny—on an idea of "educational autonomy" grounded in the First Amendment. In my view, there is no basis for a right of public universities to do what would otherwise violate the Equal Protection Clause.

[The] Court relies heavily on social science evidence to justify its deference. The Court never acknowledges, however, the growing evidence that racial (and other sorts) of heterogeneity actually impairs learning among black students. See, e.g., Flowers & Pascarella, *Cognitive Effects of College Racial Composition on African American Students After 3 Years of College*, 40 J. of College Student Development 669, 674 (1999) (concluding that black students experience superior cognitive development at Historically Black Colleges (HBCs) and that, even among blacks, "a substantial diversity moderates the cognitive effects of attending an HBC"); Allen, *The Color of Success: African–American College Student Outcomes at Predominantly White and Historically Black Public Colleges and Universities*, 62 Harv. Educ. Rev. 26, 35 (1992) (finding that black students attending HBCs report higher academic achievement than those attending predominantly white colleges).

[The] majority [also] ignores the "experience" of those institutions that have been forced to abandon explicit racial discrimination in admissions. The sky has not fallen at Boalt Hall at the University of California, Berkeley, for example. Prior to Proposition 209's adoption of Cal. Const., Art. 1, § 31(a), which bars the State from "grant[ing] preferential treatment [on] the basis of race [in] the operation [of] public education," Boalt Hall enrolled 20 blacks and 28 Hispanics in its first-year class for 1996. In 2002, without deploying express racial discrimination in admissions, Boalt's entering class enrolled 14 blacks and 36 Hispanics. Total underrepresented minority student enrollment at Boalt Hall now exceeds 1996 levels. * * *

VI. The absence of any articulated legal principle supporting the majority's principal holding suggests another rationale. I believe what lies beneath the Court's decision today are the benighted notions that one can tell when racial discrimination benefits (rather than hurts) minority groups, and that racial discrimination is necessary to remedy general societal ills. [I] must contest the notion that the Law School's discrimination benefits those admitted as a result of it. The Court spends considerable time discussing the impressive display of amicus support for the Law School in this case from all corners of society. But nowhere in any of the filings in this Court is any evidence that the purported "beneficiaries" of this racial discrimination prove themselves by performing at (or even near) the same level as those students who receive no preferences. Cf. Thernstrom & Thernstrom, *Reflections on the Shape of the River*, 46 UCLA L. Rev. 1583, 1605–1608 (1999) (discussing the failure of defenders of racial discrimination in admissions to consider the fact that its "beneficiaries" are underperforming in the classroom).

The Law School tantalizes unprepared students with the promise of a University of Michigan degree and all of the opportunities that it offers. These overmatched students take the bait, only to find that they cannot succeed in the cauldron of competition. And this mismatch crisis is not restricted to elite institutions. See T. Sowell, *Race and Culture* 176–177 (1994) ("Even if most minority students are able to meet the normal standards at the 'average' range of colleges and universities, the systematic mismatching of minority students begun at the top can mean that such students are generally overmatched throughout all levels of higher education"). [While] these students may graduate with law degrees, there is no evidence that they have received a qualitatively better legal education (or become better lawyers) than if they had gone to a less "elite" law school for which they were better prepared.

[It] is uncontested that each year, the Law School admits a handful of blacks who would be admitted in the absence of racial discrimination. Who can differentiate between those who belong and those who do not? The majority of blacks are admitted to the Law School because of discrimination, and because of this policy all are tarred as undeserving. This problem of stigma does not depend on determinacy as to whether those stigmatized are actually the "beneficiaries" of racial discrimination. When blacks take positions in the highest places of government, industry, or academia, it is an open question today whether their skin color played a part in their advancement. The question itself is the stigma—because either racial discrimination did play a role, in which case the person may be deemed "otherwise unqualified," or it did not, in which case asking the question itself unfairly marks those blacks who would succeed without discrimination.

GRATZ v. BOLLINGER

539 U.S. 244, 123 S.Ct. 2411, 156 L.Ed.2d 257 (2003).

CHIEF JUSTICE REHNQUIST delivered the opinion of the Court.

We granted certiorari in this case to decide whether "the University of Michigan's use of racial preferences in undergraduate admissions violate[s] the Equal Protection Clause of the Fourteenth Amendment [or civil rights statutes prohibiting racial discrimination]."

I A. Petitioners Jennifer Gratz and Patrick Hamacher both applied for admission to the University of Michigan's (University) College of Literature, Science, and the Arts (LSA) as residents of the State of Michigan. Both petitioners are Caucasian. Gratz, who applied for admission for the fall of 1995, was notified in January of that year that a final decision regarding her admission had been delayed until April. This delay was based upon the University's determination that, although Gratz was "well qualified," she was "less competitive than the students who ha[d] been admitted on first review." Gratz was notified in April that the LSA was unable to offer her admission. [She subsequently filed suit challenging the constitutionality of the undergraduate admissions policies, as did Hamacher.

[The University changed its admissions guidelines a number of times during the period relevant to this litigation, but the version in place at the time of the Court's decision, introduced during the 1998 academic year, employed] a "selection index," on which an applicant could score a maximum of 150 points. This index was divided linearly into ranges generally calling for admissions dispositions as follows: 100–150 (admit); 95–99 (admit or postpone); 90–94 (postpone or admit); 75–89 (delay or postpone); 74 and below (delay or reject). Each application received points based on high school grade point average, standardized test scores, academic quality of an applicant's high school, strength or weakness of high school curriculum, in-state residency, alumni relationship, personal essay, and personal achievement or leadership. Of particular significance here, under a "miscellaneous" category, an applicant was entitled to 20 points based upon his or her membership in an underrepresented racial or ethnic minority group. [Under the same category, 20 points could also be awarded based upon socioeconomic status, upon status as a recruited athlete, or upon a designation by the provost.]

[Starting] in 1999, [the] University established an Admissions Review Committee (ARC), to provide an additional level of consideration for some applications. Under the new system, counselors may, in their discretion, "flag" an application for the ARC to review after determining that the applicant (1) is academically prepared to succeed at the University, (2) has achieved a minimum selection index score, and (3) possesses a quality or characteristic important to the University's composition of its freshman class, such as high class rank, unique life experiences, challenges, circumstances, interests or talents, socioeconomic disadvantage, and underrepresented race, ethnicity, or geography. After reviewing "flagged" applications, the ARC determines whether to admit, defer, or deny each applicant.

II. [Petitioners' argument that the Fourteenth Amendment categorically prohibits the use of racial preferences to promote educational diversity fails under the holding of *Grutter*.] Petitioners alternatively argue that even if the University's interest in diversity can constitute a compelling state interest, the guidelines the University began using in 1999 do not "remotely resemble the kind of consideration of race and ethnicity that Justice Powell endorsed in *Bakke*."

To withstand our strict scrutiny analysis, respondents must demonstrate that the University's use of race in its current admission program employs "narrowly tailored measures that further compelling governmental interests." We find that the University's policy, which automatically distributes 20 points, or one-fifth of the points needed to guarantee admission, to every single "underrepresented minority" applicant solely because of race, is not narrowly tailored to achieve the interest in educational diversity that respondents claim justifies their program.

In *Bakke*, Justice Powell reiterated that "[p]referring members of any one group for no reason other than race or ethnic origin is discrimination for its own sake." [His opinion] emphasized the importance of considering each particular applicant as an individual, assessing all of the qualities that individual possesses, and in turn, evaluating that individual's ability to contribute to the unique setting of higher education. [The] current LSA policy does not provide such individualized consideration. The LSA's policy automatically distributes 20 points to every single applicant from an "underrepresented minority" group, as defined by the University. The only consideration that accompanies this distribution of points is a factual review of an application to determine whether an individual is a member of one of these minority groups. Moreover, unlike Justice Powell's example, where the race of a "particular black applicant" could be considered without being decisive, the LSA's automatic distribution of 20 points has the effect of making "the factor of race * * * decisive" for virtually every minimally qualified underrepresented minority applicant.

Also instructive in our consideration of the LSA's system is the example provided in the description of the Harvard College Admissions Program, which Justice Powell both discussed in, and attached to, his opinion in *Bakke*. The example was included to "illustrate the kind of significance attached to race" under the Harvard College program. It provided as follows: "The Admissions Committee, with only a few places left to fill, might find itself forced to choose between A, the child of a successful black physician in an academic community with promise of superior academic performance, and B, a black who grew up in an inner-city ghetto of semi-literate parents whose academic achievement was lower but who had demonstrated energy and leadership as well as an apparently abiding interest in black power. If a good number of black students much like A but few like B had already been admitted, the Committee might prefer B; and vice versa. If C, a white student with extraordinary artistic talent, were also seeking one of the remaining places, his unique quality might give him an edge over both A and B. Thus, the critical criteria are often individual qualities or experience not dependent upon race but sometimes associated with it."

This example further demonstrates the problematic nature of the LSA's admissions system. Even if student C's "extraordinary artistic talent" rivaled that of Monet or Picasso, the applicant would receive, at most, five points under the LSA's system. At the same time, every single underrepresented minority applicant, including students A and B, would automatically receive 20 points for submitting an application. Clearly, the LSA's system does not offer applicants the individualized selection process described in Harvard's example. Instead of considering how the differing backgrounds, experiences, and characteristics of students A, B, and C might benefit the University, admissions counselors reviewing LSA applications would simply award both A and B 20 points because their applications indicate that they are African–American, and student C would receive up to 5 points for his "extraordinary talent."

Respondents emphasize the fact that the LSA has created the possibility of an applicant's file being flagged for individualized consideration by the ARC. We think that the flagging program only emphasizes the flaws of the University's system as a whole when compared to that described by Justice Powell. Again, students A, B, and C illustrate the point. First, student A would never be flagged. This is because, as the University has conceded, the effect of automatically awarding 20 points is that virtually every qualified underrepresented minority applicant is admitted. Student A, an applicant "with promise of superior academic performance," would certainly fit this description. Thus, the result of the automatic distribution of 20 points is that the University would never consider student A's individual background, experiences, and characteristics to assess his individual "potential contribution to diversity." Instead, every applicant like student A would simply be admitted.

It is possible that students B and C would be flagged and considered as individuals. This assumes that student B was not already admitted because of the automatic 20–point distribution, and that student C could muster at least 70 additional points. But the fact that the "review committee can look at the applications individually and ignore the points," once an application is flagged is of little comfort under our strict scrutiny analysis. The record does not reveal precisely how many applications are flagged for this individualized consideration, but it is undisputed that such consideration is the exception and not the rule in the operation of the LSA's admissions program. Additionally, this individualized review is only provided after admissions counselors automatically distribute the University's version of a "plus" that makes race a decisive factor for virtually every minimally qualified underrepresented minority applicant.

Respondents contend that "[t]he volume of applications and the presentation of applicant information make it impractical for [LSA] to use the . . . admissions system" upheld by the Court today in *Grutter*. But the fact that the implementation of a program capable of providing individualized consideration might present administrative challenges does not render constitutional an otherwise problematic system. Nothing in Justice Powell's opinion in *Bakke* signaled that a university may employ whatever means it desires to achieve the stated goal of diversity without regard to the limits imposed by our strict scrutiny analysis.

JUSTICE O'CONNOR, with whom JUSTICE BREYER joins except as to the last sentence, concurring.

Unlike the law school admissions policy the Court upholds today in *Grutter v. Bollinger*, the procedures employed by the University of Michigan's Office of Undergraduate Admissions do not provide for a meaningful individualized review of applicants. [Although] the Office of Undergraduate Admissions does assign 20 points to some "soft" variables other than race, the points available for other diversity contributions, such as leadership and service, personal achievement, and geographic diversity, are capped at much lower levels. [The] only potential source of individualized consideration appears to be the Admissions Review Committee. The evidence in the record, however, reveals very little about how the review committee actually functions. And what evidence there is indicates that the committee is a kind of afterthought, rather than an integral component of a system of individualized review.

For these reasons, the record before us does not support the conclusion that the University of Michigan's admissions program for its College of Literature, Science, and the Arts—to the extent that it considers race—provides the necessary individualized consideration. The University, of course, remains free to modify its system so that it does so. But the current system, as I understand it, is a nonindividualized, mechanical one. As a result, I join the Court's opinion reversing the decision of the District Court.

JUSTICE THOMAS, concurring.

I join the Court's opinion because I believe it correctly applies our precedents, including today's decision in *Grutter*.

JUSTICE BREYER, concurring in the judgment.

I concur in the judgment of the Court though I do not join its opinion. I join Justice O'Connor's opinion except insofar as it joins that of the Court. I join Part I of Justice Ginsburg's dissenting opinion, but I do not dissent from the Court's reversal of the District Court's decision. I agree with Justice Ginsburg that, in implementing the Constitution's equality instruction, government decisionmakers may properly distinguish between policies of inclusion and exclusion, for the former are more likely to prove consistent with the basic constitutional obligation that the law respect each individual equally.

JUSTICE STEVENS, with whom JUSTICE SOUTER joins, dissenting.

[Because the case should be dismissed for lack of standing,] I respectfully dissent.

JUSTICE SOUTER, with whom JUSTICE GINSBURG joins as to Part II, dissenting.

II. The cases now contain two pointers toward the line between the valid and the unconstitutional in race-conscious admissions schemes. *Grutter* reaffirms the permissibility of individualized consideration of race to achieve a diversity of students, at least where race is not assigned a preordained value in all cases. On the other hand, Justice Powell's opinion in *Bakke* rules out a racial quota or set-aside, in which race is the sole fact of eligibility for certain places in a class. Although the freshman admissions system here is subject to argument on the merits, I think it is closer to what *Grutter* approves than to what *Bakke* condemns, and should not be held unconstitutional on the current record.

The record does not describe a system with a quota like the one struck down in *Bakke*, which "insulate[d]" all nonminority candidates from competition from certain seats. [The] plan here, in contrast, lets all applicants compete for all places and values an applicant's offering for any place not only on grounds of race, but on grades, test scores, strength of high school, quality of course of study, residence, alumni relationships, leadership, personal character, socioeconomic disadvantage, athletic ability, and quality of a personal essay. A nonminority applicant who scores highly in these other categories can readily garner a selection index exceeding that of a minority applicant who gets the 20–point bonus. [An] unsuccessful nonminority applicant [thus] cannot complain that he was rejected "simply because he was not the right color"; an applicant who is rejected because "his combined qualifications [did] not outweigh those of the other applicant" has been given an opportunity to compete with all other applicants.

The one qualification to this description of the admissions process is that membership in an underrepresented minority is given a weight of 20 points on the 150–point scale. On the face of things, however, this assignment of specific points does not set race apart from all other weighted considerations. Nonminority students may receive 20 points for athletic ability, socioeconomic disadvantage, attendance at a socioeconomically disadvantaged or predominantly minority high school, or at the Provost's discretion; they may also receive 10 points for being residents of Michigan, 6 for residence in an underrepresented Michigan county, 5 for leadership and service, and so on.

[The] very nature of a college's permissible practice of awarding value to racial diversity means that race must be considered in a way that increases some applicants' chances for admission. Since college admission is not left entirely to inarticulate intuition, it is hard to see what is inappropriate in assigning some stated value to a relevant characteristic, whether it be reasoning ability, writing style, running speed, or minority race. [It] suffices for me that there are no *Bakke*-like set-asides and that consideration of an applicant's whole spectrum of ability is no more ruled out by giving 20 points for race than by giving the same points for athletic ability or socioeconomic disadvantage.

JUSTICE GINSBURG, with whom JUSTICE SOUTER joins, dissenting.

I. Educational institutions, the Court acknowledges, are not barred from any and all consideration of race when making admissions decisions. But the Court once again maintains that the same standard of review controls judicial inspection of all official race classifications, quoting *Adarand*. This insistence on "consistency" would be fitting were our Nation free of the vestiges of rank discrimination long reinforced by law. But we are not far distant from an overtly discriminatory past, and the effects of centuries of law-sanctioned inequality remain painfully evident in our communities and schools. In the wake "of a system of racial caste only recently ended," large disparities endure. Unemployment, poverty, and access to health care vary disproportionately by race. Neighborhoods and schools remain racially divided. African-American and Hispanic children are all too often educated in poverty-stricken and underperforming institutions. Adult African–Americans and Hispanics generally earn less than whites with equivalent levels of education. Equally credentialed job applicants receive different receptions depending on their race. Irrational prejudice is still encountered in real estate markets and consumer transactions. "Bias both conscious and unconscious, reflecting traditional and unexamined habits of thought, keeps up barriers that must come down if equal opportunity and nondiscrimination are ever genuinely to become this country's law and practice." The Constitution instructs all who act for the government that they may not "deny to any person [the] equal protection of the laws." Amdt. 14, § 1. In implementing this equality instruction, as I see it, government decisionmakers may properly distinguish between policies of exclusion and inclusion. Actions designed to burden groups long denied full citizenship stature are not sensibly ranked with measures taken to hasten the day when entrenched discrimination and its after effects have been extirpated. See Carter, *When Victims Happen To Be Black*, 97 Yale L. J. 420, 433–434 (1988) ("[T]o say that two centuries of struggle for the most basic of civil rights have been mostly about freedom from racial categorization rather than freedom from racial oppressio[n] is to trivialize the lives and deaths of those who have suffered under racism. To pretend [that] the issue presented in [*Bakke*] was the same as the issue in [*Brown v. Board of Education*] is to pretend that history never happened and that the present doesn't exist."). Our jurisprudence ranks race a "suspect" category, "not because [race] is inevitably an impermissible classification, but because it is one which usually, to our national shame, has been drawn for the purpose of maintaining racial inequality." But where race is considered "for the purpose of achieving equality," no automatic proscription is in order.

II. Examining in this light the admissions policy employed by the University of Michigan's College of Literature, Science, and the Arts (College), [I] see no constitutional infirmity. Like other top-ranking institutions, the College has many more applicants for admission than it can accommodate in an entering class. Every applicant admitted under the current plan, petitioners do not here dispute, is qualified to attend the College. The racial and ethnic groups to which the College accords special consideration (African–Americans, Hispanics, and Native-Americans) historically have been relegated to inferior status by law and social practice; their members continue to experience class-based discrimination to this day. There is no suggestion that the College adopted its current policy in order to limit or decrease enrollment by any particular racial or ethnic group, and no seats are reserved on the basis of race. Nor has there been any demonstration that the College's program unduly constricts admissions opportunities for students who do not receive special consideration based on race. Cf. Liu, *The Causation Fallacy:*

Bakke and the Basic Arithmetic of Selective Admissions, 100 Mich. L. Rev. 1045, 1049 (2002) ("In any admissions process where applicants greatly outnumber admittees, and where white applicants greatly outnumber minority applicants, substantial preferences for minority applicants will not significantly diminish the odds of admission facing white applicants.").

The stain of generations of racial oppression is still visible in our society, and the determination to hasten its removal remains vital. One can reasonably anticipate, therefore, that colleges and universities will seek to maintain their minority enrollment—and the networks and opportunities thereby opened to minority graduates—whether or not they can do so in full candor through adoption of affirmative action plans of the kind here at issue. Without recourse to such plans, institutions of higher education may resort to camouflage. For example, schools may encourage applicants to write of their cultural traditions in the essays they submit, or to indicate whether English is their second language. Seeking to improve their chances for admission, applicants may highlight the minority group associations to which they belong, or the Hispanic surnames of their mothers or grandparents. In turn, teachers' recommendations may emphasize who a student is as much as what he or she has accomplished. If honesty is the best policy, surely Michigan's accurately described, fully disclosed College affirmative action program is preferable to achieving similar numbers through winks, nods, and disguises.

Notes and Questions

[Here add the Notes and Questions following the now omitted *Bakke* case and, for CON LAW and RTS & LIB, also add the case that immediately follows, *Wygant v. Jackson Bd. of Educ.*: CON LAW, pp. 1231–41; AMER CON, pp. 1053–57; RTS & LIB, pp. 1159–69.]

SPECIAL SCRUTINY FOR OTHER CLASSIFICATIONS: DOCTRINE AND DEBATES

ILLEGITIMACY AND RELATED CLASSIFICATIONS

CON LAW: P. 1306, at end of note 3

AMER CON: P. 1110, at end of note 3

RTS. & LIB: P. 1234, at end of note 3

The statutory provision in *Miller v. Albright* came before the Court again in NGUYEN v. INS, 533 U.S. 53, 121 S.Ct. 2053, 150 L.Ed.2d 115 (2001), a case not involving third-party standing complications, and the Court upheld the statute. KENNEDY, J., who wrote the majority opinion, did not explain his apparent change of view from *Miller*, in which he had joined O'Connor, J.'s, concurring opinion and its suggestion that the statute would not "withstand[] heightened scrutiny." Applying heightened scrutiny, Kennedy, J., found the statute substantially related to two important governmental interests: "assuring that a biological parent-child relationship exists" and "ensur[ing] that the child and the citizen parent have some demonstrated opportunity or potential to develop [a] relationship [that] consists of the real, everyday ties that provide a connection between child and citizen parent and, in turn, the United States."

O'CONNOR, J., joined by Souter, Ginsburg, and Breyer, JJ., dissented: "While the Court invokes heightened scrutiny, the manner in which it [applies] this standard is a stranger to our precedents." With respect to the first purportedly important governmental interest cited by the Court, "[m]odern DNA testing [essentially] negates the evidentiary significance of the passage of time [in establishing biological fatherhood.]" As to the second, O'Connor, J., doubted the importance of an interest in "the opportunity" for a parent-child relationship to develop in the absence of the actual development of such a relationship. And if Congress cared about parent-child relationships, it "could require some degree of regular contact between the child and the citizen parent over a period of time. [The statute] finds support not in biological differences but instead in a stereotype—i.e., 'the generalization that mothers are significantly more likely than fathers [to] develop caring relationships with their children.' [No] one should mistake the majority's analysis for a careful application of this Court's equal protection jurisprudence concerning sex-based classifications. Today's decision instead represents a deviation from a line of cases in which we have vigilantly applied heightened scrutiny."

SEXUAL ORIENTATION

CON LAW: P. 1323, at end of note 6

AMER CON: P. 1124, at end of note 4

RTS & LIB: P. 1251, at end of note 6

LAWRENCE v. TEXAS, p. 50 of this Supplement, per KENNEDY, J., overruled *Bowers* and held that a Texas statute prohibiting homosexual but not heterosexual sodomy lacked a legitimate purpose and violated a liberty right protected under the Due Process Clause. The Court passed quickly by an equal protection argument: "[P]etitioners [contend] that *Romer* provides the basis for declaring the Texas statute invalid under the Equal Protection Clause. That is a tenable argument, but we conclude the instant case requires us to address whether *Bowers* [has] continuing validity. Were we to hold the statute invalid under the Equal Protection Clause some might question whether a prohibition would be valid if drawn differently, say, to prohibit the conduct both between same-sex and different-sex participants. Equality of treatment and the due process right to demand respect for conduct protected by the substantive guarantee of liberty are linked in important respects, and a decision on the latter point advances both interests. If protected conduct is made criminal and the law which does so remains unexamined for its substantive validity, its stigma might remain even if it were not enforceable as drawn for equal protection reasons. When homosexual conduct is made criminal by the law of the State, that declaration in and of itself is an invitation to subject homosexual persons to discrimination both in the public and in the private spheres. The central holding of *Bowers* has been brought in question by this case, and it should be addressed." In characterizing the equal protection argument as "tenable," did the majority endorse it?

O'CONNOR, J., concurring, would have put the decision wholly on equal protection grounds: "When a law exhibits [a bare] desire to harm a politically unpopular group, we have applied a more searching form of rational basis review to strike down such laws under the Equal Protection Clause. [And we] have been most likely to apply rational basis review to hold a law unconstitutional under the Equal Protection Clause where, as here, the challenged legislation inhibits personal relationships. [O'Connor, J., here cited *Moreno*, *Eisenstadt v. Baird*, *Cleburne*, and *Romer*.] The statute at issue here [treats] the same conduct differently based solely on the participants. Those harmed by this law are people who have a same-sex sexual orientation. [The] Texas statute makes homosexuals unequal in the eyes of the law by making particular conduct—and only that conduct—subject to criminal sanction. [Texas] attempts to justify its law [by] arguing that the statute satisfies rational basis review because it furthers the legitimate governmental interest of the promotion of morality. In *Bowers*, we [rejected] the argument that no rational basis existed to justify [a prohibition against sodomy], pointing to the government's interest in promoting morality. [But] *Bowers* did not hold that moral disapproval of a group is a rational basis under the Equal Protection Clause to criminalize homosexual sodomy when heterosexual sodomy is not punished. [Moral] disapproval of a group cannot be a legitimate governmental interest under the Equal Protection Clause because legal classifications must not be 'drawn for the purpose of disadvantaging the group burdened by the law.' Texas' invocation of moral disapproval as a legitimate state interest proves nothing more than Texas' desire to criminalize homosexual sodomy. But the Equal Protection Clause prevents a State from creating 'a classification of persons undertaken for its own sake.'

"Texas argues [that] the law discriminates only against homosexual conduct. While it is true that the law applies only to conduct, the conduct targeted by this law is conduct that is closely correlated with being homosexual. Under such circumstances, Texas' sodomy law is targeted at more than conduct. It is instead directed toward gay persons as a class."

Scalia, J., joined by Rehnquist, C.J., and Thomas, J., dissenting, rejected the equal protection as well as the due process argument: "On its face [the challenged statute] applies equally to all persons. [To] be sure, § 21.06 does distinguish between the sexes insofar as concerns the partner with whom the sexual acts are performed: men can violate the law only with other men, and women only with other women. But this cannot itself be a denial of equal protection, since it is precisely the same distinction regarding partner that is drawn in state laws prohibiting marriage with someone of the same sex while permitting marriage with someone of the opposite sex. The objection is made, however, that the antimiscegenation laws invalidated in *Loving* similarly were applicable to whites and blacks alike, and only distinguished between the races insofar as the partner was concerned. In *Loving*, however, we correctly applied heightened scrutiny, rather than the usual rational-basis review, because the Virginia statute was 'designed to maintain White Supremacy.' [By contrast, no] purpose to discriminate against men or women as a class can be gleaned from the Texas law, so rational-basis review applies. That review is readily satisfied here by the same rational basis that satisfied it in *Bowers*—society's belief that certain forms of sexual behavior are 'immoral and unacceptable.' This is the same justification that supports many other laws regulating sexual behavior that make a distinction based upon the identity of the partner—for example, laws against adultery, fornication, and adult incest, and laws refusing to recognize homosexual marriage.

"Justice O'Connor argues that [this law discriminates] with regard to the sexual proclivity of the principal actor. [But a similar claim could be made about] any law. A law against public nudity targets 'the conduct that is closely correlated with being a nudist,' and hence 'is targeted at more than conduct'; it is 'directed toward nudists as a class.' But be that as it may. Even if the Texas law does deny equal protection to 'homosexuals as a class,' that denial still does not need to be justified by anything more than a rational basis, which our cases show is satisfied by the enforcement of traditional notions of sexual morality. Justice O'Connor simply decrees application of 'a more searching form of rational basis review' to the Texas statute. [She does not] explain precisely what her 'more searching form' of rational-basis review consists of. It must at least mean, however, that laws exhibiting 'a ... desire to harm a politically unpopular group,' are invalid even though there may be a conceivable rational basis to support them. This reasoning leaves on pretty shaky grounds state laws limiting marriage to opposite-sex couples. Justice O'Connor seeks to preserve them by the conclusory statement that 'preserving the traditional institution of marriage' is a legitimate state interest. But 'preserving the traditional institution of marriage' is just a kinder way of describing the State's moral disapproval of same-sex couples. Texas's interest in § 21.06 could be recast in similarly euphemistic terms: 'preserving the traditional sexual mores of our society.' "

"FUNDAMENTAL RIGHTS"

VOTING

"DILUTION" OF THE RIGHT: APPORTIONMENT

CON LAW: P. 1354, add after Davis v. Bandemer

AMER CON: P. 1154, add after Davis v. Bandemer

RTS & LIB: P. 1282, add after Davis v. Bandemer

VIETH v. JUBELIRER

541 U.S. 267, 124 S.Ct. 1769, 158 L.Ed.2d 546 (2004).

JUSTICE SCALIA announced the judgment of the Court and delivered an opinion, in which THE CHIEF JUSTICE, JUSTICE O'CONNOR, and JUSTICE THOMAS join.

[After the 2000 census showed that Pennsylvania was entitled to only 19 Representatives in the U.S. House of Representatives, a decrease of two from its previous delegation, the Republican-controlled Pennsylvania legislature adopted and the Republican governor signed into law a redistricting plan designed to advantage Republicans. The plaintiff Democratic voters brought suit alleging that the "meandering and irregular" districts created by the plan "ignored all traditional redistricting criteria, including the preservation of local government boundaries, solely for the sake of partisan advantage," and thereby violated the Equal Protection Clause.]

Political gerrymanders are not new to the American scene. [It] is significant that the Framers provided a remedy for such practices in the Constitution, Article 1, § 4, while leaving in state legislatures the initial power to draw districts for federal elections, permitted Congress to "make or alter" those districts if it wished.

[Eighteen] years ago, [over] the dissent of three Justices, the Court held in *Bandemer* that, since it was "not persuaded that there are no judicially discernible and manageable standards by which political gerrymander cases are to be decided," such cases *were* justiciable. [But there was no majority on what the appropriate standards were. Nor] can it be said that the lower courts have, over 18 years, succeeded in shaping the standard that this Court was initially unable to enunciate. As one commentary has put it, "throughout its subsequent history, *Bandemer* has served almost exclusively as an invitation to litigation without much prospect of redress." S. Issacharoff, P. Karlan, & R. Pildes, *The Law of Democracy* 886 (rev. 2d ed. 2002). The [only lower court] case in which relief was provided (and merely preliminary relief, at that) did *not* involve the drawing of district lines [but instead involved a North Carolina system of electing all superior court judges statewide—a system that had resulted in the election of only a single Republican since 1900]; in *all* of the cases we are aware of involving that most common form of political gerrymandering, relief was denied. [Eighteen] years of judicial effort with virtually nothing to show for it [demonstrate that] no judicially discernible and manageable standards for adjudicating political gerrymandering claims have emerged. Lacking them, we must conclude that political gerrymandering claims are nonjusticiable and that *Bandemer* was wrongly decided.

We begin our review of possible standards with that proposed by Justice White's plurality opinion in *Bandemer* because, as the narrowest ground for our decision in that case, it has been the standard employed by the lower courts. The plurality concluded that a political gerrymandering claim could succeed only where plaintiffs showed "both intentional discrimination against an identifiable political group and an actual discriminatory effect on that group" [so severe that it was] "denied its chance to effectively influence the political process" as a whole, which could be achieved even without electing a candidate. [In] the lower courts, the legacy of the plurality's test is one long record of puzzlement and consternation. [We] decline to affirm it as a constitutional requirement.

Appellants take a run at enunciating their own workable standard. [Their proposal] retains the two-pronged framework of the *Bandemer* plurality—intent plus effect—but modifies the type of showing sufficient to satisfy each. [But it too is unworkable.]

For many of the same reasons, we also reject the standard suggested by Justice Powell in *Bandemer*. He agreed with the plurality that a plaintiff should show intent and effect, but believed that the ultimate inquiry ought to focus on whether district boundaries had been drawn solely for partisan ends to the exclusion of "all other neutral factors relevant to the fairness of redistricting." [This] is essentially a totality-of-the-circumstances analysis, where all conceivable factors, none of which is dispositive, are weighed with an eye to ascertaining whether the particular gerrymander has gone too far—or, in Justice Powell's terminology, whether it is not "fair." "Fairness" does not seem to us a judicially manageable standard. Fairness is compatible with noncontiguous districts, it is compatible with districts that straddle political subdivisions, and it is compatible with a party's not winning the number of seats that mirrors the proportion of its vote.

IV. We turn next to consideration of the standards proposed by today's dissenters. [The] mere fact that these four dissenters come up with three different standards—all of them different from the two proposed in *Bandemer* and the one proposed here by appellants—goes a long way to establishing that there is no constitutionally discernible standard. [Careful assessment of the proposed standards confirms that they are either not judicially manageable or not discernible in the Constitution.]

V. Justice Kennedy [who concurs in the Court's judgment dismissing the case before it but does not join this opinion holding all allegations of political gerrymanders to present nonjusticiable political questions] recognizes that we have "demonstrated the shortcomings of the other standards that have been considered to date." [Yet] he concludes that courts should continue to adjudicate such claims because a standard *may* one day be discovered.

[Reduced] to its essence, Justice Kennedy's opinion boils down to this: "As presently advised, I know of no discernible and manageable standard that can render this claim justiciable. I am unhappy about that, and hope that I will be able to change my opinion in the future." What are the lower courts to make of this pronouncement? We suggest that they must treat it as a reluctant fifth vote against justiciability at district and statewide levels—a vote that may change in some future case but that holds, for the time being, that this matter is nonjusticiable.

JUSTICE KENNEDY, concurring in the judgment.

[The] plurality demonstrates the shortcomings of the [standards] that have been considered to date. [But the fact that] no [adequate] standard has emerged in this case should not be taken to prove that none will emerge in the future. Where important rights are involved, the impossibility of full analytical satisfaction is reason to err on the side of caution.

[Because], in the case before us, we have no standard by which to measure the burden appellants claim has been imposed on their representational rights, appellants cannot establish that the alleged political classifications burden those same rights.

JUSTICE STEVENS, dissenting.

The central question presented by this case is whether political gerrymandering claims are justiciable. Although our reasons for coming to this conclusion differ, five Members of the Court are convinced that the plurality's answer to that question is erroneous.

[In] evaluating a challenge to a specific district, I would apply the standard set forth in [cases involving the deliberate creation of majority-minority districts] and ask whether the legislature allowed partisan considerations to dominate and control the lines drawn, forsaking all neutral principles. Under my analysis, if no neutral criterion can be identified to justify the lines drawn, and if the only possible explanation for a district's bizarre shape is a naked desire to increase partisan strength, then no rational basis exists to save the district from an equal protection challenge. * * *

JUSTICE SOUTER, with whom JUSTICE GINSBURG joins, dissenting.

For a claim based on a specific single-member district, I would require the plaintiff to make out a prima facie case with five elements. First, the resident plaintiff would identify a cohesive political group to which he belonged, which would normally be a major party, as in this case and in *Davis*. [Second], a plaintiff would need to show that the district of his residence paid little or no heed to those traditional districting principles whose disregard can be shown straightforwardly: contiguity, compactness, respect for political subdivisions, and conformity with geographic features like rivers and mountains. [Third], the plaintiff would need to establish specific correlations between the district's deviations from traditional districting principles and the distribution of the population of his group. [Fourth], a plaintiff would need to present the court with a hypothetical district including his residence, one in which the proportion of the plaintiff's group was lower (in a packing claim) or higher (in a cracking one) and which at the same time deviated less from traditional districting principles than the actual district. [Fifth], and finally, the plaintiff would have to show that the defendants acted intentionally to manipulate the shape of the district in order to pack or crack his group. [A] plaintiff who got this far would [then] shift the burden to the defendants to justify their decision by reference to objectives other than naked partisan advantage.

[As] for a statewide claim, I would not attempt an ambitious definition without the benefit of experience with individual district claims, and for now I would limit consideration of a statewide claim to one built upon a number of district-specific ones.

JUSTICE BREYER, dissenting.

[T]he legislature's use of political boundary drawing considerations ordinarily does *not* violate the Constitution's Equal Protection Clause. [But there is] at least one circumstance where use of purely political boundary-drawing factors can amount to a serious, and remediable, abuse, namely the *unjustified* use of political factors to entrench a minority in power. By entrenchment I mean a situation in which a party that enjoys only minority support among the populace has nonetheless contrived to take, and hold, legislative power. * * *

Notes and Questions

1. *Current state of the law.* When confronted with a partisan gerrymandering claim, what should a lower court now do? Is Scalia, J., correct that a lower court should treat Kennedy, J., as having cast a reluctant fifth vote for the proposition that partisan gerrymandering claims are nonjusticiable? Or if the problem is that no judicially manageable standard has yet "emerged," as Kennedy, J., put it, is a lower court entitled to try to devise and apply a standard that it believes to be judicially manageable? In considering these questions, note that at least five Justices in *Vieth* had found the tests developed in *Bandemer* and by the *Vieth* dissenters specifically *not* to be judicially manageable. With all of those tests ruled out, does a challenger have any realistic hope of success?

Consider Richard H. Pildes, *The Constitutionalization of Democratic Politics*, 118 Harv.L.Rev. 28, 76–77 (2004): "Under the one-person, one-vote doctrine, state legislative districts are presumptively constitutional if the departure from equally populated districts is minimal. The state needs only a legitimate interest, not a compelling one, to justify such deviations. Nevertheless, a three-judge district federal court concluded that purely partisan purposes cannot provide even that minimal justification [and in a decision handed down after *Vieth* the] Court summarily affirmed in *Cox v. Larios*, ___ U.S. ___, 124 S.Ct. 2806, 159 L.Ed.2d 831 (2004). The affirmance [suggests] that the Court remains in flux on both *Vieth* and, more generally, on the permissible role of partisan purposes. [Perhaps] *Vieth* might come to mean that where manageable remedies exist, as in *Larios*, courts will hold unconstitutional the severe manipulation of election rules and structures."

2. *Current political practice.* By all accounts, gerrymandering is now widespread. Where one party is able to do so, it gerrymanders to its own advantage.

Where a single party lacks the dominant position to gerrymander unilaterally, so-called "bipartisan gerrymanders" often occur. See Samuel Issacharoff & Pamela S. Karlan, *Where to Draw the Line?: Judicial Review of Political Gerrymanders*, 153 U.Pa.L.Rev. 541, 572–73 (2004): "Whereas a partisan gerrymander is a declaration of war, a bipartisan gerrymander is a nonaggression pact between the parties in which they agree to divide up the state in favor of incumbent sinecure. The result on the day of the general election can be that elections are simply not competitive at all. [In] the first post-reapportionment elections in 2002, only four House incumbents lost to their challengers, and only 43 incumbents received less than 60% of the vote. [In California,] not a single challenger in the general election received over 40% of the vote. In other words, every single incumbent won by landslide margins."

3. *A proposed antitrust approach.* Consider Samuel Issacharoff, *Gerrymandering and Political Cartels*, 116 Harv.L.Rev. 593, 600–01, 643–44 (2002): "[T]he harm in gerrymandering is not really the discrimination that the Court [has]identified. [Rather], the harm is the insult to the competitiveness of the process resulting from the ability of insiders to lessen competitive pressures." In order to avoid this harm, Issacharoff maintains, the Court should forbid all purposeful districting for political advantage, "much as the antitrust laws reach not only the actual cartelization of markets but also conspiracies that set out to frustrate competition": "[T]he Court should forbid ex ante the participation of self-interested political insiders in the redistricting process [Various] approaches to nonpartisan districting, such as blue-ribbon commissions, panels of retired judges, and Iowa's computer-based models, recommend themselves as viable alternatives to the pro-incumbent status quo." Compare Peter Schuck, *The Thickest Thicket: Partisan Gerrymandering and Judicial Regulation of Politics,* 87 Colum.L.Rev. 1325, 1337 (1987) (arguments against a structure permitting gerrymandering "overlook important complexities and values in our political life, project incomplete visions of democratic representation, and invite innovative political remedies that should not be mandated by our federal courts").

See also Ronald H. Brown & Daniel H. Lowenstein, *A Democratic Perspective on Legislative Districting,* 6 J.L. & Pol. 673, 679 (1990): "The most common 'neutral' criterion Republicans try to impose [is] compactness. The usual way of levying a political attack on a districting plan is to show diagrams of selected oddly-shaped districts. This is supposed to prove that the plan is an outrageous gerrymander. [The] real reason the Republicans promote the compactness requirement is that it tends to work systematically to their [benefit]. Inner-city areas tend to contain Democratic voters concentrated in extraordinarily high percentages. Many surrounding affluent areas are predominantly but not nearly so overwhelmingly Republican. Accordingly, it may be relatively easy to draw compact districts separating these areas and thereby to accomplish the objective of a Republican gerrymander—a small number of overwhelmingly Democratic districts surrounded by a larger number of much closer but still safely Republican districts." But cf. Martin Shapiro, *Gerrymandering, Unfairness, and the Supreme Court,* 33 UCLA L.Rev. 227, 240 (1985): "If geography favors the Republicans in an ungerrymandered world, that is a purely fortuitous result, unforeseeable by either party when it chose its ideologies and clienteles. Such stacking ought to be considered extraneous to the goal of constraining the self-serving actions of the legislatures."

4. *The problem of judicially manageable standards.* Consider Pildes, supra, at 66–70: "Problems like gerrymandering require a shift in the way manageable judicial remedies are conceived. [Academics] typically demand that legal doctrines

achieve stability through clear, necessary-and-sufficient criteria of doctrinal application. [In] the gerrymandering context, these critiques translate into the view that, if the Court is going to rule excessive partisan gerrymandering unconstitutional, it must be able to specify a fair partisan distribution of districts. [But] vague constitutional constraints can produce stable political or social practices. [Given] politicians' interests in certainty and control, judicial creation of general but necessarily vague constraints, with a credible threat of application, might generate a process [in which politicians would steer clear of excessively partisan gerrymandering to avoid the threat of judicial intervention]." Do you agree?

5. *The Constitution and political democracy.* Consider Richard H. Fallon, Jr., *The Dynamic Constitution: An Introduction to American Constitutional Law* 209–10 (2004): "Many commentators believe that the Court misses a vital dimension of the problem in election law cases when it talks exclusively in the vocabulary of individual rights and fails to focus directly on issues of how best to structure political democracy under the Constitution. Perhaps for this reason, the Court's analysis in election law cases often seems shallow and unsatisfying." If so, however, is the fault that of the Court or the Constitution–or both? See id.: "If the Court thought that the Constitution embodies a general theory of democracy, it could resolve election law cases under that theory. But the Justices have been unable to discern or develop such a theory."

EQUALITY IN THE COUNTING AND RECOUNTING OF VOTES

CON LAW: P. 1359, substitute for Notes and Questions

AMER CON: P. 1158, substitute for Notes and Questions

RTS & LIB: P. 1287, substitute for Notes and Questions

1. *The holding.* What exactly was the holding of *Bush v. Gore*? The Court described its "consideration" as "limited to the present circumstances" involving "the special instance of a statewide recount under the authority of a single state judicial officer" who has "the power to assure uniformity" but has not exercised that power. In a dissenting opinion in *Smith v. Allwright*, CON LAW p. 1419, AMER CON 1207, RTS & LIB p. 1347, Roberts, J., analogized the Court's holding to "a restricted railroad ticket, good for this day and train only." Could the same be said of *Bush v. Gore*?

2. *Doctrinal support.* Do the Court's prior voting rights cases support the result in *Bush v. Gore*? Consider Pamela S. Karlan, *Unduly Partial: The Supreme Court and the Fourteenth Amendment in Bush v. Gore*, 29 Fla.St. U.L.Rev. 587, 600 (2001): "[T]he decision to stop the recount had virtually nothing to do with equal protection. It vindicated no identifiable voter's interests. The form of equality it created was empty: it treated all voters whose ballots had not already been tabulated the same, by denying any of them the ability to have his ballot counted. And its remedy perpetuated other forms of inequality that were far more severe: between voters whose ballots were counted by the machine count and voters whose ballots were not, and even between voters in counties that performed timely manual recounts [and] voters in other counties." Compare Michael W. McConnell, *Two-and-a-Half Cheers for Bush v. Gore*, 68 U.Chi.L.Rev. 657, 673 (2001), reprinted in The Vote: Bush, Gore & the Supreme Court (Cass R. Sunstein & Richard A.

Epstein eds., 2001): "It may be true that the Equal Protection Clause typically protects against discrimination against identifiable groups, but [the Court has elsewhere] summarily affirmed the principle that it also protects against 'irrational and wholly arbitrary' state action, even where the plaintiff does not allege that the unequal treatment was on account of 'membership in a class or group.' [To] treat one voter's ballot as a legal vote, and another voter's identical ballot as spoiled, in the same jurisdiction, for no conceivable public purpose, certainly states a plausible equal protection claim."

3. *The non-remedy.* Although seven Justices appear to have agreed that the recount ordered by the Florida Supreme Court was constitutionally defective, only a bare majority endorsed the remedy of halting the recount altogether, rather than allowing the Florida Supreme Court to devise an adequate vote-counting standard (or even permitting it to determine whether a timely recount was feasible). Many commentators regard this aspect of *Bush v. Gore* as the most difficult to defend on doctrinal grounds, with critics describing the Court's remedial ruling as "utterly indefensible,"[a] "transparently phony,"[b] and "Kafkaesque."[c] Even now-Judge Michael McConnell, who otherwise endorses the Court's decision, questions the remedy: "Having rested the decision on the standardless character of the recount ordered by the state court, the logical outcome was to remand under proper constitutional standards." McConnell, supra at 675. Compare Charles Fried, *An Unreasonable Reaction to a Reasonable Decision,* in Bush v. Gore: The Question of Legitimacy, 3, 16 (Bruce Ackerman ed., 2002): "[T]he Court [did] not just make it up that the Florida court had stated several times its interpretation of Florida law as requiring compliance with [the December 12] deadline. [The] Court was justified in holding [the Florida Supreme Court] to that interpretation."

4. *Further reactions.* In addition to the positions already noted, consider the following points of view:

(a) *Bush v. Gore was not only erroneous, but also partisan in motivation.* See Alan M. Dershowitz, Supreme Injustice: How the High Court Hijacked Election 2000, 174 (2001): "[The] majority justices violated their own previously declared judicial principles—principles they still believe in and will apply in other cases. In this respect, the decision in the Florida election case may be ranked as the single most corrupt decision in Supreme Court history, because it is the only one that I know of where the majority justices decided as they did because of the personal identity and political affiliation of the litigants."

(b) *The decision was sound on its peculiar facts.* Michael McConnell, supra at 673, emphasizes, "[e]ven Justice Stevens [acknowledged] that 'the use of differing standards for determining voter intent in different counties employing similar voting systems may raise serious concerns.' [Justice Stevens] declined to find a constitutional violation, however, on the ground that 'those concerns are alleviated—if not eliminated—by the fact that a single

a. Laurence H. Tribe, *eroG v. hsuB and Its Disguises: Freeing Bush v. Gore from Its Hall of Mirrors,* 115 Harv.L.Rev. 170, 268 (2001).

b. Larry D. Kramer, *We the Court,* 115 Harv.L.Rev. 4, 156 (2001).

c. Margaret Jane Radin, *Can the Rule of Law Survive Bush v. Gore?,* in Bush v. Gore: The Question of Legitimacy 110, 116 (Bruce Ackerman ed. 2002).

impartial magistrate will ultimately adjudicate all objections arising from the recount process.' " With all the pressures that would have surrounded a Florida recount, and all the ballots that would have required examination, is it doubtful that a truly impartial counting process before a truly impartial magistrate could possibly have been achieved within the time available? If so, was the fairest result simply to accept the tally recorded by the voting machines?

(c) *The decision properly initiates judicial oversight of the fairness of voting and vote-counting procedures.* See Cass R. Sunstein, *Order Without Law,* in The Vote, note 2 supra, at 205, 206–07: "[*Bush v. Gore*] has the potential to create the most expansive, and perhaps sensible, protection for voting rights since the Court's one-person, one-vote decisions of mid-century. In the fullness of time, that promise might conceivably be realized within the federal courts, policing various inequalities with respect to voting and voting technology." See also Samuel Issacharoff, *Political Judgments,* in The Vote, at 55, 69–70.

(d) *The decision reflected rough, pragmatic justice.* According to Richard A. Posner, *Breaking the Deadlock: The 2000 Election, the Constitution, and the Courts* (2001), *Bush v. Gore* originated with a reckless, partisan decision by the Florida Supreme Court to order a recount not properly authorized by state law. That recount threatened to create a national constitutional crisis: If Al Gore had prevailed, the Florida legislature would have appointed an alternative set of electors pledged to Bush, and a division would have ensued between the Republican-controlled House of Representatives and the Democrat-controlled Senate about which set of electors' votes should be counted. Given the "real and disturbing potential for disorder and temporary paralysis," *id.* at 143, Posner concludes that the Supreme Court was justified in intervening and, in view of the misconduct of the Florida Supreme Court, that its decision achieved a kind of "rough justice," even if its legal reasoning was slightly shaky.[d] Compare Ward Farnsworth, *"To Do a Great Right, Do a Little Wrong": A User's Guide to Judicial Lawlessness*, 86 Minn.L.Rev. 227, 265–66 (2001), arguing that although result-oriented judicial "lawlessness" might occasionally be defensible, there was no excuse in *Bush v. Gore*: "[There] were processes in place for resolving the controversy without judicial intervention. The Court itself had too large a stake in the outcome of the controversy to be a good arbiter of it, and the Court was too split by its usual ideological division to be able to offer a credible resolution that reflected judgment detached from the underlying stakes. [If] regarded as an exercise in stepping outside the conventional bounds of the law to do the country a favor, *Bush v. Gore* remains a study in temptation best resisted."

(e) *The Court's willingness to accept the case at all revealed the Justices' inflated sense of the Court's indispensable role.* See Kramer, supra at 153–56: "Nothing jumps off the pages of the opinion quite so starkly as the majority's

d. Posner finds the Court's equal protection rationale wholly unpersuasive and thinks the Court would have done better to rest on the alternative basis offered in Rehnquist, C.J.'s concurrence, in which Scalia and Thomas, JJ., joined. See Posner at 153–61. Rehnquist, C.J., pointed to Art. II, § 1, cl.2, which provides that each state shall choose its electors "in such Manner as the Legislature thereof shall direct." He argued that the Florida Supreme Court had adopted an "absurd" construction of state election law contrary to the "clearly expressed intent of the legislature." But cf. Tribe, supra, at 184–94 (characterizing the Art. II issue as a "red herring").

evident determination to call a halt to things before Congress could get its hands on the problem. [Unsought] responsibility?! Forced to confront?! Nothing kept the Justices from ruling that the Supreme Court was not the proper forum in which to decide a presidential election. Nothing in the law, that is." See also Jesse H. Choper, *Why the Supreme Court Should Not Have Decided the Presidential Election of 2000,* 18 Const.Comm. 335, 335 (2001): "[The] Court's adjudication was both unnecessary and unwise, creating a widely-based popular perception of partisanship by the Judicial Branch that carries the threat of diminishing the public's trust and confidence in the Justices and endangering the Court's institutional standing and overall effectiveness."

5. *Other literature.* Apart from commentary on its reasoning,[e] *Bush v. Gore* has spawned an enormous literature addressing such matters as (a) an asserted need for electoral reform in the United States;[f] (b) the decline of the political question doctrine;[g] and (c) the role of partisan ideology on the Supreme Court.[h]

RACIAL GERRYMANDERING REVISITED: "BENIGN" OR "REMEDIAL" RACE-CONSCIOUS DISTRICTING

CON LAW: P. 1373, after note 3

AMER CON: P. 1169, after note 2

RTS & LIB: P. 1301, after note 2

Following the remand in *Hunt v. Cromartie*, 526 U.S. 541, 119 S.Ct. 1545, 143 L.Ed.2d 731 (1999), the district court held a trial and determined that the legislature's predominant purpose in drawing an oddly shaped, majority-minority district—an earlier configuration of which had also been at issue in *Shaw v. Reno*—involved race, not politics. HUNT v. CROMARTIE (II), 532 U.S. 234, 121 S.Ct. 1452, 149 L.Ed.2d 430 (2001), again reversed, this time on the ground that the lower court's finding of predominant racial motivation was "clearly erroneous" in light of the evidence. Emphasizing the challengers' burden to show that "a facially neutral [districting] is law unexplainable on grounds other than race," BREYER, J., found the evidence inadequate to establish that the legislature was predominantly motivated to create a majority-minority district, as opposed to a "safe Democratic seat" that would maintain the existing partisan balance among the state's congressional delegation: "[W]here racial identification correlates highly with political affiliation, the party attacking the legislatively drawn boundaries must show at the least that the legislature could have achieved its legitimate political objectives

e. For a good introduction to the issues directly raised by *Bush v. Gore,* see *Symposium,* 68 U.Chi.L.Rev. 613 (2001), reprinted in The Vote, supra. See also *A Badly Flawed Election: Debating Bush v. Gore, the Supreme Court, and American Democracy* (Ronald Dworkin ed., 2002); Symposium, *The Law of Presidential Elections: Issues in the Wake of Florida 2000,* 29 Fla.St.U.L.Rev. 325 (2001).

f. See, e.g., Richard A. Epstein, *Whither Electoral Reforms in the Wake of Bush v. Gore?,* in The Vote, supra at 241.

g. See, e.g., Rachel E. Barkow, *More Supreme Than Court? The Fall of the Political Question Doctrine and the Rise of Judicial Supremacy,* 102 Colum.L.Rev. 237, 273–300 (2002).

h. See., e.g., Frank I. Michelman, *Suspicion, or the New Prince,* 68 U.Chi.L.Rev. 679 (2001), reprinted in The Vote, supra at 123.

in alternative ways that are comparably consistent with traditional districting principles. That party must also show that those districting alternatives would have brought about significantly greater racial balance. Appellees failed to make any such showing here."

THOMAS, J., joined by Rehnquist, C.J., and Scalia and Kennedy, JJ., dissented: "In light of the direct evidence of racial motive and the inferences that may be drawn from the circumstantial evidence, [the] District Court's finding was permissible, even if not compelled by the record."

ACCESS TO THE COURTS

CON LAW: P. 1390, after Ross v. Moffitt

AMER CON: P. 1185, after Ross v. Moffitt

RTS & LIB: P. 1318, after Ross v. Moffitt

In HALBERT v. MICHIGAN, ___ U.S. ___, 125 S.Ct. 2582, ___ L.Ed.2d ___ (2005), the question framed by the Court was whether *Douglas* or *Ross* "provide[d] the controlling instruction" for assistance of counsel to indigents under a state rule that requires defendants who plead guilty or nolo contendere to seek leave of court before bringing a first-level appeal. The Court, per GINSBURG, J., ruled that although review was discretionary, the state court of appeals sat to correct errors and did not, like the appellate court in *Ross*, base its decisions to grant review on the general importance of the questions presented: "The Court of Appeals' ruling on a plea-convicted defendants' claims [also] provides the first, and likely the only, direct review the defendant's conviction and sentence will receive," whereas the defendant in *Ross* had already had the assistance of counsel in a first-tier review. THOMAS, J., joined by Rehnquist, C.J., and Scalia, J., dissented: "The majority does not say where in the Constitution [the right that it upholds] is located—the Due Process Clause, the Equal Protection Clause, or some purported confluence of the two. [It] substitutes its own policy preferences for that of Michigan voters, and it does so based on an untenable reading of *Douglas*" as applicable to discretionary appeals.

THE CONCEPT OF STATE ACTION

DEVELOPMENTS IN THE 1980s AND 1990s

CON LAW: P. 1460, add at end of note 1

AMER CON: P. 1239, add at end of note 1

RTS & LIB: P. 1388, add at end of note 1

(d) *"Entwinement."* BRENTWOOD ACADEMY v. TENNESSEE SECONDARY SCHOOL ATHLETIC ASS'N, 531 U.S. 288, 121 S.Ct. 924, 148 L.Ed.2d 807 (2001): TSSAA was a membership corporation organized (and so designated by the state board of education in 1972) to regulate interscholastic sports among the public and private high schools in Tennessee. Almost all of the state's public high schools (290) and 55 private schools belonged. Its rules (specifically approved by the state board in 1972, and subject to subsequent review) governed such matters as student eligibility and academic standards and financial aid. Its operating committees were limited to principals elected by member schools, all of whom at the time of the action challenged in this case were from public schools, and ex-officio appointees of the state board. In 1997, TSSAA penalized Brentwood Academy, a parochial school, for violating a rule against "undue influence" in recruiting. The Court, per SOUTER, J., held that this was "state action": "The nominally private character of the Association is overborne by the pervasive entwinement of public institutions and public officials in its composition and workings.

"[Although] the terms of the State Board's Rule expressly designating the Association as regulator of interscholastic athletics in public schools was deleted in 1996, the year after a Federal District Court held that the Association was a state actor because its rules were 'caused, directed and controlled by the Tennessee Board of Education' [this] affected nothing but words." Nor is it dispositive "that the State neither coerced nor encouraged the actions complained of. 'Coercion' and 'encouragement' are like 'entwinement' in referring to kinds of facts that can justify characterizing an ostensibly private action as public instead. [When] the relevant facts show pervasive entwinement to the point of largely overlapping identity, the implication of state action is not affected by pointing out that the facts might not loom large under a different test.

"[Even] facts that suffice to show public action (or, standing alone, would require such a finding) may be outweighed in the name of some value at odds with finding public accountability in the circumstances. [For example], full-time public employment would be conclusive of state action for some purposes, but not when the employee is doing a defense lawyer's primary job; then, the public defender does 'not ac[t] on behalf of the State; he is the State's adversary.' *Polk County v. Dodson*, 454 U.S. 312, 102 S.Ct. 445, 70 L.Ed.2d 509 (1981)."

THOMAS, J., joined by Rehnquist, C.J. and Scalia and Kennedy, JJ., dissented: "We have never found state action based upon mere 'entwinement.' Until today, we have found a private organization's acts to constitute state action only when the organization performed a public function; was created, coerced, or encouraged by the government; or acted in a symbiotic relationship with the government. [Although *Evans v. Newton*] uses the word 'entwined,' [our] analysis rested on the recognition that the subject of the dispute, a park, served a 'public function,' much like a fire department or a police department. [Even] if the city severed all ties to the park and placed its operation in private hands, the park still would be 'municipal in nature,' analogous to other public facilities that have given rise to a finding of state action: the streets of a company town in *Marsh*; the elective process in *Terry*; and the transit system in *Pollak*."

CON LAW: P. 1466, at end

AMER CON: P. 1241, at end

RTS & LIB: P. 1394, at end

See *Castle Rock v. Gonzales*, p. 71 of this Supplement.

CONGRESSIONAL ENFORCEMENT OF CIVIL RIGHTS

REGULATION OF STATE ACTORS

CON LAW: P. 1495, add to fn. d

AMER CON: P. 1264, add to fn. d

RTS & LIB: P. 1423, add to fn. d

See *Cutter v. Wilkinson*, p. 191 of this Supplement.

CON LAW: P. 1497, at end of fn. f

AMER CON: P. 1265, at end of fn. f

RTS & LIB: P. 1425, at end of fn. f

On the question of the applicability of the eleventh amendment to a federal bankruptcy court's discharge of a state's claim against a debtor, pursuant to Congress's Art. I bankruptcy power, see *Tennessee Student Assistance Corp. v. Hood*, 541 U.S. 440, 124 S.Ct. 1905, 158 L.Ed.2d 764 (2004).

CON LAW: P. 1497, before note (b)

AMER CON: P. 1268, before note (b)

RTS & LIB: P. 1425, before note (b)

(i) *Required congressional record.* BOARD OF TRUSTEES OF UNIV. OF ALA. v. GARRETT, 531 U.S. 356, 121 S.Ct. 955, 148 L.Ed.2d 866 (2001), per REHNQUIST, C.J. held that Congress had no § 5 power to abrogate state immunity under the eleventh amendment and provide its employees a damages remedy under Title I of the Americans with Disabilities Act, which forbids employment discrimination against "a qualified individual" because of "disability" and requires "reasonable accommodations" to achieve this end: "[*Cleburne* held that a legislative classification based on disability] incurs only the minimum 'rational-basis' review applicable to general social and economic legislation. [Breyer, J.'s dissent suggests] that state decisionmaking reflecting 'negative attitudes' or 'fear' necessarily runs afoul of the Fourteenth Amendment. Although such biases may often accompany irrational (and therefore unconstitutional) discrimination, their presence alone does not a constitutional violation make. [Thus,] States are not required by the Fourteenth Amendment to make special accommodations for the disabled, so long as their actions towards such individuals are rational. They could quite hard headedly—and perhaps hardheartedly—hold to job-qualification requirements which do not make allowance for the disabled. If special accommodations for the disabled are to be required, they have to come from positive law and not through the Equal Protection Clause.

"Once we have determined the metes and bounds of the constitutional right in question, we examine whether Congress identified a history and pattern of unconstitutional employment discrimination by the States against the disabled. * * *

"Respondents contend that the inquiry as to unconstitutional discrimination should extend not only to States themselves, but to units of local governments, such as cities and counties. [B]ut the Eleventh Amendment does not extend its immunity to units of local government. [It] would make no sense to consider constitutional violations on their part, as well as by the States themselves, when only the States are the beneficiaries of the Eleventh Amendment.

"Congress made a general finding in the ADA that 'historically, society has tended to isolate and segregate individuals with disabilities, and, despite some improvements, such forms of discrimination against individuals with disabilities continue to be a serious and pervasive social problem.' The record assembled by Congress includes many instances to support such a finding. But the great majority of these incidents do not deal with the activities of States.

"Respondents in their brief cite half a dozen examples from the record that did involve States. [But] these incidents taken together fall far short of even suggesting the pattern of unconstitutional discrimination on which § 5 legislation must be based. [Further, the] host of incidents [in the appendix to Breyer, J.'s dissent] consists not of legislative findings, but of unexamined, anecdotal accounts of 'adverse, disparate treatment by state officials.' [Of course,] 'adverse, disparate treatment' often does not amount to a constitutional violation where rational-basis scrutiny applies. These accounts, moreover, were submitted not directly to Congress but to the Task Force on the Rights and Empowerment of Americans with Disabilities, which made no findings on the subject of state discrimination in employment.[7] And, had Congress truly understood this information as reflecting a pattern of unconstitutional behavior by the States, one would expect some mention of that conclusion in the Act's legislative findings. There is none. Although Justice Breyer would infer from Congress' general conclusions regarding societal discrimination against the disabled that the States had likewise participated in such action, the House and Senate committee reports on the ADA flatly contradict this assertion. [The Senate] Committee's report reached, among others, the following conclusion: 'Discrimination still persists in such critical areas as *employment in the private sector,* public accommodations, public services, transportation, and telecommunications.' The House Committee [reached] the same conclusion * * *.

7. Only a small fraction of the anecdotes Justice Breyer identifies in his Appendix C relate to state discrimination against the disabled in employment. At most, somewhere around 50 of these allegations describe conduct that could conceivably amount to constitutional violations by the States, and most of them are so general and brief that no firm conclusion can be drawn. The overwhelming majority of these accounts pertain to alleged discrimination by the States in the provision of public services and public accommodations, which areas are addressed in Titles II and III of the ADA.

"Even were it possible to squeeze out of these examples a pattern of unconstitutional discrimination by the States, the rights and remedies created by the ADA against the States would raise the same sort of concerns as to congruence and proportionality as were found in *Boerne*. For example, whereas it would be entirely rational (and therefore constitutional) for a state employer to conserve scarce financial resources by hiring employees who are able to use existing facilities, the ADA requires employers to 'make existing facilities used by employees readily accessible to and usable by individuals with disabilities.' The ADA does except employers from the 'reasonable accommodation' requirement where the employer 'can demonstrate that the accommodation would impose an undue hardship on the operation of the business of such covered entity.' However, even with this exception, the accommodation duty far exceeds what is constitutionally required. [The] Act also makes it the employer's duty to prove that it would suffer such a burden, instead of requiring (as the Constitution does) that the complaining party negate reasonable bases for the employer's decision.

"The ADA also forbids 'utilizing standards, criteria, or methods of administration' that disparately impact the disabled, without regard to whether such conduct has a rational basis. Although disparate impact may be relevant evidence of racial discrimination, see *Washington v. Davis,* such evidence alone is insufficient even where the Fourteenth Amendment subjects state action to strict scrutiny.

"The ADA's constitutional shortcomings are apparent when the Act is compared to Congress' efforts in the Voting Rights Act of 1965 [in which] Congress documented a marked pattern of unconstitutional action by the States. State officials, Congress found, routinely applied voting tests in order to exclude African–American citizens from registering to vote. Congress also determined that litigation had proved ineffective and that there persisted an otherwise inexplicable 50–percentage-point gap in the registration of white and African–American voters in some States. Congress' response was to promulgate in the Voting Rights Act a detailed but limited remedial scheme designed to guarantee meaningful enforcement of the Fifteenth Amendment in those areas of the Nation where abundant evidence of States' systematic denial of those rights was identified.

* * * Congress is the final authority as to desirable public policy, but in order to authorize private individuals to recover money damages against the States, there must be a pattern of discrimination by the States which violates the Fourteenth Amendment, and the remedy imposed by Congress must be congruent and proportional to the targeted violation. Those requirements are not met here."

Kennedy, J., joined by O'Connor, J., who joined the Court's opinion, concurred: "For the reasons explained by the Court, an equal protection violation has not been [shown]. If the States had been transgressing the Fourteenth Amendment by their mistreatment or lack of concern for those with impairments, one would have expected to find in decisions of the [courts] extensive litigation and discussion of the constitutional violations. This confirming judicial documentation does not exist. That there is a new awareness, a new consciousness, a new commitment to better treatment of those disadvantaged by mental or physical impairments does not establish that an absence of state statutory correctives was a constitutional violation."

BREYER, J. joined by Stevens, Souter and Ginsburg, JJ., dissented: "There are roughly 300 examples of discrimination by state governments themselves in the legislative record. I fail to see how this evidence 'fall[s] far short of even suggesting the pattern of unconstitutional discrimination on which § 5 legislation must be based.'

"The congressionally appointed task force collected numerous specific examples, provided by persons with disabilities themselves, of adverse, disparate treatment by state officials. They reveal, not what the Court describes as 'half a dozen' instances of discrimination, but hundreds of instances of adverse treatment at the hands of state officials—instances in which a person with a disability found it impossible to obtain a state job, to retain state employment, to use the public transportation that was readily available to others in order to get to work, or to obtain a public education, which is often a prerequisite to obtaining employment. State-imposed barriers also frequently made it difficult or impossible for people to vote, to enter a public building, to access important government services, such as calling for emergency assistance, and to find a place to live due to a pattern of irrational zoning decisions similar to the discrimination that we held unconstitutional in *Cleburne.*

"As the Court notes, those who presented instances of discrimination rarely provided additional, independent evidence sufficient to prove in court that, in each instance, the discrimination they suffered lacked justification from a judicial standpoint. [But] Congress, unlike courts, must, and does, routinely draw general conclusions—for example, of likely motive or of likely relationship to legitimate need—from anecdotal and opinion-based evidence of this kind, particularly when the evidence lacks strong refutation. In reviewing § 5 legislation, we have never required the sort of extensive investigation of each piece of evidence that the Court appears to contemplate. Nor has the Court traditionally required Congress to make findings as to state discrimination, or to break down the record evidence, category by category. * * * Congress could have reasonably believed that these examples represented signs of a widespread problem of unconstitutional discrimination. * * *

"The problem with the Court's approach is that neither the 'burden of proof' that favors States nor any other rule of restraint applicable to *judges* applies to *Congress* when it exercises its § 5 power. * * * Rational-basis review—with its presumptions favoring constitutionality—is 'a paradigm of *judicial* restraint.' *FCC v. Beach Communications.* And the Congress of the United States is not a lower court.

"Indeed, [*Cleburne*] made clear that the absence of a contrary congressional finding was critical to our decision to apply mere rational-basis review to disability discrimination claims—a 'congressional direction' to apply a more stringent standard would have been 'controlling.' * * *

"There is simply no reason to require Congress, seeking to determine facts relevant to the exercise of its § 5 authority, to adopt rules or presumptions that reflect a court's institutional limitations. Unlike courts, Congress can readily gather facts from across the Nation, assess the magnitude of a problem, and more easily find an appropriate remedy. Cf. *Cleburne* (addressing the problems of the 'large and diversified group' of persons with disabilities 'is a difficult and often a technical matter, very much a task for legislators guided by qualified professionals and not by the perhaps ill-informed opinions of the judiciary'). Unlike courts, Congress directly reflects public attitudes and beliefs, enabling Congress better to understand where, and to what extent, refusals to accommodate a disability amount to behavior that is callous or unreasonable to the point of lacking constitutional justification. Unlike judges, Members of Congress can directly obtain information from constituents who have first-hand experience with discrimination and related issues.

"Moreover, unlike judges, Members of Congress are elected. [To] apply a rule designed to restrict courts as if it restricted Congress' legislative power is to stand the underlying principle—a principle of judicial restraint—on its head. * * *

"The Court argues in the alternative that the statute's damage remedy is not "congruent" with and "proportional" to the equal protection problem that Congress found. [But] it is just that power—the power to require more than the minimum that § 5 grants to Congress, as this Court has repeatedly confirmed. * * * Nothing in the words 'reasonable accommodation' suggests that the requirement has no 'tend[ency] to enforce' the Equal Protection Clause, *Ex parte Virginia,* that it is an irrational way to achieve the objective, *South Carolina v. Katzenbach,* that it would fall outside the scope of the Necessary and Proper Clause, *Morgan,* or that it somehow otherwise exceeds the bounds of the 'appropriate,' U.S. Const., Amdt. 14, § 5.

"The Court's more recent cases have professed to follow the longstanding principle of deference to Congress. See *Kimel* ("Congress' § 5 power is not confined to the enactment of legislation that merely parrots the precise wording of the Fourteenth Amendment." Rather, Congress can prohibit a "somewhat broader swath of conduct, including that which is not itself forbidden by the Amendment's text") * * *.

"[The] legislation before us [does] not discriminate against anyone, nor does it pose any threat to basic liberty. And it is difficult to understand why the Court, which applies 'minimum "rational-basis" review' to statutes that *burden* persons with disabilities, subjects to far stricter scrutiny a statute that seeks to *help* those same individuals.

"I recognize nonetheless that this statute imposes a burden upon States in that it removes their Eleventh Amendment protection from suit, thereby subjecting them to potential monetary liability. Rules for interpreting § 5 that would provide States with special protection, however, run counter to the very object of the Fourteenth Amendment. By its terms, that Amendment prohibits *States* from denying their citizens equal protection of the laws."

(ii) *Prophylactic legislation*. NEVADA DEP'T OF HUMAN RESOURCES v. HIBBS, 538 U.S. 721, 123 S.Ct. 1972, 155 L.Ed.2d 953 (2003), per REHNQUIST, C.J., upheld Congress' § 5 power to abrogate eleventh amendment state immunity and provide state employees damages under the Family and Medical Leave Act which entitles eligible employees up to 12 work weeks of unpaid leave annually for any of several reasons, including the onset of a 'serious health condition' in an employee's spouse, child, or parent: "The FMLA aims to protect the right to be free from gender-based discrimination in the workplace.[2] [According] to evidence that was before Congress when it enacted the FMLA, States continue to rely on invalid gender stereotypes in the employment context, specifically in the administration of leave benefits. Reliance on such stereotypes cannot justify the States' gender discrimination in this area. *United States v. Virginia.* The long and extensive history of sex discrimination prompted us to hold that measures that differentiate on the basis of gender warrant heightened scrutiny; [the] persistence of such unconstitutional discrimination by the States justifies Congress' passage of prophylactic § 5 legislation.

"As the FMLA's legislative record reflects, a 1990 Bureau of Labor Statistics (BLS) survey stated that 37 percent of surveyed private-sector employees were covered by maternity leave policies, while only 18 percent were covered by paternity leave policies. The corresponding numbers from a similar BLS survey the previous year were 33 percent and 16 percent, respectively. While these data show an increase (sic) in the percentage of employees eligible for such leave, they also show a widening of the gender gap during the same period. Thus, stereotype-based beliefs about the allocation of family duties remained firmly rooted, and employers' reliance on them in establishing discriminatory leave policies remained widespread.[3]

"Congress also heard testimony that '[p]arental leave for fathers [is] rare. Even [w]here child-care leave policies do exist, men, *both in the public and private sectors,* receive notoriously, discriminatory treatment in their requests for such leave." (Washington Council of Lawyers) (emphasis added). [This] and other differential leave policies were not attributable to any differential physical needs of men and women, but rather to the pervasive sex-role stereotype that caring for family members is women's work.[5]

"Finally, Congress had evidence that, even where state laws and policies were not facially discriminatory, they were applied in discriminatory ways. It was aware of the 'serious problems with the discretionary nature of family leave,' because when 'the authority to grant leave and to arrange the length of

2. The text of the Act makes this clear. Congress found that, "due to the nature of the roles of men and women in our society, the primary responsibility for family caretaking often falls on women, and such responsibility affects the working lives of women more than it affects the working lives of men." In response to this finding, Congress sought "to accomplish the [Act's other] purposes [in] a manner [that] minimizes the potential for employment discrimination *on the basis of sex* by ensuring generally that leave is available [*on*] *a gender-neutral basis*[,] and to promote the goal of equal employment opportunity for women and men." (emphasis added).

3. While this and other material described leave policies in the private sector, a 50-state survey also before Congress demonstrated that "[t]he proportion and construction of leave policies available to public sector employees differs little from those offered private sector employees." (statement of Meryl Frank, Director of the Yale Bush Center Infant Care Leave Project).

5. For example, state employers' collective-bargaining agreements often granted extended "maternity" leave of six months to a year to women only. [In] addition, state leave laws often specified that catchall leave-without-pay provisions could be used for extended maternity leave, but did not authorize such leave for paternity purposes.

Evidence pertaining to parenting leave is relevant here because state discrimination in the provision of both types of benefits is based on the same gender stereotype: that women's family duties trump those of the workplace. Justice Kennedy's dissent ignores this common foundation that, as Congress found, has historically produced discrimination in the hiring and promotion of women. Consideration of such evidence does not, as the dissent contends, expand our § 5 inquiry to include "*general* gender-based stereotypes in employment." To the contrary, because parenting and family leave address very similar situations in which work and family responsibilities conflict, they implicate the same stereotypes.

that leave rests with individual supervisors,' it leaves 'employees open to discretionary and possibly unequal treatment.' Testimony supported that conclusion * * *.

"In spite of all of the above evidence, Justice Kennedy argues in dissent that Congress' passage of the FMLA was unnecessary because 'the States appear to have been ahead of Congress in providing gender-neutral family leave benefits,' and points to Nevada's leave policies in particular. However, it was only '[s]ince Federal family leave legislation was first introduced' that the States had even 'begun to consider similar family leave initiatives.'

"Furthermore, the dissent's statement that some States 'had adopted some form of family-care leave' before the FMLA's enactment, glosses over important shortcomings of some state policies. First, seven States had child-care leave provisions that applied to women only. Indeed, Massachusetts required that notice of its leave provisions be posted only in 'establishment [s] in which females are employed.'[6] These laws reinforced the very stereotypes that Congress sought to remedy through the FMLA. Second, 12 States provided their employees no family leave, beyond an initial childbirth or adoption, to care for a seriously ill child or family member. Third, many States provided no statutorily guaranteed right to family leave, offering instead only voluntary or discretionary leave programs.[a] Three States left the amount of leave time primarily in employers' hands. Congress could reasonably conclude that such discretionary family-leave programs would do little to combat the stereotypes about the roles of male and female employees that Congress sought to eliminate. Finally, four States provided leave only through administrative regulations or personnel policies, which Congress could reasonably conclude offered significantly less firm protection than a federal law. Against the above backdrop of limited state leave policies, no matter how generous petitioner's own may have been, Congress was justified in enacting the FMLA as remedial legislation.[10]

"In sum, the States' record of unconstitutional participation in, and fostering of, gender-based discrimination in the administration of leave benefits is weighty enough to justify the enactment of prophylactic § 5 legislation.

"[Here, unlike *Kimel* and *Garrett*,] Congress directed its attention to state gender discrimination, which triggers a heightened level of scrutiny

6. [The] dissent asserts that four of these schemes—those of Colorado, Iowa, Louisiana, and New Hampshire—concern "pregnancy disability leave only." But Louisiana provided women with four months of such leave, which far exceeds the medically recommended pregnancy disability leave period of six weeks. This gender-discriminatory policy is not attributable to any different physical needs of men and women, but rather to the invalid stereotypes that Congress sought to counter through the FMLA.

[Kennedy, J., after noting that "our cases make clear that a State does not violate the Equal Protection Clause by granting pregnancy disability leave to women without providing for a grant of parenting leave to men, *Geduldig* v. *Aiello*," responded: "The Louisiana statute, however, granted leave only for 'that period during which the female employee is disabled on account of pregnancy, childbirth, or related medical conditions.' Properly administered, the scheme, despite its generous maximum, would not transform into a discriminatory '4-month maternity leave for female employees only.' "

a. Kennedy, J., responded: "The Court does not argue the States intended to enable employers to discriminate in the provision of family leave; nor [is] there evidence state employers discriminated in the administration of leave benefits."

10. [The] dissent misunderstands the purpose of the FMLA's family leave provision. The FMLA is not a "substantive entitlement program," Congress did not create a particular leave policy for its own sake.

[that makes it] easier for Congress to show a pattern of state constitutional violations. Congress was similarly successful in *South Carolina v. Katzenbach.* * * *

"We believe that Congress' chosen remedy, the family-care leave provision of the FMLA, is 'congruent and proportional to the targeted violation.' [By] creating an across-the-board, routine employment benefit for all eligible employees, Congress sought to ensure that family-care leave would no longer be stigmatized as an inordinate drain on the workplace caused by female employees, and that employers could not evade leave obligations simply by hiring men. By setting a minimum standard of family leave for *all* eligible employees, irrespective of gender, the FMLA attacks the formerly state-sanctioned stereotype that only women are responsible for family caregiving, thereby reducing employers' incentives to engage in discrimination by basing hiring and promotion decisions on stereotypes.

"[In] the dissent's view, in the face of evidence of gender-based discrimination by the States in the provision of leave benefits, Congress could do no more in exercising its § 5 power than simply proscribe such discrimination. But this position cannot be squared with our recognition that Congress 'is not confined to the enactment of legislation that merely parrots the precise wording of the Fourteenth Amendment,' but may prohibit 'a somewhat broader swath of conduct, including that which is not itself forbidden by the Amendment's text.' [*Kimel.*]

"Indeed, in light of the evidence before Congress, a statute mirroring Title VII, that simply mandated gender equality in the administration of leave benefits, would not have achieved Congress' remedial object. Such a law would allow States to provide for no family leave at all. Where '[t]wo-thirds of the nonprofessional caregivers for older, chronically ill, or disabled persons are working women,' and state practices continue to reinforce the stereotype of women as caregivers, such a policy would exclude far more women than men from the workplace.

"Unlike the statutes at issue in *Boerne, Kimel*, and *Garrett,* which applied broadly to every aspect of state employers' operations, the FMLA is narrowly targeted at the fault line between work and family—precisely where sex-based overgeneralization has been and remains strongest—and affects only one aspect of the employment relationship."

"We also find significant the many other limitations that Congress placed on the scope of this measure. The FMLA requires only unpaid leave, and applies only to employees who have worked for the employer for at least one year and provided 1,250 hours of service within the last 12 months. Employees in high-ranking or sensitive positions are simply ineligible for FMLA leave; of particular importance to the States, the FMLA expressly excludes from coverage state elected officials, their staffs, and appointed policymakers. Employees must give advance notice of foreseeable leave, and employers may require certification by a health care provider of the need for leave. In choosing 12 weeks as the appropriate leave floor, Congress chose a middle ground, a period long enough to serve 'the needs of families' but not so long that it would upset 'the legitimate interests of employers.' [The] damages recoverable are strictly defined and measured by actual monetary losses, and the accrual period for backpay is limited by the Act's 2–year statute of limitations (extended to three years only for willful violations)."

KENNEDY, J., joined by Scalia and Thomas, JJ., dissented on the ground that Congress had failed "to make the requisite showing. [The] Act's findings of purpose are devoid of any discussion of the relevant evidence. See *Lizzi v. Alexander,* 255 F.3d 128, 135 (C.A.4 2001) ("In making [its] finding of purpose, Congress did not identify, as it is required to do, any pattern of gender discrimination by the states with respect to the granting of employment leave for the purpose of providing family or medical care"); see also *Chittister v. Department of Community and Econ. Dev.,* 226 F.3d 223, 228–229 (C.A.3 2000) ("Notably absent is any finding concerning the existence, much less the prevalence, in public employment of personal sick leave practices that amounted to intentional gender discrimination in violation of the Equal Protection Clause"). * * *

"The Court seeks to connect the evidence of private discrimination to an alleged pattern of unconstitutional behavior by States through inferences drawn from two sources. The first is testimony by Meryl Frank, Director of the Infant Care Leave Project, Yale Bush Center in Child Development and Social Policy. [The] second is a view expressed by the Washington Council of Lawyers * * *.

"Both statements were made during the hearings on the proposed 1986 national leave legislation, and so preceded the Act by seven years. The 1986 bill, which was not enacted, differed in an important respect from the legislation Congress eventually passed. That proposal sought to provide parenting leave, not leave to care for another ill family member. [Thus, this] evidence concerns the Act's grant of parenting leave, and is too attenuated to justify the family leave provision. The Court of Appeals' conclusion to the contrary was based on an assertion that 'if states discriminate along gender lines regarding the one kind of leave, then they are likely to do so regarding the other.' The charge that a State has engaged in a pattern of unconstitutional discrimination against its citizens is a most serious one. It must be supported by more than conjecture. * * *

"The Court next argues [that] many States did not guarantee the right to family leave by statute, instead leaving the decision up to individual employers, who could subject employees to 'discretionary and possibly unequal treatment.' The study from which the Court derives this conclusion examined 'the parental leave policies of Federal executive branch agencies,' [A] history of discrimination on the part of the Federal Government may, in some situations, support an inference of similar conduct by the States, but the Court does not explain why the inference is justified here. * * *

"The Court acknowledges that States have adopted family leave programs prior to federal intervention, but argues these policies suffered from serious imperfections. [That] the States did not devise the optimal programs is not, however, evidence that the States were perpetuating unconstitutional discrimination. Given that the States assumed a pioneering role in the creation of family leave schemes, it is not surprising these early efforts may have been imperfect. This is altogether different, however, from purposeful discrimination. * * *

"Stripped of the conduct which exhibits no constitutional infirmity, the Court's 'exten[sive] and specifi[c] record of unconstitutional state conduct,' boils down to the fact that three States, Massachusetts, Kansas, and Tennessee, provided parenting leave only to their female employees, and had no program for granting their employees (male or female) family leave. * * *

"Considered in its entirety, the evidence fails to document a pattern of unconstitutional conduct sufficient to justify the abrogation of States' sovereign immunity. The few incidents identified by the Court 'fall far short of even suggesting the pattern of unconstitutional discrimination on which § 5 legislation must be based.' *Garrett;* see also *Kimel; Boerne*. Juxtaposed to this evidence is the States' record of addressing gender-based discrimination in the provision of leave benefits on their own volition.

"* * * Given the insufficiency of the evidence that States discriminated in the provision of family leave, the unfortunate fact that stereotypes about women continue to be a serious and pervasive social problem would not alone support the charge that a State has engaged in a practice designed to deny its citizens the equal protection of the laws. *Garrett.*

"The paucity of evidence to support the case the Court tries to make demonstrates that Congress was not responding with a congruent and proportional remedy to a perceived course of unconstitutional conduct. Instead, it enacted a substantive entitlement program of its own. If Congress had been concerned about different treatment of men and women with respect to family leave, a congruent remedy would have sought to ensure the benefits of any leave program enacted by a State are available to men and women on an equal basis. Instead, the Act imposes, across the board, a requirement that States grant a minimum of 12 weeks of leave per year. This requirement may represent Congress' considered judgment as to the optimal balance between the family obligations of workers and the interests of employers, and the States may decide to follow these guidelines in designing their own family leave benefits. It does not follow, however, that if the States choose to enact a different benefit scheme, they should be deemed to engage in unconstitutional conduct and forced to open their treasuries to private suits for damages."

Scalia, J., dissenting, added: "The constitutional violation that is a prerequisite to 'prophylactic' congressional action to 'enforce' the Fourteenth Amendment is a violation *by the State against which the enforcement action is taken*. There is no guilt by association, enabling the sovereignty of one State to be abridged under § 5 of the Fourteenth Amendment because of violations by another State, or by most other States, or even by 49 other States. [T]he Court does not even attempt to demonstrate that each one of the 50 States covered by [the Act] was in violation of the Fourteenth Amendment. [This] will not do. Prophylaxis in the sense of extending the remedy beyond the violation is one thing; prophylaxis in the sense of extending the remedy beyond the violator is something else. See *Rome*. [F]or purposes of defeating [a facial] challenge, it would have been enough for respondents to demonstrate that [the Act] was *facially* valid—i.e., that it could constitutionally be applied to *some* jurisdictions. See *United States v. Salerno,* [fn. 5, CON LAW p. 486, AMER CON p. 538, RTS & LIB p. 411]. But when it comes to an as-applied challenge, I think Nevada will be entitled to assert that the mere facts that (1) it is a State, and (2) some States are bad actors, is not enough; it can demand that *it* be shown to have been acting in violation of the Fourteenth Amendment."

CON LAW: P. 1499, before note (c)

AMER CON: P. 1267, before note (c)

RTS & LIB: P. 1427, before note (c)

(i) *Fundamental rights; judging the "full breadth" of the challenged statute vs. "as applied."* TENNESSEE v. LANE, 541 U.S. 509, 124 S.Ct. 1978, 158 L.Ed.2d 820 (2004), per STEVENS, J., upheld Congress' § 5 power to authorize private citizens to sue states for damages under Title II of the ADA, which "seeks to enforce a variety [of] basic constitutional guarantees [like] the right of access to the courts at issue in this case, that are protected by the Due Process Clause": "Congress identified important shortcomings in existing laws that rendered them 'inadequate to address the pervasive problems of discrimination that people with disabilities are facing.' It also uncovered * * * hundreds of examples of unequal treatment of persons with disabilities by States and their political subdivisions. [As] *Garrett* observed, the 'overwhelming majority' of these examples concerned discrimination in the administration of public programs and services.

"With respect to the particular services at issue in this case, Congress learned that many individuals, in many States across the country, were being excluded from courthouses and court proceedings by reason of their disabilities. [And various judicial decisions] also demonstrate a pattern of unconstitutional treatment in the administration of justice.

"[T]he dissent's contention that the record is insufficient to justify Congress' exercise of its prophylactic power is puzzling, to say the least. Just last Term in *Hibbs*, we approved the [FMLA] based primarily on evidence of disparate provision of parenting leave, little of which concerned unconstitutional state conduct. We explained that because the FMLA was targeted at sex-based classifications, which are subject to a heightened standard of judicial scrutiny, 'it was easier for Congress to show a pattern of state constitutional violations' than in *Garrett* or *Kimel*, both of which concerned legislation that targeted classifications subject to rational-basis review. Title II is aimed at the enforcement of a variety of basic rights, including the right of access to the courts at issue in this case, that call for a standard of judicial review at least as searching, and in some cases more searching, than the standard that applies to sex-based classifications.

"* * * Title II reaches a wide array of official conduct in an effort to enforce an equally wide array of constitutional guarantees. Petitioner urges [that] the fact that Title II applies not only to public education and voting-booth access but also to seating at state-owned hockey rinks indicates that Title II is not appropriately tailored to serve its objectives. But [the] question presented in this case is not whether Congress can validly subject the States to private suits for money damages for failing to provide reasonable access to hockey rinks, or even to voting booths, but whether Congress had the power under § 5 to enforce the constitutional right of access to the courts. [See] *United States v. Raines*, 362 U.S. 17, 26, 80 S.Ct. 519, 4 L.Ed.2d 524 (1960).[19]

19. In *Raines*, a State subject to suit under the Civil Rights Act of 1957 contended that the law exceeded Congress' power to enforce the Fifteenth Amendment because it prohibited

"* * * Title II's requirement of program accessibility, is congruent and proportional to its object of enforcing the right of access to [courts.] Congress required the States to take reasonable measures to remove architectural and other barriers to accessibility. [It] requires only 'reasonable modifications' that would not fundamentally alter the nature of the service provided, and only when the individual seeking modification is otherwise eligible for the service. [In] the case of facilities built or altered [before] 1992, [for] which structural change is likely to be more difficult, a public entity may comply with Title II by adopting a variety of less costly measures, including relocating services to alternative, accessible sites and assigning aides to assist persons with disabilities in accessing services. Only if these measures are ineffective in achieving accessibility is the public entity required to make reasonable structural changes. And in no event is the entity required to undertake measures that would impose an undue financial or administrative burden, threaten historic preservation interests, or effect a fundamental alteration in the nature of the service.

"[Under due process,] a State must afford to all individuals '[a] meaningful opportunity to be heard' in its courts. *Boddie v. Connecticut.*[20] Our cases have recognized a number of affirmative obligations that flow from this principle: the duty to waive filing fees in certain family-law and criminal cases,[21] the duty to provide transcripts to criminal defendants seeking review of their convictions,[22] and the duty to provide counsel to certain criminal defendants.[23] Each of these cases makes clear that ordinary considerations of cost and convenience alone cannot justify a State's failure to provide individuals with a meaningful right of access to the courts.[[24]]"[a]

Rehnquist, J., joined by Kennedy and Thomas,[b] JJ., dissented: "[T]he majority identifies nothing in the legislative record that shows Congress was responding to widespread violations of the due process rights of disabled persons.

"Rather, [the] majority sets out on a wide-ranging account of societal discrimination against the disabled. This digression recounts historical dis-

"any person," and not just state actors, from interfering with voting rights. We rejected that argument, concluding that "if the complaint here called for an application of the statute clearly constitutional under the Fifteenth Amendment, that should have been an end to the question of constitutionality."

20. Because this case implicates the right of access to the courts, we need not consider whether Title II's duty to accommodate exceeds what the Constitution requires in the class of cases that implicate only *Cleburne's* prohibition on irrational discrimination.

21. *Boddie* (divorce filing fee); *M.L.B. v. S.L. J.* (record fee in parental rights termination action).

22. *Griffin v. Illinois.*

23. *Gideon v. Wainwright; Douglas v. California.*

24. The Chief Justice contends that Title II cannot be understood as remedial legislation because it "subjects a State to liability for failing to make a vast array of special accommodations, *without regard for whether the failure to accommodate results in a constitutional wrong.*" (emphasis in original). But as we have often acknowledged, Congress "is not confined to the enactment of legislation that merely parrots the precise wording of the Fourteenth Amendment," and may prohibit "a somewhat broader swath of conduct, including that which is not itself forbidden by the Amendment's text." *Kimel.*

a. The Court upheld the Sixth Circuit's affirmance of the federal district judge's denial of the state's motion to dismiss on eleventh amendment grounds. The Sixth Circuit "noted that the case presented difficult questions that 'cannot be clarified absent a a factual record,' and remanded for further proceedings."

b. Thomas, J., also wrote "separately only to disavow any reliance on *Hibbs.*"

crimination against the disabled through institutionalization laws, restrictions on marriage, voting, and public education, conditions in mental hospitals, and various other forms of unequal treatment in the administration of public programs and services. Some of this evidence would be relevant if the Court were considering the constitutionality of the statute as a whole; but the Court rejects that approach in favor of a narrower 'as-applied' inquiry. We discounted much the same type of outdated, generalized evidence in [*Garrett*].

"With respect to the due process 'access to the courts' rights on which the Court ultimately relies, [there] is nothing in the legislative record or statutory findings to indicate that disabled persons were systematically denied the right to be present at criminal trials, denied the meaningful opportunity to be heard in civil cases, unconstitutionally excluded from jury service, or denied the right to attend criminal trials.[4][[8], [9]]

"Even if the anecdotal evidence and conclusory statements relied on by the majority could be properly considered, the mere existence of an architecturally 'inaccessible' courthouse—i.e., one a disabled person cannot utilize without assistance—does not state a constitutional violation. A violation of due process occurs only when a person is actually denied the constitutional right to access a given judicial proceeding. We have never held that a person has a *constitutional* right to make his way into a courtroom without any external assistance. * * *

"The majority concludes that Title II's massive overbreadth can be cured by considering the statute only 'as it applies to the class of cases implicating the accessibility of judicial services.' * * *

"In conducting its as-applied analysis, however, the majority posits a hypothetical statute, never enacted by Congress, that applies only to courthouses. [If] we had arbitrarily constricted the scope of the statutes to match the scope of a core constitutional right, [our § 5 precedents] might have come out differently. In *Garrett*, for example, Title I might have been upheld 'as applied' to irrational employment discrimination; or in *Florida Prepaid*, the Patent Remedy Act might have been upheld 'as applied' to intentional, uncompensated patent infringements.[c] It is thus not surprising that the only

4. Certainly, respondents Lane and Jones were not denied these constitutional rights. The majority admits that Lane was able to attend the initial hearing of his criminal trial [by crawling up two flights of stairs]. Lane was arrested for failing to appear at his second hearing only after he refused assistance from officers dispatched by the court to help him to the courtroom. The court conducted a preliminary hearing in the first-floor library to accommodate Lane's disability, and later offered to move all further proceedings in the case to a handicapped-accessible courthouse in a nearby town. Respondent Jones, a disabled court reporter, does not seriously contend that she suffered a constitutional injury.

8. The majority rather peculiarly points to Congress' finding that "discrimination against individuals with disabilities persists in such critical areas as *access to public services*" as evidence that Congress sought to vindicate the Due Process rights of disabled persons. However, one does not usually refer to the right to attend a judicial proceeding as "access to [a] public servic[e]." Given the lack of any concern over courthouse accessibility issues in the legislative history, it is highly unlikely that this legislative finding obliquely refers to state violations of the due process rights of disabled persons to attend judicial proceedings.

9. The Court correctly explains that "it [i]s easier for Congress to show a pattern of state constitutional violations" when it targets state action that triggers a higher level of constitutional scrutiny. [But] Congress may not dispense with the required showing altogether simply because it purports to enforce due process rights. See *Florida Prepaid; Boerne*. * * *

c. Stevens, J., replied: "Contrary to The Chief Justice, neither *Garrett* nor *Florida Prepaid* lends support to the proposition that the *Boerne* ["congruence-and-proportionality test"] authority cited by the majority is *Raines*, a case decided long before we enunciated the congruence-and-proportionality test.

"I fear that the Court's adoption of an as-applied approach eliminates any incentive for Congress to craft § 5 legislation for the purpose of remedying or deterring actual constitutional violations. Congress can now simply rely on the courts to sort out which hypothetical applications of an undifferentiated statute, such as Title II, may be enforced against the States. All the while, States will be subjected to substantial litigation in a piecemeal attempt to vindicate their Eleventh Amendment rights. * * *

"The majority's reliance on *Boddie*, and other cases in which we held that due process requires the State to waive filing fees for indigent litigants, is unavailing. While these cases support the principle that the State must remove financial requirements that in fact prevent an individual from exercising his constitutional rights, they certainly do not support a statute that subjects a State to liability for failing to make a vast array of special accommodations, *without regard for whether the failure to accommodate results in a constitutional wrong*."

SCALIA, J., also dissented because "the 'congruence and proportionality' standard, like all such flabby tests, is a standing invitation to judicial arbitrariness and policy-driven decisionmaking. Worse still, it casts this Court in the role of Congress's taskmaster. Under it, the courts (and ultimately this Court) must regularly check Congress's homework to make sure that it has identified sufficient constitutional violations to make its remedy congruent and proportional. As a general matter, we are ill advised to adopt or adhere to constitutional rules that bring us into constant conflict with a coequal branch of Government. * * *

"I would replace 'congruence and proportionality' with another test—one that provides a clear, enforceable limitation supported by the text of § 5. * * * Section 5 authorizes Congress to create a cause of action through which the citizen may vindicate his Fourteenth Amendment rights. One of the first pieces of legislation passed under Congress's § 5 power [is now codified in § 1983]. Section 5 would also authorize measures that do not restrict the States' substantive scope of action but impose requirements directly related to the facilitation of 'enforcement'—for example, reporting requirements that would enable violations of the Fourteenth Amendment to be identified. But what § 5 does not authorize is so-called 'prophylactic' measures, prohibiting primary conduct that is itself not forbidden by the Fourteenth Amendment.

"[P]rincipally for reasons of stare decisis, I shall henceforth apply the permissive *McCulloch* standard [used in *South Carolina v. Katzenbach* and *Morgan*] to congressional measures designed to remedy racial discrimination by the States. I would not, however, abandon the requirement that Congress may impose prophylactic § 5 legislation only upon those particular States in

test requires courts in all cases to 'measur[e] the full breadth of the statute or relevant provision that Congress enacted against the scope of the constitutional right it purported to enforce.' In fact, the decision in *Garrett*, which severed Title I of the ADA from Title II for purposes of the § 5 inquiry, demonstrates that courts need not examine "the full breadth of the statute" all at once.

which there has been an identified history of relevant constitutional violations."[d]

Query: On remand, what must Lane prove in order to win?

d. In a separate concurring opinion, Ginsburg, J., joined by Souter and Breyer, JJ., responded: "Members of Congress are understandably reluctant to condemn their own States as constitutional violators, complicit in maintaining the isolated and unequal status of persons with disabilities. I would not disarm a National Legislature for resisting an adversarial approach to lawmaking better suited to the courtroom."

LIMITATIONS ON JUDICIAL POWER AND REVIEW

STANDING

THE STRUCTURE OF STANDING DOCTRINE

CON LAW: P. 1517, at end of note 7

AMER CON: P. 1280, at end of note 7

RTS & LIB: P. 1440, at end of note 7

Compare UTAH v. EVANS, 536 U.S. 452, 122 S.Ct. 2191, 153 L.Ed.2d 453 (2002), which upheld Utah's standing to challenge census calculations in a suit against the Secretary of Commerce and the Census Bureau. The named defendants could not directly redress Utah's alleged injury—denial of an additional seat in the House of Representatives. Nonetheless, the Court deemed it sufficiently likely that the President and relevant congressional officials, although not parties to the suit, would act to allocate an additional House seat to Utah if the challenge succeeded on the merits. Scalia, J., was the sole dissenter with respect to standing.

CON LAW: P. 1518, at end of note 9

AMER CON: P. 1280, at end of note 7

RTS & LIB: P. 1440, at end of note 7

The Court, per STEVENS, J., page 187 of this Supplement, cited the "prudential" element in standing doctrine as a ground for denying standing in ELK GROVE UNITED SCHOOL DIST. v. NEWDOW, an action challenging the School District's policy of commencing each school day with a recitation of the Pledge of Allegiance including the words "under God." Newdow, the father of a girl in the school system, sued to enjoin the practice, which he claimed interfered with his right to communicate his atheistic beliefs to his daughter. But the girl's mother opposed the action, and the Court found it uncertain that Newdow, who shared custody with his wife, had "a right to dictate to others what they may and may not say to his child respecting religion" as a matter of California law: "[T]he interests of this parent and this child are not parallel and, indeed, are potentially in conflict. [I]t is improper for the federal courts to entertain a claim by a plaintiff whose standing to sue is founded on family law rights that are in dispute when prosecution of the lawsuit may have an adverse effect on the person who is the source of the plaintiff's claimed standing."

Rehnquist, C.J., joined by O'Connor and Thomas, JJ., dissented, voting to uphold standing based on injury to Newdow's right to expose his daughter to his religious views, and describing the majority's standing ruling as "novel" and as "like the proverbial excursion ticket—good for this day only." On the merits, the dissenting Justices would have upheld the School District's recitation policy (see page 187 of this Supplement). (Scalia, J., did not participate.)

TIMING OF ADJUDICATION

RIPENESS

CON LAW: P. 1541, add to fn. e

See also *National Park Hospitality Ass'n v. Department of Interior*, 538 U.S. 803, 123 S.Ct. 2026, 155 L.Ed.2d 1017 (2003) (holding unripe a suit by an association of concessioners challenging a National Park Service regulation involving contract disputes that had not yet been applied to particular concession contracts and that was not binding on either an Interior Department appeals board or the courts).

†